My Morning Manna

Volume 3 — Journey Through the Psalms

Ed Nelson

Mile-Hi Publishers, Inc. • P.O. Box 19340 • Denver, Colorado 80219 • (303) 985-3825

To those persecuted believers who have been delivered from Communist oppression, whose faith has been strengthened through the hope and encouragement found in the book of Psalms. May we never forget their courageous spirit and Christian testimony.

"Remember them that are in bonds, as bound with them; and them which suffer adversity, as being yourselves also in the body."
—Hebrews 13:3

Preface

This is Volume 3 of *My Morning Manna*. It gives 366 devotionals from the book of Psalms, with devotions covering between six and seven verses a day.

Therefore, I have assigned a reading schedule between eighteen and thirty verses per day. This means that the reading assigned for the day often comprises more than just one psalm. For example, the assignment for January 1 is Psalm 1 and 2—a total of eighteen verses. Then the assignments for January 2 and 3 are to read Psalms 2 and 3. If the reader follows the assignment, he will read Psalm 2 three times. The actual devotionals on Psalm 2 involve two days.

When we come to longer psalms, the reading assignment may be longer than thirty verses. For example, I have assigned Psalm 18 to be read all the way through. It is fifty verses in length, and there are seven devotionals on this psalm. Though reading assignments will be fifty verses long, there will be "Family Reading" assignments of twenty to thirty verses. Then there will be a "Devotional Portion" of seven or eight verses. Psalm 78 and Psalm 119 are two longer psalms that will be divided into shorter reading assignments.

These devotionals cover an average of seven verses each day. If the psalm is ten verses or less, the entire psalm will comprise the devotional reading for the day. This is true even of Psalms 117, 131, 133, and 134, which are only two or three verses in length. If it is eleven verses or longer, it will be divided into two or more days, depending on its length.

As in the previous two volumes, I have arranged a Bible reading assignment to guide the believer to read through his Bible in a year. This assignment appears at the bottom of the page for each day.

My prayer is that my readers may receive some of the blessings I have enjoyed while meditating on all the psalms as I wrote this book. To me, the Psalms have been *"sweeter also than honey in the honeycomb" (Psalm 19:10)*. I have enjoyed every minute of the hundreds of hours I have labored in writing these devotionals. The Psalms deal with the problems of life and, though written centuries ago, they are relevant for every one of us today.

Ed Nelson

DAILY SCHEDULE
FOR JANUARY

Day	Devotional Reading	Through the Bible in a Year	Title
Jan. 1	❏ Ps. 1–2	❏ Gen. 1–3	The Blessed Man
Jan. 2	❏ Ps. 2–3	❏ Gen. 4–6	David Saw Man in His Rebellion
Jan. 3	❏ Ps. 2–3	❏ Gen. 7–9	David Saw Jesus Christ in His Reign
Jan. 4	❏ Ps. 3–4	❏ Gen. 10–12	Think on This—The Lord Is Our Shield!
Jan. 5	❏ Ps. 4–5	❏ Gen. 13–16	Confidence in God
Jan. 6	❏ Ps. 5–6	❏ Gen. 17–19	Prayer Preparation for the Day
Jan. 7	❏ Ps. 5–6	❏ Gen. 20–22	David's Assurance of the Lord's Favor
Jan. 8	❏ Ps. 6–7	❏ Gen. 23–24	Dealing with Sin in Repentance
Jan. 9	❏ Ps. 7–8	❏ Gen. 25–26	A Clear Conscience
Jan. 10	❏ Ps. 7–8	❏ Gen. 27–28	David's Defense
Jan. 11	❏ Ps. 8–9	❏ Gen. 29–30	Our God's Greatness Revealed in His Grace
Jan. 12	❏ Ps. 9	❏ Gen. 31–32	David, a Prophet, Sees Victory Over Antichrist
Jan. 13	❏ Ps. 9	❏ Gen. 33–35	The Lord Our Refuge in Trouble
Jan. 14	❏ Ps. 9	❏ Gen. 36–37	Think of That—God's Judgment Will Come
Jan. 15	❏ Ps. 10–11	❏ Gen. 38–40	The Dangerous Way of the Wicked
Jan. 16	❏ Ps. 10–11	❏ Gen. 41–42	Dreadful Description of the Antichrist
Jan. 17	❏ Ps. 10–11	❏ Gen. 43–45	God Is Very Much Alive
Jan. 18	❏ Ps. 11–13	❏ Gen. 46–48	Trust the Lord, Regardless of the Circumstances
Jan. 19	❏ Ps. 12–14	❏ Gen. 49–50; Ex. 1	The Pure Word of God Versus the Lies of Men
Jan. 20	❏ Ps. 13–16	❏ Ex. 2–4	From a Sigh to a Song
Jan. 21	❏ Ps. 14–16	❏ Ex. 5–7	The Fool
Jan. 22	❏ Ps. 15–17	❏ Ex. 8–10	The Need of a Holy Life
Jan. 23	❏ Ps. 16–17	❏ Ex. 11–13	Jesus Christ in the Psalms
Jan. 24	❏ Ps. 16–17	❏ Ex. 14–16	I'd Rather Have Jesus
Jan. 25	❏ Ps. 17	❏ Ex. 17–20	Praying, Submitting to His Will
Jan. 26	❏ Ps. 17	❏ Ex. 21–23	How to Handle Evil Circumstances
Jan. 27	❏ Ps. 18	❏ Ex. 24–26	Praise for Victory Over Our Foes
Jan. 28	❏ Ps. 18	❏ Ex. 27–29	Praying and Seeing His Power at Work
Jan. 29	❏ Ps. 18	❏ Ex. 30–32	The Lord Delights in His Children
Jan. 30	❏ Ps. 18	❏ Ex. 33–35	Principles of God's Government
Jan. 31	❏ Ps. 18	❏ Ex. 36–38	God's Way Is Perfect

DAILY SCHEDULE
FOR FEBRUARY

Day	Devotional Reading	Through the Bible in a Year	Title
Feb. 1	❐ Ps. 18:38-50; 19	❐ Ex. 39–40	David's Victory Through the Lord
Feb. 2	❐ Ps. 18:44-50; 19	❐ Lev. 1–4	Let the God of My Salvation Be Exalted
Feb. 3	❐ Ps. 19–20	❐ Lev. 5–7	The Witness of God's Creation
Feb. 4	❐ Ps. 19–20	❐ Lev. 8–10	The Word That Converts and Produces Growth
Feb. 5	❐ Ps. 20–21	❐ Lev. 11–13	God's Help in the Day of Trouble
Feb. 6	❐ Ps. 21–22	❐ Lev. 14–15	Strength for the Battle
Feb. 7	❐ Ps. 21; 22:1-21	❐ Lev. 16–18	A View of God's Judgment on Unrepentant Sinners
Feb. 8	❐ Ps. 22	❐ Lev. 19–21	A Good View of Calvary
Feb. 9	❐ Ps. 22	❐ Lev. 22–23	Christ's Horrible Death at Calvary
Feb. 10	❐ Ps. 22	❐ Lev. 24–25	The Physical Pain of the Cross
Feb. 11	❐ Ps. 22:14-31; 23	❐ Lev. 26–27	Christ Is Risen!
Feb. 12	❐ Ps. 22:22-31; 23–24	❐ Num. 1–2	The Risen Lord's Concern
Feb. 13	❐ Ps. 23–24	❐ Num. 3–4	The Shepherd's Provision and Comfort
Feb. 14	❐ Ps. 24–25	❐ Num. 5–7	All Belongs to the Lord, Our King
Feb. 15	❐ Ps. 24–25	❐ Num. 8–10	Christ Jesus, the King of Glory
Feb. 16	❐ Ps. 25	❐ Num. 11–13	God and I
Feb. 17	❐ Ps. 25	❐ Num. 14–15	The Leadership of God
Feb. 18	❐ Ps. 25:12-25; 26	❐ Num. 16–18	David's Trouble and His Deliverance
Feb. 19	❐ Ps. 26–27	❐ Num. 19–21	A Life of Integrity
Feb. 20	❐ Ps. 26–27	❐ Num. 22–23	Walking Consistently for God
Feb. 21	❐ Ps. 27–28	❐ Num. 24–26	The Lord, Our Light and Salvation
Feb. 22	❐ Ps. 27–28	❐ Num. 27–29	Wait on the Lord
Feb. 23	❐ Ps. 28–29	❐ Num. 30–31	Trust—Receive Help—Rejoice
Feb. 24	❐ Ps. 29–30	❐ Num. 32–33	Peace in the Midst of the Terrible Storm
Feb. 25	❐ Ps. 30–31	❐ Num. 34–36	Weeping Ends—Joy Comes
Feb. 26	❐ Ps. 30–31	❐ Deut. 1–2	A Glorious End Out of Deep Trouble
Feb. 27	❐ Ps. 31	❐ Deut. 3–4	Trusting the Lord, Our Refuge
Feb. 28	❐ Ps. 31	❐ Deut. 5–7	Our Times Are in His Hands
Feb. 29	❐ Ps. 31		Our Guide to Heaven

DAILY SCHEDULE
FOR MARCH

Day	Devotional Reading	Through the Bible in a Year	Title
Mar. 1	❏ Ps. 31–32	❏ Deut. 8–10	David Rejoices in Victory
Mar. 2	❏ Ps. 32–33	❏ Deut. 11–13	David's Great Blessing—Forgiveness by God
Mar. 3	❏ Ps. 32–33	❏ Deut. 14–16	David's Instruction Concerning Guilt
Mar. 4	❏ Ps. 33	❏ Deut. 17–20	Sing Praise Because of the Power of His Word
Mar. 5	❏ Ps. 33	❏ Deut. 21–23	The Great Power of God's Word
Mar. 6	❏ Ps. 33	❏ Deut. 24–27	Our Hope and Help is in the Lord
Mar. 7	❏ Ps. 34	❏ Deut. 28	The Lord Cares for His Own
Mar. 8	❏ Ps. 34	❏ Deut. 29–31	Our Lord Protects and Provides
Mar. 9	❏ Ps. 34	❏ Deut. 32–34	Contrasts Between the Righteous and the Evil
Mar. 10	❏ Ps. 35	❏ Josh. 1–4	Rejoice in Spite of Trials
Mar. 11	❏ Ps. 35	❏ Josh. 5–7	Praise in the Midst of Severe Trials
Mar. 12	❏ Ps. 35:18-28; 36	❏ Josh. 8–9	A Thankful Spirit During the Trials
Mar. 13	❏ Ps. 36; 37:1-11	❏ Josh. 10–12	The Sinful Man
Mar. 14	❏ Ps. 36; 37:1-11	❏ Josh. 13–15	The Blessing Coming From God's Fountain
Mar. 15	❏ Ps. 37	❏ Josh. 16–19	Fret Not—Rather Trust the Lord
Mar. 16	❏ Ps. 37	❏ Josh. 20–22	God Deals with the Wicked and Blesses the Righteous
Mar. 17	❏ Ps. 37	❏ Josh. 23–24; Jud. 1	God's Direction for the Righteous
Mar. 18	❏ Ps. 37	❏ Jud. 2–4	Truths About the Righteous Man
Mar. 19	❏ Ps. 37:27-40; 38:1-11	❏ Jud. 5–6	The End of the Wicked
Mar. 20	❏ Ps. 38	❏ Jud. 7–8; 9:1-25	Conviction of Sin
Mar. 21	❏ Ps. 38	❏ Jud. 9:26-51; 10–11	Humiliation Over Sin
Mar. 22	❏ Ps. 38:15-22; 39	❏ Jud. 12–15	David's Confidence, Contrition, and Confession
Mar. 23	❏ Ps. 39–40	❏ Jud. 16–18	Thinking About Life
Mar. 24	❏ Ps. 39–40	❏ Jud. 19–20	David's Hope Was in the Lord
Mar. 25	❏ Ps. 40	❏ Jud. 21; Ruth 1–2	From the Mire to the Choir
Mar. 26	❏ Ps. 40:6-17; 41	❏ Ruth 3–4; I Sam. 1	David's Victory in the Battle—and Our Victory
Mar. 27	❏ Ps. 41–42	❏ I Sam. 2–4	Compassion Toward Others
Mar. 28	❏ Ps. 41–42	❏ I Sam. 5–9	The Awful Price for Sin
Mar. 29	❏ Ps. 42–43	❏ I Sam. 10–13	God—Our Hope, Help, and Health
Mar. 30	❏ Ps. 42–43	❏ I Sam. 14–15	When the Outlook is Dark—Try the Uplook
Mar. 31	❏ Ps. 43–44	❏ I Sam. 16–17	Trust the Lord—Don't Get Discouraged

DAILY SCHEDULE
FOR APRIL

Day	Devotional Reading	Through the Bible in a Year	Title
Apr. 1	❐ Ps. 44	❐ I Sam. 18–20	The Right and Wrong Weapons for Spiritual Battles
Apr. 2	❐ Ps. 44	❐ I Sam. 21–24	Victory and Chastening—Both from the Lord
Apr. 3	❐ Ps. 44:17-25; 45	❐ I Sam. 25–27	Praising and Praying through Problems
Apr. 4	❐ Ps. 45	❐ I Sam. 28–31	Our King of Beauty and of Might
Apr. 5	❐ Ps. 45	❐ II Sam. 1–3	The Reign of King Jesus
Apr. 6	❐ Ps. 45:9-17; 46	❐ II Sam. 4–7	The Church: The Bride of Christ
Apr. 7	❐ Ps. 46–47	❐ II Sam. 8–11	Trust in Time of Trouble
Apr. 8	❐ Ps. 46–47	❐ II Sam. 12–13	Be Still and Know God for Victory
Apr. 9	❐ Ps. 47–48	❐ II Sam. 14–15	Praise Him
Apr. 10	❐ Ps. 48–49	❐ II Sam. 16–18	Protected by God's Presence
Apr. 11	❐ Ps. 48–49	❐ II Sam. 19–21	God's People Testifying of God's Deliverance
Apr. 12	❐ Ps. 49	❐ II Sam. 22–23	Worldly Wealth vs. God's Wisdom
Apr. 13	❐ Ps. 49	❐ II Sam. 24; I Kings 1	The Foolishness and Futility of Trusting Riches
Apr. 14	❐ Ps. 49:14-20; 50	❐ I Kings 2–3	Those Who Trust the Lord Need Not Fear
Apr. 15	❐ Ps. 50	❐ I Kings 4–6	Judgment Begins With God's People
Apr. 16	❐ Ps. 50	❐ I Kings 7; 8:1-32	Deliverance From God's Judgment
Apr. 17	❐ Ps. 50:17-23; 51	❐ I Kings 8:33-66; 9–10	Godly Lives Rejecting Hypocrisy
Apr. 18	❐ Ps. 51	❐ I Kings 11–12	David's Great Penitential Prayer
Apr. 19	❐ Ps. 51–52	❐ I Kings 13–14	Consequences of David's Sin Against God
Apr. 20	❐ Ps. 51–52	❐ I Kings 15–16	David's Resting on a Full Redemption
Apr. 21	❐ Ps. 52–54	❐ I Kings 17–18	God's Judgment Will Come on Evil Men
Apr. 22	❐ Ps. 53–55	❐ I Kings 19–20	The Antichrist Revealed
Apr. 23	❐ Ps. 54–55	❐ I Kings 21–22	Committing All to the Lord—Even When Betrayed
Apr. 24	❐ Ps. 55	❐ II Kings 1–3	Facing Trouble
Apr. 25	❐ Ps. 55:9-23; 56	❐ II Kings 4–5	Another Bitter Price for Sin
Apr. 26	❐ Ps. 55:16-23; 56	❐ II Kings 6–8	David's Confidence in the Lord
Apr. 27	❐ Ps. 56–57	❐ II Kings 9–10	Confidence in God and His Mercy
Apr. 28	❐ Ps. 56:8-13; 57–58	❐ II Kings 11–13	Passing God's Exams
Apr. 29	❐ Ps. 57–58	❐ II Kings 14–16	David's Refuge—The Lord's Mercy
Apr. 30	❐ Ps. 57–58	❐ II Kings 17–18	A Heart That Sings Through Trials

DAILY SCHEDULE
FOR MAY

Day	Devotional Reading	Through the Bible in a Year	Title
May 1	☐ Ps. 58–59	☐ II Kings 19–21	Faulty Judgment Begins in the Heart
May 2	☐ Ps. 58–59	☐ II Kings 22–24	The Certainty of Judgment
May 3	☐ Ps. 59	☐ II Kings 25; I Chr. 1	David's Consolation in Knowing his God
May 4	☐ Ps. 59–60	☐ I Chr. 2–3	God Hears and Records Sin
May 5	☐ Ps. 59:10-17; 60	☐ I Chr. 4–5	Trust Triumphs Over Trouble
May 6	☐ Ps. 60–61	☐ I Chr. 6	Beware Being Overconfident in the Flesh
May 7	☐ Ps. 60–61	☐ I Chr. 7–8	Trusting God for Victory Rather Than Man
May 8	☐ Ps. 61–62	☐ I Chr. 9–11	Lead Me to the Rock
May 9	☐ Ps. 62–63	☐ I Chr. 12–14	Trust in the Face of Trouble
May 10	☐ Ps. 62–63	☐ I Chr. 15–16	Trust the Lord at All Times
May 11	☐ Ps. 63–64	☐ I Chr. 17–20	Seek Only God—and Seek Him Early
May 12	☐ Ps. 63–64	☐ I Chr. 21–23	Satisfied With the Lord's Presence
May 13	☐ Ps. 64–65	☐ I Chr. 24–26	The Death Dealing Tongue
May 14	☐ Ps. 64–65	☐ I Chr. 27–29	Vengeance is Mine, Saith the Lord
May 15	☐ Ps. 65–66	☐ II Chr. 1–4	The Deliverance of the Blessed Man
May 16	☐ Ps. 65–66	☐ II Chr. 5–7	Praising Our God of Great Power
May 17	☐ Ps. 66	☐ II Chr. 8–12	A Coming Golden Age
May 18	☐ Ps. 66	☐ II Chr. 13–17	Deliverance With Divine Discipline
May 19	☐ Ps. 66–67	☐ II Chr. 18–20	A Wonderful Personal Testimony
May 20	☐ Ps. 67; 68:1-18	☐ II Chr. 21–23	Singing Before the Judge
May 21	☐ Ps. 68	☐ II Chr. 24–26	God Victorious Over His Enemies
May 22	☐ Ps. 68	☐ II Chr. 27–29	God's Leading Israel in Victory
May 23	☐ Ps. 68	☐ II Chr. 30–32	The Conqueror Coming to Zion's Hill
May 24	☐ Ps. 68:15-35	☐ II Chr. 33–35	The Future Deliverance of Israel
May 25	☐ Ps. 68:15-35	☐ II Chr. 36; Ezra 1–2	Jesus Christ Shall Reign
May 26	☐ Ps. 69	☐ Ezra 3–6	Christ's Suffering For Us
May 27	☐ Ps. 69	☐ Ezra 7–9	The Awful Suffering of Calvary's Cross
May 28	☐ Ps. 69	☐ Ezra 10; Neh. 1–2	The Reproach of the Crowd
May 29	☐ Ps. 69–70	☐ Neh. 3–6	The Day of Wrath to Come
May 30	☐ Ps. 69:18-36; 70	☐ Neh. 7–8	From a Sigh to a Song
May 31	☐ Ps. 70–71	☐ Neh. 9–10	An Emergency Prayer

DAILY SCHEDULE
FOR JUNE

Day	Devotional Reading	Through the Bible in a Year	Title
Jun. 1	❐ Ps. 71	❐ Neh. 11–12	Trusting the Lord in Old Age
Jun. 2	❐ Ps. 71	❐ Neh. 13; Est. 1–2	Living With Praise in Old Age
Jun. 3	❐ Ps. 71	❐ Est. 3–7	The Testimony of a Godly Old Man
Jun. 4	❐ Ps. 72	❐ Est. 8–10; Job 1	A Coming King
Jun. 5	❐ Ps. 72	❐ Job 2–5	The Kingdom of Righteousness
Jun. 6	❐ Ps. 72	❐ Job 6–8	A Future Glorious Millennial Reign
Jun. 7	❐ Ps. 73	❐ Job 9–12	The Seeming Prosperity of the Wicked
Jun. 8	❐ Ps. 73	❐ Job 13–15	The Condition of the Wicked Who Seem to Prosper
Jun. 9	❐ Ps. 73	❐ Job 16–19	Asaph Sees Life From God's Perspective
Jun. 10	❐ Ps. 73:8-28	❐ Job 20–22	Trusting the Lord—The Wise Choice
Jun. 11	❐ Ps. 74	❐ Job 23–27	The Destruction of the Enemies
Jun. 12	❐ Ps. 74	❐ Job 28–30	God Is at Work for His Own
Jun. 13	❐ Ps. 74:16-23; 75	❐ Job 31–33	God Takes Care of His Own
Jun. 14	❐ Ps. 75–76	❐ Job 34–36	God Is the Sovereign Judge
Jun. 15	❐ Ps. 76–77	❐ Job 37–39	Great Victory Through God's Power
Jun. 16	❐ Ps. 76–77	❐ Job 40–42	Praise Him—He Gives the Victory
Jun. 17	❐ Ps. 77	❐ Prov. 1; Is. 1–2	From a Sigh to a Song
Jun. 18	❐ Ps. 77	❐ Prov. 2; Is. 3–4	Victory Comes As We Believe God's Word
Jun. 19	❐ Ps. 77:10-20; 78:1-11	❐ Prov. 3; Is. 5–6	God's Greatness and His Leadership
Jun. 20	❐ Ps. 78:1-10	❐ Prov. 4; Is. 7–9	Teach the Children Spiritual Truths
Jun. 21	❐ Ps. 78:5-28	❐ Prov. 5; Is. 10–12	Reasons We Should Teach Our Children
Jun. 22	❐ Ps. 78:9-31	❐ Prov. 6; Is. 13–14	The Voice of History
Jun. 23	❐ Ps. 78:15-39	❐ Prov. 7; Is. 15–21	The Dangerous Sin of Unbelief
Jun. 24	❐ Ps. 78:30-53	❐ Prov. 8; Is. 22–23	Man Changes—God Changes Not
Jun. 25	❐ Ps. 78:40-62	❐ Prov. 9; Is. 24–27	The Lure of the World
Jun. 26	❐ Ps. 78:50-72	❐ Prov. 10; Is. 28–29	Idolatry Causes the Glory to Depart
Jun. 27	❐ Ps. 78:62-72; 79	❐ Prov. 11; Is. 30–32	God Chooses the Place for Worship
Jun. 28	❐ Ps. 79–80	❐ Prov. 12; Is. 33–35	God's Judgment on His People
Jun. 29	❐ Ps. 79:8-13; 80	❐ Prov. 13; Is. 36–37	Prayer and Our Promise to Praise
Jun. 30	❐ Ps. 80	❐ Prov. 14; Is. 38–40	God's People Need to Turn

DAILY SCHEDULE
FOR JULY

Day	Devotional Reading	Through the Bible in a Year	Title
Jul. 1	❏ Ps. 80	❏ Prov. 15; Is. 41–42	The Vine Planted and Attacked
Jul. 2	❏ Ps. 80:14-19; 81	❏ Prov. 16; Is. 43–44	God's Restoration of His Own
Jul. 3	❏ Ps. 81–82	❏ Prov. 17; Is. 45–47	Worshiping Him Who Saved Us
Jul. 4	❏ Ps. 81–82	❏ Prov. 18; Is. 48–50	Missed Opportunities
Jul. 5	❏ Ps. 82–83	❏ Prov. 19; Is. 51–53	Judgment of the Judges
Jul. 6	❏ Ps. 83	❏ Prov. 20; Is. 54–56	The Enemies of God Attack His People
Jul. 7	❏ Ps. 83	❏ Prov. 21; Is. 57–59	God's People Surrounded with Enemies
Jul. 8	❏ Ps. 83–84	❏ Prov. 22; Is. 60–63	A Godly Purpose for Praying That God Will Judge
Jul. 9	❏ Ps. 84–85	❏ Prov. 23; Is. 64–66	Longing for Home Where Jesus Is
Jul. 10	❏ Ps. 84–85	❏ Prov. 24; Jer. 1–2	Lord, I'm Coming Home
Jul. 11	❏ Ps. 85–86	❏ Prov. 25; Jer. 3–4	A Plea for Revival
Jul. 12	❏ Ps. 85:6-13; Ps. 86	❏ Prov. 26; Jer. 5–6	Wilt Thou Not Revive Us Again?
Jul. 13	❏ Ps. 86–87	❏ Prov. 27; Jer. 7–8	Praying in Severe Trial
Jul. 14	❏ Ps. 86–87	❏ Prov. 28; Jer. 9–10	Praising the Lord and Trusting Him for the Answer
Jul. 15	❏ Ps. 86:12-17; 87–88	❏ Prov. 29; Jer. 11–13	A Prayer of the Lord Jesus Christ
Jul. 16	❏ Ps. 87–88	❏ Prov. 30; Jer. 14–15	God's Glorious City—Jerusalem
Jul. 17	❏ Ps. 88	❏ Prov. 31; Jer. 16–17	Praying When Trials Are Heavy
Jul. 18	❏ Ps. 88	❏ Ecc. 1; Jer. 18–21	Our Hope is in the Lord
Jul. 19	❏ Ps. 89:1-24	❏ Ecc. 2; Jer. 22–23	God's Faithfulness Facing Man's Ruin
Jul. 20	❏ Ps. 89:1-24	❏ Ecc. 3; Jer. 24–25	The Faithfulness of God
Jul. 21	❏ Ps. 89:8-33	❏ Ecc. 4; Jer. 26–28	Praise in the Midst of Chaos
Jul. 22	❏ Ps. 89:19-41	❏ Ecc. 5; Jer. 29–30	God's Covenant with David
Jul. 23	❏ Ps. 89:25-45	❏ Ecc. 6; Jer. 31–32	Our Lord Is Faithful!
Jul. 24	❏ Ps. 89:38-52; 90	❏ Ecc. 7; Jer. 33–34	Things Are Not Always What They Appear to Be
Jul. 25	❏ Ps. 89:46-52; 90	❏ Ecc. 8; Jer. 35–37	Trusting the Lord in All Circumstances
Jul. 26	❏ Ps. 90	❏ Ecc. 9; Jer. 38–40	The Greatness of God and the Infirmity of Man
Jul. 27	❏ Ps. 90	❏ Ecc. 10; Jer. 41–43	The Frailty of Man
Jul. 28	❏ Ps. 90	❏ Ecc. 11–12; Jer. 44–46	May We Apply Our Hearts to Wisdom
Jul. 29	❏ Ps. 90:12-17; 91	❏ S. Sol. 1; Jer. 47–48	May We Neither Live Nor Labor in Vain
Jul. 30	❏ Ps. 91	❏ S. Sol. 2; Jer. 49–50	God, the Lord, Our Dwelling Place
Jul. 31	❏ Ps. 91	❏ S. Sol. 3; Jer. 51	God, the Lord, Our Protection

DAILY SCHEDULE
FOR AUGUST

Day	Devotional Reading	Through the Bible in a Year	Title
Aug. 1	❏ Ps. 91:9-16; 92	❏ S. Sol. 4; Jer. 52; Lam. 1	The Security of the Godly
Aug. 2	❏ Ps. 92–93	❏ S. Sol. 5; Lam. 2–3	It is Good to Praise the Lord
Aug. 3	❏ Ps. 92–93	❏ S. Sol. 6; Lam. 4–5; Ez. 1	Wicked Scattered—Righteous Strong Like Palms
Aug. 4	❏ Ps. 93–94	❏ S. Sol. 7; Ez. 2–5	His Future Righteous Reign
Aug. 5	❏ Ps. 94	❏ S. Sol. 8; Ez. 6–8	The Vengeance of God
Aug. 6	❏ Ps. 94	❏ Ez. 9–12	God Sees, Hears, Knows, and Will Judge
Aug. 7	❏ Ps. 94:15-23; 95	❏ Ez. 13–15; 16:1-34	The Righteous Delivered—The Wicked Doomed
Aug. 8	❏ Ps. 95–96	❏ Ez. 16:35-63; 17–18	Come, Let Us Worship
Aug. 9	❏ Ps. 95–96	❏ Ez. 19–21	Don't Grieve God with Unbelief
Aug. 10	❏ Ps. 96–97	❏ Ez. 22–23	A Missionary Hymn
Aug. 11	❏ Ps. 96–97	❏ Ez. 24–26	Sing! Give! Let!
Aug. 12	❏ Ps. 97–98	❏ Ez. 27–29	Rejoicing in His Reign
Aug. 13	❏ Ps. 97–98	❏ Ez. 30–32	Hate Evil—So He Can Reign Supreme
Aug. 14	❏ Ps. 99–101	❏ Ez. 33–35	The New Song of Salvation
Aug. 15	❏ Ps. 99–101	❏ Ez. 36–38	The Lord Reigneth for Helis Holy
Aug. 16	❏ Ps. 100–101; 102:1-7	❏ Ez. 39–40	A Day Coming With Universal Worship of Our Lord
Aug. 17	❏ Ps. 101; 102:1-14	❏ Ez. 41–43	A King's Resolutions—Part 1
Aug. 18	❏ Ps. 101; 102:1-14	❏ Ez. 44–46	A King's Resolutions—Part 2
Aug. 19	❏ Ps. 102	❏ Ez. 47–48; Dan. 1	The Heavy Burden of the Ps.ist
Aug. 20	❏ Ps. 102	❏ Dan. 2–3	Consolation Amidst the Gloom
Aug. 21	❏ Ps. 102:16-28; 103:1-7	❏ Dan. 4–5	A Glorious Future
Aug. 22	❏ Ps. 102:22-28; 103	❏ Dan. 6–8	Our Eternal and Faithful God
Aug. 23	❏ Ps. 103	❏ Dan. 9–11	Let's Praise the Lord
Aug. 24	❏ Ps. 103	❏ Dan. 12; Hos. 1–4	The Song of the Soul Set Free
Aug. 25	❏ Ps. 103	❏ Hos. 5–10	Bless the Lord, All His Dominion
Aug. 26	❏ Ps. 104	❏ Hos. 11–14; Joel 1	Exalting the God of Creation
Aug. 27	❏ Ps. 104	❏ Joel 2–3; Amos 1–2	The Universal Flood And the Earth Following the Flood
Aug. 28	❏ Ps. 104	❏ Amos 3–7	Our Great God Who Provides Every Need
Aug. 29	❏ Ps. 104:20-35; 105:1-6	❏ Amos 8–9; Oba.; Jonah 1–4	Praising God for His Creation
Aug. 30	❏ Ps. 104:26-35; 105:1-15	❏ Mic. 1–7	Praise Him for His Sustaining of the Earth
Aug. 31	❏ Ps. 105	❏ Nah. 1–3; Hab. 1–2	Rejoice—Return—Remember

DAILY SCHEDULE
FOR SEPTEMBER

Day	Devotional Reading	Through the Bible in a Year	Title
Sep. 1	❏ Ps. 105	❏ Hab. 3; Zeph. 1–3	God's Keeping and Protecting of Israel
Sep. 2	❏ Ps. 105	❏ Haggai 1–2; Zech. 1–2	God's Blessing on Joseph
Sep. 3	❏ Ps. 105	❏ Zech. 3–8	God Delivers the People of Israel
Sep. 4	❏ Ps. 105:36-45; 106:1-10	❏ Zech. 9–13	God's Saves and Keeps His Own
Sep. 5	❏ Ps. 105:39-45; 106:1-15	❏ Zech. 14; Malachi 1–3	Praise God for His Salvation
Sep. 6	❏ Ps. 106	❏ Mat. 1–3	Praising the Lord for Him and His People
Sep. 7	❏ Ps. 106	❏ Mat. 4–5	Israel and Her Sins
Sep. 8	❏ Ps. 106	❏ Mat. 6–7	The Danger of Leanness of Soul
Sep. 9	❏ Ps. 106:12-35	❏ Mat. 8–9	Turn from Rebellion and Idols
Sep. 10	❏ Ps. 106:21-48	❏ Mat. 10–11	Do Not Play with Sin
Sep. 11	❏ Ps. 106:32-48; 107:1-8	❏ Mat. 12	Flee Pride, Worldliness, and Idolatry
Sep. 12	❏ Ps. 106:40-48; 107:1-15	❏ Mat. 13	The Dangers of Sin
Sep. 13	❏ Ps. 106:40-48; 107:1-15	❏ Mat. 14–15	Praise God for His Deliverance
Sep. 14	Ps. 107	❏ Mat. 16–17	A Psalm We Need to Read
Sep. 15	❏ Ps. 107	❏ Mat. 18–19	Delivered by the Lord
Sep. 16	❏ Ps. 107	❏ Mat. 20–21	Trusting the Lord for Healing
Sep. 17	❏ Ps. 107	❏ Mat. 22–23	Our Lord Quiets the Storms
Sep. 18	❏ Ps. 107:33-43; 108	❏ Mat. 24	God Has Power to Bless or Blight
Sep. 19	❏ Ps. 107:33-43; 108	❏ Mat. 25	God's Righteous Government
Sep. 20	❏ Ps. 108	❏ Mat. 26	A Fixed Heart
Sep. 21	❏ Ps. 108; 109:1-7	❏ Mat. 27	Victory Through Christ's Victory
Sep. 22	❏ Ps. 109	❏ Mat. 28; Mk. 1	Follow David's Godly Example
Sep. 23	❏ Ps. 109:6-31	❏ Mk. 2–3	God Will Deal with Sin
Sep. 24	❏ Ps. 109:11-31	❏ Mk. 4; 5:1-20	Calling on God to Deal with Sin
Sep. 25	❏ Ps. 109:21-31; 110	❏ Mk. 5:21-43; 6	David's Need of the Lord's Mercy
Sep. 26	❏ Ps. 109:26-31; 110–111	❏ Mk. 7–8	David Gives God the Glory for Victory
Sep. 27	❏ Ps. 110–111	❏ Mk. 9	Our Glorious Priest-King
Sep. 28	❏ Ps. 111–112	❏ Mk. 10	Worship the Lord
Sep. 29	❏ Ps. 111–112	❏ Mk. 11; 12:1-27	The Wonder that Leads us to the Wisdom of Praise
Sep. 30	❏ Ps. 112–113	❏ Mk. 12:28-44; 13	Another Look at the Blessed Man

DAILY SCHEDULE
FOR OCTOBER

Day	Devotional Reading	Through the Bible in a Year	Title
Oct. 1	❏ Ps. 112–113	❏ Mk. 14	Blessings in the Life of the Blessed Man
Oct. 2	❏ Ps. 113–114	❏ Mk. 15–16	Praise the Lord
Oct. 3	❏ Ps. 114–115	❏ Lk. 1	Spiritual Power from God
Oct. 4	❏ Ps. 115	❏ Lk. 2	Rely on the Lord—Not Idols
Oct. 5	❏ Ps. 115	❏ Lk. 3–4	The Lord—Our Help and Shield
Oct. 6	❏ Ps. 115:12-18; 116	❏ Lk. 5; 6:1-38	He Will Bless Those Who Fear Him
Oct. 7	❏ Ps. 116	❏ Lk. 6:39-49; 7	God Answers Prayer
Oct. 8	❏ Ps. 116–117	❏ Lk. 8	Faith Through Dreadful Trials
Oct. 9	❏ Ps. 116–117	❏ Lk. 9	Surrender to God Because of Blessings Received
Oct. 10	❏ Ps. 117–118	❏ Lk. 10; 11:1-13	A Call to All to Praise the Lord
Oct. 11	❏ Ps. 118	❏ Lk. 11:14-54; 12:1-21	Praise Him for His Enduring Mercy
Oct. 12	❏ Ps. 118	❏ Lk. 12:22-59; 13	Deliverance by God's Help
Oct. 13	❏ Ps. 118	❏ Lk. 14–15	Delivered by God's Right Hand
Oct. 14	❏ Ps. 118	❏ Lk. 16–17	Christ, Our Cornerstone
Oct. 15	❏ Ps. 118:22-29; 119:1-16	❏ Lk. 18; 19:1-27	The Lord at Calvary Became Our Cornerstone
Oct. 16	❏ Ps. 119:1-24	❏ Lk. 19:28-48; 20	Brief Introduction to Psalm 119
Oct. 17	❏ Ps. 119:1-8; 25-40	❏ Lk. 21; 22:1-18	The Psalm of Superabounding Blessing
Oct. 18	❏ Ps. 119:1-8; 41-56	❏ Lk. 22:19-71	The Way of Genuine Happiness
Oct. 19	❏ Ps. 119:9-16; 57-72	❏ Lk. 23	The Effect of God's Word in a Committed Believer
Oct. 20	❏ Ps. 119:9-16; 73-88	❏ Lk. 24	Letting God's Word Work in our Lives
Oct. 21	❏ Ps. 119:17-24; 89-104	❏ Jn. 1	Opportunities in the Word—Opposition to the Word
Oct. 22	❏ Ps. 119:25-32; 105-120	❏ Jn. 2–3	Dealing with Sin in our Lives
Oct. 23	❏ Ps. 119:33-40; 121-136	❏ Jn. 4	Four Pictures of a Man of God
Oct. 24	❏ Ps. 119:41-48; 137-152	❏ Jn. 5	Trusting the Lord to do His Will
Oct. 25	❏ Ps. 119:49-56; 153-176	❏ Jn. 6	Hoping in God's Word
Oct. 26	❏ Ps. 119:1-16; 49-56	❏ Jn. 7	Comforted by God's Judgments
Oct. 27	❏ Ps. 119:17-32; 57-64	❏ Jn. 8	A Robbery that Awakened the Soul
Oct. 28	❏ Ps. 119:33-48; 65-72	❏ Jn. 9; 10:1-30	Blessing Through Affliction
Oct. 29	❏ Ps. 119:49-64; 73-80	❏ Jn. 10:31-42; 11	Man Created Directly by God
Oct. 30	❏ Ps. 119:65-80	❏ Jn. 12; 13:1-20	Proper Requests When We Face Trials
Oct. 31	❏ Ps. 119:81-104	❏ Jn. 13:21-38; 14–15	Clinging to God's Word in Difficult Circumstances

DAILY SCHEDULE
FOR NOVEMBER

Day	Devotional Reading	Through the Bible in a Year	Title
Nov. 1	❏ Ps. 119:89-96; 105-120	❏ Jn. 16–17	The Word: Forever Settled in Heaven
Nov. 2	❏ Ps. 119:97-104; 121-136	❏ Jn. 18–19	Wisdom from God's Word
Nov. 3	❏ Ps. 119:105-112; 137-152	❏ Jn. 20–21	The Bible—Our Guide in Life
Nov. 4	❏ Ps. 119:105-112; 153-168	❏ Acts 1–2	The Bible—Our Heritage
Nov. 5	❏ Ps. 119:1-8; 113-120; 169-176	❏ Acts 3–4	The Lord and His Word—Our Only Hope
Nov. 6	❏ Ps. 119:9-24; 121-128	❏ Acts 5–6	Believing God Will Work
Nov. 7	❏ Ps. 119:25-48; 129-136	❏ Acts 7	God's Word—The Light We Need
Nov. 8	❏ Ps. 119:49-72; 137-144	❏ Acts 8–9	The Bible—Our Delight
Nov. 9	❏ Ps. 119:73-96; 145-152	❏ Acts 10–11	Fervent Prayer When Troubled
Nov. 10	❏ Ps. 119:97-120; 153-160	❏ Acts 12–13	Revival Through the Lord, the Living Word
Nov. 11	❏ Ps. 119:121-144; 161-168	❏ Acts 14–15	Standing in Awe of God's Word
Nov. 12	❏ Ps. 119:145-168	❏ Acts 16–17	The Blessing of Great Peace
Nov. 13	❏ Ps. 119:169-176; 120–121	❏ Acts 18–19	A Great Writer Needed the Lord
Nov. 14	❏ Ps. 120–122	❏ Acts 20–21	The Dreadful Opposition of a False Tongue
Nov. 15	❏ Ps. 121–123	❏ Acts 22–24	Our Lord—Able to Keep Us
Nov. 16	❏ Ps. 122–124	❏ Acts 25–26	The Blessing of Corporate Worship
Nov. 17	❏ Ps. 123–125	❏ Acts 27–28	Seeing the Lord Above Our Circumstances
Nov. 18	❏ Ps. 124–126	❏ Rom. 1–2	A Song of Gratitude
Nov. 19	❏ Ps. 125–128	❏ Rom. 3–5	Secure in Christ
Nov. 20	❏ Ps. 126–129	❏ Rom. 6–8	The Rejoicing of the Ransomed
Nov. 21	❏ Ps. 127–130	❏ Rom. 9–10	Building with God as Partner
Nov. 22	❏ Ps. 128–130	❏ Rom. 11–13	A Fruitful Home
Nov. 23	❏ Ps. 129–131	❏ Rom. 14–16	Nations of the Earth— Beware!
Nov. 24	❏ Ps. 130–132	❏ I Cor. 1–3	Who Could Stand?—None!
Nov. 25	❏ Ps. 131–132	❏ I Cor. 4–6	A Humble Believer
Nov. 26	❏ Ps. 132–133	❏ I Cor. 7–9	Yielding Our Lives to be Used of God
Nov. 27	❏ Ps. 132–133	❏ I Cor. 10–11	God's Sure Promise to David
Nov. 28	❏ Ps. 132:8-18; 133–134	❏ I Cor. 12–14	Are You Clothed with His Salvation?
Nov. 29	Ps. 133–135	❏ I Cor. 15–16	The Blessing of Unity
Nov. 30	❏ Ps. 134–135	❏ II Cor. 1–4	Dedicated Servant Yielded to Him

DAILY SCHEDULE
FOR DECEMBER

Day	Devotional Reading	Through the Bible in a Year	Title
Dec. 1	❒ Ps. 135	❒ II Cor. 5–8	Praise Him, Ye Servants
Dec. 2	❒ Ps. 135	❒ II Cor. 9–11	The Greatness of Our God
Dec. 3	❒ Ps. 135:15-21; 136	❒ II Cor. 12–13; Gal. 1–2	Our God is Alive and Deserves Praise
Dec. 4	❒ Ps. 136	❒ Gal. 3–4	All Creation Reveals His Mercy
Dec. 5	❒ Ps. 136	❒ Gal. 5–6; Eph. 1	Israel's History Reveals His Mercy
Dec. 6	❒ Ps. 136:17-29; 137	❒ Eph. 2–4	Israel's Victories Because of His Mercy
Dec. 7	❒ Ps. 137–138; 139:1-6	❒ Eph. 5–6; Phil. 1	Cherish the Blessings of God
Dec. 8	❒ Ps. 138–139	❒ Phil. 2–4	Praise to God for His Control and Power
Dec. 9	❒ Ps. 139	❒ Col. 1–3	God Knows All about Me
Dec. 10	❒ Ps. 139	❒ Col. 4; I Thes. 1–3	God is Everywhere Present
Dec. 11	❒ Ps. 139	❒ I Thes. 4–5; II Thes. 1–2	God's Power is Manifested in Each Human Body
Dec. 12	❒ Ps. 139:17-24; 140	❒ II Thes. 3; I Tim. 1–3	Judgment Must Begin at God's House
Dec. 13	❒ Ps. 140–141	❒ I Tim. 4–6	Prayer for Deliverance from Evil
Dec. 14	❒ Ps. 140–141	❒ II Tim. 1–3	David's Confidence That God Will Deal Fairly
Dec. 15	❒ Ps. 141–142	❒ II Tim. 4; Titus 1–3	How to Face Trouble
Dec. 16	❒ Ps. 142–143	❒ Phile.; Heb. 1–3	God is With Us in No Man's Land
Dec. 17	❒ Ps. 143–144	❒ Heb. 4–7	David Turns All Over to the Lord
Dec. 18	❒ Ps. 143:7-12; 144	❒ Heb. 8–10	David's Prayer When Facing Trials
Dec. 19	❒ Ps. 144–145	❒ Heb. 11–12	The Lord, Our Help and Defender
Dec. 20	❒ Ps. 144–145	❒ Heb. 13; James 1–2	A Happy People
Dec. 21	❒ Ps. 145	❒ James 3–5; I Pet. 1	David's Great Psalm of Praise
Dec. 22	❒ Ps. 145	❒ I Pet. 2–4	God's Greatness, Goodness, and Glory
Dec. 23	❒ Ps. 145:14-21; 146	❒ I Pet. 5; II Pet. 1–3	Praise God for His Government and Grace
Dec. 24	❒ Ps. 146–147	❒ I Jn. 1–4	Praise Him Now While We Live
Dec. 25	❒ Ps. 147	❒ I Jn. 5; II Jn; III Jn.; Jude	Praising the Lord for the Coming of Jesus Christ
Dec. 26	❒ Ps. 147	❒ Rev. 1–3	How Great Thou Art!
Dec. 27	❒ Ps. 147:12-18; 148	❒ Rev. 4–8	Israel Should Praise the Lord
Dec. 28	❒ Ps. 148–149	❒ Rev. 9–12	All of Heaven—Praise Him
Dec. 29	❒ Ps. 148–149	❒ Rev. 13–16	All of Earth—Praise the Lord!
Dec. 30	❒ Ps. 149; Rev. 4:8-11; 5:8-14	❒ Rev. 17–19	Praise by His Favored Ones
Dec. 31	❒ Ps. 150; Rev. 7:9-12; 19:1-10	❒ Rev. 20–22	The Grand Finale of Praise

January 1

Read Psalms 1–2
Devotional Reading: Psalm 1

The Blessed Man

I cannot think of a better portion of Scripture to begin a new year than Psalm 1. It speaks of the blessed man and gives promise to him as a faithful believer. It also warns the wicked of the danger inherent in his errant way.

The blessed man of whom Psalm 1 speaks is first of all the Lord Jesus Christ. He is the only One who could actually say He never walked in the counsel of the ungodly, He never stood in the way of sinners, and He never sat in the seat of the scornful. But the psalm goes beyond the Lord Jesus Christ to encompass every believer who walks faithfully with the Lord to honor Him.

This first psalm is an introduction to the entire book of Psalms, actually presenting the theme of the whole book. It speaks of the godly and the ungodly, revealing the blessings of the godly, and the curses on the ungodly.

Who is the blessed man? That individual is the believer who is careful not to walk in the counsel (literally, the philosophy) of the ungodly. How important it is that we establish the right thought patterns, having the right philosophy for life. That philosophy must be acquired from and be based upon the Word of God. When we walk not in the philosophy of the world, we will be delivered from standing with sinners. Please note the downward direction—first, one *walks* in the wrong philosophy; then he *stands* in the way of sinners; and, lastly, he *sits* down with scoffers, seeming to be totally identified with them.

What makes the blessed man what he is? Verse two gives the answer: *". . . his delight is in the law of the Lord; and in his law doth he meditate day and night."*

Verse three then gives the promise that comes to this blessed man. He is *"like a tree planted by the rivers* [not just one, but many] *of water,"* thereby being nourished to strength and stability. His leaf does not wither—he prospers in the blessings of God. These first three verses are verses a believer can claim for the new year.

Through the Bible in a Year: Genesis 1–3

January 2

Read Psalms 2–3
Devotional Reading: Psalm 2

David Saw Man in His Rebellion

Psalm 2, a very instructive passage, joins Psalm 1 as an introduction to the entire book of Psalms and in God's dealing with men. Psalm 1 presents the principles by which God works with men; Psalm 2 presents the prophecy of how God will deal with man and his rebellion.

Psalm 2 gives the basis for all of the world's problems. We understand current world conditions when we understand this psalm. This world is in a life-and-death struggle between those who love the Lord Jesus Christ and the hordes of Antichrist.

To unlock the meaning of this psalm, we must take this key: the psalm encompasses four speakers.

First Speaker:	David the Psalmist—verses 1-3
Second Speaker:	God the Father—verses 4-6
Third Speaker:	God the Son—verses 7-9
Fourth Speaker:	God the Holy Spirit—verses 10-12

The psalm opens with David's question: *"Why do the heathen rage, and the people imagine a vain thing?"* He saw the world in a dreadful state of rebellion. The power of this rebellion is in the fact that *"the people imagine a vain thing" (v. 1).* The word translated *imagine* here is the same word translated *meditate* in Psalm 1:2. The people meditate on how they can overthrow God. Because the people have such a humanistic philosophy, their rulers set themselves against God (v. 2).

The focus of this rebellion is against God's *person* and His *precepts.* They hate Him and His Son, His anointed, the Lord Jesus Christ (v. 2). They also hate the precepts of His rule. They cry out, *"Let us break their bands asunder* (those of God and His anointed), *and cast away their cords from us" (v. 3).* They will speak against God's restraints. They mock the Bible and its principles: the sanctity of the home, sexual purity, obedience to parents, respect for authority, the necessity of salvation, and a holy life.

David saw the rebellion of man, and it concerned him. May we believers love the person and the precepts of our God.

Through the Bible in a Year: Genesis 4–6

January 3

Read Psalms 2–3
Devotional Reading: Psalm 2

David Saw Jesus Christ in His Reign

Yesterday we noted David's concern over the rebellion of men against God. Today we will note God's answer to the rebellion of man.

First, we read in verse four that God laughs. Man cries out that he wants to break God's bands and cast away His cords of restraint. In answer God sits in Heaven and laughs. He does not move from His place—He simply laughs and then speaks. His wrath is revealed in His speaking. His voice is all that is needed to answer the rebellion and resistance of men.

A rebel participating in the French revolution scaled the spire of Notre Dame Cathedral, tore off the cross, and threw it to the pavement far below. He spoke to a Parisian peasant, "We are going to pull down all that reminds you of God!" The peasant quietly and calmly replied, "Then, citizen, pull down the stairs."

Second, we note what God says: *"Yet have I set my king upon my holy hill of Zion" (v. 6).* Man can mock—he can rebel. But God's decree is set—Jesus Christ is King, and Jerusalem is the place from which He will reign. Men have their ideas about Jerusalem, but God has already said that it will be the city from which Jesus Christ will reign.

In verses seven through nine we hear the Lord Jesus Christ speak. He states that His reign will be according to the decree of the Father: that Christ is God's Son, and He has been appointed to rule. The heathen (nations) are His inheritance, and those who reject Him will suffer the wrath of God.

Finally, in verses ten through twelve we have the advice of God the Holy Spirit. He states that the kings and judges will be wise to serve the Lord and thus rejoice (v. 11). This world has not seen the last of Jesus Christ. He will come to earth again. God states that the blessed man will be that one who puts his trust in Him.

May we embrace Him and love Him. Then we will stand with Him against the godless world and its rebellion against God.

Through the Bible in a Year: Genesis 7–9

January 4

Read Psalms 3–4
Devotional Reading: Psalm 3

Think on This—The Lord Is Our Shield!

In Psalm 1 we see that the only One who truly met the qualifications of the *blessed man* is the Lord Jesus Christ. Then in Psalm 2 we know that this One, *"the Son,"* is the King who has been decreed by God to reign someday. Now beginning in Psalm 3 we see the problems faced by those who trust the Lord and who live now while He is absent from earth.

The psalms are filled with trouble, trial, and distress. *"Lord, how are they increased that **trouble** me! many are they that rise up against me" (v. 1). "Hear me when I call, O God of my righteousness: thou hast enlarged me when I was in **distress** . . ." (4:1).* But David had victory in his soul. He could say, *"But thou, O Lord, art a shield for me . . ." (3:3). "I will not be afraid of ten thousands of people, that have set themselves against me round about" (v. 6).* David had learned to rest on the Lord, regardless of circumstances.

There were many who said that David had no help in God (3:2). David knew that was not true. Had these foes said, "David deserves no help from God," he would have admitted that it was true. David ended this verse with the word *Selah*, meaning *think* or *meditate* on this. You will note that David used the word *Selah* in this psalm three times (vv. 2, 4, and 8). He wanted readers and singers to know about these truths.

David thought about what his enemies had said, and then he boldly announced, *"But thou, O Lord, art a shield for me" (v. 3).* He could believe God, and he knew that his Lord would be the Victor. David also had previous experience of God's answering his prayer (v. 4) and sustaining him with and through his sleep (v. 5).

When a man is saved, he may have more enemies and trouble than he ever had before. He has a sinful nature to burden him. Carnal lusts trouble him. Satan endeavors to defeat him. But he can rejoice that God is his Father, the Lord Jesus is his precious Saviour, and the Holy Spirit is his ever-present Comforter. He can go directly to the Father, Son, and Holy Spirit to receive the grace and strength which he needs. He can honestly say, *"Salvation belongeth unto the Lord" (3:8).*

Through the Bible in a Year: Genesis 10–12

January 5

Read Psalms 4–5
Devotional Reading: Psalm 4

Confidence in God

Psalms 3 and 4 stand together. Psalm 3 presents David's attitude in the morning. Even though he was fleeing from Absalom (heading of Psalm 3), he had lain down, slept, and awakened, knowing that the Lord had taken care of him (3:5). Psalm 4 reveals David's attitude in the evening—he is now ready to retire—*"I will both lay me down in peace, and sleep: for thou, Lord, only makest me dwell in safety" (4:8)*. The heading of Psalm 4 mentions *Neginoth*, which means *smitings*. It appears that in both Psalm 3 and Psalm 4 David is facing Absalom and his rebellion. The hordes are gathering against him.

David turned to the Lord in his distress (v. 1). He relied on God's mercy for his deliverance. Then he turned to ask his enemies, *". . . how long will ye turn my glory into shame?. . ." (v. 2)*. It is in verse three that he shows his real confidence in the Lord: *"But know that the Lord hath set apart him that is godly for himself: the Lord will hear when I call unto him."* Who is this *"godly"* man? It is the man who relies on God's mercy (v. 1) and who gives the Lord first place in his life.

Then David revealed that his soul was at rest. He had gladness in his heart that abounded more than did those who had realized a good corn and grape harvest (v. 7). There were those who scoffed and asked, *"Who will show good to David?"* His reply was that the Lord alone could do it by lifting up the light of His countenance upon His people (v. 6).

Therefore David knew that he could lie down and rest in safety. As David did, so can we. We can trust the Lord and leave all to Him, regardless of the problems we face. We do need to remember that to have this blessing of rest in the Lord we need to have a joyful heart. While others manifested their pessimism with the question, *"Who will show us any good?" (v. 6)*, David could triumphantly say, *"Thou hast put gladness in my heart . . ." (v. 7)*.

May each of us simply trust, rejoice, and realize victory over the enemies round about. Like David, our confidence and joy must be in the Lord.

Through the Bible in a Year: Genesis 13–16

January 6

Read Psalms 5–6
Devotional Reading: Psalm 5

Prayer Preparation for the Day

Psalms 3, 4, and 5 seem to go together. In all three, David is facing a foe that is out to destroy him. Psalm 3 speaks of David's morning prayer, while Psalm 4 presents an evening prayer. It appears that Psalm 5 is a prayer on a following morning.

David was going forth for the day and expected to meet dangerous and powerful foes. He prepared for the day by spending time in prayer. This should speak to each of us—for each day as we go forth, we do not know what the day will bring. G. Campbell Morgan stated that we face no day which is not filled with dangers.

Psalm 5 presents a contrast between David, who was made righteous by grace, and the wicked, who opposed him. David said he would pray in the morning to seek the blessing of God (v. 3). Spurgeon wrote that the morning "is the fittest time for intercourse with God. An hour in the morning is worth two in the evening. While the dew is on the grass, let grace drop upon the soul. Let us give to God the mornings of our days and the mornings of our lives. Prayer should be the key of the day and the lock of the night. Devotions should be both the morning star and the evening star."

The words, *"in the morning will I direct my prayer unto thee" (v. 3)*, carry the idea of an archer aiming the arrow at a specific target. We need to organize our prayer life so that we effectively pray for specific things.

David literally pleaded with the Lord to listen. He requested God: *"Give ear to my words, O Lord, . . . " (v. 1)*. The word for *"give ear"* literally meant to cup the ear so that the hearer could hear better. David was boldly pleading with God to hear his prayer.

In verse three David confessed that God was a hearing God. He knew that God answers prayer. Therefore, David said, *"in the morning will I direct my prayer unto thee, and will look up."* David prayed, believing God and expecting an answer. May we have this same faith.

Through the Bible in a Year: Genesis 17–19

January 7

Read Psalms 5–6
Devotional Reading: Psalm 5

David's Assurance of the Lord's Favor

David was surrounded by wicked enemies (v. 4), bloody and deceitful men (v. 6). They were liars. (To *speak leasing* in verse six means *lying*.) But in such dire circumstances, David ended this psalm by singing: *"For thou, Lord, wilt bless the righteous; with favor wilt thou compass him as with a shield" (v. 12).*

How could David sing as he did in this twelfth verse when he was facing such wicked foes? The answer is that David had a twofold refuge. He knew he could enjoy the Lord's presence by seeking refuge in prayer as he started the day (vv. 1-3). The other refuge was the privilege he had of going into the house of the Lord. He promised God he would pray (v. 2). And then he promised: *"But as for me, I will come into thy house in the multitude of thy mercy: and in thy fear will I worship toward thy holy temple" (v. 7).*

The two must go together—prayer and attendance in the house of God. Without these, no believer is able to stand against the enemies of the Lord. In this seventh verse David is looking beyond an earthly temple, for it had not yet been built. He was speaking of coming into the heavenly presence of God. The only basis by which he could come was *"in the multitude of thy [God's] mercy" (v. 7).*

Then he prayed for the Lord to lead him *"in . . . righteousness" (v. 8).* He knew that only the Lord could lead him and give him full protection, and he followed the Lord to escape the enemy.

David ended the psalm by revealing that even in the dire circumstances he was facing, the wisest and best thing he could do would be to rejoice in the Lord (v. 11). He concluded the psalm by stating that God would compass the righteous with favor *"as with a shield."* The *"shield"* here is the *"buckler"*—a large shield made to protect the whole body, twice the size of an ordinary shield. To others David appeared vulnerable, but he was not trusting himself or his followers. He was trusting the Lord. May we always rest in Him as our shield and protector.

Through the Bible in a Year: Genesis 20–22

January 8

Read Psalms 6–7
Devotional Reading: Psalm 6

Dealing with Sin in Repentance

Psalm 6 is the first of what we refer to as "The Penitential Psalms." We are not told when David penned this psalm, but we can be sure it was following something in his life that he recognized as sinful. Here is a believer, realizing he has sinned, and being burdened about it.

Remember that believers are sinners—they are sinners saved by grace—but they are still sinners. Those of us who have trusted Christ are redeemed sinners with Heaven as our home and Christ Jesus as our Saviour. But we still have a sin nature that can produce in us that of which we should be ashamed. One of the tragedies we see today is professed believers who allow sin to come into their lives but refuse to face it as sin and repent of it. How much we believers need to learn the truth of Proverbs 28:13—*"He that covereth his sins shall not prosper: but whoso confesseth and forsaketh them shall have mercy."*

David admitted he was a sinner. He was deeply grieved over his sin and in Psalm 6 revealed the agony that came to his life because of sin. In the first seven verses we see David in great distress over his sin. He even felt that he might have committed the sin unto death (v. 5). His soul was sore vexed (v. 3), even to the place of bringing terrible weakness to his body (v. 2). Spurgeon warned, "The trouble of the soul is the soul of trouble." David was greatly exercised, groaning all night, even wetting his bed with his tears (v. 6).

But when we come to verse eight, we find a renewed David. He states that *"the Lord hath heard the voice of my weeping."* He then knows the Lord will receive his prayer (v. 9), and he has confidence his mocking enemies will be ashamed (v. 10). Because he admitted his sin and repented in agony for his sin, he had come back to a place of confidence in the Lord. The renewal of David is sudden. One moment he was overwhelmed with tragedy, and the next he was proclaiming victory over his enemies. What made the difference? He had come to God with burdened prayer, weeping over his sin. May we come to the Lord with that same kind of burden and see God give victory in our lives.

Through the Bible in a Year: Genesis 23–24

January 9

Read Psalms 7–8
Devotional Reading: Psalm 7

A Clear Conscience

This seventh psalm continues as David faces persecution by wicked foes. The superscription states that this song was composed when he had heard the words of Cush the Benjamite. We do not know who Cush was, but apparently he had slandered David with horrible, malicious intent.

However, David had a clear conscience. He examined his heart (vv. 3-5). He told God that if he had done what Cush had been saying, then he deserved punishment. However, he stated that the opposite is the truth (v. 4). While he was accused of rewarding evil to those who were at peace with him, he was actually doing the opposite—delivering and helping those who were his enemies.

This brought him to the place where he could say with confidence, *"The Lord shall judge the people . . . " (v. 8).* Then he could request, *"judge me, O Lord, according to my righteousness . . . " (v. 8).* What a blessing it is when a believer knows down in his heart that he has endeavored to do the right thing. Paul stated such a confidence clearly to Felix in Acts 24:16:

> *"And herein do I exercise myself, to have always a conscience void of offense toward God, and toward men."*

David did not claim to be perfect. Of course, he made mistakes; but deep inside he knew that he had consistently endeavored to do what was right. He had wanted to glorify God. David knew that *"the righteous God" (v. 9)* tested the hearts of His people. David invited that judgment to come. Especially did he ask God to *"judge me . . ." (v. 8).* What a bold prayer!

I have had lies spread about me. When that happens, I quote to myself I Corinthians 4:5:

> *"Therefore judge nothing before the time, until the Lord come, who both will bring to light the hidden things of darkness, and will make manifest the counsels of the hearts: and then shall every man have praise of God."*

Through the Bible in a Year: Genesis 25–26

January 10

Read Psalms 7–8
Devotional Reading: Psalm 7

David's Defense

Yesterday we noted David's clear conscience from Psalm 7:1-9. Today we note his defense, beginning at verse ten: *"My defense is of God, which saveth the upright in heart."*

David knew that God would judge righteously. He stated in verse eleven: *"God judgeth the righteous, and God is angry with the wicked every day."* Be assured that God will judge the wicked. *"If he* (the wicked) *turn not, he* (God) *will whet his sword: he* (God) *hath bent his bow, and made it ready"* (v. 12).

David then gives three illustrations explaining God's moral government. God's laws permit sin to bring its own inevitable consequences. In verses fourteen through sixteen we find these three illustrations.

First, sin in its source is like a birth (v. 14). He states that the wicked *"travaileth."* Sin is conceived in the heart, and it grows within a person until it comes forth as a birth. That which was conceived in Cush's heart was *"mischief."* That word speaks of perverseness. Just as a pregnant woman swells up to bring forth a child, wickedness swells up in a man's soul until it comes forth in deceit and rottenness.

Second, sin in its course is like a bait. Verse fifteen states that Cush made a trap to ensnare. Sin works to deceive and wreck lives. Cush's problem was not that he slipped into sin, but he actually deliberately planned to trap and ensnare.

Third, sin brings its own curse. Verse sixteen states that Cush's mischief shall return upon his own head. Sin will act as a boomerang. It will swing back to ruin the sinner. Remember this: *"[W]ith what measure ye mete, it shall be measured to you again"* (Matthew 7:2).

May we daily live a life pleasing to the Lord—to honor and glorify Him.

Through the Bible in a Year: Genesis 27–28

January 11

Read Psalms 8–9
Devotional Reading: Psalm 8

Our God's Greatness Revealed in His Grace

In the previous psalms we have read of the trials David experienced. He saw his foes coming upon him, and he learned to rest on the Lord as his defense. Now as we come to Psalm 8, the whole tone is changed. David looks to the Lord as the triumphant One. He sees the Lord Jesus Christ as the reigning One.

Some have called this an "Envelope Psalm." It begins and ends with the same words: *"O Lord our Lord, how excellent is thy name in all the earth!"* The psalm begins where it ends and ends where it begins. The opening and closing statements wrap up all the truth between them.

This psalm makes a distinct contrast between our infinite God and finite man. The psalmist speaks of things such as babes and sucklings. Then he points out the vast heavens with all of their greatness (vv. 2, 3).

David gives two lines of proof that the name of the Lord is most excellent. The first is the *Greatness of God.* In verse three he considers the heavens with their moon and stars as that which God not only planned and ordained but also created with His fingers. As a shepherd boy, David had spent many a night looking at the stars in the few galaxies his eyes could see. He knew that a God with an excellent name—a great God—created all of this.

But then David asked in verse four: *"What is man, that thou art mindful of him?"* The second truth David realized was the *Grace of God.* In His grace God has been concerned about men. God is more interested in people than in planets. He has crowned man and given him dominion over all of His creation (vv. 5-8). God in His grace sent His Son, the Lord Jesus Christ, to earth. It is He who is *"the son of man"* in verse four and who is *"crowned . . . with glory and honor"* in verse five. In the New Testament there are three passages that quote from this psalm, showing that it refers to the Lord Jesus—Matthew 21:15-17; I Corinthians 15:27; and Hebrews 2:6-9.

May we worship and honor Him today who is crowned with glory and honor and whose name is the most excellent in all the earth.

Through the Bible in a Year: Genesis 29–30

January 12

Read Psalm 9

David, a Prophet, Sees Victory Over Antichrist

We will be reading Psalms 9 and 10 for the next six days. In certain ancient versions these two psalms appeared as one. It is certain that they are both dealing with the same subject. Both psalms speak of the wicked as being in opposition to the Lord and His people.

The *"wicked"* in these psalms focuses on one individual. In Psalm 9:6 David addresses him: *"O thou enemy . . . ."* The last verse of Psalm 10 calls this one *"the man of the earth . . . ."* In Psalm 10 the title, *"the wicked,"* is listed five times (vv. 2, 3, 4, 13, 15). That title is referring to a single individual twenty-seven times. The third person personal and possessive pronouns are used referring to *"the wicked"* —i. e.; *he, him his.* I have stated all of this to show that these two psalms are speaking of one wicked individual who will appear on the scene. That one is presented as the antichrist in I John 2:18—*". . . as ye have heard that antichrist shall come, even now are there many antichrists; . . ."* The Apostle Paul spoke of him in II Thessalonians 2:8, 9—*"And then shall that Wicked be revealed, . . . Even him, whose coming is after the working of Satan . . . ."* In these two psalms we see the shadow of this one who will appear on the scene.

As Psalm 9 begins, David is praising the Lord. The psalm speaks about the enemy of David, of God, and of His people. But David praises the Lord because the victory is with him. David has known suffering at the hand of a vicious enemy. King Saul has persecuted and chased him —yet what has David given in return? The Scripture shows that he has manifested kindness, grace, and love (I Samuel 24:8-19; 26:7-21). When he faces the truth of his enemies in Psalm 9, his heart does not grumble and complain. Rather, he praises the Lord. He states that he will praise God with his whole heart (v. 1). Then he announces that God will turn the enemies back (v. 3) and that wicked one who opposes him will be destroyed (v. 5). The destructions of his enemy will end forever (v. 6). David was undoubtedly looking forward as a prophet to the day when the Lord Jesus Christ will have defeated antichrist and will have chained Satan.

Through the Bible in a Year: Genesis 31–32

January 13

Read Psalm 9

The Lord Our Refuge in Trouble

Today I want us to note particularly verses seven through fourteen of Psalm 9. David has been speaking of an enemy, and he said in verse six that the destructions of the enemy would end permanently. In verse seven when he speaks of the Lord, he states the exact opposite. The enemy shall have an end, *"But the Lord shall endure forever . . . ."* With that statement the Lord introduces us to blessings that His people will receive. They have had trouble, but the day will come when they will realize that God judges:

Verse 7—"[H]e hath prepared his throne for judgment."

Verse 8—"And he shall judge the world in righteousness, he shall minister judgment to the people in uprightness."

He will not only judge in righteousness but He will also be a refuge for those who have been oppressed and in trouble (v. 9). David was no stranger to trouble and oppression, but he knew from experience the wonderful truth of our refuge in the Lord.

David expressed the blessed truth that God is interested in and concerned for His own. He prayed, *"thou, Lord, hast not forsaken them that seek thee" (v. 10).* David emphasized this fact again in verse twelve:

"When he maketh inquisition for blood, he remembereth them: he forgetteth not the cry of the humble."

Think of it—God will inquire into the suffering of His people. With this righteous judgment, He will know exactly why they suffer. Often when we suffer, we feel forsaken and forgotten, but we can know that God never forgets. He notices every sorrow that His people have to endure—He will not forget their cry. He will have mercy and consider the trouble we may be facing. Remember—God is interested. Please allow Him to prove His concern over you in your troubles and trials.

Do you think you have suffered unjustly? Do not get bitter over it. Rather, remember that God knows and will make all things right someday. Turn to Him as your refuge and do not let hurts ruin your testimony for Christ.

Through the Bible in a Year: Genesis 33–35

January 14

Read Psalm 9

Think of That—God's Judgment Will Come

In our two previous meditations, we have considered the truth that God is concerned about our trials. In His righteous judgment, God knows exactly what we are going through. David states that in spite of the trouble caused by foes that would destroy him, he will show forth God's promise and rejoice in the Lord's salvation (v. 14).

Then David sees the end of the wicked. Verse fifteen states that those who set a trap for God's people are ensnared in their own trap. Be absolutely sure that God has established laws whereby those who devise wickedness are caught in it. In verse sixteen he states it again: *". . . the wicked is snared in the work of his own hands."* And then God adds the words, *"Higgaion. Selah."* We have noted before that *"Selah"* means *"What do you think of that?"* I believe it was a musical term that meant *"repeat this refrain."* It was worth saying again. God wanted that truth brought home to the heart. The word *"Higgaion"* meant *"Think on it for a while."* Think of it! The wicked will be caught in their own traps. Haman was hanged on the very gallows he prepared for Mordecai (Esther 7:9, 10). Adoni-bezek received the same punishment he had meted out (Judges 1:6, 7). Such is the poetic justice of God—*"for whatsoever a man soweth, that shall he also reap" (Galatians 6:7).* Someone has said that Galatians 6:7 is as much a law of the soul as it is a law of the soil.

Then God makes that dreadful truth—*"The wicked shall be turned into hell . . ." (Psalm 9:17).* What an awful, solemn thought! They will look as if they are prospering, but their end is Hell.

Let's note one more truth in Psalm 9. In verses eleven and fourteen, he speaks of Zion. Remember that Zion refers to the kingdom of Israel. He uses the title *"heathen"* three times, the word *"nations"* twice, and the word *"world"* once. Psalm 9 is speaking of Zion (Israel) experiencing trouble with the nations. Israel will undergo dreadful persecution in the tribulation period; but she will be delivered by God, and the world will be ruled from Zion during the Kingdom Age.

Through the Bible in a Year: Genesis 36–37

January 15

Read Psalms 10–11
Family Reading: Psalm 10

The Dangerous Way of the Wicked

Psalm 10 begins by asking the same question which we often ask: *"Why . . . , O Lord?"* It appears that sin and wickedness are triumphing. When that happens, we are prone to ask the familiar question: *"Why, O Lord?"* The psalmist seemed to think that God was afar off and not concerned about the trouble His people faced.

Following verse one, the psalmist speaks of the awful attitudes and actions of the wicked. What a terrible indictment is given against the wicked in verses two through eleven! Those attitudes and actions are summed up in the last statement of verse four:

". . . God is not in all his thoughts."

In this psalm we have a portrait of the practical atheist. He does not deny God with his lips, but he ignores Him in his life. He does not say, "There is no God," but he lives as though God does not exist.

In verse two we find the *sinful behavior* of the wicked. That sinful lifestyle comes from a proud heart. He carries out his wickedness by persecuting the poor. However, God will take the wicked in their very devices of wickedness so that He can bring judgment on them (v. 2).

One sin that stands out above all others in the life of the wicked is the sin of pride.

*Verse 2 — "The wicked in his **pride** doth persecute the poor . . . ."*

*Verse 3 — "For the wicked **boasteth** of his heart's desire . . . ."*

*Verse 4 — "The wicked, through the **pride** of his countenance . . . ."*

Because of his pride, the ways of the wicked man *"are always grievous . . . ."* He is blinded by sin and cannot understand God's judgments—they *"are far above out of his sight . . . ."* He will just puff at his enemies (v. 5). All the while, he will be playing the part of a fool.

Proverbs 6:16-18 lists seven things that are abomination to God. The first one listed is *"a proud look."* May we as believers humble ourselves and avoid a proud look, walking in humility.

Through the Bible in a Year: Genesis 38–40

January 16

Read Psalms 10–11
Family Reading: Psalm 10

Dreadful Description of the Antichrist

In verses two through eleven we find the dreadful characteristics of the wicked man. In our meditation for January 12 we read that the wicked man is an Old Testament revelation of the antichrist—one individual. Note that in verse fifteen he is referred to as *"the evil man,"* and in verse eighteen as *"the man of the earth."* Today we are going to center our thoughts on this description of the antichrist. Yesterday we saw his pride and the fact that he will not allow God in all of his thoughts.

The next truth about him that we see today is that he is a blasphemous man. In verse seven we read that his mouth is full of cursing. Along with his cursing are deceit and fraud. So wicked is he with his mouth that God describes it by using the picture of certain venomous reptiles. It is said that they carry bags of poison under their teeth, and God says the wicked man carries under his tongue *"mischief and vanity."* Please remember that which characterizes the antichrist also characterizes all wicked men.

Next we will note that he is a brutal man. He murders the innocent (v. 8). He lies in wait like a lion to pounce upon any that he can destroy. He crouches like a lion so that he can leap with strength upon the poor (vv. 9-11). The Bible states that Satan walks about as a roaring lion. The antichrist and all wicked men follow Satan in his lionlike attitudes and actions.

I am writing this in Virginia Beach, Virginia, in July, 1991. This past week I have been appalled at the murders and violence of this area. The horrible work of the wicked is being acted out before our eyes. It seems that we are close to the time when the Antichrist himself will be revealed.

All through this section the wicked one states, *"God hath forgotten"* (v. 11). But that all changes in verse twelve where the psalmist asks the Lord to arise and act. And He always does, proving that He is King (v. 16). May we flee to the Lord.

Through the Bible in a Year: Genesis 41–42

January 17

Read Psalms 10–11
Family Reading: Psalm 10; Devotional Reading: Psalm 10:12-18

God Is Very Much Alive

Psalm 10 begins with two questions: *"Why standest thou afar off, O Lord? why hidest thou thyself in times of trouble?"* Then in the next ten verses the psalmist describes the wicked man. He is so vile and wicked that it almost seems there is no hope. But then we read verse twelve:

"Arise, O Lord; O God, lift up thine hand: forget not the humble."

The psalmist takes hope. He prays. He asks God to arise and deal with the wicked. In verse sixteen he announces: *"The Lord is King for ever and ever: . . ."* In the previous two devotionals we saw the treachery and violences of the wicked. The psalmist wondered as we may wonder: "Why does God stand afar off? Why is He not doing something?"

The wicked is saying, "God is dead!" Verse thirteen states that the wicked says of God that He will not judge and require condemnation of the wicked. At the end of the last century Frederich Nietzche arose in Europe. He rebelled against the religious faith of his parents and instituted a philosophy against God. He defined the trinity as God the Father, God the Son, and God *the devil*. His teachings spawned *nazism*. He pleaded for a superman. He had a great influence on men like Hitler. Nietzche stated that Christianity was "the one great curse—the one immoral blemish of mankind." He was the one who kept propagating the lie: "God is dead." What did God do? He watched quietly. Nietzche lost his mind and was committed to an asylum. God judged! God was not dead. When Nietzche died, a wise man wrote this couplet:

> "God is dead."   (signed) Nietzche
> "Nietzche is dead."   (signed) God

As I write this in the summer of 1991, we are seeing the breakup of the Communist regimes—these that said "Religion is the opiate of the people " and those that have tried to remove God and the Bible. But God has been working quietly while wicked men thought He was asleep.

Psalm 10 ends: *". . . the man of the earth may no more oppress."* God is not dead!

Through the Bible in a Year: Genesis 43–45

January 18

Read Psalms 11–13
Family Reading: Psalm 11

Trust the Lord, Regardless of the Circumstances

In Psalm 11 David reveals the place of his strength in a very difficult time in his life. This psalm was very likely written when David was being pursued by Saul. It may have been written while he was still in the court serving Saul. The king had developed a bitter hatred for David because of his jealousy over David's successes and popularity. Repeatedly Saul had devised ways to kill David.

David said there were those who were trying to kill him with bows and arrows (v. 2). The bow and arrow were a coward's way of trying to handle a problem. He could hide where his victim could not see him and from there shoot the arrows to kill the one he hated. Those bows were being held by Saul and others around him who hated David.

In these circumstances David cried out: *"If the foundations be destroyed, what can the righteous do" (v. 3).* His answer followed immediately— *"The Lord is in his holy temple, the Lord's throne is in heaven: . . ." (v. 4).* As in yesterday's devotional, David was saying, "God is not dead. He is still alive and is the One who is ruling."

Please note the last part of verse four and then verse five: *"his eyes behold, his eyelids try, the children of men. The Lord trieth the righteous: but the wicked and him that loveth violence his soul hateth."* No—God is not dead or asleep. He is very much alive—alert to all that is going on. When it says *"his eyelids try,"* just think of our eyelids. When we are really examining something, we narrow our eyelids to get a sharper focus. God does know what is going on. He knows the condition of the righteous and the evil of the wicked.

May we learn to trust Him no matter how difficult things seem. He will judge the wicked (v. 6), and He still looks favorably upon the righteous and their righteousness.

> Simply trusting every day,
> Trusting through a story way;
> Even when my faith is small,
> Trusting Jesus, that is all.
> —Edgar P. Stites

Through the Bible in a Year: Genesis 46–48

January 19

Read Psalms 12–14
Family Reading: Psalm 12

The Pure Word of God Versus the Lies of Men

Psalm 12 begins and ends with the same theme. David begins by crying out to God for help because godly men were disappearing from the scene. He ends the psalm by stating conditions at the time: *"The wicked walk on every side, when the vilest men are exalted" (v. 8).* It was a sad day for David. He may have written this while he was kept in Saul's court, or when he was fleeing from Saul, who desired to kill him, or maybe when he was a fugitive trying to escape the cohorts with Absalom, his traitorous son. David saw how desperate was his plight, and he cried: *"Help, Lord; for the godly man ceaseth; . . ." (v. 1).*

One of David's biggest problems involved the lies being told about him. In verses two through four David spoke of the dreadful persecution that came through the lying lips of his enemies. Their speech was simply revealing the wicked hearts they had (v. 2). These wicked men spoke three sentences in verse four—and all three were wrong.

They said, *"With our tongue will we prevail; . . ." (v. 4).* But God says, *"The Lord shall cut off all flattering lips, . . ." (v. 3).* These wicked men also said, *"our lips are our own: . . ." (v. 4).* How wrong they were! Our lips should belong to the Lord; they are not ours to do with as we desire. In the commandments God wrote: *"Thou shalt not take the name of the Lord thy God in vain; . . ." (Exodus 20:7).* Again God said in Exodus 20:16—*"Thou shalt not bear false witness against thy neighbor."* God gave us our lips, and we need to use them to honor Him. The third mistake the wicked people made was in asking, *". . . who is lord over us?" (Psalm 12:4).* They acted as though they had no lord, but they did. Every individual has someone he follows and to whom he ascribes lordship.

God contrasted the words of these vain men with His Word:

"The words of the Lord are pure words: as silver tried in a furnace of earth, purified seven times" (v. 6).

We need to rely on God's Word in this day when there is a dearth of godly men as there was in David's day.

Through the Bible in a Year: Genesis 49–50; Exodus 1

January 20

Read Psalms 13–16
Family Reading: Psalms 13–14; Devotional Reading: Psalm 13

From a Sigh to a Song

David must have written Psalm 13 when he was exhausted—tired of running, trying to escape King Saul. He had difficulty understanding why it seemed to take God so long to do something. Four times in the first two verses he asked the Lord, *"How long?"* "Why do I have to suffer like this?" "Why are You not doing something, Lord?" Have you ever thought or verbalized words like these questions?

Remember, God is working. His timing may not be our timing. We want Him to be concerned about our circumstances, but He is concerned about something far more important—our character. He permits circumstances to exist so that we can grow spiritually and have our character developed. We would like for God to change our circumstances, and we forget that He wants to see us changed. Romans 8:28 is still in the Bible:

"And we know that all things work together for good to them that love God, to them who are the called according to his purpose."

David's circumstances were so bad that he thought he might die. He did recognize the fact that death for a believer is only the sleep of the body (v. 3). You see, he did trust the Lord and knew that he belonged to God. That is revealed in verses five and six. In these two verses he speaks four times of his relationship to God: *"I"* and *"thy," "my"* and *"thy," "I"* and *"the Lord," "he"* and *"me."* David knew that God had promised him the kingdom. He trusted the Lord, and that brought him out of his despair. In verses five and six we find David coming to a place of real victory. He said in verse five, *"But I have trusted in thy mercy; my heart shall rejoice in thy salvation."* While he was in these most dire circumstances, David said he would trust and rejoice. He had changed from his sigh of desperation in verses one and two to his song of victory in verse six. Had his circumstances changed? No! Had Saul called back his soldiers? No! Circumstances had not changed, but still David could sing—because neither had God changed. He could sing because he relied on the Lord.

Through the Bible in a Year: Exodus 2–4

January 21

Read Psalms 14–16
Family Reading: Psalms 14–15; Devotional Reading: Psalm 14

The Fool

Psalm 14 speaks of the dreadful depravity of man. The fool states, *"There is no God."* He may not say it in those words, but he lives as though there is no God. David calls him a fool.

When we come to the New Testament, we realize that God is speaking of all men who are without Christ. Paul quotes from this psalm: *"There is none righteous . . . They are all gone out of the way . . . there is none that doeth good, no, not one" (Romans 3:10, 12).*

God is saying that all men have sin down inside. As I write this, a controversy is holding the attention of the news media. Should health workers be forced to have mandatory testing for AIDS? You see, they may have AIDS but look perfectly healthy. Some doctors have had AIDS but looked all right. They performed surgery, transmitted the AIDS to the patient, and now the patient is dying because of the transmission. The health worker looks very healthy on the outside, but down inside the worker has AIDS. That's a picture of a lost sinner. He may look as good as others, but down inside is the nature of sin. Remember, regardless of how good the person seems to appear, *"There is none righteous, no, not one" (Romans 3:10).*

The world refers to believers who love the preaching of the Word of God as being foolish. *"For the preaching of the cross is to them that perish foolishness; . . ." (I Corinthians 1:18).*

Then Paul makes a very important statement in I Corinthians 1:25— *"Because the foolishness of God is wiser than men . . . ."* So you see, the fool is the one who says there is no God. The wise man is the one who believes the Bible and trusts the Lord.

We see the foolishness of man when we consider the cross. Jesus is the only person who ever lived of whom it was written, *"[He] went about doing good" (Acts 10:38).* He lived a perfect life. What happened to Him? He was arrested, given a mockery of a trial, and then crucified. Man's foolishness reached its zenith when man nailed Jesus to the cross. Believe God's Word—receive Christ today.

Through the Bible in a Year: Exodus 5–7

January 22

Read Psalms 15–17
Family Reading: Psalms 15–16; Devotional Reading: Psalm 15

The Need of a Holy Life

Psalm 15 is a total contrast to Psalm 14. The fourteenth psalm speaks of the fool—the man who has tried to live as if there is no God. The fifteenth psalm presents the exact opposite—the man who longs to dwell in the presence of the Lord. David begins by asking the question, *"Lord, who shall abide in thy tabernacle? who shall dwell in thy holy hill?"* The balance of the psalm is an answer to that question. This psalm is like Psalm 1 in that the only One who can fulfill all of the qualifications is the Lord Jesus Christ, God's perfect Son. David was a good man who genuinely longed to be this one who could abide in God's presence. But as we read the story of David's life, we find many places where he failed to be all he should have been. When I was pastor of South Sheridan Baptist Church in Denver, we studied the life of David in Sunday School one year. I remember being shocked at the number of times David fell short of being a God-honoring man. And then I remember what I would say to myself and my class, "The best of men are only men at the best." David, a man after God's own heart, was still a *man*.

Please note how much the tongue has to do with our dwelling in God's presence. The one who dwells with God speaks *"truth in his heart . . . backbiteth not with his tongue . . . nor taketh up a reproach against his neighbor" (vv. 2-3)*. Certainly this reminds us of James 3:2, *"If any man offend not in word, the same is a perfect man . . . ."*

Psalm 15 should be to us a passage that challenges us to genuine holy living. I recommend you read it again slowly and ask God to make real in your lives the challenge presented here. Do remember that the only person who can expect to have these characteristics is one who is born again. He loves to be with God's people for *". . . he honoreth them that fear the Lord . . ." (v. 4)*.

> Take time to be holy, Speak oft with thy Lord;
> Abide in Him always, And feed on His Word.
> Make friends of God's children; Help those who are weak;
> Forgetting in nothing His blessing to seek.
> —William D. Longstaff

Through the Bible in a Year: Exodus 8–10

January 23

Read Psalms 16–17
Family Reading: Psalm 16

Jesus Christ in the Psalms

The title given Psalm 16 makes it a special psalm: *"Michtam of David."* The word *Michtam* means *a poem, a prayer,* or *a meditation.* Psalms 56, 57, 58, 59, and 60 have this same title. However, in each of those titles something is added, such as in Psalm 56: *"When the Philistines took him in Gath."* These were special meditations caused by events in David's life. But this sixteenth psalm must have been a special meditation, not because of some trial or tragic event, but a meditation David loved to think upon. For this reason, some have called this the "Golden Psalm." Spurgeon called it "The Psalm of the Precious Secret."

We do not need to look to human interpreters to find the key to this golden mystery. Peter said that David was speaking in Psalm 16 concerning Christ (Acts 2:25). Paul said that David wrote of Christ through whom Paul preached the forgiveness of sins (Acts 13:35-38). We can apply truths in this psalm to David and to the saints, but we certainly must see that in the psalm "Christ is all."

In verse six Christ said: *"The lines are fallen unto me in pleasant places; yea, I have a goodly heritage."* The lines, to the Hebrews, were measuring lines by which were marked out plots of land. The lines determined the heritage of a Hebrew man and his family. In this psalm, Christ spoke of His having to suffer the pangs of Hell (v. 10). He knew He would suffer and need to rest on the preserving grace of God (v. 1). In the face of all this suffering, He said that the lines measuring His heritage were pleasant.

The passage can be applied to every believer. As we rest on His grace and rely on His wisdom and will for our lives, we can say, *"The lines are fallen unto me in pleasant places."* Even in trouble and difficulties, we can know that our heritage is a goodly one.

> And when, before the throne, I stand in Him complete,
> "Jesus died my soul to save," My lips shall still repeat.
> Jesus paid it all, All to Him I owe;
> Sin had left a crimson stain,
> He washed it white as snow.
>
> —Elvina M. Hall

Through the Bible in a Year: Exodus 11–13

January 24

Read Psalms 16–17
Family Reading: Psalm 16

I'd Rather Have Jesus

In Psalm 16 David was speaking prophetically of Jesus. In verse ten he wrote, *". . . neither wilt thou suffer thine Holy One to see corruption."* The only One of whom that could be written is the One who rose from the dead. David's baby did see corruption; his resurrection is yet future. In his pentecostal sermon, Peter said that David's *"sepulcher is with us unto this day" (Acts 2:29).* In Acts 2:31 Peter said, *"He [David] seeing this before spake of the resurrection of Christ . . . ."*

Psalm 16 speaks of Christ, the only One who could say, *"I have set the Lord **always** before me . . ." (v. 8).* After over forty years of service, I would have to say, "I have **endeavored** to set the Lord before me."

The psalm is speaking of Jesus. As believers, we can rest on Him for power to see victory in our lives and can know the fullness of joy in His presence (v. 11). Sorrows will be multiplied to those who hasten after another god (v. 4). We have the assurance through Christ that we have life and will not be in Hell (John 10:28). We know the joy that comes from trusting Christ Jesus, who died for us and rose again.

The story is told of King George VI of England, a man who had put his trust in Christ. While visiting British Columbia in Canada, some officials invited Chief Whitefeather, chief of one of the tribes, to sing for the king, thinking he would probably sing a native Indian song. But the chief was a Christian, and he sang:

> I'd rather have Jesus than silver or gold,
> I'd rather be His than have riches untold;
> I'd rather have Jesus than houses or land,
> I'd rather be held by His nail-pierced hand—
> Than to be the king of a vast domain
> Or be held in sin's dread sway;
> I'd rather have Jesus than anything
> This world affords today.
>
> —Rhea F. Miller

The Canadian officials were shocked. But King George took Chief Whitefeather's hand and said, "I'd rather have Jesus, too."

Through the Bible in a Year: Exodus 14–16

January 25

Read Psalm 17

Praying, Submitting to His Will

David wrote this seventeenth psalm at a time when he was facing wicked and deadly enemies who surrounded him (v. 9). But this psalm, like many others, goes way beyond just the life of David. There are statements made in this psalm which no one but the Lord Jesus Christ could honestly speak. Please note verse three: *" . . . thou hast tried me, and shalt find nothing . . . ."*

Only Jesus Christ could say that no sin could be found in Him. Bible scholars believe this psalm could have been that which Jesus quoted in Gethsemane.

He cried unto God for deliverance. In His plea in verse one, we find another statement which no one but the Lord Jesus could have made: *"give ear unto my prayer, that goeth not out of feigned lips."* He was saying that when He prayed, His lips spoke exactly what was right and His heart was in His prayer.

How often has prayer gone out of feigned lips in my life! I pray one way and live another way. Sometimes we pray, "God, give me grace to love all the brethren," and then in a little while we are gossiping and tearing someone else down. That is praying out of feigned lips. Or we pray and tell the Lord we trust Him to supply all our needs. And soon we are worried about how our needs are going to be met. That is praying out of feigned lips.

In Gethsemane the Lord Jesus committed Himself to the will of God. He asked that the cup might pass from Him, but then He said: *"nevertheless, not my will, but thine, be done" (Luke 22:42).* You can note the same attitude all the way through this prayer in Psalm 17.

> Sweet will of God, still fold me closer,
> Till I am wholly lost in Thee.
> —Leila N. Morris

Through the Bible in a Year: Exodus 17–20

January 26

Read Psalm 17

How to Handle Evil Circumstances

Have you ever heard someone say, "I am doing fine under the circumstances"? A good question to ask that individual is, "What are you doing under the circumstances?" Those of us who know the Lord should be able to triumph over the circumstances.

Yesterday we mentioned that this psalm presents truths about the Lord Jesus Christ as He prayed in Gethsemane. He was compassed about with the wicked (vv. 9, 11). Even as the Lord knelt in Gethsemane, Judas was leading men to the place where they could arrest Jesus. Circumstances pressed hard upon our Lord.

This psalm gives some wonderful truths about having victory in difficult times. First, He states that we are kept from the paths of the destroyer by the Word of God (v. 4). If we will hide God's Word in our hearts, we will realize victory through Him.

Second, we need to trust the Lord. Verse eight expresses that trust: *"Keep me as the apple of the eye, hide me under the shadow of thy wings."* From whom did David desire to be hidden? *"The wicked that oppress . . . [his] deadly enemies"* (v. 9). God is able to deliver us from the enemies. Two characteristics of our enemies are that they seem to be prosperous (*"They are inclosed in their own fat"*), and they are proud (v. 10).

What should we do when these evil circumstances engulf us? We need to pray, *"Arise, O Lord, . . ."* (v. 13). He alone is able to defeat them (to *"disappoint him, cast him down"*) and to deliver our souls *"from the wicked"* (v. 13).

May we learn to turn to Him, knowing that He will arise and give victory over the circumstances that oppress us. Remember, Jesus did arise from the dead. We can experience His resurrection power over the enemies that would defeat us. And we can end life saying, *"As for me, I will behold thy face in righteousness: I shall be satisfied, when I awake, with thy likeness"* (v. 15).

Through the Bible in a Year: Exodus 21–23

January 27

Read Psalm 18
Family Reading: Psalm 18:1-21; Devotional Reading: Psalm 18:1-6

Praise for Victory Over Our Foes

We know that this psalm is a very important one because it is recorded twice in Scripture. David wrote this psalm in II Samuel 22. There are a few minor changes. Apparently David recorded the words as he first penned them in II Samuel. When he submitted it to the chief musician, he made some minor changes. It is a psalm well worth our time in meditation.

The superscription tells us the occasion of David's writing this psalm. David had realized victory over all his foes. Not only had he been delivered from the hand of Saul, but also he was delivered from Absalom and other foes. God had given him the victory, and in this psalm he ascribes the praise unto the Lord.

David begins the psalm by stating, *"I will love thee, O Lord, my strength."* He knew that God had given him great and blessed victory. Now he sang of this victory with a love for the Lord. In verses two and three he gives seven figures of speech by which he praises God. Someone has well said that this passage "touches the high-water mark of the Old Testament and is conspicuous among its noblest utterances." The psalmist begins with *"The Lord is my rock, . . ."* (v. 2).

Please get the picture. Here is a huge rock, very likely offering shelter in caves within it similar to the one in I Samuel 24. On top of this rock is a fortress, and at one corner of the fortress is a high tower. The Lord was this to David. But there was more. He had equipment—a buckler and a horn. The buckler was used for defense and the horn for offense. David had all of this!

David had these items that can give victory because he had the Lord. In fact, the Lord was his protection and deliverance. He rested in the Lord. *"I will call upon the Lord, . . ."* said David in verse three. So may we have victory in every difficulty.

Through the Bible in a Year: Exodus 24–26

January 28

Read Psalm 18
Family Reading: Psalm 18:6-25; Devotional: Psalm 18: 7-16

Praying and Seeing His Power at Work

David prayed in his distress, and God answered his prayer. He knew that the Lord had heard his voice and that his cry had come before the Lord (v. 6). David knew that God does answer prayer.

Note God's response. The earth shook; fire came forth; the heavens bowed (vv. 7-9)—miracles took place. The Lord is always ready to answer prayer and do His work for the believer.

Psalm 18 is speaking of more than just David. Many commentaries describe the psalm as speaking entirely of the Lord Jesus Christ. In this portion, there is no doubt it is speaking of Christ in His resurrection. What power was manifested by God in raising Jesus from the dead!

Ephesians 1:19, 20 speaks of Paul's desire for us to know *". . . what is the exceeding greatness of his power to us-ward who believe, according to the working of his mighty power, Which he wrought in Christ, when he raised him from the dead, and set him at his own right hand in the heavenly places."*

Yes, it took mighty power to raise Jesus Christ from the dead. And that same power is available to believers in prayer. Oh, that we could pray and believe God for His answer. He literally will bow the heavens and come down to aid His praying, trusting child (Psalm 18:9).

Please note there is no time space between verses six and seven. When David cried unto the Lord (v. 6), *"Then"* (v. 7) God answered. What power can be ours if we will believe and pray! It was said of Martin Luther: "That man could have of God what he would." The Queen of Scots confessed that she was more afraid of the prayers of John Knox than she was of an army of ten thousand men.

Therefore, let's pray, believing God for His power.

> Restraining prayer, we cease to fight;
> Prayer keeps the Christian's armor bright;
> And Satan trembles when he sees
> The weakest saint upon his knees.
> —William Cowper

Through the Bible in a Year: Exodus 27–29

Read Psalm 18
Family Reading: Psalm 18:16-36; Devotional Reading: Psalm 18:16-23

The Lord Delights in His Children

When we have been rescued by God, we must be careful to give Him the glory. That is exactly what David did. In verse seventeen he stated that God *". . . delivered me from my strong enemy, and from them which hated me: for they were too strong for me."* He ascribed the glory to God and confessed his own weakness. We believers also battle strong enemies; for example, sin within and Satan without. And we must rely on the Lord, who *". . . is able to do exceeding abundantly above all that we ask or think, . . ." (Ephesians 3:20).*

We should never forget that we were sinners and God redeemed us. Israel was commanded in Isaiah 51:1— *"Hearken to me, ye that follow after righteousness, ye that seek the Lord: look unto the rock whence ye are hewn, and to the hole of the pit whence ye are digged."* God is telling us to look to the Rock, Christ Jesus, in His death on Calvary. But He also tells us to remember the pit from which we were digged. May we never forget that we are only sinners saved by grace.

David thanked God for all He had done for him. He said that the Lord *". . . brought me forth also into a large place: he delivered me, because he delighted in me" (v. 19).* What a blessing is ours when we meditate on the way God has worked in our lives because He delights in us. He loves us and has given Himself for us so that we can enjoy His fellowship and His delight in us.

May we trust Him—walk in His grace and know that He delights in seeing blessings poured out on us. We are valuable to Him—and we must love Him with all of our hearts.

> Naught have I gotten but what I received;
> Grace hath bestowed it since I have believed;
> Boasting excluded, pride I abase;
> I'm only a sinner saved by grace.
> —James M. Gray

Through the Bible in a Year: Exodus 30–32

Read Psalm 18
Family Reading: Psalm 18:24-44; Devotional Reading: Psalm 18:24-30

Principles of God's Government

In verses twenty-four through thirty, the Lord gives us principles that operate in God's economy. These are principles we should take to heart and by which we should endeavor to live.

Do you sometimes feel that God is not treating you as you think you should be treated? You may not have said it just that way; but in your mind you have thought it, and with your emotions you have felt it. Often I have heard people say, "I cannot understand why God did this to me." Or some say, "I do not understand why people treat me the way they do." In verses twenty-four and twenty-five, God gives us some principles involved in His government.

First, *"With the merciful thou wilt show thyself merciful" (v. 25).* If we show mercy, He will shower mercy upon us. Jesus said, *"Blessed are the merciful: for they shall obtain mercy" (Matthew 5:7).* Why does God seem to be hard on some of us? It is because we are hard on others. An old saying we all have heard is, "What goes around comes around." That is another way of saying we will be treated as we treat others. Jesus gave the great principle of life in Matthew 7:12— *"Therefore all things whatsoever ye would that men should do to you, do ye even so to them: for this is the law and the prophets."*

Second, *"with an upright man thou wilt show thyself upright" (v. 25).* God will deal with us in an upright manner if we will deal with others that way. Have you ever noticed that often those who are the most ready to criticize others are those who are the most sensitive to criticism?

Third, God does the same with the pure, dealing with them in purity. Then God says He will be froward with the froward (v. 26). The *froward* are the self-willed, and God often has to deal severely with the self-willed to bring them to the place of bearing fruit.

Through the Bible in a Year: Exodus 33–35

January 31

Read Psalm 18
Family Reading: Psalm 18:30-50; Devotional Reading: Psalm 18:30-37

God's Way Is Perfect

David has been speaking of God's dealings with him. Yesterday we noted that in God's government, He deals with us as we deal with others. Today we see what David believes about God's Divine Government— *"As for God, his way is perfect: the word of the Lord is tried: he is a buckler to all those that trust in him" (v. 30).*

God does not make mistakes. He knows what He is doing. He has a purpose in all that He does in our lives. You may have felt that God made some mistakes in His dealing with you, but not David. He said, *"As for God, his way is perfect: . . ."* God's Word is true, and it always proves itself so when you put God to the test. *"[God] is a buckler to all those that trust in him."* The buckler was the defensive armor for the soldier. God will be our defense against all of our enemies. May we trust Him to deal in righteousness with us.

> My Father's way may twist and turn;
> My heart may throb and ache;
> But in my soul, I'm glad I know
> He maketh no mistake.
>
> My cherished plans may go astray,
> My hopes may fade away;
> But still I'll trust my Lord to lead
> For He doth know the way.
>
> Tho' night be dark and it may seem
> That day will never break;
> I'll pin my faith, my all in Him;
> He maketh no mistake.
>
> There's so much now I cannot see,
> My eyesight's far too dim,
> But come what may, I'll simply trust
> And leave it all with Him.
>
> For by and by the mist will lift
> And plain it all He'll make.
> Thro' all the way, tho' dark to me,
> He made not one mistake.
>
> —A. M. Overton

Through the Bible in a Year: Exodus 36–38

February 1

Read Psalms 18:38-50 and 19
Family Reading: Psalm 18:38-50; Devotional Reading: Psalm 18:35-43

David's Victory Through the Lord

God has provided us with the equipment needed for victory, and He has given us the victory in Christ. In verses thirty-nine and forty David wrote: *". . . thou hast subdued under me those that rose up against me. Thou hast also given me the necks of mine enemies . . . ."* David realized victory in his battles.

He had this victory because God personally had provided his defense and offense. David had the *"shield of thy salvation" (v. 35)* for defense; and God had girded him *"with strength unto the battle" (v. 39).* His victory was entirely in, by, and through the Lord. The enemies of David were subdued by the Lord (v. 39)—God gave the victory.

> *"But thanks be to God, which giveth us the victory through our Lord Jesus Christ". — I Corinthians 15:57*

> *"Now thanks be unto God, which always causeth us to triumph in Christ, and maketh manifest the savor of his knowledge by us in every place". — II Corinthians 2:14*

As we have seen in previous devotionals, this psalm is one that mingles the life of David and the prophecy of the Lord Jesus Christ, the Son of David. We see in verse forty-three a statement picturing Jesus Christ our Lord: *". . . thou hast made me the head of the heathen: a people whom I have not known shall serve me."* David experienced this in his reign, but it is certainly most applicable to the Lord Jesus. The word *heathen* does not always mean *pagan idolaters.* The original English word was *heath-men,* men who lived in wild places away from civilization. Here it is speaking of Gentile nations—not part of Israel. Our Lord Jesus has given salvation to the whole world. He has made both Jew and Gentile one by His blood (Ephesians 2:11-14). May we love Him and serve Him.

> Jesus shall reign where'er the sun
> Does his successive journeys run;
> His kingdom spread from shore to shore,
> Till moons shall wax and wane no more.
> —Issac Watts

Through the Bible in a Year: Exodus 39–40

February 2

Read Psalms 18:44-50 and 19

Let the God of My Salvation Be Exalted

Today we complete one week of devotions on Psalm 18. David had faced many enemies, but in this psalm we find the reason for his victory over the enemies—his trust in the Lord. He sums up his attitude by saying, *". . . let the God of my salvation be exalted" (v. 46).*

As believers, exalting our Lord and Saviour should be our main work. The tragedy is that so many today exalt themselves and fail to exalt the Lord Jesus. John the Baptist said, *"He must increase, but I must decrease" (John 3:30).* Remember, the Lord Jesus said of John that among men born of natural birth, he was the greatest. What made him great? He was great because he exalted the Lord.

May we learn the truth of David's statement: *"Let the God of my salvation be exalted."* David stated this because he realized all that God had done for him. And by God's constant victory in his life, David knew for certain that *"the Lord liveth . . ." (Psalm 18:46).* He is as much alive today as He was in David's day.

He is alive (v. 46). He is the One who delivers us from all our enemies, even the violent man (v. 48). May we live, believing He is to us all that He was to David then. Let's be done with living as though God is dead. Like David, we should give thanks unto the Lord among the heathen and sing praises unto His name (v. 49). Jesus Christ will reign. When He reigns, the dark reign of sin and Satan will be over. He will be exalted. We need to say with David: *"Let the God of my salvation be exalted."*

> Be Thou exalted forever and ever
> God of eternity, the Ancient of Days!
> Wondrous in wisdom, majestic in glory
> Perfect in holiness, and worthy of praise.
>
> Be Thou exalted by seraphs and angels,
> Be Thou exalted with harp and with song;
> Saints in their anthems, of rapture adore Thee,
> Thine be the glory, forever, Amen!
> —Fanny J. Crosby

Through the Bible in a Year: Leviticus 1–4

February 3

Read Psalms 19–20

The Witness of God's Creation

Psalm 19 presents God's two witnesses: the witness of His world (vv. 1-6) and the witness of His Word (vv. 7-11). The two go together. God has revealed Himself through His infinite worlds and by His infallible Word. Men have often tried to pit science against the Bible as though the two are incompatible. Actually, scientific fact and Biblical truth never contradict each other. Please note—I said "scientific fact." There are so-called scientific theories, unproved, just hypotheses, that are often opposed to the Bible. Real science is never opposed to a right understanding of Scripture. Science is an orderly presentation of the facts of the natural universe, and the Bible is an orderly presentation of God's redemption. Some poet wrote:

> 'Twas great to call a world from naught,
> 'Twas greater to redeem.

David, the shepherd boy, could look up into the sky and realize that God *is*. He wrote, *"The heavens declare the glory of God . . ." (Psalm 19:1).* How simple are the statements God gives. In Genesis 1:16 God gives a statement of only five words: *"he made the stars also."* Men have been studying the stars ever since and have written multiplied thousands of volumes about them. Yet, as I write this, only recently scientists said they had found a huge hole in the solar system about which they knew nothing. They said it could be that this "hole" contains more galaxies and more stars than men had known about before. God simply wrote: *"he made the stars also" (Genesis 1:16) "and the firmament showeth his handiwork" (Psalm 19:1).* The firmament is atmospheric heaven surrounding the earth. It contains the right gases that sustain our life. If those gases were not in the proper proportion, they could explode and destroy us all. God has placed them in the right order. Please note that the word *where* in verse three is in italics. That means it was added by the translators. It should read: *". . . their voice is not heard."* We see the heavens and the firmament, but we do not hear a voice. We simply believe because we see God's greatness in creation.

Through the Bible in a Year: Leviticus 5–7

February 4

Read Psalms 19–20

The Word That Converts and Produces Growth

Yesterday we noted that Psalm 19:1 presents the fact that God witnesses to us in His creation. Today we will consider verses seven through eleven, which present God in the revelation of His Word.

Creation reveals God's power and grace. Man can see proofs of God's greatness and yet know nothing of His person or personality. Therefore, the soul needs converting. Only the Word of God can do that.

"The law of the Lord is perfect, converting the soul . . ." (v. 7).

As men we are sinners in deep need of God's redeeming grace. Verses twelve and thirteen speak of willful sins (presumptuous) and of unwilling sins (secret). Because of sin man needs to turn around. That is accomplished by receiving the Word of God as true. In verse seven the law of the Lord is the entire truth of God's Word. It brings conversion. I Peter 1:23 states: *"Being born again, not of corruptible seed, but of incorruptible, by the word of God, which liveth and abideth forever."*

After conversion there must be growth. That growth comes also by the Word of God. *"[T]he testimony of the Lord is sure, making wise the simple" (Psalm 19:7).* Converted—turned around—born again. But then we are simple, knowing not the truth of God. We need to spend time in His Word so that we can grow. I Peter 2:2 presents that: *"As newborn babes, desire the sincere milk of the word, that ye may grow thereby."*

Psalm 19:8 tells us, *"The statutes of the Lord are right, rejoicing the heart . . . ."* The word *statutes* refers to the paths God lays out for us to walk. People are often afraid to accept and follow God's direction. However, when we do, we rejoice in our hearts. Note the progress: he who was converted was next made wise and is now made happy. The truth which makes the heart right gives joy to the right heart.

How great and powerful is the Word of God! It has power to **convict** — *"Moreover by them is thy servant warned . . ." (v. 11).* It also has power to **cleanse**—*"Who can understand his errors? cleanse thou me . . ." (v. 12).* Also, it has power to **correct** and guide us in fellowship with Him (vv. 13-14).

Through the Bible in a Year: Leviticus 8–10

February 5

Read Psalms 20–21

God's Help in the Day of Trouble

In V. Graham Scroggie's book, *The Psalms,* I read a very interesting story of thirteen men trapped in a coal mine in England in 1839. The sides of a shaft had caved in, closing off their way out of the mine. They tried every other exit possible through abandoned shafts, but there was no escape. Then they retired in a narrow space that had been cut out of the coal seam, an area 18 feet by 24 feet, 3½ feet high. There they sat down and prepared for death. They held a prayer meeting and opened it by singing stanzas that were based on Psalm 20:1-5. By this they were all strengthened and their nerves were calmed. They quoted Scripture passages, and all spoke of their faith and hope for life after death. They wept as they spoke of their loved ones who would be left behind.

But after an extended time, they were rescued—miraculously delivered from their apparent grave. The last stanza of their song fit well their deliverance. It was based on Psalm 20:5.

> In thy salvation we will joy;
> In our God's Name we will
> Display our banners; and the Lord
> Our prayers all fulfill.

When I read that story, I thanked God for coal miners in that day who trusted the Lord and knew His Word. I wonder whether we have miners today who are prepared to face tragedy. Our need is to trust the Lord—not horses, not chariots, but the Lord (v. 7). We simply need to remember the Name of the Lord our God. Those who do not trust Him will be brought down and fallen, but those who remember His Name will arise over defeat and stand upright. May their battle hymn, Psalm 20, prepare us for our battle with Satan, the flesh, and the world.

In early 1991 we saw the brief Persian Gulf War. Our technology revealed that we had "smart" bombs just as some people had been telling us. Our danger today is that we will trust in our technology rather than in the Lord. The psalmist here stressed that trust must be in the Lord and not military hardware. If America does not repent of sin and turn to God, the day will come when her technology and "smarts" will not win.

Through the Bible in a Year: Leviticus 11–13

February 6

Read Psalms 21–22
Family Reading: Psalm 21; Devotional Reading: Psalm 21:1-6

Strength for the Battle

Psalms 20 and 21 fit together. They can be called *"The Battle Songs."* Psalm 20 is a *prayer before* the battle, while Psalm 21 is *praise after* the battle. The first anticipates the battle; the second reflects upon it. Psalm 21 begins with David's praise of victory in the battle about which he prayed in Psalm 20. Psalm 21 gives to us the secret of victory. Everyone wants to know the secret of power and victory. The Philistines longed to know where Samson's strength lay. They finally succeeded when they said to Delilah, *"Entice him, and see wherein his great strength lieth . . ." (Judges 16:5).* Samson had his strength within himself—so much so that he did not really rely on the Lord for strength.

With David, this matter of strength was not a secret. He announced in Psalm 21:1: *"The king shall joy in thy strength, O Lord . . . ."* Hebrew poetry is parallel in form. The first verse is an excellent example of synthetic parallelism because the second line explains or adds something given in the first line. David had said his strength was in the Lord; then he added that his strength came by salvation in the Lord: *" . . . and in thy salvation, how greatly shall he rejoice!"* God answers prayer! This is what David was almost shouting in verse two. *"Thou hast given him his heart's desire, and hast not withholden the request of his lips."* This is such an important truth that David added the word *Selah,* which means: Think on that! Stop—Meditate! His prayer before the battle was, *"Send thee help from the sanctuary . . . (Psalm 20:2).* God had answered that prayer.

Here are three secrets to strength: (1) Strength comes from the Lord; (2) Strength comes to those who know His salvation; and (3) Strength comes in answer to prayer. Remember, *"I can do all things through Christ which strengtheneth me" (Philippians 4:13).* With strength from Him, we will be able to say with the psalmist: *"He asked life of thee, and thou gavest it him, even length of days forever and ever" (v. 4).* Everlasting life! That is our gift from Him. The mockers at the cross were right. *"He saved others; himself he cannot save" (Matthew 27:42).* He gave Himself so that we could have life forever.

Through the Bible in a Year: Leviticus 14–15

February 7

Read Psalms 21 and 22:1-21

A View of God's Judgment on Unrepentant Sinners

Yesterday we saw the place of victory in the life of the believers by the power of God. Today, in the last half of Psalm 21, we see the wrath of God that will be loosed against His foes. Psalm 21 goes far beyond the experience of David. Without question, verses eight through twelve speak of that which only God can do.

The Lord only is the One whose hand will find out all His enemies (v. 8). He and no other could make His enemies as a fiery oven (v. 9). God will deal with His enemies. With this great power at His hand, it is blessed to know that He cares for those who believe on Him. He prevents *(precedes)* believers with blessing (v. 3). How wonderful to know that He does go before us with plans for blessings to be poured out upon us!

But, also, how dreadful to realize His awful judgment on those who are His enemies! Verse nine states: *"Thou shalt make them as a fiery oven in the time of thine anger: . . . ."* These are terrible words. Those who try to weaken them by human reasonings are not doing well. Spurgeon wrote: "Reader, never tolerate slight thoughts of Hell or you will soon have low thoughts of sin." We must not allow anyone or anything to try to convince us there is no fire in Hell. If there were not, the Lord would not have used strong language as this in Psalm 21.

Today we have anemic views of God and we seem to have lost sight of the holiness and righteousness of God. The Bible does say that God is angry with the wicked every day (Psalm 7:11). The Old Testament prophets never lost sight of this truth, and neither should we. In this day when we read of "user-friendly" churches, those churches and pulpits that do not want to offend, we need to come back to Psalm 21 and see God's holiness and righteousness and its results in the character of our churches and the witness of our ministries.

There are those today who say that Hell is only annihilation—that a soul in Hell will burn up and there is no such thing as conscious, eternal punishment. Remember, God destroyed Sodom and Gomorrah, turning even bodies of residents into ashes. The Lord said in Matthew 11:24 that Sodom will come into judgment. May we get from Psalm 21 a vision of Hell and then go forth to win lost souls to Jesus Christ.

Through the Bible in a Year: Leviticus 16–18

February 8

Read Psalm 22
Family Reading: Psalm 22:1-21

A Good View of Calvary

Today we begin reading and meditating in the shepherd psalms, Psalms 22, 23, and 24. All three present the Lord Jesus Christ, each giving a different aspect of His shepherding work. The New Testament speaks of Christ as being the *"Good Shepherd" (John 10:11);* the *"Great Shepherd" (Hebrews 13: 20-21);* and the *"Chief Shepherd" (I Peter 5:4).*

Psalm 22 presents the Good Shepherd giving His life for the sheep; Psalm 23 presents the Great Shepherd leading and protecting the sheep; and Psalm 24 presents the Chief Shepherd coming again to reward His saints.

Psalm 22 provides the most vivid and detailed description of the cross in the Bible. It begins by giving one of the cries Jesus offered from the cross: *"My God, my God, why hast thou forsaken me?"* It also ends with the contents of another cry from Calvary: *"It is finished."* Please note that the word *"this,"* the last word of the psalm, is in italics. That means it has been added. The psalm ends, *"he hath done."* In the Hebrew the masculine and neuter pronouns are the same. Since this is in the middle voice, it could actually be translated, *"It is finished."* This is a psalm of the cross!

Twice in the first six verses we read the word *"But."* In verse three the psalmist speaks of the holiness of God. Because He is holy, sin must be punished. The second *"But"* is in verse six, where it speaks of the fact that Jesus became *"a reproach of men"* because He bore their sins.

In verse six, Jesus said, *"I am a worm."* The word for *"worm"* here is the worm that was crushed to make the scarlet dye, that which was used in the most expensive garments. Remember, his worm had to be crushed. Jesus Christ was crushed at Calvary so that by His shed blood we could be clothed in the garments of salvation. Men thought of Jesus as though He were just a worm and men could rid the world of Him. But in this vile deed, they were used of God to bring salvation. Pray that you will see Calvary's cross clearly as we read Psalm 22 for four days.

Through the Bible in a Year: Leviticus 19–21

February 9

Read Psalm 22
Family Reading: Psalm 22:7-31; Devotional Reading: Psalm 22:7-13

Christ's Horrible Death at Calvary

Psalm 22 presents another proof of the inspiration of the Word of God. It was written at least a thousand years before our Lord Jesus hung on the cross. Yet it pictures in most graphic detail that which took place at the cross. Remember that the cross was not a Jewish method of capital punishment. The Jews executed by stoning. Crucifixion came as the most hideous death Roman emperors could devise for those guilty of crime. A thousand years before the world knew about a death on a cross, God predicted and pictured such a death in Psalm 22.

This psalm gives experiences David had—but it goes far beyond David and prophesies the death of God's Son, Jesus Christ. Verses nine and ten reveal Him as the Son of God, the One who was virgin born and had a special relationship with God the Father even before His birth.

Verses seven and eight speak of the mockery Christ endured on the cross. Verse seven states that they laughed Him to scorn. Matthew 27:39-41 reveals He was reviled by those passing by and mocked by the chief priests, scribes, and elders. Verse eight is quoted in Matthew 27:43: *"He trusted in God; let Him deliver Him now . . . ."*

In verse twelve the psalmist speaks of the bulls of Bashan besetting him round about. The bulls of Bashan were the big bulls that fed on the rich pasture lands. Bulls will surround a victim and then attack. In verse sixteen he speaks of being compassed about by dogs, and in verse twenty-one of being attacked by lions and unicorns. All of this tells us not only of the mocking of the human crowd round about the cross, but also of the attacking of demonic hordes, the beings from Hell. Then we read in verse thirteen, *"They gaped upon me with their mouths, as a ravening and a roaring lion."* In I Peter 5:8, we read that the devil acts *"as a roaring lion."* You see, as Jesus hung there in those three hours at darkness, He was attacked by Satan and all His hosts. He underwent the agonies of Hell for us. Oh, may we thank Him for His grace and love Him for His willingness to bear the agonies of the cross for us.

Through the Bible in a Year: Leviticus 22–23

February 10

Read Psalm 22
Family Reading: Psalm 22:7-31; Devotional Reading: Psalm 22:14-31

The Physical Pain of the Cross

Today we will note some of the physical anguish of the cross. First the Lord said He was to be poured out like water. His physical strength was gone. Water poured out has no power to bring itself back again into its previous form.

"[A]ll my bones are out of joint . . ." (v. 14). Have you ever had one bone out of joint? The pain is terrible. Some say that the greatest and most intolerable pain the body can endure is that of a bone out of place or a dislocated joint. Think of it! The Lord Jesus did not have just one bone out of joint but *all* of them (v. 14).

"My heart is like wax; it is melted in the midst of my bowels" (v. 14). He experienced a heart attack—dreadful additional pain (v. 14). *"My strength is dried up . . . my tongue cleaveth to my jaws . . ." (v. 15).* He experienced horrible dehydration—to the place where He was brought *"into the dust of death" (v. 15).*

"For dogs . . . pierced my hands and my feet" (v. 16). The dogs were the Gentile soldiers that surrounded the foot of the cross. They drove the spikes through His hands and feet. These extremities, the hands and feet, contain the most numerous nerves and blood vessels of any part of the body. And their nerves are intimately connected with the nerves of the whole body. This means our Lord felt the sharpest pangs shoot through every part of His body.

"I may tell all my bones: . . ." (v. 17). As He hung there, His body distended on the rack of the cross and His bones became visible through the thin veil of the skin.

Dreadful physical pain! It should bring tears to our eyes. However, there was something much worse. He was suffering spiritually the anguish of Hell and separation from His Father (v. 1). He did it for us.

> In the old rugged cross, stained with blood so divine,
> A wondrous beauty I see;
> For 'twas on that old cross Jesus suffered and died,
> To pardon and sanctify me.
>
> —George Bennard

Through the Bible in a Year: Leviticus 24–25

February 11

Read Psalms 22:14-31 and 23
Family Reading: Psalm 22:22-31

Christ Is Risen!

What a change we find in Psalm 22:22! It is the same voice we hear that we heard in verses 1-21; but it is not the same tune. The first twenty-one verses were a sob of agony; but beginning at verse twenty-two we have a song of triumph. Verse twenty-one ends with horrible death. He speaks of being heard *"from the horns of the unicorns."* The unicorn was a wild ox with great branching horns which are almost as sharp as needles on the points. Executioners would take a poor, wretched, condemned victim, bind him by his feet and shoulders upon those sharp horns, and then turn the wild animal loose to run about in the wilderness until the man died. Even from such a terrible picture the psalmist says the Lord heard him. Crucifixion was the horrible death Jesus suffered— anguish as bad as that of the victim on the sharp horns of the wild ox.

But then the anguish ends. Verse twenty-one states that He has been heard. Prayer gives place to praise. What has been a sob now becomes a song. No longer is the focus on the cross but rather on the throne. *"I will declare thy name unto my brethren: in the midst of the congregation will I praise thee" (v. 22).* Jesus died that awful death at Calvary, but death could not keep his foe. Jesus Christ arose and is alive evermore. He gives absolutely no hint of previous suffering. He is now the conqueror returned from the battle.

"In the midst of the congregation" is translated *"in the midst of the church"* in Hebrews 2:12. Here is our blessed Lord brought up from death, taking His place in the midst of the company of the redeemed and leading our hearts in praise. The risen, ascended Lord is seen here gathering around Himself that special company, that unique body of those He calls, *"my brethren."* As our resurrected Lord, He leads us to reach out to win a lost world to Christ. He speaks of those who come to Him as *"the great congregation" (v. 25).* That *"great congregation"* is the church of Jesus Christ. It involves *"all the ends of the world . . ." (v. 27).* What a glorious victory followed the cross—Christ and His glorious church! It is *"a glorious church, not having spot, or wrinkle, or any such thing . . . holy and without blemish" (Ephesians 5:27).*

Through the Bible in a Year: Leviticus 26–27

February 12

Read Psalms 22:22-31 and 23–24
Family Reading: Psalms 22:22-31

The Risen Lord's Concern

Yesterday we began with the Lord risen from the dead (v. 22). Today we will see His activity and concern as our risen, ascended Lord.

Next, we see His concern for the afflicted. He does not hide His face from our afflictions, but rather He hears our cries (v. 24).

Then we see who makes up the *"great congregation" (v. 25).* It will be comprised of the meek who shall eat and find their satisfaction in the Lord. There are those who seek Him. Of these in the great congregation He states, *"your heart shall live forever" (v. 26).*

In verse twenty-seven He begins to speak of the missionary burden and activity of this *"great congregation."* Yesterday we saw that this congregation is the New Testament church. The church has a responsibility to take the message of Christ's death and resurrection to the whole world. Verse twenty-seven says, *"All the ends of the world"* and *"all the hundreds of the nations"* shall turn to the Lord and worship before Him. This message of His death and resurrection must be heard. We who are believers are to *"declare his righteousness unto a people that shall be born, that he hath done this" (v. 31);* redemption is complete (v. 31).

In verse twenty-nine we read a solemn warning: *"none can keep alive his own soul."* While we proclaim, *"they shall praise the Lord that seek him" (v. 27),* we must also warn that those who reject Christ have absolutely no hope. That soul will be lost forever who does not turn to the Lord.

Calvary has insured us that Jesus Christ is Redeemer and also Ruler. *"For the kingdom is the Lord's: and he is the governor among the nations" (v. 28).* His rule will be one that will bring contentment—*"All they that be fat upon earth shall eat and worship . . ." (v. 29).* His reign will be one of righteousness and peace.

Let's proclaim the cross as our only hope of reconciliation with God, and let's proclaim His resurrection as our hope for a future resurrection and a life of victory today as we submit to His Lordship.

Through the Bible in a Year: Numbers 1–2

February 13

Read Psalms 23–24
Family Reading: Psalm 23

The Shepherd's Provision and Comfort

Psalm 23 is probably the most familiar portion of all Scripture. Go to the church for a funeral and the director will hand you a small folder in which very likely Psalm 23 will be quoted. Spurgeon called it "The Pearl of Psalms." It has been the subject of countless sermons, and hundreds (possibly thousands) of books have been written on this psalm. I knew one pastor who preached a series of thirty-six sermons on Psalm 23 and felt he had only begun to plumb its depths.

It is the psalm of life—the living presence of the Lord Jesus Christ. Psalm 22 speaks of His death and resurrection. Then Psalm 23 presents His priesthood at the right hand of God the Father. It is the psalm for us in the church age.

This is the psalm of the Shepherd. Sheep need a shepherd. The Bible says, *"All we like sheep have gone astray . . ." (Isaiah 53:6).* We go astray like sheep—therefore, also like sheep, we need a shepherd. We believers have our Shepherd, the Lord Jesus Christ, *"that great Shepherd of the sheep,"* who works in us so that we will do that which is *"well-pleasing in His sight" (Hebrews 13:20-21).* All believers can confidently say, *"The Lord is my shepherd."* Because He is our Shepherd, we can also say, *"I shall not want."* I shall not want for rest or refreshment (v. 2); I shall not want for restoration or righteous direction (v. 3). Because I am His sheep, He provides my every need.

In verse four, God assures us that even in the valley of the shadow of death, our Shepherd goes with us. It states that He goes with us *"through"* this dreadful valley. He does not go with us just *"to"* or just *"in"* the valley—but *"through"* it. What a comfort to know that He is there. His rod, to defeat the enemy, and His staff to help us walk with and for Him—both will comfort us. Remember that death is only a shadow, and shadows never hurt us.

May we today long to know our Shepherd, the Lord Jesus Christ, and love Him.

Through the Bible in a Year: Numbers 3–4

February 14

Read Psalms 24–25
Family Reading: Psalm 24

All Belongs to the Lord, Our King

We are taking one week to consider three Psalms that unite to present truths about our Lord. Psalm 22 presents our Saviour; Psalm 23, our Shepherd; and Psalm 24, our Sovereign. Psalm 22 speaks of God's grace; Psalm 23, God's guidance; and Psalm 24, God's glory. Psalm 22 is related to the Past; Psalm 23, to the Present; and Psalm 24, to the Future. Think of this again—Psalm 22 presents the Good Shepherd dying for our sin in John 10:11; Psalm 23 reveals the Great Shepherd directing us and *"working in us"* (Hebrews 13:20-21); and Psalm 24 announces the Chief Shepherd coming again to give His rewards (I Peter 5:4).

Psalm 24 begins by announcing that everything belongs to the Lord. Years ago a preacher by the name of John Welwood was going to preach near the southern border of Scotland. He gathered a crowd on some land owned by Patrick Walker. Mr. Walker did not want preaching on his land and so he walked five miles to put a stop to Mr. Welwood's preaching that day. When he arrived he heard the believers singing from Psalm 24: *"The earth is the Lord's and the fullness thereof."* He stood on the edge of the crowd and then heard Welwood say: "Though the earth be the Lord's and the fullness thereof, yet the poor fools of the world will not allow a bit of earth to preach the gospel upon." Those words pierced Walker's heart and he sat down, listening to Welwood the whole day. He accepted the Lord, went home and established a family altar time for his family. He joined other believers in getting out the Word of God.

The psalmist asks two questions: *"Who shall ascend into the hill of the Lord? or who shall stand in His holy place"* (v. 3)? The answer is in verse four: Those who are godly or Christlike will *"ascend"* and *"stand."* They need purity of life—outwardly with clean hands and inwardly with a pure heart. They need to live not for self in vanity but truthfully without deceit.

The Lord owns all. We simply must submit to Him and let Him direct us. Then we shall receive the *"blessing from the Lord, and right-eousness from the God of [our] salvation" (v. 5).* May we recognize His Lordship and submit all to Him.

Through the Bible in a Year: Numbers 5–7

February 15

Read Psalms 24–25
Family Reading: Psalm 24

Christ Jesus, the King of Glory

This twenty-fourth psalm was sung in the Temple worship on the first day of the week, Sunday. On each day a different psalm was assigned: Monday—Psalm 48; Tuesday—Psalm 82; Wednesday—Psalm 94; Thursday—Psalm 81; Friday—Psalm 93; Saturday—Psalm 48; Sabbath—Psalm 92. It is interesting that Psalm 24 was assigned to Sunday, the day of the Lord's resurrection. This psalm was probably written to commemorate David's bringing the ark from the house of Obed-Edom to the newly captured fortress of Jerusalem.

However, the psalm goes beyond David's day. It is speaking of the Lord Jesus Christ. He is the only One who could fulfill the qualifications of verse four—having clean hands and a pure heart, having never lifted up His soul to vanity nor sworn deceitfully. He is the One who received for us the blessing and righteousness (v. 5).

In addition the doors mentioned in verses seven and nine are *"everlasting doors"*—not earthly doors. Jesus Christ, the King of Glory, is the only One who could ever gain entrance for Himself and us, His children. This is a psalm celebrating His resurrection and His ascension. Five times in verses seven through ten, the Holy Spirit presents Christ as the King of Glory.

Twice the challenge goes forth: *"Who is this King of glory" (v. 8)?* The first answer presents *"[t]he Lord strong and mighty . . . mighty in battle" (v. 8).* It speaks of Christ coming from Calvary, rising from the dead, and ascending to glory. He lifts up His nail-scarred hands— emblems of the victory over all the sin and temptations of earth. The everlasting doors being lifted-up, Christ enters Heaven and is seated at God's right hand. Then comes the church age. Christ returns and raptures His saints. Again the challenge comes in verse ten: *"Who is this king of glory?"* Christ points to the great host of believers He is bringing with Him. They have been bought by His blood and are clothed in His righteousness. Again, the everlasting gates and doors are lifted up and we believers will have the same triumphal entry He had. *"So shall we ever be with the Lord" (I Thessalonians 4:17).*

Through the Bible in a Year: Numbers 8–10

February 16

Read Psalm 25

God and I

Psalm 25 could be called the "God and I" psalm. In verse one David prays, *"Unto thee, O Lord do I lift up **my** soul."* He spoke of himself personally. It would be good for you to underline and count every time you find a form of the first personal pronoun in this psalm; *i.e.,* "I," "me," "mine," "my." What made David a man after God's own heart (I Samuel 13:14)? It was that he had a definite, very personal relationship with God. He recognized that he answered to God, that he needed to trust the Lord for strength, and that his personal relationship to God was the most important thing in his life.

David prayed a prayer that should be the desire of our hearts: *"Show me thy ways, O Lord; teach me thy paths. Lead me in thy truth, and teach me" (vv. 4-5).* We need to know His ways—the principles of life that God gives us. We must understand His path—His specific direction. David told God that he wanted to be led of God (v. 4). He wanted His will so much that he wanted God to show him the Lord's ways.

Not only did David *want* to be led of the Lord, but he also was *willing* to be led: *"Lead me in thy truth, and teach me: for thou art the God of my salvation . . ." (v. 5).* Only as we study His truth, the Word of God, will we fully understand His leading and direction. We do not need some new revelation—we must simply read and accept the Bible. It is His holy, inspired Word, and it will be used to help us know His will.

David was also *waiting* to be led: *"[O]n thee do I wait all the day"* (v. 5). God is never in a hurry. Most of us are unwilling to wait on the Lord. Rather, we rush into that which is not really His will.

Then David looks over the past and three times he prays, *"Remember" (vv. 6-7).* David must have been facing difficult times and deep distress. He asked God to deal with him now according to mercies he had shown over and over again in David's life. He thought about the sins of his youth and turned them over again to God. He recognized the goodness of God and the fact that God always dealt in mercy.

May we today recognize that we too must have "God and I" time—that personal blessed relationship with our Lord.

Through the Bible in a Year: Numbers 11–13

February 17

Read Psalm 25

The Leadership of God

Psalm 25 was written when David was facing severe trials. It may have been composed when Absalom was at the height of his rebellion. Certainly this psalm presents a clear indication of why David was referred to as a man after God's own heart. When trouble surrounded him, David fled to his refuge in the Lord.

Verse eight tells us that the Lord's actions come out of His righteous character. What the Lord does follows inevitably from what He is. Scroggie states: "Because He is *upright,* He directs men *right up.*" He is upright; therefore, He teaches sinners in the way.

David gives us principles to be realized for God to guide us. In verses 8-10, he speaks of teaching *"sinners in the way,"* of teaching the meek *"His way,"* of guidance *"in judgment,"* and of the *"paths of the Lord."* Again in verse twelve we read, *"Him shall He teach in the way that he shall choose."* The first principle is that if a person is to be led by God, he must be saved. David states that the Lord is good (v. 8). Remember, Paul said that *"the goodness of God leadeth thee to repentance" (Romans 2:4).* Guidance must begin with our salvation.

Second, to be guided we must be submissive. *"The meek will He guide in judgment, and the meek will He teach His way" (v. 9).* Too often we come to God to ask His will and we already have our minds made up. Remember, He leads the meek—those submitted to Him.

Third, to be led we must be consecrated to the Lord. The paths of the Lord are for those who *"keep his covenant and his testimonies" (v. 10).* If we have our character lined up with God's Word, we will be in a place where God can lead us.

Fourth, to be led we must have a right attitude toward the Lord. *"What man is he that feareth the Lord? Him shall He teach in the way that he shall choose" (v. 12).* The Lord is willing and anxious to lead us, but we must have our eyes fastened on Him and be willing to follow Him. You see, *"The secret of the Lord is with them that fear Him, and He will show them His covenants" (v. 14).*

God is ready to guide us. May we consistently meet His conditions.

Through the Bible in a Year: Numbers 14–15

February 18

Read Psalms 25:12-25 and 26
Devotional Reading: Psalm 25:15-22

David's Trouble and His Deliverance

In Psalm 25:15-19, we see David's terrible plight.

Verse 15—His feet were entrapped in a net
Verse 16— *"I am desolate and afflicted"*
Verse 17— *"my distresses"*
Verse 18— *"mine affliction, and my pain"*
Verse 19— *"mine enemies . . . are many"; "cruel hatred"*

David was lonely and humbled before the Lord and his people. What was the cause of it? Verse 17 has the answer: *"The troubles of my heart are enlarged."* He is reflecting here on the fact that his heart embraced sin—it goes back to the sins of adultery and murder involving Bathsheba and her husband, Uriah. These two sins of adultery and murder had stalked David's steps ever since. He had sinned with his heart and now he must pay with pains in his heart. In verse eighteen he prays, *"Forgive all my sins."* That sin with Bathsheba still haunted him. And it always would. Proverbs 6:33 says of the adulterer: *"A wound and dishonor shall he get; and his reproach shall not be wiped away."* David was experiencing the dishonor as a king who had lost the respect of his people. It is not said of any other sin that the reproach will never be wiped away. Adultery leaves an awful mark on the life. It can be forgiven but scars will remain. David was burdened about his sin. He had prayed in verse seven: *"Remember not the sins of my youth, nor my transgressions . . . ."* He was carrying a load because of his sin.

David knew that the only One to whom he could go was the Lord. By turning all over to Him, David could realize the blessing of not being ashamed (vv. 1 and 20). He could claim God's redemption—delivering Israel from all its troubles. The word *"redeem"* in verse twenty-two means to deliver from the power of sin. David knew that he and the nation needed God's redeeming grace and mercy. He knew that he personally needed integrity and uprightness.

These same blessings are needed today! If we are going to have His power and blessing, we must live in conformity to His Word. God can do it. May we trust His redeeming and keeping power.

Through the Bible in a Year: Numbers 16–18

February 19

Read Psalms 26–27
Family Reading: Psalm 25:15-22

A Life of Integrity

In Psalm 25 David confessed his sin. In Psalm 26 David pleads his righteousness. Sometimes we forget that David did have righteousness. We meditate so much on his great sin with Bathsheba that we forget David did live a righteous life. David had committed a great sin, but he did not continue to live in that sin. What David did once, the king of Babylon did regularly. The fact is, God recognized David's righteous life for He measured later kings by how they followed David's example. Note Jehoshaphat (II Chronicles 17:3), Ahaz (II Chronicles 28:1), Hezekiah (II Chronicles 29:2), and Josiah (II Chronicles 34:2).

David stated in this psalm that he had *"walked in . . . integrity" (v. 1)* and he planned to continue walking in integrity (v. 11). He was so confident of his walk that he readily asked God to examine him and prove him (v. 2). David confidently said, *"I have walked in thy truth" (v. 3).*

In verses four through six, David gives two principles that each believer must apply to his life in order to walk in integrity. The first principle is that of separation. David said, *"I have not sat with vain persons . . ." (v. 4).* These are people who have no character. He added, *"neither will I go in with dissemblers" (v.4).* These are hypocrites, acting something they are not. David further stated he *"hated the congregation of evil doers . . ." (v. 5).* The original language gives the idea of those involved with pornography—lewd, lustful individuals. David also said he would *"not sit with the wicked" (v. 5).* These were lawless and rebellious people. If we are to live a consistent Christian life, we must separate ourselves as David did.

The second principle is that of sanctification. David said he would *"wash [his] hands in innocency" (v. 6).* "Sanctify" means to make holy; purify; set apart or reserve for the Lord. The two must go together— separation from the world and sanctification to the Lord. May both of these principles be active in our lives.

Through the Bible in a Year: Numbers 19–21

February 20

Read Psalms 26–27
Family Reading: Psalm 26

Walking Consistently for God

Yesterday we mentioned that Psalm 26 is a psalm of David's living a life of integrity. One main reason he could live such a life was that he had found sure footing by trusting the Lord.

Verse 1—*"I shall not slide"*
Verse 12—*"My foot standeth in an even place"*

David was now sure footed. He was established on the Rock. A slippery hillside is a dangerous place to be. This last summer we attended a baptismal service in Moscow on the banks of the Moscow River. One of our men brought a video camera and was moving about to take pictures. I was standing on top of a small grassy hill where I could see the service below. He came walking swiftly over the hill past me so he could get better pictures. But the green grass was slippery and his feet went out from under him. The camera was broken, and we could not get it repaired in Russia. He needed sure footing—an even place.

We all need that sure footing spiritually. Many Christians have not separated from the evil as David did in verses four and five. They do not have a good testimony as David did in verse six, and they do not love to fellowship with God's people in his house as David did in verse eight. They are on slippery ground. They need to plant their feet on the solid Rock, Christ Jesus, and live for Him.

We must come to the place where we say "No" to the world, and "Yes" to the Lord. The songwriter confessed:

> I cannot give it up,
> This friendly world I know,
> The innocent delights of life
> The things I cherish so.

But then the song writer saw the cross and wrote further.

> Nay, world, I turn away;
> Though thou seem fair and good
> That friendly outstretched hand of thine
> Is stained with Jesus' blood!

Through the Bible in a Year: Numbers 22–23

February 21

Read Psalms 27–28
Family Reading: Psalm 27

The Lord, Our Light and Salvation

Psalm 27 begins with a statement of confidence in the Lord. It ends with an exhortation to others to wait on the Lord and thus realize His strength. It is divided into two sections. The first section comprises verses one through six, verses that present the victory of faith. The second section, verses seven through fourteen, seems to be dominated by fear. The two blend together.

David begins the psalm with a great statement of confidence. He states that the Lord is his personal help: *"The Lord is **my** light and **my** salvation . . . the Lord is the strength of **my** life . . ." (v. 1)*. With those statements he asks twice *"whom shall I fear?"* My fears will be shattered when I know the Lord as *my* light, *my* salvation, and *my* strength. As *my* light, He will dispel the darkness; as my salvation, He will deliver me from my enemies; and as my strength, He will empower me for whatever battle I will face.

The psalmist had known difficult times—times when his enemies and foes endeavored to destroy him and surrounded him as a host (vv. 2-3). Yet David could say, *"I will be confident."* He was going to trust the Lord, no matter what the circumstances.

There was one great desire that permeated David's life—that was that he might *"dwell in the house of the Lord all the days of "his life" (v. 4)*. He longed to be in the presence of the Lord. More than that, he had a deep longing to see the beauty of the Lord. He knew that the Lord would deliver him from the host of enemies and foes that were around him. He expressed his confidence that *"in the time of trouble, he [the Lord] shall hide me in his pavilion . . ." (v. 5)*. Oh that we believers would all realize God's protection and deliverance. The Lord is our light—we do not need to be overcome by darkness. The Lord is our salvation. The Lord is our strength—we do not have to be defeated by our weakness.

But the Lord does more—He hides us in the time of trouble (v. 5). What a blessing that He will protect and care for us, seeing us through every trial.

Through the Bible in a Year: Numbers 24–26

February 22

Read Psalms 27–28
Family Reading: Psalm 27

Wait on the Lord

The last verse of Psalm 27 is one we all should memorize and quote often: *"Wait on the Lord: be of good courage, and He shall strengthen thine heart: wait, I say, on the Lord."*

David had been facing the enemies who had come upon him to eat up his flesh (v. 2). He pleaded with God not to deliver him unto the will of his enemies (v. 12). These enemies were ready to lie about him and were breathing out cruelty against him.

What was David to do in such dire circumstances? He learned the lesson of faith—the lesson of waiting on the Lord. God does not always do for us immediately that which we request.

When he was in the valley of despair, David wisely prayed for guidance. In verse eleven he prayed that the Lord would lead him in a plain path. He did not pray for an easy path. He could trust the Lord even though he was about to be ambushed by his enemies. If we walk with Him by faith, we will have the plain, level path we need.

In verse thirteen the psalmist wrote, *"I had fainted, unless I had believed to see the goodness of the Lord in the land of the living."* You will note that these words *"I had fainted"* are in italics, meaning that these words were added by the translators. But, you say, we would not have a complete sentence without them. We would not say, *"Unless I had believed to see the goodness of the Lord in the land of the living."* No—then you would not have a declarative sentence. But it could be an exclamatory sentence: *"Oh, if I had not believed to see the goodness of the Lord in the land of the living!"* How often have I heard someone say, "I don't know what I would have done had it not been that I had faith in the Lord! When my business fell apart; when all my savings were wiped out; when my loved one was taken—Oh, the tragedy if I had not known the Lord! But I did know Him—I waited on Him—and I had peace."

"Wait, I say, on the Lord!"

Through the Bible in a Year: Numbers 27–29

February 23

Read Psalms 28–29

Trust—Receive Help—Rejoice

In Psalm 28 David realized fully that he needed to rely on the Lord. In verse one he stated that his cry would be to the Lord, his Rock. He asked God to deliver him from being like men in the world—they speak one thing with their mouth but something else is in their hearts. It is peace in the mouth but mischief in the heart (v. 3). Honey on the lips and hatred in the soul! How each of us needs to pray for deliverance from such wicked acting. Why do the worldly people do this? Verse five has the answer: *"They regard not the words of the Lord nor the operation of His hands."*

David praised the Lord that his prayer had been answered (v. 6). Then, in verse seven, he gave some wonderful truths. He saw the Lord as his strength and shield—his strength to accomplish those things that he could not ordinarily do, and his shield to protect him from his enemies. The Lord is all to us: strength for our work and a shield for our protection.

Now note the confidence David manifested in the rest of verse seven: *"My heart trusted in Him, and I am helped: therefore my heart greatly rejoiceth: and with my song will I praise Him."* *"My heart trusted"*—past tense; *"I am helped"* and *"my heart rejoiceth"*—present tense; *"I will praise Him"*—future tense. This is always the sequence of a spiritually blessed life—trust, help, joy, and praise. If you are not praising, it is because you do not have joy; if you do not have joy, it is because you have not recognized His help; if you do not have help, it is because you have not trusted. We must trust the Lord and the process begins. May we trust Him today, recognize His help today, and thus have His joy producing the song that praises Him.

In verses eight and nine David revealed that he had a burden for others. He was praying for the Israelites who had been charmed into coming under the authority of one who would destroy the nation—that one was Absalom. David prayed, *"Save thy people, and bless thine inheritance."* He was burdened for others. Our prayer life always needs to have a strong note of intercession. David was concerned about his plight, but he was not blinded to the needs of others.

Through the Bible in a Year: Numbers 30–31

February 24

Read Psalms 29–30

Peace in the Midst of the Terrible Storm

Psalm 29 is a nature psalm. Thus far in the book of Psalms we have noted two other nature psalms: Psalms 8 and 19. Psalm 8 speaks of God's testimony at night when we can see the moon and the stars. Psalm 19 speaks of our Lord's being revealed as the bright sun. Here in Psalm 29 we see the Lord in the storm. Ewald wrote, "This psalm is elaborated with symmetry of which no more perfect specimen exists in Hebrew." McGee stated, "This is Hebrew poetry of the highest order."

Psalm 29 mentions the Lord eighteen times. Add to that the pronouns referring to Him and the titles of God (v. 3) and king (v. 10), and we find references to God twenty-five times in eleven verses. And the word *"glory"* appears four times. It is clear that David saw God's glory even in the storm.

God is in the storm. He was in this storm David saw and He is in the storms that come to each of our lives. Do you believe that?

The storm that inspired David to write this hymn formed first in dark clouds over the waters of the Mediterranean Sea (v. 3). Probably King David sat on the porch of his newly built palace in Jerusalem and saw the storm far to the northwest. He watched it as it moved from Lebanon to the north (v. 5), across Sirion (Mt. Hermon) down into Palestine. Then he saw it come across Jerusalem moving to the south, all the way to the wilderness of Kadesh (v. 8), the desert wilderness south of Beersheba. He saw the lightning's brilliant flash (v. 7) and heard the thunder's frightening roll (v. 4 and all the verses giving the *"voice of the Lord"*). The voice of the Lord came through the desolation. In verse eight he speaks of the *"wilderness"* twice. But God is able to deliver in spite of the desolation. Even through the trial God will bring fruit: He brings the *"hinds to calve."*

Through it all, David knew that the Lord was in charge, sitting *"upon the flood; [and as a] king forever" (v. 10)*. David knew the strength and peace of the Lord (v. 11). Those who trust the Lord will have strength and peace beyond the fury of the storm. May we trust God even in the storms that come.

Through the Bible in a Year: Numbers 32–33

February 25

Read Psalms 30–31
Family Reading: Psalm 30

Weeping Ends — Joy Comes

Psalm 30 was written for the dedication of the house of God. David was praising the Lord for delivering him from a dreadful trial. He had been ill—*"I cried unto thee and thou hast healed me" (v. 2).* God performed a miracle in David's body. David uses it as a picture not only of physical healing but also of spiritual healing. Verse three speaks of lifting up David's soul *"from the grave"* and delivering him from going *"down to the pit."* We should always praise the Lord for saving us!

Why was David healed? Was it accomplished so that David could boast about it? Was it so that he could magnify some healer? No, it was accomplished so that David could remember the holiness of the Lord (v. 4). Too often we forget why God has saved us.

Verse five is a great verse—one that I recommend you memorize. God's anger endures but a moment. God does need to discipline us so that we may grow in the Lord. It may seem as though His discipline is for an extended time. I have heard folks say, "It seems that it has been longer than a moment for me; I have prayed and prayed—yet the sorrow and heartache continue. Years have gone by and still I see no answer. A moment? No, I have had a lifetime of it." I say, "Wait a minute—think about it. A lifetime—how long is that compared to eternity?" You see, even a lifetime to us is only a moment to God.

"Weeping may endure for a night" (v. 5), but remember, joy will replace it in the morning. And the idea here is that weeping does leave but joy comes to stay. The Lord announces, *"I am the bright and morning star" (Revelation 22:16).* His coming heralds the morning—and then there will be no more sorrow, pain, or suffering for the believer.

David realized he had to be careful not to let God's blessings be taken for granted and not to succumb to coldness and indifference. He wrote: *"In my prosperity I said, I shall never be moved" (v. 6).* When God's people prosper in one way, they are often tried in another way. Few of us can handle unmingled prosperity. Comforts and abundance breed carnal security and self-confidence. May we look to the Lord and not worldly security.

Through the Bible in a Year: Numbers 34–36

February 26

Read Psalms 30–31
Family Reading: Psalm 30

A Glorious End Out of Deep Trouble

David had prospered. He now was king of Israel. In this thirtieth psalm, David, by faith, dedicates the Temple. He was looking forward to a future date when the Temple would be erected. God had prospered him. He took the shepherd boy from the hills of Judah and made him king over all the land. In verse seven he stated: *"Lord, by thy favor thou hast made my mountain to stand strong . . . ."* Notice, however, that even though David said God had done it, he did call it *"my mountain."* He was strong. His land was at peace. Not a nation on earth would dare raise up arms against him.

It is in times like this that God may begin to deal with us. In the last of verse seven, David said: *"Thou didst hide thy face and I was troubled."* The Lord needed to bring David to a place of surrender and trust.

In verse six he said, *"In my prosperity, I shall never be moved."* When things go our way, we often neglect spiritual truth and spiritual requirements. But God dealt with David. Now in verse seven he says that he *"was troubled."* In fact, I would gather from verses three and nine that David became ill—so ill that he was close to death. The word *"troubled"* in verse seven is a strong word, expressing confusion, helplessness, and terror. David went through some deep waters that God was using to accomplish His purpose. David said that God hid His face; he felt that God had left him to face the problems alone. But, as He always does, the Lord saw David through these trials.

David learned his lesson. In verse eight he reveals that he cried unto the Lord. He learned that safety lies in keeping in constant touch with God. He could claim that God would hear and have mercy. What a blessing to know that our God is not like human friends. They will be offended if we slight them or neglect them—but not God for He is ready to take us back no matter what we have done. David ended the psalm by saying that God had turned his mourning into dancing and gladness (v. 11). Therefore David said he would praise the Lord for whatever glory he had among the kingdoms of the world. He would give thanks to the Lord forever (v. 12).

Through the Bible in a Year: Deuteronomy 1–2

February 27

Read Psalm 31

Trusting the Lord, Our Refuge

Psalm 31 follows the thunderstorm and judgment of Psalm 29 and the praise for deliverance of Psalm 30. If we look at this psalm dispensationally we see that it prophesies future troubles for the godly in Israel and their prayer for deliverance. However, we can look beyond the dispensational aspect and find that the truths here expressed fit all of us who belong to the Lord. We as God's people have our trials, our spiritual enemies, and many adversities. Just like Israel our refuge is prayer and confidence in God. As we trust the Lord, we find that He delivers and our hearts well up with praise.

David had a deep desire: *"In thee, O Lord, do I put my trust; let me never be ashamed" (v. 1).*

He knew that his defense was in the Lord: *"Deliver me in thy righteousness" (v. 1).* David told the Lord that he trusted Him. He requested that the Lord would be his strong rock, a defense that would save him. Following his request, that God would be his rock, David confessed, *"For thou art my rock and my fortress" (v. 3).* He was claiming God's promises. Then he requested that the Lord would lead and guide him.

David's danger appears in verse four. He saw that a net had been laid for him and that there were those who were trying to ensnare him. He stated that the Lord was his strength.

Therefore in verse five David prayed that he would surrender everything to God. The prayer makes up the last cry of Christ from the cross: *"Into thy hands, I commend my spirit . . ." (Luke 23:46).* These same blessed words have been used by hundreds of martyrs since then. Stephen prayed, *"Lord Jesus, receive my spirit" (Acts 7:59).* The church bishop pronounced the last words on John Huss: "And now we commit thy soul to the devil." Huss calmly responded, "I commit my spirit into Thy hands, Lord Jesus Christ: unto Thee I commend my spirit whom Thou hast redeemed." Then he was burned to death. These were the last words of Polycarp, of Bernard, of Jerome of Prague, of Luther, and of many, many others. May we too step into eternity with these blessed words of David.

Through the Bible in a Year: Deuteronomy 3–4

February 28

Read Psalm 31

Our Times Are in His Hands

David had faith to believe God. In verse fifteen he told the Lord, *"My times are in thy hand."* When he claimed this truth, he was in very dire straits.

He was in serious trouble (v. 9).
His whole being was filled with grief (v. 9).
It seemed to him his life had been grief and sighing (v. 10).
He was a reproach, even to his neighbors (v. 11).
He was forgotten and no one cared (v. 12).
His life seemed to be like a broken vessel, no longer any good and thrown out as useless (v. 12).
He believed men were plotting against his life (v. 12).

Where could he turn? Verse fourteen has the answer: *"But I trusted in thee, O Lord; I said, Thou art my God."* The title *Lord* is *Jehovah,* the God who keeps His covenant. The title *God* is *Elohim,* the God of creation. Absalom may have led the rebellion, and David's throne may seem to have been toppled, but David still had God. All circumstances looked dreadful—but David could say, *"My times are in thy hand."* All that happened to him was under the controlling hand of God. Oh, that we might constantly have that same faith.

What a prayer: *"My times are in thy hands."* We need to say that daily. It means that we are trusting Him alone and that we are submitting all to Him. Whatever He wills, we will accept.

> Time has no aimless strands;
> God's warp and woof combine;
> Life's loom is in His holy hands;
> Each shuttle knows its line.
> —Author Unknown

When circumstances seem to overwhelm and throw us down, we need to sing and practice:

> Turn your eyes upon Jesus;
> Look full in His wonderful face;
> And the things of earth will grow strangely dim,
> In the light of His glory and grace.
> —Helen Howarth Lemmel

Through the Bible in a Year: Deuteronomy 5–7

February 29

Read Psalm 31

Our Guide to Heaven

Although February 29 occurs only once every four years, we have provided a brief devotional in this book for leap years.

In Psalm 31 we have noted David's praise for the Lord in the middle of difficult circcumstances. He asked the Lord to *"guide"* him (v. 3). He expressed his love for the Lord and His Word. May we, like David, rest in the Lord and seek His guidance through His Word.

Thy Word

The heav'ns declare Thy glory, Lord,
In ev'ry star Thy wisdom shines;
But when our eyes behold Thy Word,
We read Thy Name in fairer lines.

The rolling sun, the changing light,
And nights and days, Thy pow'r confess;
But the blest volume Thou didst write,
Reveals Thy justice and Thy grace.

Sun, moon, and stars convey Thy praise
Round the whole earth, and never stand;
So, when Thy truth began its race,
It touch'd and glanc'd on ev'ry land.

Nor shall Thy spreading Gospel rest,
Till thro' the world Thy truth has run;
Till Christ has all the nations blest
That see the light or feel the sun.

Great Sun of Righteousness, arise;
Bless the dark world with heavenly light;
The Gospel makes the simple wise;
Thy laws are pure, Thy judgments right.

Thy noblest wonders here we view,
In souls renewed and sins forgiven;
Lord, cleanse our sins, our souls renew,
And make Thy Word our guide to Heaven.

—Issac Watts

March 1

Read Psalms 31–32
Family Reading: Psalm 31

David Rejoices in Victory

David confessed a sin that most, if not all, of us need to confess at times. David admitted that he had rushed ahead in haste. He wrote, *"For I said in my haste, I am cut off from before thine eyes: . . ." (v. 22).* How often have I had to come to God and confess the very same sin— acting in haste. Had I just not rushed ahead, I would have acted much more wisely. In his haste, David stated something that was not true. He said that he was cut off from before the eyes of the Lord. Here he was, a man who had trusted the Lord; and now he thought God had cut him off. Through his experiences he had learned that God hides His own from the pride of man and keeps them in a pavilion from the strife of tongues. God is interested. David had to confess the Lord as the One who heard his supplications and met his need (v. 22).

From this experience, David has some good advice for all believers: *"[L]ove the Lord . . ." (v. 23); "be of good courage . . ." (v. 24).* David knew that *"the Lord preserveth the faithful, and plentifully rewardeth the proud doer" (v. 23).* There it is—good advice! Love the Lord and be of good courage. There will be times when discouragement comes and everything points to defeat. That is when we need to follow David's advice. When we follow that advice, then the Lord will strengthen our hearts and give great victory even when circumstances look defeating.

David was back in Jerusalem when Psalm 31 was written. In verse twenty-one he praised the Lord because God had shown *"His marvelous kindness in a strong city."* That *"strong city"* was Jerusalem. David was glad to be back in Jerusalem. Undoubtedly he had despaired of ever being able to see Jerusalem again. The rebellion of Absalom had grown, and David experienced more defections from his followers. Absalom had become much stronger. Even Ahithophel, David's friend and counselor, had joined with Absalom to see David defeated. Would he ever be able to go back to Jerusalem?

But here he was back in the *"strong city."* He could now sing, *"Oh how great is thy goodness" (v. 19).* God gave him a strong deliverance. Psalm 31 begins with tears (v. 2) and ends in triumph (v. 21).

Through the Bible in a Year: Deuteronomy 8–10

March 2

Read Psalms 32–33
Family Reading: Psalm 32

David's Great Blessing—Forgiveness by God

Psalm 32 is the second psalm that begins with the word *"blessed."* The first was Psalm 1. The word *"blessed"* means *"happy"* or *"joyful."* Both verses one and two begin with the word *"blessed."* David was ecstatic—filled with joy! Why? Because he knew his sin was forgiven. I can almost hear him shout: *"BLESSED IS HE"* and *"BLESSED IS THE MAN!"* David was a happy man because his sin had been forgiven.

This psalm was written after David's great sin of adultery with Bathsheba and the murder of her husband, Uriah. The words were penned after Nathan told him of God's displeasure with David because of his sin (a sin David thought was secret). This psalm is a record of David's confession and the forgiveness that came.

Sin is described in the first two verses with four different titles:

Transgression (v. 1)—Rebellion against authority, transgressing over the boundary of authority; defiance. It is what a child manifests when he says "No" to a parental command.

Sin (v. 1)—Missing the mark, to stumble; to fall; to come morally short. It is sin by practice. The defiance results in practice that is contrary to God.

Iniquity (v. 2)—The very basis of evil; "moral crookedness."

Guile (v. 2)—Deceit; insincerity. It involves the idea of cunning work against others. David used "guile" in his dealings with Uriah. He wanted Uriah to go home to be with his wife. When Uriah refused, he plotted a way to have him killed in battle. DECEIT!!

The *transgression* is pardoned—what a blessing! There is no greater joy to anyone in this life than to know his transgression is forgiven. Nothing in this life can equal the value of that conscience that knows God has forgiven. *Sin* is covered—not to be seen by God again. *Iniquity* is not imputed—not charged to the sinner's account. The spirit has had *guile* removed. There must be no deceit. We need to face sin for what it is. Oh, that we might come clean with God! When we do, He pours out the blessing of forgiveness for our transgression and covering for our sin.

Through the Bible in a Year: Deuteronomy 11–13

March 3

Read Psalms 32–33
Family Reading: Psalm 32

David's Instruction Concerning Guilt

Yesterday we mentioned that Psalm 32 is the second psalm that begins with the word *"blessed."* Psalm 1 begins, *"Blessed,"* and speaks of the man who *never* went astray. That man would have to be the Lord Jesus Christ. Psalm 32 praises the Lord for giving this blessed joy to one who *did* go astray. Therefore, the blessing of this psalm can be known by you and me and all others (*See* Isaiah 53:6).

In the superscription we find that Psalm 32 is a "Maschil." That word means "instruction." Therefore, we should stop and pray, "Lord teach me what you have for me to learn in this psalm." Here are some truths that you and I should learn from Psalm 32:

1. God does forgive sin. David realized that blessing and shouted about it in verses one and two.

2. It is folly for us to try to cover up sin. Because David kept silent (v. 3), serious physical problems resulted. Guilt because of his sin ate him up. His bones waxed old (v. 3); he seemed dried up on the inside (v. 4); he knew God's hand was heavy against him (v. 4).

3. Confession of sin brings wonderful relief. David confessed his sin and God forgave him (v. 5). That was such an exciting truth that David wrote the word *"Selah,"* which means *"repeat that again"* so that we can meditate on it.

4. David recommended that everyone free himself from the guilt of unforgiven sin (v. 6). *"In the flood of great waters"* (the time of trials that will come), we will be blessed and prepared if we know that our transgressions are forgiven and our sin covered.

5. Following forgiveness, one can really begin to live for the Lord and know God's leading and direction.

6. Sorrows will beset those who try to cover sin; but joy will come to those who are willing and ready to confess sin. *"Many sorrows shall be to the wicked; but he that trusteth in the Lord, mercy shall compass him about"* (v. 10). Therefore when transgressions are forgiven, we can be glad in the Lord and shout for joy (v. 11).

Through the Bible in a Year: Deuteronomy 14–16

March 4

Read Psalm 33

Sing Praise Because of the Power of His Word

Psalms 32 and 33 go together. They both call for praise. Psalm 32 deals with the need of a soul getting right with God and shows us the throne of God's grace. Psalm 33 is a song of the praise and worship of those who are the righteous and upright and presents the throne of God's government. We need to rejoice in the Lord.

The psalmist calls for believers to pull out all the stops as we praise the Lord. We are to praise Him with the harp, the psaltery, and with our singing (vv. 2-3). The instruments must be played loudly and skillfully.

What are we to praise? We are to praise God's Word. His Word is right and true (v. 4). Nothing is better for us than to accept God's Word as that which has the right principles for our lives.

We find two important truths about the power of the Word of God (vv. 4-7). First, there is its moral power. The Lord always expresses that which is right for *"He loveth righteousness and judgment: the earth is full of the goodness of the Lord" (v. 5)*. We need to come back to this truth that God's Word is that which is right and righteous. When we depart from His Word, we lose our moorings and we find ourselves without sail or rudder or anchor. America threw the Bible out of the public school system. The results have been dreadful. We lost our moral base as a nation. We now have a generation of secular-minded people who feel they do not need God or the Bible. They are rearing children to live for the world and apart from God. What we need in America is to come back to our roots in the Bible.

Second, there is the creative power of His Word. Verse six states, *"By the word of the Lord were the heavens made; and all the host of them by the breath of his mouth."* In Genesis 1 we note that God spoke, and creation took place. Oh, the power of His Word—let's read it to be wise, believe it to be safe, and practice it to be holy.

Oh, the power of His Word—He spoke and the earth and heavens came into existence. His Word manifests power—by His Word a person is saved with transforming power. *"Being born again, not of corruptible seed, but of incorruptible, by the word of God, which liveth and abideth forever" (I Peter 1:23)*.

Through the Bible in a Year: Deuteronomy 17–20

March 5

Read Psalm 33

The Great Power of God's Word

Yesterday we closed our devotional with the recognition of the creative power of God's Word—power manifested in the fact that God spoke and worlds came into existence. *"For he spake, and it was done; he commanded, and it stood fast" (v. 9).*

Hebrews 11:3 states it this way: *"Through faith we understand that the worlds were framed by the word of God, so that things which are seen were not made of things which do appear."* All creation took place just by the Word that God spoke. He created the heavens and gathered the waters together by speaking: *"And God said, Let the waters under the heaven be gathered together unto one place, and let the dry land appear: and it was so" (Genesis 1:9).*

What power! What should be the result of knowing this manifest power of His Word? Each of us should fear Him and stand in awe of Him (v. 8). As we realize the greatness of His power, we should stand amazed and praise Him. Man has been trying to explain the earth and its forming. However, man often leaves God out. Why not go to God to learn about creation. He was there when it happened. Accept His Word and know that by His Word everything came to be.

Nations should recognize Him. *"The Lord bringeth the counsel of the heathen to nought . . ." (v. 10).* God's counsel stands forever (v. 11). Solomon in Proverbs stated it this way: *"There are many devices in a man's heart; nevertheless, the counsel of the Lord, that shall stand" (Proverbs 19:21).* Lenin and his successors in the former Soviet Union thought they could eliminate the counsel of the Lord. They believed their devices would stand, but their devices failed. In the final analysis, God's Word and authority will prevail.

Nations that rebel at the Word of God will have their whole nation and program come to nought. The Bible stands true. It states: *"Blessed is the nation whose God is the Lord; and the people whom he hath chosen for his own inheritance" (v. 12).* Our United States of America was blessed because it gave religious freedom. But now it is turning away from its mooring, and there will be national consequences that will take place. May we praise, honor, worship, and serve our great God.

Through the Bible in a Year: Deuteronomy 21–23

March 6

Read Psalm 33

Our Hope and Help is in the Lord

The psalmist recognizes that God looks at all men. *"From the place of his habitation he looketh upon all the inhabitants of the earth" (v. 14).* God sees all men as they are, and He states that men are all alike. *"He fashioneth their hearts alike; he considereth all their works" (v. 15).*

All men are alike—sinners in need of a Saviour. He is speaking here of the nations, the heathen (v. 10). Whether they be of Alaskan Eskimo or African ethnic origin, whether they be an American in his fancy house or an Asian in his primitive surroundings, all have the same problem of sin and all need the same solution—knowledge of and trust in the Lord.

Then the psalmist discusses something nations need to learn: *"There is no king saved by the multitude of a host . . . A horse is a vain thing for safety . . ." (vv. 16-17).* Nations need to trust the Lord, not their armaments. I am writing this in 1991. This year we have seen the defeat of Sadam Hussein in the Persian Gulf War. The alarming thing is that our technology and our well-trained armies are being praised, but I hear hardly any praise to God. With all of this, homosexuality is being recognized as a viable alternative lifestyle, and thousands of innocent babies are being murdered by abortion. My friend, the day will come that America will not win because she continues in her sins against Almighty God. Verse eighteen states, *"Behold, the eye of the Lord is upon them that fear him, upon them that hope in his mercy."* Here is our need—to recognize that our military might will not succeed because God will bring judgment against sin.

No king is saved by the multitude of his host. The Midianites discovered that when they faced Gideon and his tiny band of 300. Sennacherib learned that in the days of Hezekiah and Isaiah. We dare not trust that God will intervene and deliver as he did in Hezekiah's day.

May we do what verse twenty states: *"Our soul waiteth for the Lord . . . ."* Then we can claim Him as *"our help and shield" (v. 20).*

Through the Bible in a Year: Deuteronomy 24–27

March 7

Read Psalm 34

The Lord Cares for His Own

Psalm 34 is a well-known portion of Scripture. Believers often quote many of its verses. It is important to note the superscription to the psalm: *"A Psalm of David, when he changed his behavior before Abimelech; who drove him away, and he departed."* This psalm was written after the events of I Samuel 21 took place. David went to Ahimelech the priest and did not manifest the character he should have manifested as one in right relationship to God. He lied to Ahimelech and then went to Achish, king of Gath. Achish (the "Abimelech" of the superscription) did not want David and may have killed him except that he lied again by acting like a madman. The Philistines expelled him from the land. He was hunted by Saul with his life constantly in danger.

It was in these dire circumstances that David wrote the words of Psalm 34. With all of the troubles he faced, he wrote, *"I will bless the Lord at all times: his praise shall continually be in my mouth" (v. 1).* He was trusting and praising the Lord. Then David gives advice to everyone who reads the psalm: *"O magnify the Lord with me, and let us exalt his name together" (v. 3).*

Verses 4-7 form a testimony from David and others who have trusted the Lord. David testified that he sought the Lord and that God delivered him from all his fears (v. 4). Then verse five is the testimony about others who looked unto the Lord and were enlightened by the Lord. David had not done that—he had not looked to the Lord. He had looked at the Philistines and became afraid. I Samuel 21:12 states that David *"was sore afraid of Achish the king of Gath."* Here is the man who had not feared the bear or the lion or Goliath. But now he is fearful. Why? Because he placed his eyes on himself rather than on the Lord.

Then in verse six, David wrote, *"This poor man cried, and the Lord heard him and saved him out of all his troubles."* He knew he could go to no one but the Lord. God had delivered him. He saw the miraculous work of *"the angel of the Lord" (v. 7).* That Angel is ready to encamp about anyone who fears Him. Our God is in the business of delivering His own from their troubles. *"The angel of the Lord"* is referring to the ever-present presence of the Lord. May we thank Him for His care.

Through the Bible in a Year: Deuteronomy 28

March 8

Read Psalm 34

Our Lord Protects and Provides

Verse seven speaks of the *"angel of the Lord."* Who is this angel? I believe it is a preincarnate manifestation of the Lord Jesus Christ. Only twice in the Psalms do we find the title *"the angel of the Lord"* —Psalm 34:7 and Psalm 35:5. In Psalm 34, we see the Angel of the Lord protecting His saints. In Psalm 35, we find Him pursuing the sinner. David rejoiced in God's protection and advised all to *"taste and see that the Lord is good: blessed is the man that trusteth in him."*

Does the Angel of the Lord still camp around those who fear Him? Yes, I believe He does. Even today if our eyes could be opened to see the invisible realm about us, we would see something similar to the mountain full of horses and chariots of fire that Elisha's servant saw (II Kings 6:17). The angels are *"ministering spirits, sent forth to minister for them who shall be heirs of salvation" (Hebrews 1:14).*

In verse nine he informs us of one important blessing— *"there is no want to them that fear him."* David had fled from the land of the Philistines to the cave of Adullam (I Samuel 22:1). As he sat there in the cave with those who had come with him, he probably heard the roar of a young lion off in the distance. That young lion was hungry—but here David was driven out of Gath with nothing, and he looked around and noted that God had supplied every need. Men had joined him from farm areas and had brought with them produce for food. Hunters had joined his group and brought venison and birds they had killed. David knew that the Lord provides.

Please note that those who trust the Lord shall not want any good thing. Of course, often with our discontented spirits, we want things that are not for our need or for our good. But we can always be sure that the Lord provides and our needs will be met.

The first ten verses of Psalm 34 form a song of praise. Then beginning at verse eleven he presents a sermon to help all those who read the psalm to know the life God wants us to live. We will note tomorrow what David instructs us to do as he says: *"I will teach you the fear of the Lord" (v. 11).*

Through the Bible in a Year: Deuteronomy 29–31

March 9

Read Psalm 34

Contrasts Between the Righteous and the Evil

Today we come to the last part of Psalm 34. It begins at verse eleven as a sermon by the psalmist. He asks in verse twelve who it is that loves life and desires to have a long life. He then gives solid instruction that those needs may be met in a life. First, he states that an individual needs to guard his speech so that he does not speak evil of others or tell lies. In verse thirteen he states that the person who wishes to have a long life needs to depart from evil and do good.

Then the psalm contrasts the difference between the righteous and those who do evil.

Righteousness	Evil Doers
1. The eyes of the Lord are over the righteous and He is ready to hear their prayers (v. 15).	1. The face of the Lord is against them that do evil (v. 16).
2. The righteous cry to the Lord and He delivers them out of all their troubles (v. 17).	2. The remembrance of the evil ones will be cut off (v. 16).
3. The righteous will be kept by God, even through many afflictions (vv. 19-20).	3. Evil shall slay the wicked and they will be desolate (v. 21).

In the last two verses we note another contrast. *"They that hate the righteous shall be desolate"* (v. 21), but *"none of them that trust in him shall be desolate"* (v. 22).

I am writing this during the last week of August, 1991. Newscasters are calling this week the time of the death knell of communism in Russia. Men who hated the Lord and his people, imprisoning them for the Gospel's sake, are now in prison themselves. Those who love the Lord are free to preach the Gospel of Jesus Christ. Amen! David closed this psalm by saying this would be the case. The ones hating the righteous are desolate; yet not one of those trusting the Lord will be desolate.

Through the Bible in a Year: Deuteronomy 32–34

March 10

Read Psalm 35
Family Reading: Psalm 35:1-20

Rejoice in Spite of Trials

Psalm 35 should be read carefully by believers today. There are parts of this prayer that David offered during the dispensation of law that we should not pray in this age of grace. However, the psalm does give us instruction in handling problems.

You see, David was facing the problem of slander and gossip, even by those he had thought were his friends. In verse fourteen David wrote: *"I behaved myself as though he had been my friend or brother."* These *"friends"* included King Saul and members of his court. After David had slain Goliath, the women of Israel began to sing, *"Saul has slain his thousands, and David his ten thousands" (I Samuel 18:7).* Of course this produced great jealousy in the life of Saul. There were others in his court such as Doeg, the Edomite, who would do all in their power to see David ruined.

In Psalm 35 David opens his heart to us in the light of the vicious lies and slander being spoken against him. David revealed that his strength was in turning to the Lord. He opens the psalm with prayer. He asks God to be his defense and his offense. Men were striving against him (v. 1) and he asks God to fight for him and to stand up as his defense in the time of trial (v. 1).

David stated that in spite of all the accusations and insinuations against him, his soul would be joyful in the Lord (v. 9). Thus he ends the psalm with praise: *"And my tongue shall speak of thy righteousness, and of thy praise all the day long" (v. 28).* Here is our answer to problems and trials. Turn the problems and the enemies over to the Lord and rejoice in the Lord's grace with praise to Him for His goodness. Then we shall have the victory.

David turned his enemies over to the Lord. In his prayer he asked that God's justice be done. David was not going to do anything, but he did pray: *"Let them be confounded and put to shame" (v. 4); "Let them be as chaff before the wind: and let the angel of the Lord chase them" (v. 5); "Let their way be dark and slippery" (v. 6); "Let destruction come upon him at unawares" (v. 8).* David asked God to render justice.

Through the Bible in a Year: Joshua 1–4

March 11

Read Psalm 35
Family Reading: Psalm 35:8-28

Praise in the Midst of Severe Trials

In the first ten verses of Psalm 35 we find David praying for help because of the trials he was undergoing. Verses eight and nine are words of praise to the Lord. Then in verses eleven through eighteen we read again how David's enemies brought severe trials upon him. This section also ends with praise: *"I will give thee thanks in the great congregation: I will praise thee among much people" (v. 18).*

David records the ways these enemies attacked him (vv. 11-18). At least one enemy David had considered to be a friend and had even mourned over his friend's problem as much as if David had lost his mother (v. 14). Very likely this individual was Saul. David was loyal to Saul—he had no plans whatsoever to touch the Lord's anointed.

"False witnesses" rose up against David (v. 11). He said that *"they laid to my charge things that I knew not."* This is the device of the ungodly. It was used against our Lord Jesus Christ, and we may expect that it may be used against us. David had not even thought such things. Then verse twelve states, *"They rewarded me evil for good to the spoiling of my soul."* This is devilish and men have learned well how to do the works of Satan. David experienced their Satanic-inspired action, but did he retaliate with similar action? Oh, no—verse thirteen reveals what David did. He humbled himself in the garments of grief and prayer—in sackcloth. He prayed for those who despitefully used him. Oh, that we could learn that lesson. We should obey Luke 6:31: *"And as ye would that men should do to you, do ye also to them likewise."* Please note that this statement of David's actions appears in the same psalm as the prayers of condemnation.

David was innocent of these things. He actually carried a burden to pray for these enemies when they were sick (v. 13). Even then they continued to lie about David and mock him (vv. 15-16). They did this behind his back.

What did David do? Please observe that there is not a single note of bitterness in David's writing about this. Instead he praised the Lord. May we have grace to follow in David's footsteps.

Through the Bible in a Year: Joshua 5–7

March 12

Read Psalms 35:18-28 and 36

A Thankful Spirit During the Trials

In Psalm 35 we learn that David had been undergoing great trials. His so-called friends had turned against him and had rewarded him evil for good (v. 12). David reveals the attitude that gave him blessed victory in his life (vv. 18-28). He gave thanks to the Lord before the people (v. 18). Further he promised God he would speak of God's righteousness and give praise to the Lord all day long (v. 28).

Why could he do this? It seems so contrary to human nature—yet David did exactly that. One reason he could do it is that he recognized the omniscience of God. Men were slandering David and God knew it (vv. 21-22). Our Heavenly Father knows all our sorrow. Spurgeon said: "Omniscience is the saint's candle which never goes out." In Luke 18:7, the Lord Jesus asked, *"And shall not God avenge his own elect which cry day and night unto him?"* God sees. Therefore David could pray, asking God to *"keep not silence"* and to *"be not far from him" (v. 22).*

The sense of God's nearness and presence brings comfort, courage, and confidence. David knew well that God is righteous in all His judgments, and he was willing to rest on the blessed truth of God's omniscience and proper judgment.

David's enemies were powerful and persistent. They did not cease to fight Him and His causes. They spoke not peace, and they used deceit to try to destroy David (v. 20). But David turned to the Lord. He knew that God saw all things and understood perfectly what was taking place. It seemed as though the Lord were asleep. David asked that God would stir Himself up and awake. It is important to note that David requested the Lord to judge him. So David trusted the Lord and sought to judge himself so that he might be the person God would want him to be.

David ends the psalm on a high note. He speaks of shouting for joy because of his righteous cause (v. 27). He has faced the problems and has come through the difficult trial with the realization that he must continually praise the Lord. You see, in the midst of severe trials, David turned to the Lord and gave thanks. It is easy to sing when the trouble ceases—but David thanked God in the midst of the trouble.

Through the Bible in a Year: Joshua 8–9

March 13

Read Psalms 36 and 37:1-11

The Sinful Man

Psalm 36 is a revelation of what man is before God and what God can be to man. Verses one though four present the sinful man. Then beginning at verse five we see the attitude and response of the saved man.

Today we will note the sinful man and tomorrow we will look at the saved man. Please keep in mind that there are only two divisions of men in the Bible—the wicked and the righteous, the saved and the lost. A man is either just or unjust. He is not "pretty good" or "slightly bad." He is either justified or condemned. In the Bible we find that in God's sight things are either black or white. There are no grays in God's eye. It can be no other way, for God asks, *"What communion hath light with darkness?" (II Corinthians 6:14).*

The sinful man's principle—(v. 1). The word *"transgression"* in verse one is translated many other places *"rebellion."* Sinful man is a rebel against God. He may try to have a religion outwardly but he is just a practical atheist. He says in his heart that he does not fear God.

The sinful man's pride—(v. 2). He flatters himself in his own eyes. He does not feel any accountability to God. He has the idea that he can live in his sin and it will not be found out. He has persuaded himself that God will not interfere with him. When we lose the fear of God, we open the door to all kinds of wickedness. This psalm is a picture of many Americans today. They have become totally secular, leaving God out of their plans. We removed the Bible from our schools and brought in sex education. Now schools pay security people to patrol the campuses where crime is rampant. As man goes on in his pride, his iniquity becomes more hateful (v. 2).

The sinful man's practice—(vv. 3, 4). His mouth spews out wickedness and deceit. He does not manifest wisdom and ceases to be good. He meditates, even in his bed, on what he can do to rebel against God. The last part of verse four gives the very core of his problem: *"He abhorreth not evil."* A righteous, saved man is going to abhor evil and endeavor to walk away from sin, but not the wicked man. In his pride and self-sufficiency he lives apart from God. Oh, may believers turn from sin and honor the Lord.

Through the Bible in a Year: Joshua 10–12

March 14

Read Psalms 36 and 37:1-11
Family Reading: Psalm 36

The Blessing Coming From God's Fountain

The first four verses of Psalm 36 reveal the condition of sinful man. Then, beginning in verse five, the Lord presents an absolute contrast by revealing the goodness of God toward the righteous. Please note:

God's mercy is in the heavens (v. 5).
God's faithfulness reaches unto the clouds (v. 5).
God's righteousness is like the great mountains (v. 6).
God's judgments are a great deep that cannot be fathomed (v. 6).
God's loving kindness excels beyond anything known (v. 7).

Because of these great attributes of God, the children of men turn from sin and put their trust under the shadow of the Lord's wings (v. 7). What is the result? *They shall be abundantly satisfied with the fatness of thy house; and thou shalt make them drink of the river of thy pleasures" (v. 8).* The word "pleasures" is the word "edene"—speaking of the delights Adam and Eve had in Eden before the fall. It is God's desire to restore that pleasure for the believer. Philips has written: "Pleasure, after all is God's invention." The devil has never been able to invent one single pure and satisfying pleasure. The devil's formula, a characteristic of the artificial amusements and pastimes he concocts for men and women, is a deadly one—an ever increasing dose is required for an ever diminishing return."

The Lord will cause them to drink from the river of His pleasures (v. 8). What is the river of God's pleasures? I believe it is the Holy Spirit's testimony to the preciousness of Christ. Psalm 46:4 assures *"there is a river, the streams whereof shall make glad the city of God . . ."* Psalm 65:9 tells us that the earth is enriched by the river of God.

Psalm 36:9 is a great verse: *"For with thee is the fountain of life: in thy light shall we see light."* The river of God's pleasures dwells within the believer to spring up as a fountain full of blessing (John 4:13-14). David then prays that this river will keep flowing and pouring out blessing (v. 10). May that river of blessing, indwelling our lives as believers, spring up as a refreshing fountain continually.

Through the Bible in a Year: Joshua 13–15

March 15

Read Psalm 37
Family Reading: Psalm 37:1-22

Fret Not—Rather Trust the Lord

Psalm 37 is a portion of Scripture in which all of us should meditate. We are so prone to worry and fret. This psalm follows most naturally Psalm 36. The last verse of Psalm 36 reveals that the workers of iniquity will fall. Then Psalm 37 begins, *"Fret not thyself because of evil doers."* It is so much better to be a believer trusting the Lord than to be fretting over what appears to be the prosperity of the wicked.

This is the burden of Psalm 37. The great riddle of prosperity of the wicked and the afflictions of the righteous is dealt with in the light of the future. Worrying and fretting over this are definitely forbidden. The command is given, *"Fret not" (v. 1).* The remedy for this fretting is given in verses 3-8: *"Trust in the Lord" (v. 3); "Delight thyself in the Lord" (v. 4); "Commit thy way unto the Lord" (v. 5); "Rest in the Lord" (v. 6); "Fret not thyself" (v. 8).* These five commands give us the positive approach that will overcome the danger of worrying.

How prevalent is this matter of worry even among believers! Dr. Harvey Springer was for many years the pastor of the First Baptist Church of Englewood, Colorado. The church building was strategically located with thousands of cars passing it each day. On one exterior wall in big letters so all those passing the building could read it easily were these words: "WHY PRAY WHEN YOU CAN WORRY?" The sign made me think—and I am sure it also made many others stop and think. We need to trust the Lord, delight in Him, rest in Him, and quit our fretting. God will take care of those who trust Him.

David begins the psalm by explaining that none should envy the lot of the wicked. In the end, everyone will realize that the harvest that will come to a wicked man is not something to desire and prize. In fact, we should to pity the wicked man *"who will be cut down like the grass" (v. 2).* *"[T]he wicked shall fall by his own wickedness" (Proverbs 11:5).*

"Delight thyself also in the Lord; and He shall give thee the desires of thine heart" (v. 4). There is the answer. A problem arises—do not become occupied with the problem. Set your eyes on the Lord and you can be lifted above your problem.

Through the Bible in a Year: Joshua 16–19

March 16

Read Psalm 37
Family Reading: Psalm 37:8-28

God Deals with the Wicked and Blesses the Righteous

Following the negative command, *"Fret not" (v. 1),* are five positive statements that God gives so believers can have victory. It is better for us to occupy ourselves with pleasing the Lord than to spend our time fretting over other people who do evil. Those five positives are as follows: *"Trust in the Lord" (v. 3);* *"[D]o good" (v. 3);* *"Delight in the Lord" (v. 4);* *"Commit thy way unto the Lord" (v. 5);* and *"Rest in the Lord" (v. 7).*

The reason that God gives in support of having the positive attitudes is that the triumph of the wicked is short lived. The wicked *"shall soon be cut down"* or *"cut off" (vv. 2, 9, 10).* The righteous *"rest" (v. 7)* while the wicked plot and rave against the righteous (v. 12). Why should the righteous rest? The answer is found in God's response. He laughs at the wicked because He knows the end of the wicked (v. 13). God sees the future as well as the present.

God reveals that there is a principle of retribution at work in the world. Verse fourteen states that the wicked draw the sword and bend their bow. But the next verse presents the truth of retribution; the sword slays the wicked and his bow is broken. Evil comes back like a boomerang upon the head of the evildoer. How many atrocities have been committed against men in the day in which we live. I read about the way Saddam Hussein treated the Kuwaitis and even some of his own staff who disagreed with him. We can be assured as the Scripture says (and as history proves in the case of Hitler, Lenin, and Stalin) that the sword will enter into their own heart.

Verse sixteen reveals another great truth from God. The value of riches is determined by their effect on character. *"A little that a righteous man hath is better than the riches of many wicked" (v. 16).* The godly seem to be poor, but they have an eternal inheritance (v. 18), and they shall not be forsaken by God (v. 19). We often get our values confused. Riches in this life cannot equal the value of wisdom from God. In Job 28:12-19, we find that neither gold, nor silver, nor crystal, nor precious jewels can begin to equal the value of wisdom from God.

Through the Bible in a Year: Joshua 20–22

March 17

Read Psalm 37
Family Reading: Psalm 37:18-40

God's Direction for the Righteous

Psalm 37 is for the saved people, not the unsaved. Verse twenty-three reveals very clearly this fact: *"The steps of a good man are ordered by the Lord, and He delighteth in His way."* In writing to the saved people and commanding them not to fret (vv. 1, 7, 8), David presented a strong contrast between the wicked and the righteous. In verses twelve through twenty-two he gives us the attitude and end of the wicked, and he does so again in verses thirty-five and thirty-eight.

The wicked in all of his prosperity may look very attractive, but he shall perish (v. 20). He shall be as the fat of lambs which the fire can consume so quickly. In fact, he shall be just like the smoke that comes from the fat—it soon disappears and is not to be found. How foolish to trust the things of the world to give happiness and satisfaction.

Note the contrast: *"The wicked borroweth and payeth not again: but the righteous showeth mercy, and giveth" (v. 21).* What a shameful thing for a man to borrow, knowing that he cannot pay back. It is even worse if such a man calls himself a Christian. Only a week ago I heard of such a believer—he owed money to a brother in the Lord and absolutely refused to pay him back. A genuinely righteous man will do the opposite. He will pay his bills and then look for opportunities to be merciful and give to help others in need. To do this, he will be careful not to incur so many debts and bills that he would be unable to give to others.

Then note the wonderful truth: *"The steps of a good man are ordered by the Lord" (v. 23).* God leads His own children. It was George Mueller who said, "Not only the *steps* of a good man are ordered by the Lord, but also the *stops* of such a man are ordered by God." This good man, being led of the Lord, may stumble and fall (v. 24); however, the Lord is ever present to pick him up. *"The Lord upholds him with his hand" (v. 24).*

May we learn to look daily to the Lord for His leadership. He is anxious to direct our steps and our stops.

Through the Bible in a Year: Joshua 23–24; Judges 1

March 18

Read Psalm 37
Family Reading: Psalm 37:18-40

Truths About the Righteous Man

Today we are going to consider nine verses that present five truths in Psalm 37:25-33.

First, we read David's observation as an older man who had watched people for many years. He noted that the righteous are never forsaken and they will receive adequate income to supply their needs. He had never seen any seed of the righteous begging bread. To be the seed of the righteous, one would have to live righteously. Those who come from Christian parentage and live to glorify God will have every need provided (v. 25).

Second, the righteous individual is merciful and concerned about being a help to others (v. 26).

Third, the Lord protects and preserves the righteous who do good and depart from evil. The righteous (those who are saved—declared righteous because of Calvary) dwell forever (v. 27). They have an eternal home in Heaven.

Fourth, a righteous man speaks wisdom which comes from a worshiping fear of the Lord (v. 30 and Proverbs 9:10). The righteous talk of judgment. A righteous man recognizes the fact that God's judgment is sure and will come; therefore, he speaks about it and lives in anticipation of it.

Fifth, the righteous man has the law of God in his heart (v. 31). He meditates on and desires to obey the law of God. In Psalm 1:2 we saw that the delight of the blessed man is in the law of the Lord—he meditates in that law day and night. In Psalm 37:31 we realize why he delights in that law—he has it engraved in his heart. The righteous man has the promise that the Lord will keep the righteous in His hand and not condemn him (v. 33). God will settle accounts, and the righteous man will realize how gracious and just God is. May we constantly delight in the Word of God and let it fill our memory, guide our feet, and rule our hearts.

Through the Bible in a Year: Judges 2–4

March 19

Read Psalms 37:27-40 and 38:1-11
Family Reading: Psalm 37:18-40

The End of the Wicked

David ends Psalm 37 by making it very clear that the person who has chosen righteousness and walks in the way of the Lord is the one who will be the winner in the long run. David pleaded with us not to fret even though it appears the wicked are prospering (v. 7). However, in verse thirty-four he states that the wicked will be cut off and the righteous will be exalted. I like verses thirty-seven and thirty-eight:

> *"Mark the perfect man, and behold the upright: for the end of that man is peace: But the transgressors shall be destroyed together: The end of the wicked shall be cut off."*

David identifies the *"perfect"* man as being the *"upright"* man. He is the one who has placed his faith in the Lord and is resting on God's atoning sacrifice for the forgiveness of and the cleansing from his sins. Mark that man! Why? Because his end is peace. God is telling us, "Time is on God's side." Man's life will end. The *end* of the righteous is peace and the *end* of the wicked shall be cut off. The righteous man has built his house on the rock. The rains can fall and the floods can rise, but the house will stand. The wicked have built on the sand. When the floods rise, the house on the sand with no foundation will fall, and great will be its fall (Matthew 7:24-27).

Also in verse thirty-four God gives one more precept—a command like those listed in verses one through eight: *"Wait on the Lord."* Just wait—God will vindicate! I am writing this in September of 1991. Right now we are witnessing an amazing part of history enacted before us. Bolshevistic communism in Russia has come to its end, we are told. Statues of Lenin are falling. There is talk of removing Lenin's tomb from Red Square. The hammer and sickle flag has been replaced. All around us we hear men say, "It is unbelievable what is happening." God is showing us the truth of Psalm 37. The end of the wicked is being cut off. And we have not had to wait until the Lord comes again. Believe it, friend—Psalm 37 is true. The end of the wicked shall be cut off. THEREFORE—*"Fret not thyself because of evildoers"* (v. 1).

Through the Bible in a Year: Judges 5–6

March 20

Read Psalm 38

Conviction of Sin

Psalm 38 is one of the penitential psalms. David is distressed and broken-hearted because of his sin. The superscription states this psalm was written "to bring to remembrance." He remembers his sin and manifests the conviction of his soul over that sin. Three times in the Scriptures, David is referred to as *"a man after God's own heart."* This psalm reveals an attribute that made David a man after God's heart. He was willing to face sin, admit sin, and seek God's grace for his life.

The first four verses reveal David's conviction over his sin. He acknowledged that God's arrows were piercing him (v. 2), that he had no rest in his being (v. 3), and that the burdens he bore because of his sin were too heavy for him (v. 4). In this psalm David is manifesting genuine sorrow and repentance because of his sin. Others in Scripture were sorry for sin but they did not really repent. Esau is one of those who was sorry about the dreadful results of his sin but not sorry about his sin itself. Cain said, *"My punishment is greater that I can bear" (Genesis 4:13).* But Cain did not admit his sin was wrong and he manifested no sorrow over it.

The worst attitude a person can have about sin is to try to ignore its seriousness. When King Saul was confronted by Samuel, he excused his sin and asked that he be honored in spite of the sin. In I Samuel 15:30 Saul said, *"I have sinned: yet honor me now, I pray thee, before the elders of my people, and before Israel."* He showed no remorse—no evidence of conviction about his sin. I have seen this attitude revealed today, and I must guard against having this same attitude enter my heart.

We need to be like David—convicted over sin and filled with sorrow because of it. Have you faced your sins, admitted them, and then trusted Christ for forgiveness and cleansing? If you have not, do so today, and then continue to examine your heart and confess sin to the Lord constantly. Oh, may we look at sin as David did: *"I am troubled; I am bowed down greatly; I go mourning all the day long" (v. 6).* So often today men who should know better commit sin and keep going on as though nothing serious has taken place. Let's hate sin and be ready to confess and forsake it when we see its ugly head in our lives.

Through the Bible in a Year: Judges 7–8 and 9:1-25

March 21

Read Psalm 38

Humiliation Over Sin

In the first four verses of Psalm 38 we noted David's heart being convicted of sin. In verses five through fourteen we read of David bowing before God in a sense of deep humiliation because of his sin. In verse six he said: *"I am troubled; I am bowed down greatly; I go mourning all the day long."*

David had sinned grievously with Bathsheba and Uriah. He wrote this psalm to warn his readers that sin does take an awful toll and does leave terrible scars. From this psalm we learn that David suffered with some serious physical malady. In verse seven he wrote, *"My loins are filled with a loathsome disease: and there is no soundness in my flesh."* It is strange that as we read the story of David's life in Samuel and Chronicles we find no mention of this disease. Though those historical writers did not mention it, David himself wanted to let everyone know that there is a price to pay for sin. He called it a "loathsome disease." The word "loathsome" means "feverish." David was inflamed with fever. So serious was this disease that his lovers, friends, and relatives did not come close to him (v. 11). What disease is it that causes others to stand afar off? It is leprosy. Is it possible that David is telling us here that he was afflicted with leprosy?

Whatever it was that plagued David, it was serious! He was broken over it. As a man after God's own heart, David was willing to confess sin and be humble before God because of it. Read this psalm carefully and realize that David is warning us about the danger of sin. Remember it brought even the great King David to a very low place before God.

Not only was David deserted by friends, he was also derided by foes: *"They that seek my hurt speak mischievous things, and imagine deceits all the day long"* (v. 12). David was so overwhelmed by this that he sat quietly as a man who was deaf and dumb. His mouth was stopped; he could not talk. Did David anticipate such an end when he first began to play with sin? No—but now he knew. Oh, may we learn well—do not play with sin.

Through the Bible in a Year: Judges 9:26-51 and 10–11

March 22

Read Psalms 38:15-22 and 39

David's Confidence, Contrition, and Confession

In Psalm 38:15-22, we find David turning to the Lord. In the previous fourteen verses he spoke of his sick condition. Then in verse fifteen he announces that his hope is in the Lord and in the fact that the Lord hears and answers prayer. In these last eight verses David turns to the Lord as the only answer in his need.

First, we see David's **confidence**: *"For in thee, O Lord, do I hope: thou wilt hear, O Lord, my God" (v. 15).* He used two different titles for God in this verse — *"Lord"* and *"Lord my God."* The first title is *"Jehovah"*—the One who keeps His covenants with His own. The second title is *"Elohim"*—the One who is the Creator. David knew the Lord would keep His covenant with him, and he knew that the Creator has the power to do all that is necessary to make things right. His confidence was in the Lord.

Second, we see David's **contrition**. In verse seventeen he wrote, *"For I am ready to halt, and my sorrow is continually before me."* Yesterday we stated that David had become seriously ill. Here we learn that he believes his spiritual condition was a reason for his sickness. In his heart he was concerned about his sin.

Third, we see David's **confession**. Verse eighteen reads: *"For I will declare my iniquity; I will be sorry for my sin."* What an important step this was in David's life. He had to come to the place where he admitted his sin—confessed it to God. *"He that covereth his sins shall not prosper, but whoso confesseth and forsaketh them shall have mercy" (Proverbs 28:13).* David confessed his sins so that he could realize the mercy of God. On the basis of his confession, David could expect God to answer his prayer: *"Make haste to help me, O Lord my salvation" (v. 22).*

Even with all his problems, David still had to face constantly the derision and antagonism of his enemies: *"But mine enemies are lively, and they are strong: and they that hate me wrongfully are multiplied" (v. 19).* Sin takes an awful toll. May we hate sin and constantly dwell in the realm of confessed sin. Let's keep very short accounts with God.

Through the Bible in a Year: Judges 12–15

March 23

Read Psalms 39–40
Family Reading: Psalm 39

Thinking About Life

Psalm 39 is a very good follow-up to Psalm 38. In Psalm 38 David revealed his sickness and his trouble. In Psalm 39 we find that he thought about his life and realized how empty life is without the Lord.

David began Psalm 39 by making a vow that he would be careful about his speech. He could have railed about the enemies who opposed him. I do think he went too far in his statement that he would not speak out at all—even about that which was good (v. 2). When we try to keep total silence, we certainly go beyond what God intended.

Verse three tells us what David did that changed his life. His heart was stirred about his problems but he did not speak. His heart was "hot" and the fire burned while he mused (thought). David did some thinking. After thinking, he spoke—but he manifested wisdom, for he spoke to God and not to men. And what did he speak? He asked God to reveal the end of life and how much time he had. He told God that life is short. He recognized life as only a handbreadth and that life is full of vanity. People do not like to be reminded of death but as David thought, he realized his life was very short.

He mused. That is what all of us need to do—think about life. David saw life as vanity, even his riches (v. 6). We need to think about life today. But we are so taken up with amusements that we do not think. Look at that word—*amuse*. The letter "a" is the negative. "*A muse*"—it means "not to think." And that's what men want today—something to keep them from thinking about life. David thought about the right things: the brevity of life; the emptiness of all that is in the world; the need to live each day for the Lord.

In verse six David spoke of the rich man. Even he with all his wealth found his life vain if lived apart from the Lord. The comforts and power of wealth are but a "vain show" to the rich unless they have the Lord. David saw this clearly. He himself was wealthy but he realized it was all a "vain show."

May we, like David, stop and think life through.

Through the Bible in a Year: Judges 16–18

March 24

Read Psalms 39–40
Family Reading: Psalm 39

David's Hope Was in the Lord

In Psalm 39:7 David announced: *"Lord . . . my hope is in thee."* In the darkness of his trial he turned to the Lord. He expressed what Peter did when the Lord asked the twelve, *"Will ye also, go away?" (John 6:67)*. Peter's answer was in the form of a question: *"Lord, to whom shall we go?" (John 6:68)*. Peter was saying that there was no hope except in the Lord. That has always been true and is especially so in the day in which we live. Where else or to whom else can we turn?

David realized that he had brought many of his problems on himself. He saw that his transgressions had caused him trouble. He stood silent before the Lord (v. 9). The silence of verse nine is different from that in verse two. In verse two it was the silence of resistance against the providence of God. In verse nine it is the silence of submission to the will and way of God. Please note that David asked for forgiveness of his sins (v. 8) before he asked for the removal of suffering (v. 10). We must face the fact of our sins and seek God's forgiveness before we can claim deliverance from suffering. David realized that God's hand was upon him because of his sin. In verse eleven he recognized that God was dealing with him because of iniquity. David knew that his life had been filled with vanity (v. 11).

May we with David pray that we may *"recover strength"* and know that things are right with God before we step into eternity (v. 13).

David ended the psalm with a prayer in which he pleaded for God to hear. He asked God not to hold His peace at David's tears. It seems that God is moved by our tears. Spurgeon wrote: "No prayer will ever prevail with God more surely than the liquid petition, which being distilled from the heart, trickles from the eyes, and waters the cheeks. Then is God won, when he hears the voice of your weeping."

In verse thirteen, David pleaded with God that he might recover from sickness and have his strength again. God answered that prayer. He did recover. In fact, the recovery was so complete that the historians never recorded David's illness.

Through the Bible in a Year: Judges 19–20

March 25

Read Psalm 40

From the Mire to the Choir

Psalm 40 is a portion of Scripture that is filled with blessing. I wish we could spend several days meditating in it. It presents the Lord Jesus Christ. Hebrews 10:5-9 quotes from Psalm 40 and applies it to the Lord. The whole psalm reveals Christ in His offering before God—as the sacrifice acceptable to God.

The first three verses not only present a testimony of the Lord Jesus Christ, but they also give us the testimony of David and what should be the testimony of every believer.

All of us have sunk into the mire of sin. It acts like quick sand sucking us in, ready to devour and destroy us. I can imagine nothing more frightening than to be in a deep pit being sucked down by miry clay. But what a blessing David experienced. The Lord reached down into that deep pit and lifted him out. He did the same for every one of us. We were in the pit of sin and the Lord lifted us. It took a long arm to reach down into the pit of sin where I was entrapped. But *the Lord's hand is not shortened that it cannot save . . ." (Isaiah 59:1).* He is able to reach down and lift anyone out who will do what David did in crying for help. God lifted David up and we find that:

> The pit was exchanged for a rock,
> A slippery place was exchanged for a secure place,
> And no footing was exchanged for sure footing.

What was the result? David was given a new song. He went from the mire to the choir. And that made him a soul winner. Many could see what God had done for David and many trusted in the Lord.

The same has happened to every believer in Jesus Christ. We have been delivered from the pit of sin. We need to sing songs of joy about our salvation. We need to use our testimony to witness to others about Christ. May we never forget the pit from which we are lifted. And may we trust Him to use our testimony to win others to Christ. The promise is that many shall hear our song and fear and trust the Lord.

Through the Bible in a Year: Judges 21; Ruth 1–2

March 26

Read Psalms 40:6-17 and 41

David's Victory in the Battle—and Our Victory

In Psalm 40:6 David revealed God's attitude about ritual worship: *"Sacrifice and offering thou didst not desire."* So many today have only a ritual for worship; they lack the one all-important truth—the need to have a personal relationship with God. Again in verse six David said, *"Mine ears hast thou opened."* The word *"opened"* is literally the word *"bored."* He said, "God has bored and thus opened my ears." David had at last come to the place of understanding. He was able to hear and understand the Word of God.

Understanding God's Word brought another new blessing to David's life—he became willing to do the will of God. Verse eight states, *"I delight to do thy will, O my God."* What a victory for David to come to the place of submission to the will of God. With that victory he witnessed to others. He preached righteousness (v. 9) and declared God's faithfulness and salvation (v. 10). He did not hide God's lovingkindness nor His truth (v. 10).

We would think with such a victory David's battle would be over. Oh, not so! He had been delivered from some enemies, but not from all. We must never put off our armor when a battle is won. Life is not one battle but rather a campaign. David said that he was compassed about with innumerable evils (v. 12). Note the power of these evils—David was not able to look up. Note the number of them—more than the hairs of his head. Note the result in David's life—his heart failed him.

What was David's answer to these innumerable evils? He prayed and trusted the Lord (vv. 13-15). David knew he could not win the battles in his own strength. He pleaded with God for deliverance. In verse fourteen David prayed that those who wished him evil would be destroyed. David knew that He had God on his side and he could win any battle. One, with God, is a majority.

You and I must follow David's example. Daily we must be watchful concerning the enemies. Our only hope and strength is in the Lord and His power. In verse seventeen David stated the truth for himself and for you and me: *"Thou art my help and my deliverer."*

Through the Bible in a Year: Ruth 3–4 and I Samuel 1

March 27

Read Psalms 41–42

Compassion Toward Others

The book of Psalms is divided into five sections. Psalm 41 completes the first section. At the end of this psalm we note the words *"Amen, and Amen."* These words reveal the fact that one section has ended and a new section will begin.

When David wrote this psalm, he was extremely ill. In fact, some of his so-called friends thought he was going to die (v. 8). Someone has said, "Great men are simple men; you can read them like a book. You know what they will do in any given situation." This was surely true of David. Here he was—not only very sick in his body but also lacking rest in his soul (v. 4). But in this difficult situation he did exactly what he has done before. He prayed and praised the Lord.

David begins this psalm with *"Blessed is he that considereth the poor" (v. 1).* He was poor in body and soul, but still he praised the Lord. And he could confidently say that he knew God would bless those who consider the poor. David had shown grace and mercy to others, and now he knew that God would bless him in his time of need. He believed God would do the following for those who have compassion toward others:

1. Deliver him in time of trouble (v. 1);
2. Preserve and keep him in life (v. 2);
3. Blessed him upon earth (v. 2);
4. Delivered him from his enemies (v. 2);
5. Strengthen him in the time of weakness (v. 3); and
6. Comfort him in the time of sickness (v. 3).

As we have strength, may we do for others—thus being able to claim God's blessing in our need. Job 42:10 records, *"And the Lord turned the captivity of Job, when he prayed for his friends: also the Lord gave Job twice as much as he had before."* Job became burdened for others. David also prayed for others (vv. 8-10). May we have this fervent trust in the Lord—and so see the need of other lives touched.

Through the Bible in a Year: I Samuel 2–4

March 28

Read Psalms 41–42
Family Reading: Psalm 41

The Awful Price for Sin

Sin demands an awful price. David is constantly revealing a price he paid because of his sins with Bathsheba and Uriah. That is true in Psalm 41. In verse five he speaks of his enemies. Then in verse six he narrows it down to one of the enemies: *"And if **he** came to see me . . . ."* *(v. 6)*. Very likely this individual was Absalom, David's son. He had access as a son to come to see the king. But all the while he was visiting King David, he was plotting the seizure of the kingdom. David said that when *"he"* came to see David, *he* spoke vanity (literally falsehood). David was very ill and Absalom would profess to be coming to comfort him, but *"his heart was gathering iniquity to itself"* *(v. 6)*. He was plotting the overthrow of his father. When he left his father's bedside, he would tell *"abroad"* *(v. 6)*. What would he tell? Very likely he would say that an evil disease was clinging to David and that he would not rise from his bed of sickness (v. 8).

Another enemy enters the scene in verse nine. It was David's own familiar friend in whom he trusted. Undoubtedly this was Ahithophel who defected to Absalom. (Note II Samuel 15:12, 31; 16:22-23; 17:1-2; 17:23). Ahithophel had developed a deep-seated hatred of David, he counseled Absalom to erect a tent where he could go in to the concubines of David in the sight of all Israel (II Samuel 16:21-22). Ahithophel was the grandfather of Bathsheba, and he never forgave David for his adulterous sin. In his bitterness he rebelled against David.

What a price David paid! Psalm 41:1-9 tells of this price. He had a memory of sin and thus an accusing conscience. He had deep remorse over his sin, and now the consequences resulting from sin could literally drive him to depression—even insanity or suicide as it does with many.

Where could David turn? What could he do? The answer comes in verses ten through thirteen. He turned to the Lord and His mercy. *"But thou, O Lord, be merciful unto me . . ."* *(v. 10)*. He is the One to whom we must turn, and His mercy is the grace we must trust in our need. Then we, too, can join with David in ending the psalm: *"Blessed be the Lord God from everlasting, and to everlasting"* *(v. 13)*.

Through the Bible in a Year: I Samuel 5–9

March 29

Read Psalms 42–43

God—Our Hope, Help, and Health

Psalm 42 is a blessing to anyone who is going through a deep trial. The psalmist's soul was cast down; his very being was threatened; it looked as though death was nigh. Many believe this psalm was written by King Hezekiah when he was facing death. His sickness followed immediately after the time Sennacherib, King of Assyria, threatened to overthrow Hezekiah and take the kingdom. Isaiah 36–38 tells of the Assyrian threat and the serious illness Hezekiah faced. Miraculously God defeated the Assyrians and healed him of his disease.

Hezekiah was a great king who had brought revival to the nation and who had dealt definitely and severely with false religious worship and idolatry (II Chronicles 29–31). He led the nation in the greatest and most blessed passover since the reign of David (II Chronicles 30:26). He longed to honor the Lord.

But now he was ill and thought he was dying. He spoke of it as though he were drowning in the swift waters of Jordan (vv. 6-7). Through all of this he knew that his only help, his only health, his only healing was by hoping in the Lord. He started the psalm by saying that he longed for the presence and blessing of God. *"As the hart panteth after the water brooks, so panteth my soul after thee, O God. My soul thirsteth for God, for the living God . . ." (vv. 1-2).* What a dreadful experience! To make it worse, his enemies cried out, *"Where is thy God?" (v. 3).* He was in dire straits.

It was in this dry, barren time and this time when his tears flowed freely that Hezekiah said his soul panted after God. He longed for the blessing of the house of God (v. 4) He needed the fellowship of the Lord and of the Lord's people. It is the same with us today. We must not forsake the assembling of ourselves together (Hebrews 10:25). Assembling together will help us hold fast the profession of our faith and provoke one another to good works (Hebrews 10:23, 24).

Hezekiah gave the answer to his distress: *"Hope thou in God" (v. 5)* and *"praise him who is the health of my countenance (v. 11)."* This is not only the answer for Hezekiah but also our answer today. We get the *help* of His countenance and it gives *health* to our countenance.

Through the Bible in a Year: I Samuel 10–13

March 30

Read Psalms 42–43

When the Outlook is Dark—Try the Uplook

In Psalm 42 the psalmist came to the place where he could claim victory in the Lord. Verse nine tells us where he finally stood. *"I will say unto God my Rock . . . . "* He set his feet on the Rock. Now he had a place to stand. The floods and the billows had gone over him (v. 7), but he found the Rock and claimed its stability

> When all around my soul gives way,
> He then is all my hope and stay.
> On Christ the solid Rock, I stand;
> All other ground is sinking sand.
> —Edward Mote

Yes, praise God, the psalmist stood on the Rock. He could say, "Lord, you are a Rock. I am weak and shaking—but You are a Rock that does not change or move."

The psalmist knew that the Lord will commend His loving-kindness in the daytime. More than that, the Lord would also be there in the night seasons—*"in the night his song shall be with me"* (v. 8). Then the psalmist knew that he could pray with an expectant heart because he was praying to the God of his life.

In verse nine the psalmist gives us part of his prayer. He would say unto God, *"Why hast thou forgotten me? Why go I mourning . . . ?"* He was doing what believers often do. We come to God and plead the fact of His nature. He is the Rock of Ages. We can rely on Him in His nature. He never changes and is always interested in His own.

Though he had settled upon the Rock, the psalmist realized he would still face the taunts and reproaches of enemies: *"As with a sword in my bones, mine enemies reproach me: while they say daily unto me, Where is thy God?" (v. 10).* This is what hurt the psalmist the most. Things that had happened caused men to blaspheme God.

He ends Psalm 42 by giving us the way of victory in times of trouble. *"Hope thou in God: for I shall yet praise him" (v. 11).* This is instruction for the discouraged and encouragement for the depressed. No matter how dark the outlook, try the uplook. Whether we can see it or not, the sun is still shining. Hope in God—Praise Him.

Through the Bible in a Year: I Samuel 14–15

March 31

Read Psalms 43–44

Trust the Lord—Don't Get Discouraged

Psalm 43 is a continuation of Psalm 42. It was written by the same writer and has reference to the same occasion. The psalm is very personal with the writer using *"I," "me,"* and *"my"* fifteen times.

The psalmist reveals where his strength will come from when he faces the enemies. He refers to his enemy as an *"ungodly nation"* and as a *"deceitful and unjust man" (v. 1)*. Against such an enemy the writer's strength will come from God (v. 2). Therefore, in his prayer he asks God to be his judge and his advocate who will plead his cause (v. 1). Then in the same verse he asks that God be his deliverer—Saviour. He knows the only one to whom he can turn is the Lord. We all need to learn to trust the Lord as did the psalmist.

He told the Lord that he desired to be led by God's light and God's truth (v. 3). He knew that the Lord would lead to His holy hill and to His fellowship in His tabernacle. When we look to the Lord for leadership we can be sure He is going to lead us. We will be kept in His presence and protection.

The psalmist stated that he needed the leading of the truth of God. Hezekiah's enemy, the nation of Assyria, was bombarding the citizens of Jerusalem with anti-God, anti-truth philosophy. Hezekiah said he needed to depend on the truth for leadership. This is also true in our day when Satan has blasted the world with his anti-God philosophy and worked to devaluate the Bible. May we trust the Bible for leadership.

To know that we are being led by God's light and truth will bring the blessed result of *"exceeding joy"* (v. 4). That will cause us to praise the Lord with the music from our hearts. And our praise will be unto *"God my God."* How personal the relationship becomes when we know his salvation and strength.

Therefore—why should my soul be disquieted (discouraged)? Why be anxious for anything (Philippians 4:6)? God is still on the throne. He is still judge and advocate. *"If God be for us, who can be against us?" (Romans 8:31)*. There is no ground for discouragement for his light and his truth will lead.

Through the Bible in a Year: I Samuel 16–17

April 1

Read Psalm 44

The Right and Wrong Weapons for Spiritual Battles

Psalm 44 gives each of us many spiritual truths for today which we can apply to our lives to help us grow in His grace.

First, we can take the truth revealed in the past and apply it to our lives. In verse one the psalmist said he had heard what God did in the past. We hear of past victories by reading the Word of God.

Second, he states that God planted Israel in the land (v. 2). That word *"planted"* suggests life, growth, and fruitfulness. It is God who drives out the heathen—He drives out our spiritual foes, the sins of the flesh that plague our spiritual growth and blessing.

Third, he states that the Israelites were not victors because of their own strength (v. 3). Their sword did not bring victory—their arm was too weak to defeat the enemy. It was God's right hand and His arm that won the battle against the foes. And we must not forget *"the light of his countenance"* had much to do with each victory Israel experienced. Verse three ends by stating that the victories came to Israel because of God's grace— *"because thou hadst a favor unto them."*

How true is verse three in the spiritual realm today. When we admit our weakness and depend upon His might, we can see the vanquishing of our foes. Paul knew this for he wrote, *"And he said unto me, My grace is sufficient for thee: for my strength is made perfect in weakness. Most gladly therefore will I rather glory in my infirmities that the power of Christ may rest upon me." (II Corinthians 12:9)*

In verse six we learn that to trust in conventional weapons is useless in spiritual warfare. Paul wrote in II Corinthians 10:3, *"For though we walk in the flesh, we do not war after the flesh."* May we learn to fight our spiritual foes with the weapons of His strength.

The psalmist made it very clear—God is the One who commands deliverances for Jacob (v. 4). It is through Him that we will push down our enemies. It was in God that the Israelites and the psalmist could boast of strength and grace (v. 8). God is sovereign. God is sufficient! In verse six we find that to trust in conventional weapons would be useless. Such weapons do not win battles in spiritual warfare!

Through the Bible in a Year: I Samuel 18–20

April 2

Read Psalm 44

Victory and Chastening—Both from the Lord

We are not told when Psalm 44 was written nor by whom it was given to us. From the psalm we understand that the people of God were in dire straits. They looked to history and realized that their fathers had seen victory over fierce foes. From the history of Israel they realized that victory could come only through spiritual weapons and God's delivering power.

Today it is important that believers understand this same truth. Paul expressed it clearly in Ephesians 6:12: *"For we wrestle not against flesh and blood, but against principalities, against powers, against the rulers of the darkness of this world, against spiritual wickedness in high places."* Therefore we must do what the psalmist did in psalm 44:8: *"In God we boast all the day long and praise thy name forever."*

When we come to verse nine of this psalm, we find a change. The verse begins with the word *"But."* The first eight verses present what the Israelites learned from their history. But verse nine introduces a new thought—the problems Israel was then facing. God was not blessing. They seemed to be cast off and were put to shame. Sin had come in to the nation and God was permitting them to suffer the consequences. When this psalm was penned, Israel was experiencing shame, reproach, and confusion (vv. 9-16). God had permitted this to come so as to chasten Israel and thus bring correction to the nation (Proverbs 3:11-12).

In verses one through fourteen, please note the pronouns that refer to God—*"Thou," "Thy," "Thee," and "Thine,"* appear twenty-one times. In the history of Israel the psalmist said, *"Thou didst drive out the heathen with thy hand"* (v. 2). In those present dire circumstances the psalmist said, *"Thou hast cast off"* (v. 9). Again in verse ten he states that it was God who made them retreat before their enemies. God blesses, but God also chastises so that blessing can come. The chastisement of verses nine through sixteen was severe and certainly bitter to accept. But God did have a purpose in it. May we today look to Him for victory and blessing. He is ready to bless if we will but trust Him.

Through the Bible in a Year: I Samuel 21–24

April 3

Read Psalms 44:17-25 and 45

Praising and Praying through Problems

Yesterday we considered the truth in Psalm 44:9-16, the passage that reveals the condition of Israel at the time of the writing of the psalm. They were undergoing God's chastising discipline. Beginning at verse seventeen the psalmist reminds God that through this chastisement Israel had not:

1. Forgotten the Lord—v. 17
2. Departed from His covenant—v. 17
3. Backslidden from God's way—v. 18
4. Departed into idolatry—v. 20

The above list represents a great claim by Israel. Was it a true claim? Apparently so—for in verse twenty-one the psalmist states that God would know if it were not true. We may fool man with our boasting, but we cannot fool God. The fact is, the Israelites were suffering for the Lord (v. 22). They could honestly say that their troubles were a discipline from God. We ought always to make sure our suffering is for Christ's sake and not because of our sins.

The psalmist knew well what would happen if Israel had forgotten God or turned to idolatry. He knew that God would search all this out because God alone knows the secrets of the heart. He realized that whatever suffering came, it was for the sake of the Lord (v. 22). He keenly felt the necessity of turning to the Lord.

The psalmist longed for God's presence and blessing. He felt as though God was not present with them. He prayed for the Lord to return. In the last verse he prayed for the Lord to redeem them for His own mercies' sake.

This psalm begins with *praise* and ends with *prayer.* In between there are *problems!* However, all through the psalm we find the presence of faith. Someone has wisely said, "Deity makes all the difference in difficulty." Psalm 44 drives this truth home. We will do well to learn this most valuable lesson.

Through the Bible in a Year: I Samuel 25–27

April 4

Read Psalm 45

Our King of Beauty and of Might

Psalm 45—what a great psalm to explore! I wish we could spend a week in this psalm, but our schedule will allow us only three days. As I read it I feel just as the psalmist did in verse one: *"My heart is inditing a good matter . . . ."* That word *"inditing"* means *"bubbling up"* or *"overflowing."* The psalmist said his heart was overflowing with blessings. That is exactly what this psalm should do for us—cause us to overflow with praise for our Lord and Saviour Jesus Christ.

The psalm was undoubtedly written for the wedding of one of the kings of Judah. Some think it was written by David for the wedding of Solomon. Others think it may have been written by Isaiah for the wedding of Hezekiah. We do not know just when it was written, but we do know about whom it was written—it is speaking of King Jesus Christ and His bride, the church. Verses six and seven are quoted in Hebrews 1:8-9, with the author applying them to Jesus Christ. The psalmist said his heart was overflowing and the words were pouring forth from his tongue *"as the pen of a ready writer" (v. 1).*

As the psalmist rejoiced, he sang first of the beauty of the Lord. *"Thou art fairer than the children of men" (v. 2).* That is the way the believer sees Him. But how does the world look at Him? Isaiah 53 expressed the attitude of the world: *"When we shall see Him, there is no beauty that we should desire Him."* What makes the difference in the two views? Psalm 45:2 reveals what it is— *"Grace is poured into thy lips."* Because of grace, we see all the beauty in our Lord.

He comes not only in His beauty but also in His might as the Conqueror. Verse three commands Him to gird His sword upon His thigh. A bridegroom carrying a sword? Yes, this Bridegroom wins His bride through a war. The war involves the battle won at Calvary, thus purchasing the bride. Then the bride, the church, is won during the church age. And another battle will be fought at the end of the church age—the battle is in the valley of Megiddo. Our Bridegroom, clothed with the glory and majesty of Megiddo, is the One who can give us the victory today if we will submit to Him as our King.

Through the Bible in a Year: I Samuel 28–31

April 5

Read Psalm 45

The Reign of King Jesus

We learn of God's government in Psalm 45:6-8 from which we note three truths:

1. **The Permanence of His Government**. *"Thy throne, O God, is forever and ever" (v. 6).* In Revelation we should ascribe to Him *"glory and dominion"* forever and ever (Rev. 1:6); praise and honor should be given the Lord forever and ever (Rev. 5:13); the Lord lives forever and ever (Rev. 4:9 and 5:14); and the saints shall reign with the Lord forever and ever (Rev. 22:5). On earth kingdoms come and go, but His throne will exist throughout all the ages of eternity.

2. **The Perfection of His Government**. *"The sceptre of thy kingdom is a right sceptre: Thou lovest righteousness and hatest wickedness" (vv. 6-7).* The founding fathers of the United States of America hoped to build a nation that would be an ideal with a love for righteousness and a hatred of iniquity. They inscribed their faith in God, recording it on the face of our coins, and built some great institutions on Biblical principles. They devised a government they hoped would inspire righteousness. But what happened? It has seemed to fail. The worst ?? are actively working in our country claiming the Bill of Rights for freedom and civil liberty. Praise God, we can look forward to a perfect government with Jesus Christ at the helm.

3. **The Pleasantness of His Government**. There will be the *"oil of gladness" (v. 7).* We look forward to the glorious day of the reign of Jesus Christ. Today every new administration in our government promises to abolish corruption, to rid the nation of drugs, to cut taxes, to have a better police force and safer streets—and every administration fails. But when Jesus Christ establishes his government, it will be one of integrity, holiness, and humility. How we all need to look forward to that day when Jesus shall reign! May we love Him and live righteously, looking forward to that day when we shall participate with Him in His righteous reign.

Through the Bible in a Year: II Samuel 1–3

April 6

Read Psalms 45:9-17 and 46

The Church: The Bride of Christ

Today we consider the last part of Psalm 45. Through verse eight we read of the king, the Bridegroom. Beginning at verse nine we read of the queen, the bride. Since the first eight verses speak of Jesus Christ, we know of whom these last nine verses speak—Christ's bride, the church. Revelation 21:2, 9 speak of the bride—she is made up of the "saved" (v. 9). Therefore these last verses of Psalm 45 speak of the church, the bride of Christ.

What do we learn of the church from Psalm 45?

First, the church needs to *desire the Word of God.* Verse ten invites the church to *"Hearken . . . consider, and incline thine ear."* For one to come into the church, he must be saved. That requires the Word of God. *"So then, faith cometh by hearing, and hearing by the the Word of God" (Romans 10:17).* The members of the church are saved by the Word of God, and they also grow by the Bible. In Acts 20:32, Paul commended the Ephesians to the Word of God *"which is able to build you up and give you an inheritance."* So the Bible is necessary to have us grow in grace.

Second, the church needs to *depart from the old life. "Forget also thine own people, and thy father's house" (v. 10).* Just as a bride needs to leave her father and mother, to forsake all others, and to be faithful to her husband, so must the church live for the Lord and love Him.

Third, the church is *desired by the King, our Lord.* He greatly desires the beauty of the bride (v. 11) and he speaks of the beauty of the church being primarily within (v. 13). Her beauty is not in outward apparel but rather in the inward working of God's Spirit. (*See* I Peter 3:3-4.)

The psalmist speaks of the beauty of the bride (vv. 13-14). She is glorious within, and her clothing is of gold (v. 13). She is brought to the king in raiment of needlework. The Lord is speaking here of that beauty that comes from within. The church is clothed in needlework—that which is beautiful. The Lord wants that beauty of character displayed in us. How is the needlework (embroidery) coming in our lives? We need to surrender to Him in order to grow and thereby be effective.

Through the Bible in a Year: II Samuel 4–7

April 7

Read Psalms 46–47

Trust in Time of Trouble

Psalm 46 is a blessing to read in time of trouble. It is believed the psalm was written in the days of Hezekiah. The king of Assyria came up against Judah, and Hezekiah tried appeasing Sennacherib by paying him money (II Kings 18:13-16). That did not stop Sennacherib, however, and he did all he could to terrify the inhabitants of Jerusalem and to defy the Lord. Hezekiah refused to comply with the Assyrian's demands. Encouraged by the prophet Isaiah, Hezekiah turned to the Lord in prayer, asking God to deliver him and his nation. God answered that prayer by sending an angel at night to smite the camp of the Assyrians, killing 185, 000 Assyrian soldiers that night. It was probably then that Psalm 46 was written.

The king and the people faced trouble but found God to be their refuge and strength (v. 1). Because of this the psalmist announced confidently, *"Therefore will not we fear . . ." (v. 2).* Then in verse four we read, *"There is a river, the streams whereof shall make glad the city of God . . . ."* That river, calm and progressing, is the river of life through Christ and the river of the power of the Holy Spirit. (*See* John 7:38-39.) Because the Holy Spirit indwells the believer, the river is within the believer and flows out in supernatural power. That river is flowing and the streams of each of our lives are making up its force. These streams join together to make glad the city of God (v. 4). God is in the midst of the city—therefore that city will not be moved (v. 5). The city in Hezekiah's day was Jerusalem, and she was delivered from the rantings and the onslaught of Sennacherib. Verse six states the heathen raged. Whenever God blesses, the heathen opposition will arise; but God's voice is stronger than the armies of the nations.

Israel did not need to fear, though she was under the attack of the powerful Assyrian army: *"The Lord of hosts is with us; the God of Jacob is our refuge" (vv. 7, 11).* The words *"with us"* are the translation of the Hebrew word *"immanu"* from which we get our English word *"Immanuel"* meaning *"God with us"* (Matthew 1:23). We have our Lord Jesus Christ *"with us"* today, our Immanuel who gives us the victory. Always—in trouble or triumph—we need to look to the Lord.

Through the Bible in a Year: II Samuel 8–11

April 8

Read Psalms 46–47

Be Still and Know God for Victory

In Psalm 46:8, God invites all to *"behold the works of the Lord, what desolations he hath made in the earth."* As we read the Bible we find time after time where God gave His people blessed victory. And God is still in the victory business. The day will come when He will have wars cease and armaments all destroyed (v. 9).

Today we are in a battle with Satan and the flesh.

Satan— *"Put on the whole armor of God, that ye may be able to stand against the wiles of the devil. For we wrestle . . . against principalities, against powers, against the rulers of the darkness of this age . . ." (Ephesians 6:11-12).*

The Flesh— *"For the flesh lusteth against the Spirit, and the Spirit against the flesh . . ." (Galatians 5:17).*

How can we have victory over these two enemies? Psalm 46:10 gives the answer: *"Be still and know that I am God."* To *"be still"* means *"to get quiet and wait."* That is one of the hardest things for us to do. We are prone to talk, to defend ourselves, to justify our failures, and to condone our defeats. But remember, God made it definite: *"Be still."* And activity is no sure sign of progress. Jesus commended Mary for sitting quietly and rebuked Martha because she was too busy (Luke 10:38-42). We are not only to sit still but also to know that He is God. It is those who *"wait upon the Lord* [that] *shall renew their strength" (Isaiah 40:31).* We must wait before we work, sit before we serve, and know before we teach. We must take time to be holy.

By waiting on the Lord we can claim the blessed assurance of the two verses we noted yesterday, verses seven and eleven: *"The Lord of hosts is with us, the God of Jacob is our refuge."* The Lord has His hosts—multiplied angels of God ready to do His bidding and minister to us, the heirs of salvation (Hebrews 1:14). But these promises in Psalm 46 do not say the angels will be with us—that would be a big help and encouragement. These promises say the **Lord** of these hosts will be with us. Had Sennacherib realized what he would face, he would have stayed home. Think of it: *"The **Lord** of hosts is with **us** "*—with believers today. You and I can face our problems with confidence.

Through the Bible in a Year: II Samuel 12–13

April 9

Read Psalms 47–48
Family Reading: Psalm 47

Praise Him

Psalm 47 is a millennial psalm which speaks of the day when God shall be recognized as *"king of all the earth" (v. 7)* and who *"reigneth over the heathen" (v. 8)*. It is closely related to Psalm 46 which ends with the words: *"The Lord of hosts is with us."* God longs for us to have victory, and by His Sovereignty He gives that victory.

Psalm 46 speaks of the terror that came to Judah when Sennacherib invaded the land and attacked King Hezekiah. But the king rested on the fact that *"The Lord of hosts is with us"* and saw Sennacherib and his hosts defeated. In fact, 185,000 Assyrian soldiers died in one night because the angel of the Lord smote them (II Kings 19:35). Therefore, in Psalm 47 we find Hezekiah able to praise the Lord for He *"is king over all the earth" (v. 7)* and He *"reigneth over the heathen" (v. 8)*.

The psalm centers around two themes: Praise and Power. Actually it presents man's praise of God's power. Today there seems to be a terrible absence of praise coming from the hearts of God's people. The admonitions of Psalm 47 need to be heeded today. The people were to clap their hands and shout unto God with the voice of triumph (v. 1). They were also to sing praises to God, their King (v. 6). Praise was and is the order of the day for God's people.

Their praise was to be *"with understanding" (v. 7)*. We have all heard the statement, "What a person doesn't know won't hurt him." The world may consider this a good statement—but it certainly is not true when we think of the spiritual realm. God holds every believer accountable for what he could know. The more of God's Word we know, the happier we are. The more we understand, the more intelligently we can pray and *believe God*. The more thankful we can be.

Are we praising the Lord? That is a good question! We should praise Him daily. He gives us victory (v. 3) and stands ready to lead and provide for us (v. 7). *"He is greatly exalted" (v. 9)*. We should praise Him for all He has done for us and for all He will do through us. He sits on His throne to reign over all the earth and in every believer's life (v. 8). Our greatest joy and power will come when we learn to praise Him.

Through the Bible in a Year: II Samuel 14–15

April 10

Read Psalms 48–49
Family Reading: Psalm 48

Protected by God's Presence

All Scripture has a *Primary Interpretation,* much has *Prophetic Implication,* and nearly all has a *Practical Application.* Psalm 48, in speaking of Zion and Jerusalem, does not refer to the church and Heaven. Rather, it refers to an earthly city and earthly people. It speaks of an historical event and points forward to the millennial reign of Christ.

We do not know for certain where the psalm was written, nor by whom. Psalm 47 speaks of the king and Psalm 48 presents his city. We are told that it is *"the city of our God" (v. 1)* as well as *"the city of the great King" (v. 2).* The city of which these verses speak is Jerusalem for verses eleven and twelve tell us it is mount Zion. Jerusalem sits as a mountain surrounded on the east, south, and west by deep valleys, thus making it a difficult city for invading armies to attack. It could be approached only from the north. Jerusalem sits as the highest place in the country. The psalmist said that it was *"beautiful for situation" (v. 2).*

Even with its ideal location, sitting on the summit of steep, precipitous inclines that were topped with high city walls, Jerusalem fell to attacks by outsiders. It is the most sacked city in the world, having been completely destroyed eighteen times. With all of her natural protection, Jerusalem needed more. Verse three states that *"God is known in her palaces for a refuge."* She needed to depend on God for protection and deliverance. Invaders attacked Jerusalem because Israel had sinned. But some of these armies would assemble and then be troubled and turn away (vv. 5-6). God's presence would defeat them.

Kings assembled together against Jerusalem (v. 4). They saw the huge walls that surrounded the city but felt sure they could overcome the difficulty posed by the walls. But they could not overcome the truth of verse three that in the palace God was trusted. When Sennacherib tried to frighten Jerusalem into submission, Hezekiah gave his people a message of faith and confidence that we could summarize with these words: "In God we trust." (*See* II Chronicles 32:7-8.)

Hezekiah and his people saw the victory. So can we today if we will realize Christ is our victory and we can trust Him.

Through the Bible in a Year: II Samuel 16–18

April 11

Read Psalms 48–49
Family Reading: Psalm 48

God's People Testifying of God's Deliverance

The first eight verses of Psalm 48 present the truth that God's city Jerusalem was protected by His presence. The Lord revealed His power in His protection. He broke the ships of Tarshish simply by sending a strong wind from the east (v. 7). Believers hear of God's power; and by believing, they see God at work in mighty power. Then they know that God will establish His city forever (v. 8).

Beginning at verse nine we read that these people, delivered by God's power, reflect upon the deliverance God has given. In the temple they think of His loving-kindness, realizing that His loving-kindness was manifested in their miraculous deliverance.

When God gives deliverance, a testimony should be given so that others may know. Psalm 48 reveals that this took place following the deliverance of Jerusalem. Verse ten says that the praise of the miraculous deliverance went *"unto the ends of the earth."* They praised the Lord that His right hand, full of righteousness, had been revealed. God desires our witness of deliverance. Verse thirteen presents what God would have us do— *"tell it to the generations following."* The Lord wants us to testify of His deliverance today and to have it recorded so that successive generations can hear of it. We should give testimony of our salvation so that others may hear it and be blessed and challenged.

The deliverance of God should bring joy: *"Let mount Zion rejoice, let the daughters of Judah be glad . . ." (v. 11).* Those in Jerusalem could go out after the siege of the city and behold what God had done. In fact, that is exactly what God wanted them to do. He commanded them to *"walk about Zion" (v. 12).* As they walked around the city, they were to *"tell the towers"*— that is, they were to count the towers and thus learn that the city had miraculously escaped. All the towers of the wall were still in place—but out on the hills lay the dead bodies of the Assyrians. Their liberty was no dream—it was real—they had been delivered. And so have we. Believers today can go to the empty tomb and know that by the resurrection we have been delivered. We can know that our God *"will be our guide even unto death" (v. 14).*

Through the Bible in a Year: II Samuel 19–21

April 12

Read Psalm 49

Worldly Wealth vs. God's Wisdom

The superscription states that Psalm 49 is *"A Psalm for the sons of Korah."* There are ten psalms with the designation *"for the sons of Korah."* Korah was the man who perished as God's wrath was displayed against his arrogance and pride. (*See* Numbers 16:24-35.) Korah's pedigree is given in Numbers 16:1—he was the great-grandson of Levi and was related to Moses and Aaron. Very likely he thought that such an outstanding heritage gave him the privilege of manifesting rebellion against the leadership of Moses. But God dealt severely with him —the earth opened and swallowed up Korah and many others.

This is an important psalm. Everyone is invited to listen to it. *"Hear this, **all ye people**; give ear, **all ye inhabitants** of the world: Both low and high, rich and poor **together"** (vv. 1-2).* All of us need to hear these truths.

The psalmist emphasizes the vanity of worldly wealth and earthly honor. What he presents in this psalm form the words of wisdom and understanding (v. 3). These truths are like a parable—a dark saying (v. 4). They are so contrary to the philosophy of the world that they are difficult for the average person to understand. This psalm teaches that we should not trust in worldly wealth—rather, we should rest in the Lord. The world teaches that we must take care of ourselves—demand our rights, accumulate wealth. Such philosophy is contrary to God's wisdom and understanding. This psalm is dedicated to giving us a right philosophy of life as it regards material prosperity and wealth.

Trials of life will come. In verse five the psalmist asks why he should fear in *"the days of evil"*—the days of trial or maybe even death. His question is worded with confidence; he need not fear when the trials come, for he has accepted the words of wisdom and understanding.

Therefore the psalmist states that he need not fear (v. 5). Why did the psalmist not fear? Verse fifteen has the answer: *"But God will redeem my soul from the power of the grave."* Here is wisdom and understanding. Trust the Lord—He will meet your every need.

Through the Bible in a Year: II Samuel 22–23

April 13

Read Psalm 49

The Foolishness and Futility of Trusting Riches

What does Psalm 49:5-12 reveal about man?

First, it reveals his *fear* (v. 5). The psalmist wrote that the one who trusts the Lord need not fear when iniquity is compassed about his heels. The figure here is of an Eastern traveler walking the dirty roads. Just as the dust compasses around the heels of the traveler, so sin has a way of compassing around every one of us. But if our trust is in the Lord, we need not fear as other men.

Second, it reveals man's *foolishness (vv. 6-8)*. Money and worldly wealth cannot purchase redemption. Anyone who thinks his money can buy Heaven is a fool. It is not the possession of wealth but the trust in wealth that the psalmist is condemning. It is not money but the love of money that is the root of all evil (I Timothy 6:10). It is not the use of money but its misuse that is sinful. Verse seven states clearly that no man with his wealth can redeem a brother or pay the price of ransom from the prison house of sin. Redemption requires a much greater price than anything worldly wealth can provide. *"Forasmuch as ye know that ye were not redeemed with corruptible things, as silver and gold . . . but with the precious blood of Christ . . ." (I Peter 1:18, 19).* The wisdom spoken of in verse three cannot be purchased with gold, silver, precious jewels, or crystal (Job 28:12-17).

Third, Psalm 49 reveals the *futility* of man trusting worldly wealth or human honor. Wealth cannot guarantee that man will live forever and not see corruption (v. 9). All men die—the wealthy and the fool and the brutish person. They leave their wealth to others (v. 10). Verse eleven gives their foolish reasoning: *"Their inward thought is that their houses shall continue forever . . . ."* Man cannot take it with him. You will never see a moving van following the hearse. Men today have the idea that they are proprietors of wealth rather than stewards. They think that they can retain or dispose of wealth as they please. We all must remember that God has the last say in all such matters.

Money and wealth give honor in this life—but nothing for eternity. Man does not abide for ever—he is like the beasts that perish (v. 12). To think that man decides his own destiny is folly (v. 13).

Through the Bible in a Year: II Samuel 24; I Kings 1

April 14

Read Psalms 49:14-20 and 50
Family Reading: Psalm 49:14-20 and 50:1-15

Those Who Trust the Lord Need Not Fear

Psalm 49:14 presents the fate of the wicked:

> *"Like sheep they are laid in the grave; death shall feed on them;*
> *and the upright shall have dominion over them in the morning;*
> *and their beauty shall consume in the grave from their dwelling."*

Like sheep that die, the wicked are laid in the grave where death with all of its corruption will feed on them. Their beauty in this life will be consumed. The righteous whom they despised will have a "morning," while all they have is the darkness of death. They rejected the Lord as their Shepherd—now they have death as their shepherd.

Then the psalmist states his hope:

> *"But God will redeem my soul from the power of the grave:*
> *for he shall receive me" (v. 15).*

In the first fifteen verses of this psalm, the writer is speaking of his own understanding. He answers the question of verse five for himself: *"Wherefore should I fear in the days of evil?"* Beginning at verse sixteen he gives advice to others concerning their lives. He exhorts them: *"Be not afraid when one is made rich, when the glory of his house is increased."*

Rich men seemingly have power because of their wealth. Should we be afraid of the rich? No, because when the rich man dies he takes nothing with him (v. 17). The rich man's faith is often placed in the wrong thing and focused on the wrong world. In reality, he is eternally doomed —he shall go where *"they shall never see light" (v. 19).* He is also eternally decided—he *"is like the beasts that perish" (v. 20).*

Therefore, those who trust the Lord have the true wealth—and they need not fear.

> His love has no limit, His grace has no measure,
> His power no boundary known unto men;
> For out of His infinite riches in Jesus
> He giveth and giveth, and giveth again.
> —Annie Johnson Flint

Through the Bible in a Year: I Kings 2–3

April 15

Read Psalm 50

Judgment Begins With God's People

Psalm 50 pronounces judgment on Israel because of her unbelief. God states that *"a fire shall devour before Him" (v. 3)* and that God *"shall call to the heavens from above, and to the earth, that he may judge his people" (v. 4).* The judgment will be from the heavens and *"God is judge himself" (v. 6).*

God announces this judgment to which He is going to call all the earth (v. 1). The judgment will take place at Zion, one of the mounts in Jerusalem (v. 2). Note that verse two says, *"God hath shined."* Undoubtedly, the Lord will manifest His blazing glory out of Zion.

Who is going to be judged? First, it will be the nation of Israel. Verse five reads, *"Gather my saints together unto me; those that have made a covenant with me by sacrifice."* These are the people of God— the nation of Israel who had been the object of God's choosing and loving-kindness. They had their relationship with God on the basis of sacrifice. He identifies these *"saints"* of verse five as *"Israel"* in verse seven. In that verse God states that He will testify against Israel.

The fact that God is going to judge Israel presents the truth revealed in I Peter 4:17: *"For the time is come that judgment must begin at the house of God: and if it first begin at us, what shall the end be of them that obey not the gospel of God?"* God always begins judgment with His people. Their guilt will be in proportion to their privilege. The more God blesses, the more He requires; and the more He gives, the more He expects in return. In Matthew 11:20-24, the Lord speaks of Chorazin, Bethsaida, and Capernaum—three cities that had great privileges but that ignored their privileges. God said that Sodom, Tyre, and Sidon, would have repented had they had the same privileges. Remember—our privileges give us greater responsibilities.

Verse six states that this judgment will be a righteous judgment. God is the judge and His judgment can be only righteous. He will play no favorites. He knows what His people have done. More than that, He knows what they are, for He sees not only actions but also motives. His judgment will be impartial and righteous. May we as His people today repent of sin and surrender all to Him.

Through the Bible in a Year: I Kings 4–6

April 16

Read Psalm 50

Deliverance From God's Judgment

As we saw yesterday, Psalm 50 is about the judgment of God. Verses seven through twenty give us a description of those to be judged. The godly are described in verses seven through fifteen. Then in verse sixteen God begins a description of the godless. We will consider verses seven through fifteen and God's judgment of the godly.

God does say He will judge His people. In verse seven He states that He will testify against Israel. He knows what Israel has done, and in verse eight He commends them for the right things they did. They saw that the burnt offerings were continually before Him.

However, in verses nine through thirteen, the Lord rebukes Israel for allowing the sacrifices and burnt offerings to become only a ritual. They were offering these to God as though they were doing Him a favor. In verse nine He states that He will not take bullocks or he goats out of Israel's folds. God does not need their gift of animals for every beast of the field is His and He owns the cattle on a thousand hills (v. 10). He knows all the fowls and owns wild beasts (v. 11). If He were hungry, He would not beg of us, for the world and its fullness are His (v. 12). Though he did not reprove them for their sacrifices, God is saying He desires more than just sacrifices. God looks for the sacrifice of praise and thanksgiving. While Israel persevered in their ritualistic observances outwardly, that which the Lord desired He did not receive. You see, thanksgiving and praise are expressions of dependence. Man likes to think he has some part in making himself acceptable to God.

Right here, in verse fifteen, God gives a challenging promise: *"Call upon me in the day of trouble; I will deliver thee, and thou shalt glorify me."* What a promise! We must look to Him and trust Him. He alone has power to deliver us.

God wants His people to be *thankful* (v. 14—*"Offer unto God thanksgiving."*)

God wants His people to be *trustworthy* (v. 14—*"Pay thy vows unto the Most High."*)

God wants His people to be *trusting Him* (v. 15—*"Call upon me in the day of trouble."*)

Through the Bible in a Year: I Kings 7 and 8:1-32

April 17

Read Psalms 50:17-23 and 51
Devotional Reading: Psalm 50:17-23

Godly Lives Rejecting Hypocrisy

Psalm 50:17-23 has a tremendous message for us today. This is a psalm of judgment. In verse sixteen God begins pronouncing judgment on the wicked. He has been speaking of those who use ritual worship, leaving the Lord out. Now, in verse sixteen, he warns of the awful danger of being wicked while declaring God's statutes and while taking His covenant in their mouths. Hypocrites!—and of the worst kind, for they use God's Word as a hiding place for their wickedness. They claim to declare His statutes and to take God's covenant in their mouth. Actually with their hypocritical attitude they are hating instruction and casting God's words behind them. They hate to be taught and they hate what is taught. Outside the church, they do not hesitate to be critical of the church and its members. It is this kind of church member that undoes all the good of the rest.

Please note the actions of these hypocritical rebels. They approve of the thievery of the thief, and they use their mouths to speak evil and deceit. They also use slander against close relatives (vv. 18-20). But worst of all, they manifest the worst kind of unbelief. They look at God as though He would be just an extension of what they are (v. 21). This is idolatry, making God like the creature He created.

In verses nineteen through twenty-one man is speaking and God is silent. When we come to the last two verses we find that God speaks and man remains silent. He begs them to *"consider this"*—that is, to think seriously. He warns them that He can judge and tear them to pieces. Then He gives another wonderful promise in verse twenty-three. He promises salvation to those who offer praise and have a life of testimony for the Lord. Actually the Lord is saying here that two evidences of salvation are praise to God and a godly behavior.

God gives man a choice. He can continue on with his rituals and hypocrisy, or he can turn to the Lord, trusting Him alone for salvation. We are in the age of grace today. The Lord offers us the privilege of worshiping Him in spirit and in truth—if we will trust only Him and not some form or ritual.

Through the Bible in a Year: I Kings 8:33-66 and 9–10

April 18

Read Psalm 51

David's Great Penitential Prayer

Psalm 51 is an important passage of Scripture. It was composed by David immediately after Nathan the prophet showed David his sin (II Samuel 12:7-12). David had been under a great burden of guilt. In Psalm 32 he wrote that day and night, God's hand was heavy upon him and said: *"My moisture is turned into the drought of summer" (Psalm 32:4).* He had been under this load of guilt for about a year. The baby had already been born (II Samuel 11:27); therefore we know it was at least nine months and probably it was about a year or more.

David opens Psalm 51 with a cry for mercy: *"Have mercy upon me, O God . . ." (v. 1).* David knew he needed the mercy of God. He recognized that he had done wrong. He did not blame his heredity, society, or circumstances. He knew that he was at fault. I suggest you underline every time you find these personal or possessive pronouns in this psalm —*I, me, my, or mine.* I did so just before I wrote this devotional and I found the use of these pronouns thirty-five times in the first sixteen verses. David made the psalm intensely personal, saying that **he** was the one who sinned.

David viewed his sin in three ways. First, he recognized his sin as a blotted record that needed to be changed (v. 1). Transgression is a violation of the law. David wanted the record expunged.

Second, he also saw the iniquity of his sin as a polluted robe that needed to be washed (v. 2). Iniquity is that which is morally wrong— the word is close to inequity, that which is not equal. Iniquity is the perversion of morals. David had certainly perverted morals in committing his horrible sin.

Finally, he saw his sin as leprosy from which he needed cleansing (v. 2). The word *"sin"* means *"missing the mark."* David did not hide his sin. He openly confessed it and said that it was ever before him. He had a conscience burning over the burden of his sin. He was truly sorry for his sin and turned to God for cleansing.

Today we all need to meditate in Psalm 51 and look to God for mercy in dealing with our sins.

Through the Bible in a Year: I Kings 11–12

April 19

Read Psalms 51–52

Consequences of David's Sin Against God

In this great psalm of confession of sin, David acknowledged that his sin was against God. In verse four he said, *"Against thee, thee only, have I sinned, and done this evil in thy sight."* Had he sinned against anyone else? Of course he had! He had sinned against his family; against Bathsheba; against Uriah, her husband; against Ahithophel, Bathsheba's grandfather and David's close friend over the years; against the baby that was born; and against the people over whom he reigned as king. But all of these fade almost into insignificance when compared to the fact that David sinned against God. David saw his sin as being against God— *"Against thee, thee only, have I sinned."* David was genuinely sorry for his sin. He was not just concerned over the fact that his sin was found out, but he was sorry for the sin itself.

In his exposition of this psalm, John Philips lists seven consequences of David's sin. (*Exploring The Psalms—Volume 1,* pages 407-409). The outline he gives is so valuable that I have made this devotional two pages in length so that you could have this outline.

1. Sin's Defilement— *"Purge me with hyssop, and I shall be clean: wash me, and I shall be whiter than snow" (v. 7).*

    David felt dirty and defiled. He believed only God could cleanse.

2. Sin's Deafness— *"Make me to hear joy and gladness; that the bones which thou hast broken may rejoice" (v. 8).*

    David, the sweet psalmist, had left his harp and the sound of joy. His inner agony of soul had destroyed all of that. David had become deaf to the voice of God. He needed again to be able to hear God speak. The need in his life was to hear the word of God and obey it.

3. Sin's Disgrace— *"Hide thy face from my sins, and blot out all my iniquities" (v. 9).*

    It is fearful to men to have their sins known. On television you will see a suspected criminal brought before the cameras. They will often cover their face with a newspaper or coat—anything to hide so others cannot see them. But they usually forget that God sees all we do. David was ashamed of his sin and he wanted it blotted out.

4. Sin's Damage — *"Create in me a clean heart, O God; and renew a right spirit within me" (v. 10).*

   The word translated *"create"* is the same word used in Genesis 1:1 — to create supernaturally, to make something out of nothing. David wanted a new heart. He needed what Jesus told Nicodemus he needed — the very thing we all must have — the New Birth (John 3:3-5).

5. Sin's Doom — *"Cast me not away from thy presence; and take not thy Holy Spirit from me" (v. 11).*

   David was afraid he could receive the eternal doom of the wicked. Today we have the New Testament promises that believers *"are kept by the power of God through faith unto salvation"* (I Peter 1:5).

6. Sin's Depression — *"Restore unto me the joy of thy salvation . . ." (v. 12).*

   David needed deliverance from depression. Much of today's depression is caused by sin. David knew he needed the Lord and not a psychiatrist.

7. Sin's Defeat — *"[A]nd uphold me with thy free spirit" (v. 12).*

   David did not want to fall into sin again. He knew he must have God's deliverance so that he could live a life of victory.

Through the Bible in a Year: I Kings 13–14

April 20

Read Psalms 51–52

David's Resting on a Full Redemption

David had pled with God for mercy in the light of his great sin. In verse twelve he asked God to restore the joy of his salvation. The joy was gone and he longed for that joy again. Then he prayed, *"[U]phold me with thy free spirit" (v. 12).* He admitted that he could not keep himself from sin—God needed to do that. Every child of God must learn to depend on the Lord for deliverance from sin.

David wanted to teach transgressors the ways of God and to see sinners converted (v. 13). He knew that he could not do that unless the joy of his salvation was restored. With God's restoration David would sing aloud of the Lord's righteousness (v. 14). Please note that he said the subject of his song would be the Lord's righteousness—not His mercy. David saw the message of the gospel that Paul would preach over a thousand years later. He saw the truth of justification by faith—being declared righteous because of our trust in the Lord. David knew that the sacrifices of the Old Testament were only pointing to Christ the Lamb Who would pay our sin debt.

> Not all the blood of hearts
> On Jewish altars slain,
> Could give the guilty conscience peace
> Nor take away the stain.
> But Christ the Heavenly Lamb
> Took all our guilt away;
> A sacrifice of nobler name,
> And richer blood than they.

David said that he would continue preaching to sinners and warning them (v. 13), that he would keep on singing (v. 14), and, that he would keep on praising the Lord (v. 15). Amen! That is the mark of one who has had his joy restored. David had repented and turned to the Lord. His joy was restored so that he could preach righteousness, sing of grace, and praise the Lord for His righteousness and mercy.

David rested on a future finished redemption and looked forward to the time when Christ will reign from Mt. Zion (v. 18). When we solve the sin problem, we have the promises of God to guide us in His service.

Through the Bible in a Year: I Kings 15–16

April 21

Read Psalms 52–54

God's Judgment Will Come on Evil Men

Psalm 52 was written when David realized that Doeg, the Edomite, had told Saul that David was with Ahimelech. We note this fact in the superscription. David warns that Doeg would be destroyed forever (v. 5). The superscription calls this a "Maschil"—*i.e.,* a psalm of instruction. Psalm 52 presents the fact that God's justice will prevail.

Doeg had seen Ahimelech give David shewbread and Goliath's sword (I Samuel 21:1-10). Doeg reported this to Saul and thus caused the execution by Saul of Ahimelech and all the priests of Nob (I Samuel 22:9-23). Doeg was an evil man. Exalting such a man as Doeg to a high place of management shows the definite evil in the heart of Saul.

David painted Doeg's picture here. He showed him to be a proud boastful man (v. 1). Doeg's problem was his tongue. The Scripture records that what Doeg spoke to Saul was true. But he spoke the truth with malice in his heart. Malicious talk may be true, but it is spoken with the wrong motive. Doeg's motive was to destroy David, and he was proud of it! Words are for use—not abuse. They are like a sharp razor that can be used to shave or to slay (v. 2). Doeg's heart was evil— he loved *"evil more than good; and lying rather than to speak righteousness" (v. 3).*

David states in verse one that *"the goodness of God endureth continually."* God's justice will prevail. Judgment will fall on the man with evil motives in his heart. The Doegs of this world will be dealt with! David committed the whole matter to the Lord. He trusted God's mercy (v. 8). And he waited on God, all the while praising the Lord for His faithful work (v. 9). May we, too, leave vengeance with God, knowing that in His time he will deal with men and their motives.

> However the battle is ended, though proudly the victors come,
> With fluttering flags and prancing nags.
> And echoing roll of drum,
> Still truth proclaims this motto,
> In blazing letters of light,
> No matter is ever settled until it's settled right.
>
> —Selected

Through the Bible in a Year: I Kings 17–18

April 22

Read Psalms 53–55
Family Reading: Psalm 53

The Antichrist Revealed

Psalm 53 is very similar to Psalm 14. However there are some major differences. In Psalm 14, we find the title "Lord" ("Jehovah"— the covenant keeping God) used four times. Psalm 14 deals with God's people, the Israelites, and their relationship to God. In Psalm 53 the title "God" (the Hebrew word is "Elohim") is used in all seven references to deity. "Elohim" is the title of creation but not the title of relationship.

The second major difference is that Psalm 53:5 is changed from what we read in Psalm 14:5-6. In Psalm 14, the psalmist is writing about individuals and their personal relationship to God. Therefore it is quoted in Romans 3. Psalm 53 is speaking of those who stand against God under the leadership of the Antichrist. Note the reference to one individual in verse five: *"for God hath scattered the bones of Him that encampeth against thee . . . ."* Whereas Psalm 14 has its counterpart in Romans 3, Psalm 53 presents truth revealed to us in Revelation. This one, the Antichrist, is going to be received by men who are fools in their rejection of God. As the end time approaches when the men will enthrone the Antichrist, we are going to find men to be filthy—*"they are all together become filthy . . ." (v. 3)*. They will also be fierce—they *"eat up my people as they eat bread" (v. 4)*. Today we are living in a day of filth and ferocity. The air waves have been used to spread foul, filthy language. And fierce men are taking others hostage, killing one another without regard for life.

This world today is heading toward the day of the Antichrist. But we must always remember that the Lord will triumph and all trials will end with a song on the part of those who believe in the Lord (v. 6).

Psalm 53 ends with the hope of salvation for Israel. The first word of verse six is *"Oh,"* and from it, a word of emotion, we get the picture of a people excited about salvation. He not only speaks of salvation but also of security with his statement, *"When God bringeth back the captivity of His people"*—words of assurance that God will do it. Then *"Jacob shall rejoice and Israel shall be glad."* The future for Israel is as bright as the promises of God.

Through the Bible in a Year: I Kings 19–20

April 23

Read Psalms 54–55
Family Reading: Psalm 54

Committing All to the Lord—Even When Betrayed

David wrote Psalm 54 *"when the Ziphims came and said to Saul, Doth not David hide himself with us?"* Ziph was a little town fifteen miles to the southeast of Hebron. It was part of Judah, the tribe to which David belonged. They should have been allies with David, but they were traitors. Twice we read of their treacherous effort to betray David into the hands of Saul (I Samuel 23:19-23; I Samuel 26:1-3).

What did David do? Psalm 54 tells us. It is a "Maschil"—a psalm of instruction. Therefore this Psalm gives us instruction as to what we should do in similar circumstances. Any one of us may feel betrayed by others at various times. David's example here was that he prayed and then expressed his confidence in God. The psalm divides itself into two parts—the prayer (vv. 1-3), and the answer (vv. 4-6). (Note that the answer also includes a prayer in verses five and six.)

In his prayer David appeals to God's name and to His strength (v. 1). He uses three titles for God. In verses one, three, and four he addresses Him as *"God"—Elohim.* This is the Creator. David knew that the God who created all things could not be intimidated by a man like Saul. In verse four David also calls him *"Lord" ("Adonai")* the God who controls. In verse six he spoke to Him as *"LORD" ("Jehovah")* the God who has a covenant relationship with the believer. David rested on Him as God of Creation, of Covenant, of Control. He trusted Him. He knew that God was his Helper (v. 4) and his Deliverer (v. 7). Therefore, he could believe that God would vindicate him with his enemies. David committed the whole matter to the Lord and trusted in Him.

David's trust was in the Lord. He stated that His God was His helper. *"Behold, God is mine helper . . ." (v. 4).* David believed that God would give Him victory and blessings, even when he was being pursued by a jealous king and being betrayed by a traitorous village. David not only recognized the help of God but also the righteousness of God. God will reward evil unto those who rebel against God's will. It was God's will that David become king. But Saul would not submit to God's will. David was ready and willing to trust the righteous God.

Through the Bible in a Year: I Kings 21–22

April 24

Read Psalm 55

Facing Trouble

Psalm 55 was probably written by David when he was greatly burdened by Absalom's rebellion. The superscription states that it is a "Maschil," a psalm of instruction. In this psalm we find instruction for every one of us. The psalm speaks of David's trouble, and all of us can identify with that for we all face troubles and problems at some time. Job wrote, *"Yet man is born unto trouble, as the sparks fly upward" (Job 5:7).* Another word in the superscription is "Neginoth," which means smitings. This psalm speaks of some severe smitings that David received.

We will look at this psalm for three days. However we will look just now at a brief outline of the entire psalm. David speaks of a foe, a traitor, one whom he considered to be a very close friend. That one would be Ahithophel (II Samuel 15:12 and 16:23). In this psalm we see David's Distress (vv. 1-8), David's Indignation (vv. 9-15); and David's Confidence (vv. 16-23). First David thinks of himself; then he thinks of his foes; but victory comes when he centers his thinking on God in verses 16-23.

In this difficult circumstance David felt as though God had abandoned him. In verse one he begs God, *"[H]ide not thyself from my supplication."* Because of his sin, David thought the heavens were as brass. He pled with God, *"Give ear to my prayer . . . hear me . . ." (vv. 1-2).* Then he told God how hurt and fearful he was over the treatment given him by men (vv. 3-5). He believed that they oppressed him out of hearts filled with hatred (v. 3). This caused him such grief that he felt pain, fear, and terror—so severe that horror had overwhelmed him (vv. 4-5).

What did he think was the answer? He fantasized and thought rest would come if he could flee away (vv. 6-8). *"Oh that I had wings like a dove! for then would I fly away, and be at rest" (v. 6).* But changing circumstances is not the answer. He needed to learn to face his troubles and rest on the Lord.

Have you felt that you would like to escape? Read and reread this Psalm. Then memorize and quote frequently verse twenty-two.

Through the Bible in a Year: II Kings 1–3

April 25

Read Psalms 55:9-23 and 56

Another Bitter Price for Sin

In yesterday's devotional we gave an outline of Psalm 55. Verses nine through fifteen were titled "David's Indignation." That is exactly what we see here—an indignant king concerned about his country. When he wrote the psalm, he was escaping for his life. It was the time of his flight from Jerusalem when Absalom was wooing and winning the populace to his rebellion (II Samuel 15:13-14).

David knew that Ahithophel, his close friend and astute counselor, was now counseling Absalom (II Samuel 15:31). David prayed, *"Destroy, O Lord, and divide their counsel" (v. 9).* That prayer was answered when Hushai disagreed with the counsel of Ahithophel (II Samuel 17:1-14). David prayed that prayer because of his concern for the people of Jerusalem: *"for I have seen violence and strife in the city" (v. 9).* He amplified that concern in verses ten and eleven where he speaks of mischief, wickedness, deceit, and guile moving about through the streets of the city. Absalom was winning the people with lies and wickedness. This grieved the heart of the king.

But David's greatest grief was over the fact that his most trusted friend had turned on him. He wrote of this awful treachery in verses twelve through fourteen. The traitor was his closest advisor, Ahithophel. David said of him that he was one who companied with the king as an equal and was the king's guide and acquaintance, one with whom the king had sweet counsel and with whom the king went into the house of God (vv. 13-14). David said that this one was not his enemy and was not one who hated David (v. 12). However, the record shows that Ahithophel aligned himself with the traitor Absalom. There had to be bitterness in his heart. Without question this was another payment David made for his sin with Bathsheba—Bathsheba was Ahithophel's granddaughter. In his sin with Bathsheba and Uriah, David produced bitterness in Ahithophel, a bitterness that caused his rebellious, traitorous actions later.

What do we learn here? We learn that we must not lust after sin. Sin carries a heavy load. David paid another bitter price for sin when he experienced the turning away of his close friend, Ahithophel.

Through the Bible in a Year: II Kings 4–5

April 26

Read Psalms 55:16-23 and 56

David's Confidence in the Lord

David was troubled over the traitorous actions of his son Absalom. He became much more concerned when he learned that his closest counselor and friend, Ahithophel, had joined in the rebellion. In his deeply troubled state, however, David expressed his confidence in the Lord.

1. *David's Confidence* (vv. 16-18)

   First, David said he would pray. *"I will call upon God" (v. 16)*. He confidently announced that the Lord would save him. Even though he had this confidence, David said, *"Evening, and morning, and at noon will I pray" (v. 17)*. *See* I Thessalonians 5:17. He had confidence in God, but he knew he needed to pray and wait on God.

   Second, David reviewed his life and saw how God had answered prayer in the past. In verse 18 he states that God had delivered his soul in peace from the battle.

   Third, David took confidence in the fact that there were many who stood with him (v. 18). David had confidence in the Lord and ended the Psalm with *"I will trust in thee" (v. 23)*.

2. *David's Concern* (vv. 19-21)

   David was concerned about the men involved in the rebellion and he revealed what kind of men they were. First, they were *lost,* unbelieving men. They had not changed and did not fear God (v. 19).

   Second, they were *loathsome* men. Verse twenty states, *"He hath put forth his hands against such as be at peace with him: he hath broken his covenant."* Absalom and Ahithophel had violated laws of fellowship and friendship.

   Third, they were *lying* men. David speaks of the words of Ahithophel as being *"smoother than butter, but war was in his heart; his words were softer than oil, yet were they drawn swords" (v. 21)*.

   What was David's answer? His answer will also help us today when we feel friends have turned against us: *"Cast thy burden upon the Lord and He shall sustain thee: He shall never suffer the righteousness to be moved" (v. 22)*.

Through the Bible in a Year: II Kings 6–8

April 27

Read Psalms 56–57
Family Reading: Psalm 56

Confidence in God and His Mercy

The superscription to Psalm 56 states that David composed it when he was taken by the Philistines in Gath. The account of that experience is given us in I Samuel 21:10-15. Verse twelve of that passage states that David was *"sore afraid of Achish the king of Gath."* It is very likely that he and his servants were considering executing David. Without question, at this time David was a prisoner in enemy hands. David called this psalm a "Michtam" which means "to cut" or "to engrave." He desired this psalm to be preserved as a permanent writing—valuable for all believers to use for meditation.

Both Psalms 55 and 56 deal with trouble—Psalm 55, trouble with family and friend; and Psalm 56, trouble with foes. Psalm 56 does not carry the depression of Psalm 55. In Psalm 56 David is optimistic—for he is dealing with foes who are literally also the foes of God.

I Samuel 21:10 reveals David fled to Gath because of his fear of Saul. When he crossed the border into Philistia, he withdrew himself from the circle of God's blessing. Israelites would experience blessing from the Lord in Canaan land. But when they went beyond that, they had no promise of God's continued blessing.

David realized what he had done. He began to plead for God's mercy. Verse one records his cry: *"Be merciful unto me, O God."* That needs to be the cry of every child of God. David revealed his confidence in the Lord in verses three and four:

"What time I am afraid, I will trust in thee. In God will I praise His Word, in God I have put my trust; I will not fear what flesh can do unto me."

David was confident in the Lord and His Word; he was equally sure of the weakness of man. He knew that God is merciful. Therefore he knew that he could reckon on God's strength and see all his fears melt and vanish before him. He turned to the Lord, claimed His mercy, and then had restful confidence in the Lord.

Through the Bible in a Year: II Kings 9–10

April 28

Read Psalms 56:8-13 and 57–58
Family Reading: Psalm 56:8-13 and 57

Passing God's Exams

David would become king. To do so meant he had to graduate from God's school. He found, as any will who are willing to attend God's school, that any individual whom God wants to use and exalt will face some definite and severe testings. Do not forget—God knows what He is doing. The tests are to see if we can face testings and be victorious.

David stated in verse eight, *"Thou tellest my wanderings."* The Lord knew all about the problems David faced. God knew that Saul would pursue David. He knew that David would become so frustrated that he would seek shelter with the Philistines, the enemies of Israel.

Then David added, *"[P]ut thou my tears into thy bottle: are they not in thy book?" (v. 8).* David was saying, *"I know God will remember my tears. He sees them and will keep them for remembrance."* Do not forget that God knows your problems, understands your difficulties, and is deeply concerned for you. He will remember your tears. No matter how difficult our circumstances, God knows them and understands our need.

David knew that enemies would be defeated in as much as he trusted in the Lord. He knew that the enemies would be turned back as he cried unto the Lord, and the reason he knew was that *"God is for me" (v. 9).* Then he proclaimed the value of the Word of God. Twice in verse ten he stated that he would *"praise his word."* He took God at His Word and trusted the Lord. Therefore he could announce with confidence: *"I will not be afraid what man can do unto me" (v. 11).*

Therefore David felt constrained to keep the promises of God. He stated that the vows of the Lord were upon him and that he would continue to give praise to the Lord (v. 12). Why could David be so confident? It was because he could see God's blessing and victory in the past (v. 13). Therefore he could request the Lord to deliver his feet from falling so that he could walk before God in the light (v. 13). May we also thank Him for past deliverance and then walk in the light as he is in the light.

Through the Bible in a Year: II Kings 11–13

April 29

Read Psalms 57–58
Family Reading: Psalm 57

David's Refuge — The Lord's Mercy

Psalm 57 was probably written when David was in the cave of Engedi (I Samuel 24). Saul had firm plans to kill David. When he heard that David was in the wilderness of Engedi, Saul took 3,000 men to seek David and to kill him. Saul lay down to sleep in the very cave where David and his men were hiding. David could easily have killed Saul, but he only cut off a piece of Saul's garment with Saul's own sword.

According to the superscription he wrote this psalm as an "Altaschith," which means "destroy not." He refused to touch the Lord's anointed. There are only four "Altaschith" Psalms — 57, 58, 59, and 75. David wrote this "To the chief musician" which meant he wanted it to be sung in Temple worship.

David relied on the Lord and His mercy. He begins the Psalm with two pleas for mercy (v. 1). He knew that he was in deep trouble and serious danger. Verse one reveals his cry for mercy, yet it also reveals his trust in the Lord: *"[F]or my soul trusted in thee: yea, in the shadow of thy wings will I make my refuge . . . ."* The psalm begins with "calamities" (v. 1), but it ends in the calm of God's glorious power.

Surrounded by Saul's men, who like their leader were liars and men with bitter and sharp tongues, David knew His only refuge was under the shadow of the wing of the Lord. He had to rely on the Lord, and in this psalm he expresses clearly his total trust in Jehovah. He knew that the Lord would *"send from Heaven"* and save him *"from the reproach of him [Saul] that would swallow me up"* (v. 3). He also knew that God would not only send His mercy but also His truth — truth that would silence the deceit and lies of the sharp tongues of his enemies. David had confidence. He could rest in the hiding of the Lord. God protects His own — and David knew that truth very well.

David prayed that God would be exalted (vv. 5, 11). David was undergoing severe trials, but he prayed that the trials would be used to exalt God. When trials come, we must walk by faith, recognizing that God is sovereign. We must *trust* where we cannot *trace.*

Through the Bible in a Year: II Kings 14–16

April 30

Read Psalms 57–58
Family Reading: Psalm 57

A Heart That Sings Through Trials

As we noted in yesterday's devotional, David had just gone through a harrowing experience. Saul was out to kill him, but he rested in the Lord's protective mercy. Instead of Saul killing David, David was presented the opportunity to kill Saul. But David refused to touch the Lord's anointed. He looked to the Lord for his deliverance and also left Saul to God for Him to deal with in His time.

What a blessing came to David. He manifested his great confidence in the Lord. He announced, *"My heart is fixed, O God, my heart is fixed (v. 7).* One would think he would have said, "My heart is fluttered" or "My heart is angry." But David was resolved to trust and serve the Lord. No enemy could turn him from trusting in the Lord. In verse seven David stated, *"I will sing and give praise."* Sing? At a time like this? David sang and it revealed the peace existing in his soul.

> Sing, though sense and carnal reason
> Fain would stop the joyful song:
> Sing, and count it highest treason
> For a saint to hold his tongue.
> —Selected

It alarms the world when they see people singing in the midst of trouble. Whether saints conquer or are conquered they can still sing. When my wife and I were going to Russia the first time, Brother Georgi Vins instructed us, "If you get arrested, just sing gospel songs and ask for the American Ambassador." After years in prison, he had learned that singing in prison puzzled the officials. They could not understand such peace of soul that would produce singing right in the time of difficulty. It is a great blessing to have the heart so fixed (literally—"prepared") that songs will spring forth in spite of the dreadful circumstances. Not only will the songs be a blessing to *"the people"* (the people of God—David's people the Jews) but also to *"the nations" (v. 9).* Our songs will reach out to the people outside of Christ to bring them to exalt the Lord (vv. 5 and 11).

Through the Bible in a Year: II Kings 17–18

I Met God in the Morning

I met God in the morning,
When the day was at its best,
And His presence came like sunshine,
Like a glory in my breast.

All day long the presence lingered;
All day long He stayed with me;
And we sailed in perfect calmness
Over a very troubled sea.

Other ships were blown and battered,
Other ships were sore distressed,
But the winds that seem to drive them
Brought to us a peace and rest.

Then I thought of other mornings,
With a keen remorse of mind,
When I too had loosed the moorings
With His presence left behind.

So I think I know the secret
Learned from many a troubled way;
You must seek Him in the morning
If you want Him through the day.

—Selected

May 1

Read Psalms 58–59
Family Reading: Psalm 58

Faulty Judgment Begins in the Heart

Psalm 58 deals with judgment. It opens with David asking two questions about judgment. He asks if the judgments of the congregation are righteous, and he asks if the judges are judging rightly. He calls the judges *"sons of men" (v. 1)*. Though they are judges, they are men and are therefore prone to making faulty judgments. Then in verse two David states how flawed are the judgments of men. In their hearts they work wickedness and then weigh the violence that is in the earth. Justice is depicted as a blindfolded woman with scales in one hand and a sword in the other. Judges should hand out justice—but these weighed out violence. They acted as if they were dealing justly but they were engaged in violence.

This psalm is relevant for the day in which we live. One of our greatest problems in America is the faulty judgments that have been given by our court systems. We hear constantly of cases of injustice. Often our criminals make a farce of the judicial system by using technicalities to find legal loopholes. Judges often free dangerous men and thus make a mockery of justice.

David had been hunted and pursued by Saul. Later he had been driven out by Absalom. All of these attacks had spanned decades. David had been fleeing as a fugitive for a long time. He wondered: *"[Do] ye judge uprightly, O ye sons of men?" (v. 1)*.

He knew from whence false and faulty judgment came. It began in the heart of sinful man. Verse three states, *"The wicked are estranged from the womb: they go astray as soon as they be born, speaking lies."* This deceitful attitude takes place right at birth. We are born sinners, and sin has stained our judgment. David believed that unjust judges and rulers were as dangerous as snakes. *"Their poison is like the poison of a serpent: they are like the deaf adder* [cobra]*"* that cannot hear but can be charmed by the moving of the pipe (vv. 4-5). Faulty judgment is deadly. We see the serpent in Genesis 3 which released his deadly venom by bringing sin into the world. The result of that sin in the garden is that it has come into the life of every one of us. Our only remedy is trusting the Lord.

Through the Bible in a Year: II Kings 19–21

May 2

Read Psalms 58–59
Family Reading: Psalm 58

The Certainty of Judgment

Psalm 58 deals with the judgment of the wicked. Their judgment will be sure, and it will be fair because God is the Judge. Today we will consider two truths which are part of an outline given by LeMoyne Sharpe in his book, *Preaching Through the Psalms, Volume 2*. Those two truths are: The Sentence Predicted, and The Satisfaction Produced.

1. The Sentence Predicted (vv. 6-9)

    The psalmist prayed with confidence that God would break the power of the wicked. He compares them to young lions whose teeth must be broken. When the lions' teeth are gone, their power is gone. David wanted the plans of the wicked to be defeated. Note the requests he makes: *"Let them melt away . . ." (v. 7); "let . . . them pass away . . ." (v. 8); "take them away . . ." (v. 9)*. He uses five excellent illustrations in his prayer for them to become ineffective: he asks that they be as waters that evaporate, as arrows that are broken, as snails that die in a dry climate, as the natural abortion of a birth, and as a wind that takes the thorns away so they cannot be fuel for a fire. In this way David describes the total defeat of Israel's enemies.

2. The Satisfaction Produced (vv. 10-11)

    "The righteous shall rejoice . . ." (v. 10). Do they rejoice over the horrible fate of the wicked? No, I believe not. They rejoice over the fact that our God will bring order out of chaos. It will be absolute proof that *". . . whatsoever a man soweth, that shall he also reap"* *(Galatians 6:7)*. The vengeance of verse ten is God's, not man's. All wickedness must sooner or later be judged. Anyone who is righteous will rejoice at the triumph of good over evil.

    Verse eleven crowns the psalm with the truth that God is judge. He will reward the righteous, and He will judge the wicked. Please note that twice in verse eleven he states, *"Verily."* It is definitely true that He will be Judge, with the righteous receiving a reward and the unrighteous receiving the judgment upon sin.

Through the Bible in a Year: II Kings 22–24

May 3

Read Psalm 59

David's Consolation in Knowing his God

There can be no doubt concerning the time that David wrote Psalm 59. The heading states clearly that it was "when Saul sent, and they watched the house to kill him." We read of this in I Samuel 19:11: *"Saul also sent messengers unto David's house, to watch him, and to slay him . . . ."* Saul was obsessed with jealousy. David had defeated Goliath, and the Israelites began singing, *"Saul hath slain his thousands, and David his ten thousands" (I Samuel 18:7).* This displeased Saul, and he began to eye David constantly, becoming David's enemy continually (I Samuel 18:9, 29). From that time on, Saul, in his jealousy, was constantly plotting ways to kill David.

David prayed, asking God for deliverance (Psalm 59:1). In the first two verses of Psalm 59 David prayed: *"Deliver me . . . defend me . . . deliver me . . . save me . . . ."* Why did he need to pray this? Verse three states that the mighty lay in wait for him and gathered themselves together against him. David knew the reason. It was not because of his sin, transgression, or fault (vv. 3-4). It was because of Saul's jealousy.

What was David's consolation in the midst of the trials that he faced? It was that he knew God. He was a young man, but he had come to know God. We catch a very definite realization of this fact by noting the four names that he uses to speak to God.

1. *"God" (v. 1)* — Elohim — God, the Creator
2. *"LORD" (v. 3)* — Jehovah — Covenant-keeping God
3. *"LORD God" (v. 5)* — Jehovah Sabaoth — the Lord of hosts
4. *"God of Israel" (v. 5)* — Elohim of Israel — the mighty God who has also become Jehovah, keeping covenant with Israel

David knew God. He could claim victory from his all-powerful God and rest in what He would do to the enemies. Paul's prayer was, *"That I may know him . . ." (Philippians 3:10).* This needs to be our prayer. We need to come to know God and see His power and victory overcome in our lives.

Through the Bible in a Year: II Kings 25; I Chronicles 1

May 4

Read Psalms 59–60
Family Reading: Psalm 59

God Hears and Records Sin

David knew his God. We saw that truth yesterday. Because he knew God, he could identify the enemies and see them in their right perspective. These enemies were like dogs. They had been dispatched by Saul to catch and kill David. They watched him at his house (I Samuel 19:11 and the heading of Psalm 59). More than that, they were sent to *"go round about the city" (v. 6)*. David and Michal knew that he had best flee at night. At daybreak David would be easily spotted and slain (I Samuel 19:11-12). David trusted the Lord to be awake even in the night season to help him (v. 5).

David saw these enemies as barking dogs, belching *"out with their mouth . . ." (v. 7)*. He knew that *"swords are in their lips . . ." (v. 7)*. These men were jealous along with King Saul. They were in the court; but since David had risen above them, jealousy took over. Their words were like daggers, revealing their inner hatred of David. These foes poured out lies and curses. Then they asked a question in verse seven: *"[W]ho . . . doth hear?"* Their attitude was, "We can get away with it. Who will hear and recognize our sin?" How foolish! They forgot that God hears and records what is being said.

I will never forget when I attended a Moody Institute of Science demonstration at Lowry Air Force Base in Denver years ago. The room was filled with airmen as the man on the platform was explaining tape recording, something very new at that time. He told the men that someone had been moving about, recording what the airmen were saying as they had come in and waited in the auditorium for the demonstration. As he held up a reel of tape, he announced, "I have you recorded on this tape. Would you like me to play this so that all can hear?" Spontaneously, a loud "NO!" came from the airmen. Then he said, "But remember, God also has heard and recorded all that you said."

Yes, we must recognize that God hears our speech and knows our actions. Our only hope can be realized by coming to Christ and receiving His pardon, thereby erasing our record of sin and declaring us righteous in God's sight.

Through the Bible in a Year: I Chronicles 2–3

May 5

Read Psalms 59:10-17 and Psalm 60

Trust Triumphs Over Trouble

In the midst of these dreadful trials that David experienced, he wrote, *"The God of my mercy shall **prevent** me . . ." (v. 10).* The word *prevent* is an Old English word that would mean *precede* today. David said, "The God of my mercy shall *go before me."* He had confidence that the Lord would see him through these dangerous times.

Having this confidence, David prayed that the Lord would extend the judgment over a period of time. He asked that God would *"Slay them not . . ." (v. 11).* David did not request immediate judgment. Rather, he asked that God extend it out over a longer period of time (v. 11). He wanted his people to see clearly that God does bring judgment. The people might have a tendency to forget immediate judgment. These wicked would continue with their words, their cursing and lying, and thus be taken in their own pride. Their wicked words would come home to roost and bring them condemnation. David prayed that they would be consumed. Their hearts would become harder in sin. Thus judgment would become more definite and settled.

There are some people today who have difficulty understanding why David prayed these imprecatory prayers. We must realize these were not expressions of personal revenge, but they represented instead David's zeal for righteousness. He declared his belief that God must punish wickedness and iniquity. Also, they looked forward to the time when God will bring judgment upon an unbelieving world.

David's prayer revealed that even these wicked ones would recognize God's justice. They had howled like a pack of dogs after the prey (vv. 6-7). The time would come when they would act like a cur dog whining for meat. Judgment would be sure.

With all of this, David ended the psalm with praise. He said he would sing of God's power and God's mercy (v. 16). His song would be in the morning for he would see his enemies of the dark defeated. He knew that God was his strength and defense. David probably began this psalm while his house was surrounded at night. He may have written these last words as he sat in some cave, knowing he was safe in the arms of God. His trust triumphed over trouble.

Through the Bible in a Year: I Chronicles 4–5

May 6

Read Psalms 60–61
Family Reading: Psalm 60

Beware Being Overconfident in the Flesh

Psalm 60 should challenge each of us to claim continuous victory in the Lord. The heading informs us that this psalm was written when David was winning battles in Syria. The title *Aram,* given twice in the heading, means *Syria.* David had been winning battles to the north of Palestine, especially in two cities of Syria, Naharaim and Zobah. All the while he thought that the land over which he already reigned, the land of Canaan possessed by Joshua, was safe. He thought that the enemies had been subdued and the land was secure.

However, apparently, while David was in Syria to the north winning battles, Edom — a strong and vicious enemy — decided to attack in the far south. Joab had to return from Syria, taking a contingent of soldiers, and he met the Edomites in the valley of salt. There Joab won a great victory, and then David stationed troops there. (For further understanding of this, please read II Samuel 8, I Kings 11 — noting particularly verses fifteen and sixteen, and I Chronicles 18).

David was stunned by the attack in the south, the very area that he thought was secure. The enemy, however, is ever watchful to find a weak place. The attack came and David said that God had made Israel *"drink the wine of astonishment . . ." (Psalm 60:3).* He accepted this as God's discipline for him and his people. Thank God that David recognized God was doing it. Please note that he said eight times in the first four verses, *"Thou hast."* He had no doubt that God was dealing with him.

David recognized the fact that the battle with Edom came because of spiritual failure on his part. It was the law of cause and effect. The *effect* of a surprise attack in what was considered a secure area came out of the *cause* of an overconfidence in the flesh.

May we learn that there is no area of our lives so strong that Satan or the flesh will not rise up to do battle. Wise is the man who sees God's discipline in the attacks that come. David faced this problem as a discipline from the Lord. He said, *"God hath spoken in his holiness . . ." (v. 6).* Therefore, David relied on the Lord for victory.

Through the Bible in a Year: I Chronicles 6

May 7

Read Psalms 60–61

Trusting God for Victory Rather Than Man

In Psalm 60 David was facing the fact that the Edomites had attacked the southern part of his kingdom. He thought that everything was secure; therefore, he went to do battle with Syria in the north. He had become overconfident in the flesh and did not rely on the Lord. He recognized that the Lord was the One who had permitted the battle to come in the southern part of his kingdom.

In verses six through nine David reasserted the fact that the land belonged to him. He said that God had spoken in His holiness. David recognized that God had permitted the attack for his benefit. God is holy, and His acts are performed in holiness. However, David also claimed that what he had received from God he was going to maintain for God. He said, *"Gilead is mine, and Manasseh is mine; Ephraim also is the strength of mine head; Judah is my lawgiver" (v. 7).* All of these he now claimed anew for God.

When Satan comes in to attack your life, don't despise. Claim your family, your business, and your testimony for God. David said, "It is mine; Satan is not going to have it." Satan tried to use Edom, but David claimed the strong city of Petra, the fortified stronghold of Edom (v. 9). So complete would be David's victory over Edom that he said: *"over Edom I will cast out my shoe . . ." (v. 8).* Edom would become like a slave who cleans and shines the master's shoes. David was so confident that he reckoned the victory over Edom as already accomplished.

Then we find David admitting that he had acted in the flesh. In verse ten he said God had cast them off and that God had not accompanied his armies. David's prayer was, *"Give us help from trouble: for vain is the help of man" (v. 11).* This is so important. Oh, that we could all learn it. We all need God's help. God will use men, but we must look to the Lord and not to men. David trusted the Lord — not Joab's military genius. Therefore, he could say: *"Through God we shall do valiantly: for he it is that shall tread down our enemies" (v. 12).* May we today recognize how vain is the help of man and how much we need the Lord's help.

Through the Bible in a Year: I Chronicles 7–8

May 8

Read Psalms 61–62
Devotional Reading: Psalm 61

Lead Me to the Rock

Psalm 61 is one of encouragement in the midst of trials. The psalm was written when David was at Mahanaim with Barzillai and others providing the physical needs of David and his men (II Samuel 17:27-29; 19:31-32). The rebellion of Absalom had already been defeated with Absalom's death (II Samuel 18:15-17). Barzillai, the great man, was treating the king with royal style, but David was burdened deeply over the death of Absalom (II Samuel 18:33) and was longing to be back home in Jerusalem, back where he could abide in the Lord's tabernacle (Psalm 61:4).

With this burden on his heart and this longing in his soul, David prayed fervently to the Lord: *"Hear my cry, O God" (v. 1).* That word *cry* speaks of deep agony. David was fervently praying, not just "saying his prayers." He cried out in distress. He asked God, *"[A]ttend unto my prayer" (v. 1).* The word *attend* expresses the idea of action. God acts upon all prayers that He hears.

David realized that his problems had arisen because of his sin. He prayed in verse two: *"Lead me to the rock that is higher than I."* He knew he needed the Lord, for he himself had been a failure. Out of the Moody–Sankey revivals came the following hymn which expressed all that was in David's soul in Psalm 61.

> Oh, safe to the rock that is higher than I,
> My soul in its conflicts and sorrows would fly;
> So sinful, so weary, Thine, Thine would I be,
> Thou blest Rock of Ages, I'm hiding in Thee.
> —William O. Cushing

David begins the psalm pleading in prayer. He ends the psalm singing praise unto His name. An old hymn expresses it well.

> In this old troubled world, our God is near us,
> And when we bow in prayer, He'll always hear us.
> From every stormy wind, His love will hide us.
> In this old troubled world our God will guide us.

Through the Bible in a Year: I Chronicles 9–11

May 9

Read Psalms 62–63
Family Reading: Psalm 62

Trust in the Face of Trouble

In Psalm 62 David again deals with the problems, troubles, and trials that he faced. This psalm was probably written at the time of Absalom's rebellion. David faced those who were deliberately planning his demise and total defeat. They imagined mischief with plans to slay all of David's men, having him and his army destroyed as though they were a leaning wall or a fence with rotten posts about to fall over (v. 3). They consulted to cast David down from his throne (v. 4). That means men joined together in making plans for his defeat. In doing so, they delighted in lies (v. 4). They not only lied but also delighted in their deceit. With hypocrisy they spoke blessing with their lips while they cursed inwardly (v. 4). Absalom led them in all of this. He was a crafty leader who becomes a type of the Antichrist, the one who will come *". . . with all deceivableness of unrighteousness . . ."* and who will *". . . send them strong delusion, that they should believe a lie" (II Thessalonians 2:10-11).* Remember that the devil *". . . is a liar, and the father of it" (John 8:44).*

Facing such wicked and crafty enemies, David expressed his trust in the Lord. In verse one of Psalm 62 he wrote: *"Truly my soul waiteth upon God: from him cometh my salvation."* The word translated *truly* in verse one is also translated *only* in verses two, four, five, and six, and is translated *surely* in verse nine. The idea in all of these verses is that David was trusting God alone. It was on Him alone that David waited (vv. 1, 4), and He alone was David's rock and salvation. David said that God was the exclusive object of his trust.

Many trust in God but do not trust in Him alone. There is blessing awaiting the individual who trusts God and Him only. We must not interject actions of the flesh to help God out. He is the only One whom we must trust. The person who stands with one foot on a slippery rock and the other foot upon quicksand will sink and perish as surely as the person who stands with both feet in the quicksand. Someone has said, "I may tremble on the Rock, but the Rock never trembles under me." This is exactly what David meant when he said, *"The rock of my strength, and my refuge, is in God" (v. 7).*

Through the Bible in a Year: I Chronicles 12–14

May 10

Read Psalms 62–63
Family Reading: Psalm 62

Trust the Lord at All Times

As we saw yesterday, Psalm 62 expresses David's trust in the Lord. Verses five and six repeat almost exactly what the psalmist wrote in verses one and two. There are two notable differences between these verses. In verse five David expected God's salvation while in verse one he only knew it could come from God. In verse two the psalmist said he would *"not be greatly moved."* However, in verse six he stated confidently that he would *"not be moved"* at all. The world's expectations may rarely come to pass; they may promise, but there is no performance. David's faith, however, had grown until in verses five and six he was confident God would work. "The more faith is acted upon, the more active it becomes" (LeMoyne Sharpe). We are to exercise ourselves unto godliness, and spiritual exercise develops spiritual muscles (I Timothy 4:7).

Note how personal was David's relationship to the Lord. He claimed the Lord as *"my salvation" (vv. 1, 2, 6, 7); "my rock" (vv. 2, 3, 7); "my defense" (vv. 2, 6); "my expectation" (v. 5); "my glory," "my strength,"* and *"my refuge" (v. 7).* Because of this personal relationship which resulted in David's deep, abiding trust in the Lord, he could give advice to his people: *"Trust in him at all times; ye people, pour out your heart before him . . ." (v. 8).*

When should we trust the Lord? *"At all times,"* regardless of circumstances (v. 8).

Why should we trust the Lord? *"God is a refuge for us" (v. 8).*

David contrasts the value of trusting the Lord with trusting men. In verse nine he states that if we put *man-trust* on a scale, it will weigh lighter than vanity—absolutely no weight at all. He recommended that men trust not in might (oppression), nor in money because even if riches increased, he pleaded, *"set not your heart upon them" (v. 10).* God had spoken twice (vv. 1 and 2 and again in vv. 5 and 6). His message was, *"power belongeth unto God" (v. 11).* Therefore, let us learn to trust in Him alone.

Through the Bible in a Year: I Chronicles 15–16

May 11

Read Psalms 63–64
Family Reading: Psalm 63

Seek Only God — and Seek Him Early

The superscription identifies Psalm 63 as having been written by David when he was in the wilderness of Judah. Very likely this psalm was penned at the time when David had to flee Jerusalem because of Absalom's rebellion. It could well have been written at the very time he and his men were fleeing from Jerusalem. That would mean that he found Zadok and the Levites carrying the ark of the covenant. David commanded Zadok to take the ark back to Jerusalem (II Samuel 15:24-29).

The psalm opens with the words: *"O God, thou art my God; early will I seek thee: my soul thirsteth for thee, my flesh longeth for thee in a dry and thirsty land, where no water is" (v. 1).* David was saying, "I need the Lord." Zadok and Abiathar brought the ark of the covenant. Very likely they cried: "King David, we have the ark. All is well." However, David asked them to return the ark. That ark was a token of the presence of God and His glory among His people. The ark itself was not God, rather it was just a sacred object, an emblem of God's presence when it was in its proper place. David said, "I need God!" No emblem could replace the Lord, no matter how holy its associations.

David said he would seek the Lord *early* (v. 1). Very likely he was saying, "Early in this part of my wanderings in the wilderness, I will seek the Lord." David knew that *early in a problem* was the time to turn it over to the Lord. Someone has said, "The wise man does at first what the fool does at last." We must never try to carry what only God can handle. I like the words of the song, "Take your burden to the Lord and leave it there!"

We can also say we need to seek the Lord *early in life.* Over ninety percent of conversions to Christ take place before a person is twenty-five years old. Or we can say we must seek the Lord *early in the day.* Please read again the poem *"I Met God in the Morning"* (at the beginning of the month of May in this book). How important it is to have a daily time of devotions reading the Bible and praying each day.

Through the Bible in a Year: I Chronicles 17–20

May 12

Read Psalms 63–64
Family Reading: Psalm 63

Satisfied With the Lord's Presence

What a beautiful portion of Scripture is Psalm 63! David revealed his longing and his delight. He was in the wilderness of Judah, certainly a very dry and thirsty land. He knew that the answer for him personally and for his kingdom, the nation of Israel, was to turn all matters over to God. He longed to see God's power and His glory, just as he had seen God in the sanctuary (v. 2). He recognized God's lovingkindness to be better than life; therefore, he praised God. He said that he would constantly and continuously bless the Lord.

We see the contrast between verses one and five. In verse one David states that he thirsts for God and that his soul longs to see God. However, in verse five David announced that his soul would be satisfied as with marrow and fatness. Strange words? To the world they seem strange. Here is a king, fleeing for his life; and yet he says he is satisfied and that he would praise God with joyful lips. Why was he satisfied? The answer is simple—he trusted the Lord, and every need of his soul was met.

He was resting in the Lord and would even find comfort and strength meditating on God through the night. His soul was resting in the Lord entirely, waiting on God for His blessing (v. 6). David, fleeing in the wilderness, could say, *"In the shadow of thy wings will I rejoice"* *(v. 7)*. He sought the Lord, and the Lord was all he needed. David had fled, leaving behind everything that he possessed. Now in the wilderness he was a beggar, depending on the generosity of others to supply his needs. Yet he was praising and singing because he trusted the Lord.

A wealthy business man had been generous to the Lord's work and to the Lord's people while his business prospered. In the great depression he lost everything and was poverty stricken. Someone asked him, "Don't you wish you had some of that money you gave away?" "Oh, no!" he answered. "That's all I really have now." His treasure had been laid up in Heaven. May we also be satisfied with all that the Lord is to us.

Through the Bible in a Year: I Chronicles 21–23

May 13

Read Psalms 64–65
Family Reading: Psalm 64

The Death Dealing Tongue

Psalm 64 presents the deadly danger of a bitter tongue. David was facing the enemy who spoke against David by shooting deadly arrows with his tongue. It could have been at the time when Doeg betrayed David to Saul (I Samuel 22:9-10), or it could have been when Ahithophel desired to shame and kill David (II Samuel 16:20–17:3). Whenever the problem existed, David recognized that the men were using their tongues as sharp swords and their words as bitterly poisoned arrows (v. 3). They actually sharpened their tongues so that they could cut David to shreds.

I can remember turning the grindstone for my father so that he could sharpen his sickles and scythes for cutting hay or weeds. The big grindstone wheel would turn through a trough of water at the bottom to cool it and would bring an edge that would cut readily. These wicked men sharpened their tongues just as we sharpened blades on the farm. With their sharpened tongues they cut mercilessly away at the character of David.

David knew that his best defense was prayer. Therefore he cried unto God with his voice. He pled that God would preserve his life (v. 1). He knew that these poisoned tongues were busy spreading their venom. They were literally executing insurrection from the hearts of the workers of iniquity (v. 2). They may take the innocent victim by surprise, for *"suddenly do they shoot at him, and fear not" (v. 4).*

The wicked band together in their hatred of the righteous. David said they would *"encourage themselves in an evil manner . . ." (v. 5).* Isn't it amazing that the wicked will encourage each other in their wickedness—but so often the righteous discourage each other in their desire to live righteously. David stated that the wicked laid snares to entrap him (v. 5). Then he said they asked, *"Who shall see them?"* That is their big mistake. Thinking that no one sees them, they go on in their sin, but they forget that God sees them and knows their every thought and word. Tomorrow we will note that the wicked will have their own wickedness turn on them.

Through the Bible in a Year: I Chronicles 24–26

May 14

Read Psalms 64–65
Family Reading: Psalm 64

Vengeance is Mine, Saith the Lord

Yesterday we noted in the first five verses of Psalm 64 that the wicked turn their poisonous tongues on the righteous. They plan together to destroy the righteous, encouraging each other in their iniquity.

Beginning at verse seven David shows that God does deal with the wicked. These workers of iniquity bend their bows and shoot their arrows at the righteous (v. 3). Verse seven reveals God's poetic justice: *"But God shall shoot at them with an arrow."* Note also that just as they *"suddenly"* shoot at the righteous (v. 4), so shall they be *"suddenly"* wounded (v. 7). When men use wicked words and lying tongues, they find that their tongues will fall on themselves (v. 8). Retribution will often be in kind. They shot at the righteous secretly; God will shoot at them openly. A greater Archer than they will take sure aim, for the Archer never fails to hit His target.

As I write this the big news in America is that citizens by the millions have been frightened by AIDS. What is AIDS? It is God's sure arrow hitting those who refused to obey God and his restrictions. God's arrow has hit swiftly and surely. No one is going to get away with sin. God's Word still reads: *"Vengeance is mine; I will repay, saith the Lord" (Romans 12:19).* In the Old Testament God said, *"Be sure your sin will find you out" (Numbers 32:23).* Those who have been fearless in sin will become fearful in judgment.

What was David's final answer to the attacks of the wicked? Verse ten states that the *"righteous shall be glad in the Lord, and shall trust in Him; and all the upright in heart shall glory."* David was saying, "The wicked will not win the final battle." Judgment is coming. Their words will return to them and they will be called to account for every word (Matthew 12:36). The righteous must not use poisonous words to answer poisonous words. Rather they must quietly trust in Him regardless of the problem. May the Lord give each of us grace to know that we must glorify the Lord in spite of any attacks from wicked individuals.

Through the Bible in a Year: I Chronicles 27–29

May 15

Read Psalms 65–66
Family Reading: Psalm 65

The Deliverance of the Blessed Man

Psalm 65 is a psalm of praise and thanksgiving. It begins with, *"Praise waiteth for thee, O God, in Sion" (v. 1),* and it ends with the truth that the pastures and the valleys shouting for joy and singing (v. 13). It was very likely written for the feast of first fruits in a year that promised a blessed harvest.

The psalm reveals how approachable is our God. The first words are *"Praise waiteth for thee, O God . . . ."* The word *"waiteth"* is from a Hebrew word which means "dumb" (silent). The idea is that praise may be given to God even when only our hearts but not our voices speak. Worship of the Lord can come from a silent adoring heart as well as from a singing, praising voice. Sometimes we get the idea that worship can only be accomplished with our singing or audible praise or clapping of the hands. However, there are times when words seem inadequate to express our gratitude and praise to God.

The last of verse one also stated David's promise, *"[U]nto thee shall the vow be performed."* The heart that praises the Lord will be careful to perform any vows that have been made. Because of His grace, the believer can know the blessed fact of verse two—that God hears prayer. That fact makes real the privilege of all flesh coming to God. On what do we bare the blessing of praise and prayer? The answer is given in verse three where we find pardon for all our transgressions—*"[T]hou shalt purge them away."*

Then in verse four David speaks again of the blessed man. This man is chosen by God and has the privilege of approaching God. The privilege enjoyed only by the High Priest of the Old Testament is now a reality in the life of every believer in this New Testament age. We believers all have equal access to God. Those who praise in verse one, have their prayers answered in verse two, claim their sins pardoned in verse three, and then have their souls satisfied with the goodness of God's house in verse four. David praised the Lord for gracious deliverance, for generous provision, and for glorious peace. May we realize and rest in these same blessed truths.

Through the Bible in a Year: II Chronicles 1–4

May 16

Read Psalms 65–66
Family Reading: Psalm 65

Praising our God of Great Power

Yesterday we noted the truth that the man who praises God, Who has power to pardon transgressions, is the man who is satisfied with the goodness of God's eternal temple. Beginning at Psalm 65:5 the psalmist reveals why a believer can approach God (v. 4) with praise and prayer. We can know that our God has power.

1. He has power to *convert* (v. 5). He may use *"terrible things in righteousness"* to turn us around, but being the *"God of our salvation"* He will turn us around. Many are the testimonies of those who were turned around because of terrible things in righteousness.

2. He has power to *create* (v. 6). He, Who set the mountains firmly in place, is the God with power that can meet every need.

3. He has power to *control* (vv. 7-8). He controls the seas and their restless waves. He controls people and quiets their tumultuous lives. In verse eight the word *"tokens"* is composed of two Hebrew words which are the first and last letters of the Hebrew alphabet. Just as our Lord is the Alpha and Omega (Revelation 1:8) of the Greek alphabet, He is also the beginning and the end in the Hebrew. This One makes the *"outgoings of the morning and evening to rejoice"* *(v. 8).* He is speaking of the East (the outgoings of the morning) and the West (the outgoings of the evening). The sun rises and sets at His command.

4. He has power to *crown (vv. 9-13). "Thou crownest the year with thy goodness" (v. 11).* In these verses the psalmist is speaking of the blessing of harvest. God crowns the year with good things. He provides the moisture to water the crops abundantly; the pastures are also made green so that the flocks have every need met. All of this brings the voice of praise and singing up from the land (v. 13). God's people have great reason to praise and pray and realize His power in every situation.

Through the Bible in a Year: II Chronicles 5–7

May 17

Read Psalm 66

A Coming Golden Age

Years ago I remember hearing of a certain ministry called, "The Miracle Book Club." I never had the privilege to observe this club and its ministry—I knew only its title. Undoubtedly the "Miracle Book" was the Bible and the club's purpose was to bring people not only to know the Bible as the Written Word of God but also to know the Living Word Himself, the Lord Jesus Christ.

As we look at Psalm 66 we realize the Bible surely is the "Miracle Book." Here is a psalm written centuries before Christ was born—yet it speaks of an age to come when *"All the earth shall worship"* the Lord and *"shall sing"* unto Him (v. 4). Several commentators believe this psalm was written by Hezekiah following his overthrow of Sennacherib's army. That could well be, but the psalm is speaking of more than that. It, along with Psalms 65, 67, and 68, is looking forward, prophesying a future golden age.

There will be a day when all the lands will make a joyful noise unto God (v. 1). God's enemies will submit themselves unto Him (v. 3). Paul spoke of this in the book of Philippians when he wrote of the Lord Jesus: *"Wherefore God also hath highly exalted him, and given him a name which is above every name: that at the name of Jesus every knee should bow, of things in heaven, and things in earth, and things under the earth; and that every tongue should confess that Jesus Christ is Lord, to the glory of God the Father" (Philippians 2:9-11).*

I am writing this at the end of November, 1991. Next week President Bush has called for talk between the Arab nations and Israel. As I write this, Israel is saying she will not honor the date the United States of America has set. Our President, along with whole world, is wanting peace in the Middle East. One thing a Bible believer can tell them is that some day there will be peace. All lands (v. 1) and all the earth (v. 4) will worship the Lord together. We must realize this peace will come, but it will come only through the Prince of Peace, the Lord Jesus Christ, when He establishes His millennium of peace.

Through the Bible in a Year: II Chronicles 8–12

May 18

Read Psalm 66

Deliverance With Divine Discipline

In Psalm 66:5-12, we see *God's power, protection, and providence.*

The Lord had led Israel manifesting **His power**. In verse six we realize that *"He turned the sea into dry land: they* [Israel] *went through the flood on foot . . . ." (See* Exodus 14 and Joshua 3). The psalmist then states that at the crossings on dry ground Israel rejoiced in Him. But His power is not manifested only to Israel—it is also manifested to all the nations. *"[H]is eyes behold the nations: Let not the rebellious exalt themselves" (v. 7).* That word "behold" means "to inspect with a piercing stare." God sees the actions, the motives behind the actions, and the attitudes involved. Therefore the rebellious are fools to try to exalt themselves.

In verses eight and nine, the psalmist says that Israel should praise the Lord for **His protection**. He has taken care of His people, Israel. He kept their soul and suffered not their feet to be moved (v. 9). Israel is God's great object lesson to the whole world. Frederick the Great demanded that Count Zinzendorf defend the inerrancy and accuracy of the Bible in one word. The Count immediately replied, "Jew!" A nation scheduled by many for extermination continues to exist—and will exist to the end of the age.

Then in verses ten through twelve we read of **God's providence**. The psalmist states that it was God Who put them to the test: *"Thou . . . hast proved us . . . thou hast tried us" (v. 10); "Thou broughtest us . . . thou laidst affliction upon our loins" (v. 11); "Thou hast caused men to ride over our heads . . . but thou broughtest us . . ." (v. 12).* God used affliction to purify His people. Egypt was as much in God's plan as Canaan. The way to Heaven does lead through trials and tests. But what is the end?—*"Thou broughtest us out into a wealthy place" (v. 12).* Below I quote LaMoyne Sharpe in *Preaching Through the Psalms.*

> The distress might be grievous, but the Deliverer is Great, and the deliverance will be glorious. God has not promised us smooth sailing, but He has promised us a safe landing.

Through the Bible in a Year: II Chronicles 13–17

May 19

Read Psalms 66–67
Family Reading: Psalm 66:5-20

A Wonderful Personal Testimony

Beginning at verse thirteen there is a distinct change in Psalm 66. Through the first verses the psalmist invites all to turn to the Lord, and then he recounts God's blessings on Israel. In verses thirteen through twenty, the psalmist gives a personal testimony of what God has done for him.

First, the writer states he will go into the house of the Lord and offer burnt offerings. Without question he was a leader in Israel and he desired to lead his people to Calvary. Also in verse thirteen he wrote that he would pay his vows. He had undergone the trials of verses ten and eleven. He must have made God some promises during that proving time. He was like so many of us who promise God that we will do certain things if He will deliver us through the test. But he was unlike so very many who forget their vows when they are on the victory side. How many times I have known believers to make vows to God; and then, after being delivered by God, they seem to forget those vows! The psalmist states that he promised the vows when he was in trouble (v. 14). Now, he says he will fulfill those vows by offering rams, bullocks, and goats to the Lord (v. 15). He thought that repaying his vows was so important that he wrote *"Selah"* (v. 15)—think on this and repeat it, I will pay my vows!

Second, he states that he is anxious to give his testimony of what God had done for his soul (v. 16). If Hezekiah wrote this psalm he could tell of the healing of his body and the deliverance of the nations. But to the psalmist, the important truth was what God had done for his soul—what God had done for him spiritually.

Third, he declares that God does answer prayer (v. 20). He warned us all that a big hindrance to prayer is to regard iniquity in our hearts (v. 18). What does it mean to *"regard iniquity"*? It involves the idea of practicing sin secretly, or lusting to commit sin, or of delighting in sins of the past. It means that we lack a hatred of sin. The psalmist did not allow this in his life, for he blessed God Who answered his prayer (v. 20). May this testimony be ours also.

Through the Bible in a Year: II Chronicles 18–20

May 20

Read Psalms 67 and 68:1-18
Family Reading: Psalm 67

Singing Before the Judge

Psalm 67 fits well with Psalm 66, which we observed to be a psalm about the Millennium. This, too, is a millennial psalm speaking of Israel's great missionary endeavor during the Millennium.

The psalm opens with the blessing that God gave Aaron and his sons to use in their pronouncing blessing upon the children of Israel (Numbers 6:23-26). This is a blessing strictly for Israel (Numbers 6:27). Therefore, this psalm deals with the missionary endeavor that will be carried on by Israel during the Millennium.

I believe we can take this psalm and apply it to our ministry today. We should consider missions to be the primary emphasis of the local church. Every church should have missions at the very center and fore-front of its ministry. The Bible teaches we are born to reproduce. The Bible actually is a great missionary textbook. Someone has well said, "Every person is either a missionary or a mission field."

What is the goal of missions?

v. 2—*"That thy way may be known upon earth, thy saving health among all nations."*

vv. 3-5—That *"all the peoples"* may praise the Lord.

God is the Judge of the whole earth. This psalm states that people will stand and sing before the Judge. How can this be—singing before the Judge? The answer is simple. In this case Christ is not only the Judge but also the advocate—the attorney pleading their case. The believer is one who has accepted Christ and will not stand before the Judge at the Great White Throne. With Christ now as his attorney, his salvation is secure. His judgment will not determine his eternity but rather his reward for the Christian life he has lived. And he can daily come to God and be forgiven if he will apply I John 1:9. Saved—daily forgiven—no wonder he can sing before the judge.

Through the Bible in a Year: II Chronicles 21–23

May 21

Read Psalm 68
Family Reading: Psalm 68:1-18

God Victorious Over His Enemies

Psalm 68 had been called "one of the masterpieces of the world's lyrics." Moulton says, "It is difficult to read this mighty marching song without the feet longing to tramp and the hands to wave." The first verse signals that it is a marching song. The verse is a quote of Numbers 10:35, which was Moses' prayer when the Ark set forward to lead the camp of Israel.

Verses one through six present God's Victorious March. The psalmist prays Moses' prayer: *"Let God arise, let his enemies be scattered" (v. 1)*. When the Israelites marched with the ark before them, the enemies were stricken with terror. Please note that these enemies are *"His enemies"*—the enemies of God. When the Lord leads His people into battle, their enemies flee because they realize they are powerless before Him. *"Resist the devil, and he will flee from you" (James 4:7)*. *"Now thanks be unto God, which always causeth us to triumph in Christ" (II Corinthians 2:14)*.

Verse two reveals how completely these enemies will be defeated. They will be driven away as smoke before the wind. They will perish at the presence of God; just as wax melts before the fire, so the enemies will melt away, unable to stand before the Lord.

While the wicked enemies are facing defeat, the righteous will have the privilege of stability, rejoicing in God's presence and singing praises unto His Name (vv. 3-4). We believers can be certain we are going to face foes that are out to defeat us. Our victory is in trusting the Lord and relying on His leading and power. Conflict is an essential condition of a spiritual life. The enemies are strong and persistent. They include Satan and his hordes, the world and its attractions, and the flesh and its corruption. But God is able to give us victory. He manifests His grace to the fatherless, the widows, the solitary, and those bound with chains (vv. 5-6). He brings them victory in a place of rejoicing. With that victory, he also assures that the rebellious will continue to dwell in a dry land (v. 6).

Through the Bible in a Year: II Chronicles 24–26

May 22

Read Psalm 68
Family Reading: Psalm 68:1-23

God's Leading Israel in Victory

Beginning at verse seven, the Lord reveals the history of Israel, proving how great a God our Lord is. Victory comes to the people of God because of His Divine Presence. *"O God, when thou wentest forth before thy people . . ." (v. 7).* His Divine Presence brought with it His Divine Power. *"When thou didst march through the wilderness . . . The earth shook, the heavens also dropped . . . even Sinai itself was moved at the presence of God . . ." (vv. 7-8).* Following verse seven we find the significant word, *"Selah"*—"Think of that!" Amen! It is well worth stopping to think. The world had never seen the likes before. A nation was marching out of the wilderness led by the cloud pillar during the day and the fire pillar at night. That was God's Shekinah Glory—His Divine Presence.

We also see God's Divine Providence—*"Thou, O God, didst send a plentiful rain . . ." (v. 9).* God provided the moisture and confirmed His promises to a weary people.

This passage summarizes the story of Israel from the Exodus to the entry into Canaan, omitting the sins of Israel (vv. 7-14). Verses seven through ten cover the period of Exodus and Numbers—the period when Israel was in the wilderness. The nation of Israel, *"Thy congregation"* and *"the poor" (v. 10),* dwelt in the wilderness and witnessed God's power and provision. Then in verses eleven through fourteen, David reviews quickly the time when the Israelites moved into Canaan. They saw victory after victory with kings and armies fleeing (v. 12). They had lived among *"the pots,"* the brick kiln of Egypt, but now they would abide under the wing of a dove (v. 13). The dove here speaks of the Holy Spirit ministering and meeting their needs.

Today we can sing:

> Guide me, O Thou great Jehovah,
> Pilgrim through this barren land;
> I am weak but thou are mighty,
> Hold me with Thy powerful hand.
> —William Williams

Through the Bible in a Year: II Chronicles 27–29

May 23

Read Psalm 68
Family Reading: Psalm 68:7-26; Devotional Reading: Psalm 68:15-20

The Conqueror Coming to Zion's Hill

Today we come to the high point of Psalm 68, verses seventeen and eighteen.

In the previous two devotionals on Psalm 68, we have seen God's presence, providence, and power leading His people. Now we see that the battle is won and the Conqueror enters the sanctuary on the hill of God to dwell there (vv. 17-18). David saw beyond all the battles Israel faced and viewed the day when Christ will rule. In verses fifteen and sixteen he reveals the importance of Mt. Moriah, God's hill in Jerusalem, a part of Mt. Zion. The hills of Jerusalem are very low hills. They cannot begin to compare in size or height with the hill of Bashan (v. 15). Bashan was at the northern extremity of Palestine—it included towering Mt. Hermon. As great and tall as the hills of the north were, when they see how exalted God makes the little hill of Jerusalem they are going to leap up and down with envy of the seeming insignificant hill God has chosen to be His dwelling place. Think of it—just as God exalted the humble hill of Zion above the mighty mountains of the earth, so now God has exalted His Church to outshine the kingdoms of the world. "It is much more honorable to be Holy to God than to be High in the world"—LaMoyne Sharpe.

In verse seventeen we find the Conqueror, the Lord, entering Zion with a multitude. David, the poet, draws a line from Sinai to the Sanctuary. Verse eighteen has been used by Paul to speak of the fact of Our Lord's ascension, His entering the Sanctuary in Heaven, taking with Him the souls of all the believing dead of past ages (Ephesians 4:8). In verse eighteen the psalmist states that the Lord gives gifts to the Church, and He also transforms the rebels of earth who will receive Him. He is the Conqueror and will have believing rebels changed so he can dwell among them (v. 18). David then cries out, *"Blessed be the Lord, who daily loadeth us with benefits" (v. 19).* AMEN!

Through the Bible in a Year: II Chronicles 30–32

May 24

Read Psalm 68:15-35
Devotional Reading: Psalm 68:20-28

The Future Deliverance of Israel

In Psalm 68:20, the Hebrew word translated *"salvation"* is actually plural. Verse twenty should actually read: *"He that is our God is the God of salvations . . . ."* God has saved the Jewish people repeatedly over the years of their history. And the Lord will continue to deliver—the salvations are not over yet. The Jews still must face the great tribulation, by far the worst tribulation of all.

In the next verses, the psalmist writes of future deliverances. Verse twenty-one states that God shall wound the head of His enemies. Then He mentions *"one"* who goes *"on still in his trespasses."* He could well have been looking forward to the time of the beast who will gather nations together against Israel.

In verse twenty-two the Lord said, *"I will bring again from Bashan, I will bring my people again from the depths of the sea."* The sea is recognized as a Bible type of the Gentile nations. The psalmist here prophecies that the people of Israel will be regathered, a prophecy we see being fulfilled today. The psalmist continues on in verse twenty-three to state that Israel will be revenged: *"That thy foot may be dipped in the blood of thine enemies, and the tongue of thy dogs in the same."* To a Jew the most horrible indignity would be to die in blood and lie unburied on the battlefield and then to have wild scavengers feed on the blood and the body. The psalmist is saying that no nation that persecutes the Jews will go unpunished. Hitler learned that. And as I write this in 1991 we see the break up of the Soviet Union, a superpower that persecuted the Jews.

At verse twenty-four we begin to see the truths of the coming millennium of peace unfold. It will be a time when God rules as king. This is speaking of the reign of Jesus Christ (Revelation 11:15). It will be a time of rejoicing (v. 25). The Lord will be continuously praised (v. 26). The nation of Israel will be joined—he names four tribes, two in the south and two in the north, declaring that the whole nation Israel will be the center and the world will rejoice in peace.

Through the Bible in a Year: II Chronicles 33–35

May 25

Read Psalm 68:15-35
Devotional Reading: Psalm 68:29-35

Jesus Christ Shall Reign

In these last verses of Psalm 68 we find prophecy concerning the coming reign of Christ. It will be a time when wars will cease: *"Scatter thou the people that delight in war" (v. 30).*

The Lord will reveal His strength through the nation of Israel. All of Israel, south and north, will be brought together (v. 27) and God will give them His strength (v. 28). Why will wars cease and God's strength be revealed? These blessings will come because all men recognize the temple at Jerusalem (v. 29). Nations from around the world will bring their presents in homage to the King, the Lord Jesus Christ. There will be no false religions to lead men astray. The whole world will recognize God's king, our Lord Jesus Christ, in Jerusalem.

There can be no genuine brotherhood of man until men recognize and accept the fatherhood of God. When all recognize that Jesus Christ is indeed the king, then we will see accomplished the end of war: *"Rebuke the company of spearmen, the multitude of the bulls, with the calves of the people, till every one submit himself with pieces of silver . . ." (v. 30).*

Not only will nations submit to His kingship but they will also be converted. Princes will come from Egypt; Ethiopia will stretch out her hands unto God (v. 31). The kingdoms of the earth will sing praises unto the Lord (v. 32). What a choir that will be! I enjoy hearing Russian believers harmonize in praises unto God. They will be there. The Japanese, the Indians, the tribes people, the English, the Germanic people, the Scandinavians, the Americans—the whole world singing praises unto God.

The Lord will show Himself ruler. His voice will be as one from Heaven (v. 33). His strength will be seen in the clouds (v. 34). Oh, what a day of rejoicing. Battles over—all worshiping our king, the Lord Jesus Christ. He gives the strength and the power to His people (v. 35). We look forward with joy and anticipation to the fulfillment of Psalm 68.

Through the Bible in a Year: II Chronicles 36; Ezra 1–2

May 26

Read Psalm 69
Family Reading: Psalm 69:1-21; Devotional Reading: Psalm 69:1-7

Christ's Suffering For Us

Psalm 69 is the second most quoted psalm in the New Testament, Psalm 22 being the one quoted the most. Psalm 69 joins with Psalm 22 in presenting the truths of the sufferings of Christ. Although this psalm is ascribed to David, we cannot find any situation in David's life which corresponds with the sufferings presented in this psalm. Psalm 69 is a prophetic psalm. It speaks of the sufferings of Christ (vv. 1-21); then it presents the wrath that will come upon an unbelieving world culminating in the dreadful battle of Armageddon (vv. 22-28); and finally, it reveals Christ ruling during the millennium over a world of peace (vv. 29-36).

Verse nine is quoted in John 2:17 and in Romans 15:3 as referring to Christ. Verse twenty-one is definitely speaking of the sufferings of Christ at Calvary (Matthew 27:34, 48). Acts 1:20 quotes verse twenty-five as referring to the betrayal of Judas at the time of the crucifixion. This psalm is definitely a prophecy of Christ in His sufferings.

The psalm begins with the words, *"Save me, O God . . . ."* This is the same One of Whom we read in the previous psalm that He is our salvation (Psalm 68:19-20). Yet here He must pray, *"Save me, O God."* This pictures the terrible price paid for our salvation. The sufferer sank *"in deep mire"* and was standing in *"deep waters, where the floods"* overflowed him (v. 2). As our sins were placed on Him at Calvary, these sins became as mine. He was not in His element—sin was totally foreign to Him. He was bearing our sin (I Peter 2:24). He was not only dying *for us*—He as dying *as us.* He suffered the awful reproach of that wicked crowd gathered around the cross. His tears fell in Gethsemane (v. 3); men manifested their hate against Him—a hatred that had no reason to cause it (v. 4). He said, *"I restored that which I took not away."* He was restoring man's sinless state (lost in Genesis 3) by being made sin Himself. David speaks of himself in verse five. We are the foolish ones whose sin is not hid. But, we can thank God, He bore our reproach and our shame (v. 7). Let's read this psalm as though we are on the most holy ground.

Through the Bible in a Year: Ezra 3–6

May 27

Read Psalm 69
Family Reading: Psalm 69:7-28; Devotional Reading: Psalm 69:7-14

The Awful Suffering of Calvary's Cross

Psalm 69 is a prophecy of the sufferings of Christ. Today we will note various ways in which He suffered at Calvary.

1. He was *reproached* (v. 7).

   "Because for thy sake, I have borne reproach: shame hath covered my face." As He hung there on the cross, His body was naked for the crowd to see. Crucifixion was designed by wicked minds who wanted to bring shame to those who died this ignominious death.

   The reproach that came upon the Lord was literally your reproach and mine. The psalmist reveals that the reproaches of all of us who reproached God fell on the Lord Jesus Christ (v. 9).

2. He was *rejected* (v. 8).

   Even His own human relatives rejected Him. It is interesting to note the accuracy of the Bible in verse eight. His brothers were the children of His mother—but not His Father. Here again we see the truth of the virgin birth of Christ.

3. He was *reviled* (vv.11-12).

   Verse eleven states that He became a proverb to others. They mocked Him and cried out, *"He saved others; himself he cannot save" (Matthew 27:42).* Those that sat in the gate (the men in leadership) spoke against Him (v. 12). They mocked and derided Him.

4. He was *ridiculed* (v. 12).

   Verse twelve states He was the song of drunkards. They dragged His Name into their vile, worldly speech. They mocked Him in their taverns! What an awful thought. He Who has been the theme of Seraph's songs, Who was welcomed on earth by a heavenly choir, was the song of drunkards laughing and slopping their drink in their beards. And all the while they are mocking—He loved them—He Gave Himself for them. What suffering and shame our glorious Lord endured!

Through the Bible in a Year: Ezra 7–9

May 28

Read Psalm 69
Family Reading: Psalm 69:13-36; Devotional Reading: Psalm 69:13-21

The Reproach of the Crowd

Psalm 69 presents the sufferings of Christ for the sins of mankind. Yesterday we saw how He was reproached, rejected, reviled and ridiculed. At verse thirteen we find a change—His prayer to God, His Father. He said that His prayer came *"in an acceptable time" (v. 13).* No time for prayer is more acceptable to our Father than when we are undergoing suffering. The psalmist speaks of the trouble he faces as mire (v. 14), as a flood of deep water (vv. 14-15), and as a pit (v. 15). His prayer is that he not sink in the mire, the hatred of those about him (v. 14). Since this psalm so distinctly pictures Jesus Christ on the Cross, the prayer of verses thirteen through sixteen could well be the basis of His prayer in Gethsemane.

In this prayer He reveals His confidence in the mercy and lovingkindness of God. Verse sixteen defines God's mercy and kindness. The Lord here magnifies the mercy of God. He offers not just kindness but loving kindness; not just mercy, but tender mercy; not just tender mercy, but tender mercies (v. 16). He speaks in the superlative when He talks of God's mercy and grace. Goodness and mercy had followed Him all the days of His life, and He was certain the Father would not abandon Him now. Therefore, He could pray with confidence: *"And hide not thy face from thy servant; for I am in trouble: hear me speedily" (v. 17).*

In His prayer He saw the scorn of His enemies. They brought reproach, shame, and dishonor upon Him. This scorn had broken His heart and brought sorrow to His soul. *"Reproach hath broken my heart; and I am full of heaviness" (v. 20).* He found none to take pity and no comforters (v. 20). This awful hatred and scorn is revealed in verse twenty-one where we read, *"They gave me also gall for my meat; and in my thirst they gave me vinegar to drink."* What a dreadful crowning act of heartlessness. Jesus had been hanging on the cross for hours. Matthew states this offer was made just after Jesus had cried, *"My God, My God, why hast thou forsaken me?"* John places the offer immediately following Jesus' cry, *"I thirst."* Instead of manifesting mercy, that crowd further manifested its scorn. Oh, do you see our Saviour's suffering for us? Thank God now for what Jesus underwent for you and me.

Through the Bible in a Year: Ezra 10; Nehemiah 1–2

May 29

Read Psalms 69–70
Family Reading: Psalm 69:18-36; Devotional Reading: Psalm 69:22-28

The Day of Wrath to Come

Psalm 69:22-28 is a dreadful portion of Scripture. It presents the curse that will come upon men because of man's rejection of Christ at Calvary and the centuries following. The Cross was both the high point in man's guilt before God and the high point of God's grace. Man could never do anything worse than crucify God's only begotten Son. God could do no more to reveal His compassion and forgiving love than to take the cross, the product of the hatred of vile men and transform it into God's means of salvation.

Psalm 69 had been presenting the cross. Verses twenty-two through twenty-eight reveal the ultimate end of those who continue on in their sin of rebellion against God. These verses take us to the future when God's wrath will be poured out in the valley of Megiddo. During this present age of grace, God had been holding His wrath in abeyance. But the day will come when He will restrain His wrath no longer. These verses reveal God's wrath poured out on rebellious men. The cross, as presented in the first twenty-one verses, presents God's wrath poured out on sin. Then in these next seven verses, God reveals His wrath poured out on those who have continued in rejection of Christ.

First, the homes will be judged. The *"table"* (v. 22) speaks of the home, and their habitation will be desolate (v. 25). The breakdown of the home now is a preparation for the day of wrath poured out.

Second, disease will wrack the bodies of those who gloated over His sufferings. Their eyes will be darkened and their loins will shake (v. 23). Plagues and pestilence will characterize the coming day of wrath. We see that day approaching even now as AIDS continues to ravage mankind.

Third, the awful results of sin will be manifest. Indignation and wrathful anger will be the order of the day (v. 24).

What is the reason this day of wrath will come? Because they persecute the Lord Jesus Christ (v. 26). Thank God we are still in the age of grace and we can love Him.

Through the Bible in a Year: Nehemiah 3–6

May 30

Read Psalms 69:18-36 and 70
Family Reading: Psalm 69:18-36 and 70; Devotional Reading: Psalm 69:29-36

From a Sigh to a Song

Psalm 69 presents first the sufferings of the cross (vv. 1-21). Then we read of the coming day of wrath (vv. 22-28). Today we complete Psalm 69 with verses twenty-nine through thirty-six revealing the coming Millennium of peace. This millennial age will follow the Tribulation period and the battle of Armageddon.

Verse thirty-five gives the key to that age: *"For God will save Zion, and will build the cities of Judah."* This will be the day when the Lord Jesus Christ will establish His reign from Jerusalem. His prayer in verse twenty-nine will be answered: *"O God, set me up on High."* He will be *"The mighty God, The Prince of Peace" (Isaiah 9:6).*

What an age that will be! It will be a time of *praising* the Lord. *"I will praise the name of God with a song, and will magnify Him with thanksgiving" (v. 30).* But even more, it will be a time of *pleasing* the Lord. *"This also shall please the Lord better than ox or bullock that hath horns and hoofs" (v. 31).* The praise and offerings will come from surrendered hearts that have come out of the Great Tribulation. In spite of distressing circumstances, these souls kept praising and thanking the Lord. That is what pleases our God.

The kingdom will be inhabited by the humble (v. 32). They will seek the Lord and find life in Him. The poor, honored and helped, and the prisoners, released from the bondage of sin, will all be there. And because of all this, the seed of the Lord, those who have been born again by faith in Him, shall come to their inheritance and live in that inheritance.

Who will praise the Lord? It will involve the whole of creation: the heaven, the earth, and the seas (v. 34).

So we end another psalm that is like others in the book of Psalms—it began with a sigh and ends with a song.

Through the Bible in a Year: Nehemiah 7–8

May 31

Read Psalms 70–71
Family Reading: Psalm 70 and 71:1-16; Devotional Reading: Psalm 70

An Emergency Prayer

Psalm 70 is a prayer given by David in a time of great need. Three times he asks God to make haste. These five verses are almost identical to the last five verses of Psalm 40. Someone has conjectured that these verses were pulled out of Psalm 40 and placed in a separate Psalm so that all could have a prayer ready for use in any emergency.

Several years ago, my dear wife Guyla and one of our daughters was in one car following me and two of our sons home from church. My wife and daughter looked on in horror as the car I was driving was slammed from behind by two drunk drivers that were racing down a two-lane road. And, to make matters worse, none of us were wearing seat belts. I knew I was hurt, and I was afraid that the boys were seriously hurt. It seemed forever before an ambulance came, and even longer to reach the hospital. It was as though everyone was moving in slow-motion.

Have you ever felt that way with God? Have you asked Him to meet some need, but it seems He does not come to help. David cried, *"Make haste, O God . . . ."* He was under great persecution. Men were harassing him, mocking him, endeavoring to destroy him. He asked God to intervene—and to do it quickly!

David revealed the very essence of prayer in verse five: *"But I am poor and needy . . . ."* As we pray we admit to God, "I cannot handle this on my own—I need your help." Our own self-sufficiency keeps us from prayer. Therefore when we fail to pray, we are saying in a silent way, "I can handle things—I do not need help." We need daily to recognize our own inadequacy—then we will be willing to turn to the Lord in our need. May we today realize we need to join with David. He was persecuted—but he realized he needed to turn to the Lord and thus *"obtain mercy and find grace in time of need" (Hebrews 4:16).*

Through the Bible in a Year: Nehemiah 9–10

June 1

Read Psalm 71
Devotional Reading: Psalm 71:1-8

Trusting the Lord in Old Age

Psalm 71 is the psalm of an elderly man. The psalmist speaks of *"old age" (v. 9)* and states that he is an old man in verse eighteen: *"Now when I am old and greyheaded, O God . . . ."* He is more than just an old man—He is a *godly* old man who has trusted the Lord over the years. He certainly knew the Scriptures well. In this psalm of twenty-four verses he gives fifty quotations from or references to other psalms. We are not told who the author is, but I would suppose it to be David. Whoever wrote Psalm 71 was someone very familiar with Scripture. Every verse, in whole or in part, is found somewhere else in the Psalms.

What a testimony this elderly man had! We see it first in this psalm in his faith through life's testings. That faith is revealed in verse one: *"In thee, O Lord, do I put my trust . . . ."* The psalmist reveals his trust by stating what the Lord is to him: *"my strong habitation" (v. 3); "my rock and my fortress" (v. 3); "my hope" (v. 5); "my trust" (v. 5);* and *"my strong refuge" (v. 7).* The psalmist's *hope* was in the Lord (vv. 5 and 14). Thus he revealed his testimony of faith in spite of the trials that he experienced.

Old people experience testings that try their faith. They are retired, not having the challenge of daily employment. Health fails. I went to see my dentist recently because, while eating a piece of *bread* I cracked a tooth. When I asked him why the tooth broke just because I bit into some tough bread, he said, "Ed, it is simply that you are getting old and you are falling apart." Yes, health fails and old friends die. The income is greatly reduced and the mind seems to fail. At such a time it is easy to feel lonely, defenseless, maybe unwanted. It was just at such a time the psalmist reaffirmed, *"In thee, O Lord, do I put my trust . . . ."* And he prayed *"Deliver me" (v. 4).* He reminded the Lord that He was the One who gave the psalmist life from his mother's womb. Thus he could put his confidence in the Lord.

Through the Bible in a Year: Nehemiah 11–12

June 2

Read Psalm 71
Devotional Reading: Psalm 71:9-16

Living With Praise in Old Age

The psalmist was a godly old man. He had determined to live with praise and not with discontent. Some people think it strange if the elderly live with praises rather than with griping and complaining. The psalmist prayed in verse eight that his mouth might be filled with the praise of the Lord and His honor. Apparently there were those who thought he was very strange. Verse seven records that he was a *"wonder unto many."* But this old man was different. He gave thanks in everything. Remember—we may find it difficult to give thanks *for* some circumstances, but we can give thanks *in* them. God is still on the throne and He is still our refuge (v. 7). We are often concerned about our comforts—but God is concerned about our character.

Like other elderly, this old man felt some pressure. He prayed, *"Cast me not off in the time of old age . . ." (v. 9).* Often old people feel cast off. They feel useless and burdensome to relatives and friends. But the psalmist knew he could trust the Lord not to forsake him when his strength failed.

The psalmist had reason to pray as he did. He was facing severe persecution. Enemies spoke against him (v. 10)—in fact they seemed to plot against him. Their idea was that in his waning years he would feel that God had forsaken him and there was none to help (v. 11). But the psalmist's trust was in the Lord. He continued his prayer: *"O God, be not far from me: O my God, make haste for my help" (v. 12).* And then he said, *"But I will hope continually, and will yet praise thee more and more" (v. 14).* His trust was in the Lord and persecution could not sway him.

An elderly child of God found that his mind seemed to be failing. He could not remember Scripture promises as he once did. With trembling voice, he said fearfully to a friend, "I have forgotten them." The friend answered wisely, "Never mind so long as God has not forgotten them!" Amen! Our God is a God of love and kindness. He will not cast us off in old age because our bodies weaken and our minds seem to falter. The psalmist wisely said, *"I will go in the strength of the Lord God" (v. 16).*

Through the Bible in a Year: Nehemiah 13; Esther 1–2

June 3

Read Psalm 71
Devotional Reading: Psalm 71:17-24

The Testimony of a Godly Old Man

Many pagan cultures have no place for old people. In our own United States there are many voices pleading for the right to take the life of the elderly in order to make room for the younger and to reduce expense. May God deliver us from applying the law of the jungle, thereby just letting old people die. This godly old man reveals the importance of an old saint's testimony.

Here was an old man who had lived for the Lord from his youth. *"O God, thou hast taught me from my youth; and hitherto have I declared thy wondrous works" (v. 17).* I remember reading in one of D.L. Moody's sermons about a man testifying that he had lived in deep sin for years and then gotten saved. He was a token of God's grace. Another man stood up to give a testimony that he had never gone into dreadful depths of sin. He had godly parents who had taught him the ways of the Lord. He received Christ as a young lad and had gone on to live for Christ. Moody noted that the first testified of God's power to save. The second was really a greater testimony for it revealed God's power to save and keep.

This godly old man in Psalm 71 could give the testimony of that second man—that God had saved and kept him. Then he stated he was going to keep going on for the Lord. He wanted to show God's power to everyone (v. 18). This godly man had been through some difficult trials—he had seen *"great and sore troubles."* But he said the Lord would deliver him through them (v. 20).

How is a godly old man going to act and react? He is going to rejoice in the Lord with praise (v. 22) and with singing (v. 23). He will testify of God's grace and power. While he has blessed victory, those who have ridiculed and harassed him will be confounded (v. 24). May all of us grow old gracefully.

Through the Bible in a Year: Esther 3–7

June 4

Read Psalm 72

A Coming King

Please note the inscription of Psalm 72: "A Psalm for Solomon." This is a psalm written to challenge Solomon about the type of kingdom that would bring honor to the Lord. From the psalm we realize this psalm comprises a prayer of David (v. 20), and we also recognize that he is praying for a king other than himself: *"Give the king thy judgments, O God, and thy righteousness unto the king's son" (v. 1).*

David's prayer literally was given for two different individuals. The inscription tells us it was offered for Solomon. But as we read the psalm, we surely will recognize that the prayer is also referring to the Lord Jesus. Statements are made in the psalm which can relate only to our Lord Jesus Christ:

> Verse 5—*"They shall fear thee as long as the sun and moon endureth, throughout all generations."*
> Verse 11—*"Yea, all kings shall fall down before him: all nations shall serve him."*
> Verse 17—*"His name shall endure forever . . . ."*

The three verses listed above along with others in Psalm 72 reveal clearly that David is praying for One greater than Solomon. It was the Lord Jesus Christ who said of Himself: *"A greater than Solomon is here" (Matthew 12:42).* Therefore, in this psalm, we must conclude that David prayed for Solomon, but he also prophesied of the Lord Jesus Christ.

David prayed the right prayer. Every king does need God's judgments and righteousness (v. 1). His judging of the people must be with righteousness (v. 2). He does need to see established an abiding peace based on righteousness (v. 3). Solomon started out wisely and with great potential. But he was only a man, and in the latter years his kingdom did fail. But the One to whom David looked, the King of Kings, will establish a kingdom that will have all the characteristics given in Psalm 72. May we look forward to that kingdom.

Through the Bible in a Year: Esther 8–10; Job 1

June 5

Read Psalm 72

The Kingdom of Righteousness

Psalm 72 challenges Solomon to lead his kingdom in righteousness. However, the psalm goes beyond the kingdom of Solomon to the everlasting kingdom of our Lord Jesus Christ.

In the kingdom our Lord will establish, righteousness will be the key to its blessing and success. In the first seven verses we find the words *"righteousness"* or *"righteous"* four times. He will judge in righteousness (v. 2), and peace shall come by righteousness (v. 3). The kingdom will be such that the righteous shall flourish, the result being that abundant peace will also flourish *"so long as the moon endureth" (v. 7).* Peace is secured by righteousness. Verses three and seven reveal that peace comes by righteousness. Please note that righteousness comes before the peace. True peace is the product and consequence of righteousness. There can and will be no genuine peace until our Lord reigns in righteousness.

Verse 4—*"He shall judge the poor of the people, he shall save the children of the needy . . ."*

Verses 12-13—*"For he shall deliver the needy when he crieth; the poor also, and him that hath no helper. He shall spare the poor and needy, and shall save the souls of the needy."*

The reign of our Lord will be over the whole earth. *"[A]ll kings shall fall down before him: all nations shall serve him" (v. 11).* He will meet the needs of all, the poor and the needy. His mission will be first and foremost one of redemption (v. 14). Then God states that the blood of these redeemed ones will be precious in his sight (v. 14). Think of it—His Blood is precious to us: *"Forasmuch as ye know ye were not redeemed with corruptible things, as silver and gold, . . . but with the precious blood of Christ . . ." (I Peter 1:18-19).* His blood is precious to us—and our blood is precious unto Him. He loves and cares for us after we have been redeemed. May we praise Him for His faithfulness.

Through the Bible in a Year: Job 2–5

Read Psalm 72

A Future Glorious Millennial Reign

Psalm 72 is a psalm for Solomon. In verse sixteen, the psalmist (very likely, David) wrote of the prosperity of Solomon's reign: *"There shall be an handful of corn in the earth upon the top of the mountains; the fruit thereof shall shake like Lebanon: and they of the city shall flourish like grass of the earth."* What a harvest! A handful of corn will be sown on the top of the mountains. That is the most unlikely place to plant seed. The earth there is shallow and the wind can easily blow the seed away. But God so blessed that this little seed produced great plants that shook Lebanon and brought prosperity to the cities.

God did bless Solomon. From all outward appearances, his kingdom prospered greatly. *"King Solomon passed all the kings of the earth in riches and wisdom" (II Chronicles 9:22).* He had gold in abundance in all of his palaces—even the cooking vessels and drinking vessels were of gold (II Chronicles 9:20). But—wait—apparently he built it on debt that demanded excessive taxes. When he died and Rehoboam, his son, succeeded him to the throne, *"all Israel came and spake to Rehoboam, saying, Thy father made our yoke grievous . . . [a] heavy yoke that he put upon us . . ." (II Chronicles 10:3-4).* This heavy taxation was the start of the fall of the kingdom after Solomon's death.

America—take heed!! God has blessed our nation like He did Solomon's nation. But debt is bearing down upon us. Listen to the warning by Thomas Jefferson: "That neither the representatives of a nation nor the whole nation itself assembled can validly engage debt beyond what they may pay in their own lifetime . . . . If the debt should once more be swelled . . . we shall be committed to the English career of debt, corruption, and rottenness closing with revolution."

In Psalm 72 nothing is said about debt. These closing verses speak of a very prosperous reign. So again, as in the two previous days' devotions, we can see that the reign is not only that of Solomon's but really that of our Lord Jesus Christ. What a day to look forward to—the Millennial Reign of Christ—a reign marked by abundance and prosperity—physically, materially, and spiritually.

Through the Bible in a Year: Job 6–8

June 7

Read Psalm 73

The Seeming Prosperity of the Wicked

Psalm 73 joins with two previous psalms (Psalm 37 and Psalm 49) discussing the same problem: the seeming prosperity of the wicked and the suffering of the godly. This psalm was written by Asaph, the man who was the chief musician for David. He was a godly man who left an imprint on his family so that they continued to be singers in Israel for succeeding reigns. They were key people in the revivals under Hezekiah (II Chronicles 29:13), during Josiah's reign (II Chronicles 35:15), and with Zerubbabel's return from captivity (Ezra 2:41).

Asaph wrote Psalms 73-84. Psalm 73 begins the third book of Psalms, the book of worship. Therefore, we note that Asaph, the musician, is the key to setting the right atmosphere and attitude for worship. Music does have a great influence in our lives. When a church permits the wrong music to be used in its worship, be assured it will not be long until the theology will follow the downward plunge. Asaph and his family were godly people who pointed Israel toward revival in their music.

Asaph begins this psalm by stating the problem and how it affected him. In verse two he states that his feet were almost gone for his steps had brought him to slippery places. What was it that caused him to be in such a dangerous position that he almost lost his faith? He gives the answer to that in verse three: *"For I was envious at the foolish, when I saw the prosperity of the wicked."* The word *"foolish"* in that verse means *"arrogant."* There are those who prosper in this life and allow their prosperity to make them proud and arrogant. Asaph saw this—he could not understand it. Why do these proud people seem to prosper? This question brought him to the slippery place of verse two where his firm foundation seemed to be sliding from under his feet.

As a little boy, I almost drowned one time by disobeying my parents and walking on slippery mud next to an irrigation ditch. Don't step on spiritually slippery places as Asaph did.

Through the Bible in a Year: Job 9–12

June 8

Read Psalm 73

The Condition of the Wicked Who Seem to Prosper

In verse three, Asaph confessed he was envious of the wicked. He listed seven reasons for his envy.

1. The wicked seem to be free from the fear of death. Verse four—*"For there are no bands in their death . . . ."* They appear to die in peace and at ease. But be assured from Scripture that their death brings dreadful terrors.

2. They seem to be free from the troubles of this life. Verse five— *"They are not in trouble like other men; neither are they plagued like other men."* Their wealth seems to produce influence and power that delivers them from those things that plague the poor.

3. They appear to be in prosperity. Verse three—*"I saw the prosperity of the wicked."* We must remember that true prosperity comes when the soul prospers. (Note III John 2 and Joshua 1:8.)

4. Verse seven states, *"They have more than heart could wish."* It was right here where the psalmist may have had a touch of envy. The wicked seemed to have everything going their way.

5. They become proud. Verse six—*"Therefore pride compasseth them about as a chain . . . ."* When men become proprietors and not stewards of their riches, they become proud of what they have.

6. Their pride and self-sufficiency produces corruption and violence. *"They speak loftily" (v. 8).* They lift their voices in rebellion.

7. They speak against God. *"They set their mouths against the heavens . . . ." (v. 9).* In this speech that they spread throughout the earth they ask, *"How doth God know? and is there knowledge in the Most High?" (v. 11).* They say, "If there is a God, He must be blind and deaf, ignorant and impotent."

No wonder the psalmist stated his perplexity in verse twelve: *"Behold, there are the ungodly, who prosper in the world . . . ."* How can this be? We will consider the psalmist's solution in tomorrow's devotional.

Through the Bible in a Year: Job 13–15

June 9

Read Psalm 73
Family Reading: Psalm 73:8-28

Asaph Sees Life From God's Perspective

Today we will note Psalm 73:13-22. These verses tell us of the big conversion that came to Asaph. He had looked at the way it appeared the wicked were prospering. This perplexed him so severely that he thought his cleansing of his heart was in vain (v. 13). While the wicked prospered, Asaph, who desired to live for the Lord, experienced plagues and chastening in his life (v. 14). He knew he must not announce what he was thinking and feeling for it could hurt other children of God (v. 15). He tried to accept the position and life style of the wicked as his own. But as a child of God, he found that trying to think like the wicked was *"too painful"* for him (v. 16).

He could not understand this problem. Finally, he went into the sanctuary of God, the Temple, and meditated on these problems and on God's philosophy. It was then that he received an answer to the question which had plagued him (v. 17).

His conversion came as he saw life from God's perspective. He understood *"their end"* (v. 17). Though they were prospering, there would be a judgment. Their *"end,"* their eternity, would be different. In fact, he saw that these prospering wicked were standing on *"slippery places"* (v. 18). The end would be destruction (v. 18). Though they appear prosperous now, they will suddenly be brought to a place of desolation (v. 19). They are living in a dream world now, but they will awaken with a shock to realize their image is despised by God (v. 20).

As Asaph viewed this problem from God's perspective, he realized how foolish he had been. His heart was grieved—he was pricked in his reins (v. 21). He recognized how foolish he had been. He felt more dumb than a brute beast (v. 22). He now recognized that God is in charge and He is well able to manage the affairs of the world.

Through the Bible in a Year: Job 16–19

June 10

Read Psalm 73:8-28

Trusting the Lord—The Wise Choice

Psalm 73:23 begins with the word *"nevertheless."* Literally it means "in spite of." Asaph was saying that in spite of his foolish questions and doubting, the Lord had remained faithful. He recognized that he was continually with God. Though he had wandered from the Lord in his thinking, God had not abandoned him. The Lord had held him by his right hand (v. 23). Please note that it was the *Lord* holding—not the psalmist.

Verse twenty-five puts it all in the right perspective. Each of us must recognize that our relationship with the Lord is the most important part of life. *"Whom have I in Heaven but thee? And there is none upon earth that I desire beside thee" (v. 25).* Heaven without the Lord would not be Heaven. And life on earth without the Lord would be Hell on earth.

What does the Lord do? He guides with His counsel on earth and afterward receives us to glory (v. 24). There is nothing better than that. He will guide us past the slippery places on earth. Then He will open the gates of glory and receive us. Why should we ever be concerned about the worldly prosperity of the wicked on earth?!

On earth *"My flesh and my heart faileth" (v. 26).* But even when that happens, I have the Lord to care for me. He is the strength of my heart and also my portion forever (v. 26).

Asaph began this psalm with the statement, *"Truly God is good to Israel . . ." (v. 1).* He recognized the blessing God is to the believer. Then he states his problem—why do the wicked prosper? And then he brings everything back into perspective—recognizing his own foolishness to question this. In verse twenty-seven he states that those who are wicked will perish, even though for a time they appear to prosper. He ends the psalm with his responsibility—*"It is good for me to draw near to God: I have put my trust in the Lord God . . . " (v. 28).* The rich man puts his trust in money—the psalmist puts his trust in the Lord. In the end the psalmist will have made the wise choice.

Through the Bible in a Year: Job 20–22

June 11

Read Psalm 74

The Destruction of the Enemies

Psalm 74 is a "maschil"—that means it is a psalm of instruction. It teaches us the proper attitude in a time of discouragement and seeming difficulty and defeat.

Psalm 74 is recounting a change in Israel: *"A man was famous according as he had lifted up axes upon the thick trees. But now they break down the carved work . . ." (vv. 5-6).* Once they were famous for building; now they are famous for destroying. This is a picture of the day in which we live. In America men have tediously built, but now we have those who want to see how rapidly they can tear down. The rock musicians, the Playboy and Penthouse magazines, the movie crowd, the liquor crowd, and the Hugh Hefners do all they can to wreck our nation with immorality and sin.

The psalmist cries out in verse one, revealing his perplexity. He speaks of a great affliction: *"Why hast thou cast us off for ever?" (v. 1).* And he then presents the blessing of a close relationship represented in the words, *"the sheep of thy pasture" (v. 1).* The Shepherd and His sheep. Note the relationship: He precedes the sheep (John 10:4); He protects the sheep (Psalm 23:4); and He provides for the sheep (John 10:9). The sheep and the shepherd are closely related because of the Shepherd's purchased redemption (v. 2). In verse three the psalmist claims the active protection of the Lord: *"Lift up thy feet unto the perpetual desolations."*

Verse four presents the action of the enemy as an insult to God. The enemy roars like a wild animal with no respect for sacred things. Then in verses five through eight we see the method of destruction. It is much easier to tear down than it is to build. These enemies use axes, hammers, and fire (vv. 6-7). Why? Verse eight states they did it because their hearts were not right. Defiled hearts are always the prelude to spiritual destruction. May we walk with God and thus be builders and not destroyers.

Through the Bible in a Year: Job 23–27

June 12

Read Psalm 74

God Is at Work for His Own

What a destruction the enemy was accomplishing. They tore down the temple and burned up all the synagogues in the land (vv.7-8). This was undoubtedly a Satanically inspired destruction—endeavoring to force God out of the land. It is interesting to note that the Bolsheviks in taking over Russia in 1917 declared that Satan was "the first revolutionist whose blessed work delivered men from the slavery of God."

Then the psalmist wrote: *"We see not our signs: there is no more any prophet" (v. 9)*. They needed the Scriptures but they had departed from them. This is surely a picture of the United States of America today. Our nation has departed from the Word of God. If we come to the Bible we need no signs. The real need in Israel was a prophet who would give the people the Word of God.

It seemed that God was silent. The psalmist cried out: *"O God, how long shall the adversary reproach? Shall the enemy blaspheme thy name for ever?" (v. 10)*. We mentioned the Bolshevik revolution and the Soviet Union coming out of it. The Soviets mocked God, tried to rule religion out of the country—and for decades it seemed God was silent. But as I write this in January of 1992, we can now see God has worked. An open door for the gospel exists in the former Soviet Union. God now has revealed His arm.

In verse twelve the psalmist changes his tune. He acknowledges God's *"working salvation in the midst of the earth" (v. 12)*. Then he pulls from Israel's history miraculous evidences of God's power. He speaks of dividing the sea (v. 13)—the division of the Red Sea in Exodus 14. Verse fifteen refers to the drying up of Jordan so Israel could pass over to Canaan. God did it all.

The psalmist is saying: "Though it seems God is silent, I have assurance He is working." May we have that kind of faith regardless of the circumstances. We can rest in his power and concern for us.

Through the Bible in a Year: Job 28–30

June 13

Read Psalm 74:16-23 and Psalm 75

God Takes Care of His Own

In Psalm 74:13-15, the Lord speaks of God's grace in salvation. The psalmist sang of miracles the Lord had worked in order that it His people could be redeemed.

In verse sixteen the praise of the psalmist changes from seeing the Lord as a God of grace to beholding Him as the God of nature. He is the One Who regulates day and night (v. 16) and Who gives us the light and the sun. The Lord has set all the boundaries of the earth—the boundaries of the sea and the land (v. 17). Summer and winter were made by Him. He is the Sovereign over His people and all His creation—He is Lord.

Therefore the psalmist calls upon the Lord to do four things:

1. Remember His People (vv. 18-19)

   Surely God would not desert His own. But the psalmist calls His attention to His people. The enemy had reproached and the people had acted foolishly. The psalmist refers to God's people as His turtle dove (v. 19)—a defenseless people. Because of their weakness the psalmist pleads with the Lord not to forget these people.

2. Respect His Promise (v. 20)

   The psalmist was in Babylon where there were laws and customs of a foreign forbidden people. What a contrast between these pagan laws and the laws of God. The psalmist knew that God's promises were His pledge and He would keep them.

3. Rekindle Praise in the poor and needy (v. 21)

4. Resurrect His Power (v. 22)

   "Arise, O God . . . ." In resurrection power God can bring forth blessing and victory. Though the tumult seemed to increase in volume daily, God's power could easily overcome all that the enemies would desire. The psalmist urged God to manifest His mercy so that the miseries of the people could be overcome. May we, too, rest on the mercy of God.

Through the Bible in a Year: Job 31–33

June 14

Read Psalms 75–76
Devotional Reading: Psalm 75

God Is the Sovereign Judge

Psalm 75 can be understood as an answer to the question given in Psalm 74:10: *"O God, how long shall the adversary reproach?"* In Psalm 75 God reveals that He is Sovereign and that He operates according to His timetable.

Because He is Sovereign and will accomplish His purpose, the psalmist begins Psalm 75 with praise. In verse one he gives thanks for the wondrous works of God. The psalmist thanks God for Who He is—the fact that His name is near. God's Sovereignty is revealed in His person.

Verses two and three present God's Sovereignty revealed in His power. He states that He will judge uprightly and that He bears up the pillars of the earth. Note in these verses that God emphasizes that He will do it. *"When I shall receive the congregation I will judge uprightly . . . I bear up the pillars of it."* Then he adds *"Selah"* in verse three, meaning that these statements are so important they bear being repeated. God will work—be assured of it—He will work in His time.

Verses four and five warn against pride. He commends, *"Lift not up your horn on high" (v. 5).* The lifting up of the horn gives the picture of an animal showing his strength by lifting his horn threateningly at others. These verses speak of an individual manifesting his pride with a stiff neck. Verses six and seven reveal that promotion is from God.

Promotion does not come from the east or west or south—*"God is the judge . . ." (v. 6-7).* Notice that verse six does not mention the north. Scripture indicates that the north is God's dwelling place. (Note Isaiah 14:13; Ezekiel 1:4; and Job 26:7.)

As Judge, God deals with the wicked. Very likely this psalm was written by one of the children of Asaph when Sennacherib and Rabshakeh were defying God. The psalmist said these wicked folk would face the judging hand of God (v. 8). He stood assured by God that *"all the horns of the wicked would be cut off" (v. 10).* He ends the psalm with praise to the Lord for His delivering the righteous (vv. 9-10).

Through the Bible in a Year: Job 34–36

June 15

Read Psalms 76–77
Devotional Reading: Psalm 76

Great Victory Through God's Power

Psalm 76 is a companion passage to Psalm 75. Both reveal faith singing. In Psalm 75 the song is of victories to come; in Psalm 76 it is of victories already won. It would seem that this psalm fits with the immediately preceding psalms and therefore is speaking of the victory Hezekiah and Israel had over Sennacherib and his hosts from Assyria.

The psalm begins by stating that God is known in Judah and His Name is great in Israel. The world does not know God, but His people know Him in a wonderful way. Jerusalem is the city where God's Tabernacle was; therefore, the psalmist refers to mount Zion as God's dwelling place (v. 2).

Verse three is a great passage. It tells us that the battles are won in God's Tabernacle. The word *"there"* is referring back to the words *"his tabernacle"* in verse two. The battle was not won on the battlefield but rather in the Tabernacle in Zion. Think of it—the armies, the navies, and the air power move forward to fight battles. Generals are lauded and applauded—but really the battle is being won by some dear saints meeting with God in prayer. Sennacherib wrote Hezekiah a threatening, sarcastic letter, flaunting his worldly power and prestige. Hezekiah made his way to the Temple of God and there spread the letter out before the Lord in prayer (Isaiah 37:14-15). God answered his prayer (Isaiah 37:21-22; 33-38). Where was the battle won?—right there in the Temple when Hezekiah prayed. The stouthearted were spoiled, dying on the field (Psalm 76:5), just as God recorded in Isaiah 37:36 when 185,000 Assyrian soldiers were killed by God.

Our God wins battles. We can watch Him break the arrows, the shield, and the bow (v. 3). We must praise Him as did the people of God in Psalm 76. May we, like the psalmist, recognize: *"At thy rebuke, O God of Jacob, both the chariot and horse are cast into a dead sleep" (v. 6).* May we learn to trust Him for the victory.

Through the Bible in a Year: Job 37–39

June 16

Read Psalms 76–77
Devotional Reading: Psalm 76

Praise Him—He Gives the Victory

Psalm 76 is a song of the fact that God had given the victory. And what a great victory it was! The enemy came up against God's people in hordes with chariots and horses. After the battle their arrows, their bows, their shields, and their swords were all broken. The horses were cast into a deep sleep, the sleep of death. Their soldiers lay prone, their stout hearts cold, their hands of war stiff, they were sleeping their last sleep (vv. 3-6).

How is it possible to have such a victory? We saw yesterday that this victory came only because God was on their side (v. 4). They worshiped Jehovah, and he fought their battles for them. The truths of this psalm apply to the deliverance of our great country, the United States of America. There is no explanation for the victory of the colonial army unless you believe that God miraculously intervened. Story after story coming out of the Revolutionary War reveals that Jehovah fought for America.

This psalm repeats the truth of verse four that God is the One Who delivers His people.

v. 7—*"Thou, even thou, art to be feared . . . ."*

v. 8—*"Thou didst cause judgment to be heard from Heaven . . . ."*

God slew the aggressors and saved the afflicted. Verse nine states that *"God arose to judgment to save all the meek of the earth."* When Heaven speaks, earth trembles. God has a way of getting man's attention.

Verse ten presents a truth emphasized in Scripture: *"Surely the wrath of man shall praise thee . . . ."* God told Pharaoh that He had raised him up (Exodus 9:16). God called Nebuchadnezzar *"the man that executeth my counsel"* (Isaiah 46:11). God uses the wrath of man to cause praise. Therefore, His people should bring offerings to Him (v. 11), and all rulers must revere him (v. 12).

> Oh, worship the king, all glorious above,
> Oh, gratefully sing His power and His love;
> Our shield and Defender, the Ancient of Days
> Pavilioned in splendor and girded with praise.
>
> —Robert Grant

Through the Bible in a Year: Job 40–42

June 17

Read Psalm 77

From a Sigh to a Song

This psalm reveals the way to find comfort in the midst of severe trials. It divides itself into two sections. Verses one through nine are filled with a sigh, but in verses ten through twenty, the psalmist bounces back with a song. The first nine verses present a *Present National Disaster* while verses ten through twenty give the blessing of *Past National Deliverance*.

The *"day of trouble" (v. 2)* is the common lot of all men. Job recorded for us, *"[M]an is born unto trouble, as the sparks fly upward" (Job 5:7)*. You and I, all men, are going to face some measure of trouble. It comes to good people because even they are sinners with imperfections and resulting disappointments. The psalmist was undergoing deep trouble. His *"sore ran in the night, and ceased not: [his] soul refused to be comforted" (v. 2)*.

What did he do? He went directly to the throne of God. *"I cried unto God with my voice, even unto God with my voice; and he gave ear unto me" (v. 1)*. He repeated this in verse two: *"In the day of my trouble, I sought the Lord . . . ."*

What does this tell us? First, it reveals that the psalmist recognized he could approach God. He could do what Hebrews 4:16 invites us to do: *"Let us therefore come boldly unto the throne of grace, that we may obtain mercy, and find grace to help in time of need."* Second, it reveals the willingness of God to help. *"God is our refuge and strength, a very present help in trouble" (Psalm 46:1)*.

The psalmist was deeply troubled. He could not speak because of his great burden (v. 4). His mind dwelt on things in the past (v. 5). He probably thought of mighty deliverances such as Gideon and Samson experienced. He lay awake at night giving thought to the tests he was enduring. The night seemed full of doubts and dreads and fears. Minutes dragged and hours seemed as though they would not pass (v. 6). This is the sigh the psalmist experienced. We will note tomorrow how that sigh is turned into a song.

Through the Bible in a Year: Proverbs 1; Isaiah 1–2

June 18

Read Psalm 77

Victory Comes As We Believe God's Word

Yesterday we noted the sorrowful sigh of the psalmist in verses one through six. Today we continue to look at that sigh. In verses seven through nine, we find the psalmist asking a series of questions.

1. Has God Rejected His people forever (v. 7)? This involved two questions in verse seven. The two questions imply the fact that the psalmist wants a negative answer: "No—God has not cast off forever and God will continue His favor."

2. Has God Repudiated His mercy forever (v. 8)?

3. Has God Revoked His promise forever (v. 8)? Again the answer is implied: "No." God's promises are valid. The present dreadful situation is not permanent?

4. Has God forgotten His grace? Has He stopped His tender mercies (v. 9)? All these questions involve the idea, "Has God changed?" "Is God less than God?" "Is He fickle—changeable?"

What is the psalmist's answer? It comes in verse ten where the sigh changes to the song. The psalmist admits the problem is with him—not with God. He states: *"This is my infirmity."* He confesses it as sin. Then he states that he would *"remember the years of the right hand of the most High" (v. 10).* He is saying, "I will look to God's Word—I will read of His acts in the past." Faith is restored by turning back to the Word of God. *"[F]aith cometh by hearing, and hearing by the Word of God" (Romans 10:17).* Faith is built by believing the Word, and faith is maintained by staying in the Word.

Doubts come. Where should we go? We must go to the Word. I love the story of the elderly lady saved at a revival meeting after reading John 3:16. The doubts came as she lay in bed. Was she really saved? After thinking for a moment, she decided the doubts were from Satan. Since Satan loves darkness, and since the darkest place in the room was under the bed, then Satan would be under the bed. She opened her Bible to John 3:16, put her finger on the verse, shoved it under the bed, and said: "Here—read it for yourself." Amen! Our faith is founded on the Word of God.

Through the Bible in a Year: Proverbs 2; Isaiah 3–4

June 19

Read Psalms 77:10-20 and 78:1-11
Devotional Reading: Psalm 77:10-20

God's Greatness and His Leadership

In Psalm 77 we have seen that the problems of the psalmist were of his own making. Psalm 77:10 gives his words of confession: *"This is my infirmity."* He recognized that God had not changed; therefore, the change must be in his own life. He repented and then remembered the Lord and His works (vv. 10-11). But he did more than remember. He also meditated on the wonderful truths that he recalled and then gave a witness for the Lord (v. 12).

Then the psalmist made several observations about the Lord:

1. God's way is revealed in the sanctuary (v. 13). This means that when we sincerely worship God, we will understand what He is doing. God works according to His holiness. He has not forgotten His lovingkindness; He may be waiting to bring His love and His holiness into harmony.

2. God is a great God. The psalmist asks, *"Who is so great a God as our God?" (v. 13)*. God's greatness is seen in His redemption (v. 15), His sovereignty over creation (vv. 14, 16-18), and His leadership (v. 20).

3. God manifests Himself in miraculous power. The voice of thunder, the flash of lightning, and the shaking of the earthquake all combine to speak of God's greatness (v. 18).

An interesting statement is made in verse nineteen: *"Thy footsteps are not known."* He has been speaking of the rolling back of the waters of the Red Sea. He performs miracles and lets them speak for themselves. Men see what He has done; and if they are thinking clearly, they will know that the miracle is from the Lord. Then the psalmist states that the people of the past were led by the hand of God.

> All the way My Saviour leads me;
> What have I to ask beside?
> For I know whate'er befall me,
> Jesus doeth all things well.
>
> —Fanny J. Crosby

Through the Bible in a Year: Proverbs 3; Isaiah 5–6

June 20

Read Psalm 78:1-10

Teach the Children Spiritual Truths

Psalm 78 is the first and longest of the Historical Psalms—the others are 105, 106, and 135. It is an instructive ("maschil") psalm of Asaph, probably written by Asaph himself during David's reign. The history given in the psalm ends with the kingdom under David (vv. 70-72). The psalm repeatedly gives Israel's sin and then presents God's mercy toward Israel.

The first eight verses form an introduction to the psalm and thus reveal that the purpose of the psalm is to teach lessons for the present by studying the past. History should teach us. Unfortunately, too often the only thing we learn from history is that we do not learn from history. In these first eight verses we find that it is God's plan for the children to be informed about the past.

Verse two speaks of this portion of Scripture as a parable. LaMoyne Sharpe calls Psalm 78, "The Parable of God's Prodigal People." A parable is a simple earthly story with a spiritual meaning that can be understood only by thoughtful study. These truths are ones that *"we have heard and known, and our fathers have told us" (v. 3).* God used these truths to establish the children. The psalmist emphatically said that he would not hide the truths from the children (v. 4). One of the worst attitudes a parent can have is for that parent to say, "I am not going to force religion on my children. I will let them make up their own minds when they get old enough." Why should the parents not present their spiritual values to their children? The world does; the godless schools do; and their peers push their views on them. Parents need to teach their children.

Spurgeon has said, "The best education is education in the best things. Teach your child what you will, but if he does not learn the fear of the Lord, he will perish for the lack of knowledge."

Psalm 78 states that the fathers should teach their children, these children should teach their children, and these grandchildren should in turn teach their children (vv. 5-6). What should they teach? They should teach their children to put their hope in God, to keep His commandments, and not to disobey God (vv. 7-8).

Through the Bible in a Year: Proverbs 4; Isaiah 7–9

June 21

Read Psalm 78:5-28

Reasons We Should Teach Our Children

Today we are going to look at reasons the psalmist gave that parents should teach their children about the things of God. Verse five states that parents should make these things known unto their children. Verses seven and eight give four major reasons why the parents should do this.

1. *"That they might set their hope in God . . ."* (v. 7). Every individual, as he matures into adulthood, is going to set his hope in something. Sooner or later that person will discover whether he has a foundation on which to base his hope. The vast majority of people will find that the things in which they hope are without foundation. *"For other foundation can no man lay than that is laid, which is Jesus Christ"* (I Corinthians 3:11).

2. *"That they might . . . not forget the works of God . . ."* (v. 7). Parents need to instruct their children in the truths of God's Word. How important it is that children's minds be filled with impressions from the stories of Noah in the Ark, or Moses in his childhood and life, or David and Goliath, or Daniel in the lion's den. A child's mind absorbs these stories, and they become a vital part of his life.

3. *"That they might . . . keep His commandments"* (v. 7). Remember, children are not going to be able to keep His commandments if they do not know what they are. *"Wherewithal shall a young man cleanse his way? By taking heed thereto according to thy word . . . Thy word have I hid in mine heart, that I might not sin against thee"* (Psalm 119:9, 11).

4. That they *"might not be . . . a stubborn and rebellious generation"* (v. 8). Please note that verse eight states that they should not become like their fathers. Stubborn and rebellious fathers produce stubborn and rebellious children. Wouldn't it be wonderful if we could say that each generation will improve the preceding one? But we cannot say that. Actually the opposite is the case. Decline is more general than progress. We had better train and teach our children while they are young and tender, because when they grow up they may become cold and indifferent.

Through the Bible in a Year: Proverbs 5; Isaiah 10–12

June 22

Read Psalm 78:9-31

The Voice of History

In the last two days in these devotions we have looked at Psalm 78:1-8 and seen that God wants us to pass our faith on to our children. In verse nine the psalmist begins using the history of Israel to show that the families had not passed their faith on to their children.

The first example is Ephraim (vv. 9-11). What happens to a nation which does not seek to give its spiritual heritage to the children? *"Ephraim, being armed and carrying bows, turned back in the day of battle" (v. 9)*. They did not keep His covenant (v. 10)—that is they did not *"set their hope in God" (v. 7)*. *"They refused to walk in His law" (v. 10)*—that is they failed to *"keep his commandments" (v. 7)*. They forgot His works (v. 11)—the direct opposite of God's command in verse seven where they were *not* to *"forget the works of God."* They forgot *"His wonders that he had showed them" (v. 11)*—the product of stubborn and rebellious hearts (v. 8).

The next thing this psalmist-historian mentions is that God did wondrous things for Israel:

He delivered them from Egypt (v. 12)—a picture of salvation.
He led them miraculously through the Red Sea (v. 13).
He led them with the pillars of cloud and fire (v. 14).
He brought water to drink out of the rock (vv. 15-16).

How did Ephraim react to God's grace and lovingkindness?

1. *"They tempted God by asking meat for their lust" (v. 18)*.
2. *"They spoke against God" (v. 19)*.

What was their problem? They sinned against light. They provoked God, even though he had done so much for them. Remember: "Truth received **binds** *the souls* to God; Truth rejected **blinds** *the soul* to God." May we love His truth and honor Him.

Through the Bible in a Year: Proverbs 6; Isaiah 13–14

June 23

Read Psalm 78:15-39

The Dangerous Sin of Unbelief

In Psalm 78:17-31 the psalmist reveals the goodness of God and the ingratitude of Israel. We see man's sin and God's judgment. Israel provoked the most High in the wilderness (v. 17), they tempted God (v. 18), and they spoke against God (v. 19). This speaking against God was manifested by their asking the question: *"Can God furnish a table in the wilderness?" (v. 19).*

Can you believe it? Unbelief had so gripped their hearts that they asked, *"Can God?"* No one should ever ask that question. The very question reveals unbelief. This sin of unbelief is a terrible sin which grieves the heart of God. He is God. There is nothing too hard for God. There are things He will not do because He is holy. But He is omnipotent (all powerful)—no one should ever ask, "Can God?" Yet that is exactly what Israel asked in the wilderness.

Verse twenty-one states that God was angry because they asked, *"Can God furnish a table in the wilderness . . . can he give bread also? can he provide flesh for his people?" (vv. 19-20).* Yes!! A thousand times—yes! God can!

God was angry *"because they believed not in God" (v. 22).* The psalmist listed several things God did: He opened the doors of Heaven raining down manna to give them bread (vv. 23-24); He provided flesh for His people by sending a strong wind to stop the quail in flight (vv. 26-29).

Though God provided for Israel, the Israelites were not estranged from their lust (v. 30). While the meat was still in their mouths, a plague came from God which killed a large number of their men (v. 31; Numbers 11:33). What was their reaction? Verse thirty-two gives the answer: *"For all this they sinned still, and believed not for his wondrous works."* How prone we are to forget God's goodness and grace and allow our flesh to continue to sin against God! May we yield ourselves to the Lord so that we can be used of Him with a faithful spirit—a life that believes God.

Through the Bible in a Year: Proverbs 7; Isaiah 15–21

June 24

Read Psalm 78:30-53

Man Changes—God Changes Not

Beginning with verse thirty-four, the psalmist records the temporary repentance and turning of Israel and the longsuffering and mercy of God. The Lord would bring judgment and Israel would seem to repent. But their repentance was only superficial. Yet God continued to manifest His grace and mercy.

"When he slew them, then they sought him: and they returned and inquired early after God . . . Nevertheless they did flatter him with their mouth, and they lied unto him with their tongues" (vv. 34, 36).

When Israel suffered, they sought the Lord. But they were not as sorry for their sins as they were over their suffering. Their prayers and repentance were not genuine, and the repentance was soon forgotten when the peril was removed. Their penitence was only a pretense.

But God remained the same. His compassion and mercy did not change. Verse thirty-eight states that *"he, being full of compassion, forgave their iniquity, and destroyed them not: yea, many a time turned he his anger away . . . ."*

Why did Israel fail so miserably? Because the Lord *"remembered that they were but flesh; a wind that passeth away, and cometh not again" (v. 39).* Man's life is brief. He is like a wind that does not return. Israel continued to provoke God and grieve him in the wilderness desert (v. 40). Even when they turned back they limited God (v. 41). That word *"limited"* means the drawing of a line. It was the word used to describe David's scribbling on the doors (I Samuel 21:13) and Ezekiel's marking foreheads (Ezekiel 9:4). When Israel limited God, they drew a line telling God he could go that far and no farther. The word means "to draw a circle around." They enclosed God in a circle. Oh, may we be careful to always realize how great God is; we must not limit Him.

Through the Bible in a Year: Proverbs 8; Isaiah 22–23

June 25

Read Psalm 78:40-62

The Lure of the World

This is the sixth day we have had our devotion from Psalm 78. I remind you that this whole psalm was written to teach our children the truths of God and His works. In the passage today we note temptations that come to God's people.

The first one we will note is the *love* of the world. We saw yesterday that they turned back toward the world and *"tempted God, and limited the Holy One of Israel" (v. 40).* We saw yesterday that limiting the Holy One is to circumscribe God and His working in our lives. They did not want the Lord in control—thus *"They remembered not his hand, nor the day when he delivered them from the enemy" (v. 42).* They did not remember God's deliverance—they forgot *"the rock [from] whence [they] were hewn, and the hole of the pit [from] whence [they] were digged" (Isaiah 51:1).*

Oh, that we would never forget what God did for us the day we were saved. I love to pray with a friend of mine, Pastor Rod Bell. Every time I have prayed with him he has thanked the Lord for the day he was saved and delivered from the pit of sin. We should all thank God constantly for our salvation.

The psalmist called on them to remember the deliverance of Israel: the miracles in Egypt—the rivers turned to blood (v. 44); the frogs and the flies that plagued Egypt (v. 45); the plague of locusts (v. 46); and the hail that destroyed the crops of Egypt (v. 47). All of these plagues in verses forty-three though forty-eight took place in Egypt, which is the Old Testament type of the world.

Later God permitted evil angels to trouble Israel and pestilence to plague them (vv. 49-50). Then the psalmist comes back to Egypt and speaks of the smiting of the firstborn in Exodus 12 (v. 51). This is the world. It allures us to destroy us. We must call it what the psalmist, calls it: *"the enemy" (v. 42).* May we be delivered from the lure of the world.

Through the Bible in a Year: Proverbs 9; Isaiah 24–27

June 26

Read Psalm 78:50-72

Idolatry Causes the Glory to Depart

In Psalm 78 we have seen how God judged Israel because of the lust of their flesh and the lure of the world. Today we are going to see God's judgment of Israel because of the lies of the Devil. The history of Israel is one continuous line of victories followed by backsliding, defeat, then repentance, revival, and back to some victory. However, it was a continuous downward trend.

In verse fifty-one we read of the victory when God delivered Israel by the blood in Exodus 12. Then we pass over the history of Israel quite rapidly in verses fifty-one through fifty-five. The backsliding and resulting sin that is recorded beginning at verse fifty-six probably reveals to us the time of the judges. Verse fifty-eight states: *"For they provoked him to anger with their high places, and moved him to jealousy with their graven images."* Israel stooped to idolatry. Because of this sin of idolatry, God *"was wroth, and greatly abhorred Israel . . . he forsook the tabernacle of Shiloh . . . and delivered his strength into captivity, and his glory into the enemy's hand"* (vv. 59-61).

In spite of all His grace and goodness to them, Israel continued to follow false gods and false teachers. God made it clear in Isaiah 42:8: *"My glory will I not give to another, neither my praise to graven images."* Idolatry was always a problem to Israel. Their false worship came because of the lies of the Devil. Judgment came because they followed false teachers. God *"gave his people over also unto the sword, and was wroth with his inheritance. The fire consumed their young men; and their maidens were not given to marriage"* (vv. 62-63).

In verse sixty-four God speaks of the day in I Samuel 4:19-21 when Phinehas the priest died and his widow named the baby that was born *"Ichabod,"* which means, *"the glory is departed."* It is true that the glory had departed from Israel. God had withdrawn His hand of blessing. What a sad picture! May we today continue to honor the Lord and not allow the glory to depart.

Through the Bible in a Year: Proverbs 10; Isaiah 28–29

June 27

Read Psalms 78:62-72 and 79

God Chooses the Place for Worship and the Leaders

In Psalm 78 we first saw the *TESTIMONY*. This is the testimony that fathers should give to their children, who in turn should give it to the grandchildren and succeeding generations.

Second, we saw the *TRIUMPH*. This triumph reveals how God delivered His people Israel with His salvation (vv. 12-16).

Third, we read many verses on the *TRAGEDY*. The tragedy involved the backslidings of Israel—their stubborn rebellion against God again and again. This rebellion covered generation upon generation and one period of history after another. Tragic, but true—Israel failed to honor the Lord God who had done so much for them. The period of tragedy included the time Israel was in the wilderness with the *TABERNACLE*.

Today we look at a fourth section of Psalm 78—the time of the TEMPLE. This involves verses sixty-five through seventy-two. The Lord again led the people in mighty victory. I believe verse sixty-six is speaking about the time God used Israel to defeat the Philistines in the days of Samuel, Saul, and David. God *"put them to a perpetual reproach" (v. 66).*

Then we find that God turned from the tabernacle's place in Shiloh of Ephraim to placing the temple in Zion of Judah (vv. 67-68). Joshua himself was of the tribe of Ephraim. During the days of Joshua and the Judges, the tribe of Ephraim was the predominant tribe. But that tribe, which became the northern kingdom, Israel, was the first to fall into apostasy. So the Lord chose Judah where David set up the ark in Mt. Zion. The temple site was placed on the high places in Jerusalem.

God not only chose a new place for the ark but also chose a new leader for the nation. That leader was David His servant (v. 70). What a title of honor!—*"David his servant."* David fed and led the people with integrity and skillfulness (vv. 71-72). The previous psalm ended with Moses and Aaron leading God's flock. God uses men to lead His work. He chooses men like Moses, the meekest man on the earth, and David, a servant, a man after God's own heart (I Samuel 13:14).

Through the Bible in a Year: Proverbs 11; Isaiah 30–32

June 28

Read Psalms 79–80
Family Reading: Psalm 79

God's Judgment on His People and the Heathen

Psalm 79 resembles closely Psalm 74. Both speak of desolation coming because of Israel's backsliding. Psalm 79 opens with these words: *"O God, the heathen are come into thine inheritance . . ." (v. 1).* Psalm 74 deals primarily with the destruction of the Temple, while Psalm 79 speaks of the terrible carnage that takes place as Jerusalem is destroyed.

The *"inheritance"* in verse one involves the people of God. The *"Holy Temple"* had been defiled and Jerusalem had been destroyed (v. 1), and the people were dealt with in a dreadful manner. Their dead bodies were not buried but rather were given to the birds of prey and to the carnivorous beasts for food (v. 2). It is a sickening sight to behold. Blood of the citizens of Jerusalem was poured out again; *"There was none to bury them" (v. 3).*

The psalmist asks three questions: *"How long, Lord? Wilt thou be angry forever? Shall thy jealousy burn like fire?" (v. 5).*

The answer is, "Yes, the anger of the Lord will burn like fire and dust will be forever." What a terrible end! Why will there be such an end as this for Israelites? Undoubtedly it was because of their sin. These foreigners invaded their land and destroyed God's inheritance.

Therefore the psalmist prayed for these wicked intruders. *"Pour out thy wrath upon the heathen that have not known thee, and upon the kingdoms that have not called upon thy name" (v. 6).*

The wicked nations came upon God's people. But God will deal with those who attack His people. God is never pleased with those who devour Jacob and lay waste His dwelling place.

Remember that in this New Testament age we should pray for the salvation of those who resist God and His people. God will deal with them but we should pray He will do so in grace.

Through the Bible in a Year: Proverbs 12; Isaiah 33–35

June 29

Read Psalms 79:8-13 and 80
Devotional Reading: Psalm 79:8-13

Prayer and Our Promise to Praise

Today we consider the psalmist's prayer and his promise in Psalm 79. Yesterday we noted the fact that God allowed the heathen to act as His agents in judgment upon Israel because of the sins of Israel. But the Bible teaches, even though God must judge the sins of His people, He does not forsake His people. Through Jeremiah God explained His judgment of His people: *"Fear thou not, O Jacob my servant, saith the Lord: for I am with thee; for I will make a full end of all the nations whither I have driven thee: but **I will not make a full end of thee, but correct thee in measure**; yet will I not leave thee wholly unpunished"* *(Jeremiah 46:28).*

Psalm 79 shows us that the Lord will judge His own because of their sin—but He will also severely judge those who persecute and judge His people. In the psalmist's prayer beginning at verse eight, he speaks of the weakness of the Hebrew people: *"O remember not against us former iniquities."* Then he pleads the *"tender mercies"* of God—not just mercy, but tender mercies. May we always remember that the hand that deals discipline on His people is the hand of a loving, tender God.

Then the psalmist prays for help (v. 9). He appeals to the *"God of our salvation"* and his prayer is *"for thy name's sake."* That is the way we are to pray—in the name of the Lord Jesus Christ. We are not to come in the name of the virgin Mary, nor in the name of Buddha or Mohammed, but in His Name (John 14:13-14).

The believer should not only plead His Name, but also His nearness. He is our God, ready to revenge (v. 10).

Following this fervent prayer of the psalmist we have the promise he claimed: *"So we thy people and sheep of thy pasture will give thee thanks for ever" (v. 13).* God is near and ready to deliver. O that we might always be ready to praise Him for His goodness and grace. We can cry to Him for help—may we never fail to praise Him for the help He gives.

Through the Bible in a Year: Proverbs 13; Isaiah 36–37

June 30

Read Psalm 80

God's People Need to Turn

Psalm 80 was written at a time when Israel was realizing a great national calamity. The nation was being ravaged because God had removed His favor and protection. Very likely the psalm was written at the end of the Babylonian captivity. This psalm came to be one that was used annually. Psalm 79 was sung at the spring festival of passover. Psalm 80 was sung during the fall feast of tabernacles, the most joyous of all the annual feasts of Israel.

The psalmist begins with a plea that the Lord, the Shepherd of Israel, would hear the prayer and would save the nation. He called on the Lord to arise, feed the people, and protect the land. The Lord's blessing had been removed, and thus Israel's principal defense was gone. The Lord, the Shepherd, had led Israel like a flock. The psalmist calls on God as the One who dwells between the cherubims (v. 1). The ark of the covenant, representing God's divine presence, was placed between the cherubims in the *"Holiest of all"* (Hebrews 9:3). But now the temple has been destroyed. Therefore the psalmist is pleading to the Lord as the one who is in Heaven rising up in His strength to save the people (v. 2).

The psalmist pleaded: *"Turn us again, O God, and cause thy face to shine; and we shall be saved" (v. 3).* So strong was the burden on the heart of the psalmist that he prayed that same prayer, "Turn us again," three times in this psalm (vv. 3, 7, 19). That prayer reveals that the people had turned away from the Lord. The psalmist knew it was the people who needed to turn. For God's face to shine, the people needed to turn around and not have their back toward Him.

This is the need in the church today. We must admit that we have turned against the Lord. Oh, that we could be broken and that we would turn again toward His face.

> Turn your eyes upon Jesus,
> Look full in His wonderful face;
> And the things of earth will grow strangley dim
> In the light of His glory and grace.
> —Helen H. Lemmel

Through the Bible in a Year: Proverbs 14; Isaiah 38–40

July 1

Read Psalm 80

The Vine Planted and Attacked

In verse seven we have the second time the refrain is sung: *"Turn us again, O God of hosts, and cause thy face to shine, and we shall be saved."* The psalmist was conscious that the Israelites had turned aside unto sinful ways. They had turned from God, and now they were experiencing the bitter fruit of their departure. The Lord did not withdraw His favor first—rather Israel turned away from Him. They asked that the Lord would cause His face to shine, thus revealing that they realized their need was to be saved from their sins, not just from other nations.

We need to pray this same prayer in the United States of America. Our nation is worried about the awful AIDS epidemic and its results. They are anxious to fight the enemy but manifest little desire to turn from their sin that causes the AIDS. We need salvation from our sins much more than we need salvation from our enemies.

In verse eight the psalmist changes from picturing God as a Shepherd to picturing Him as a Husbandman. The psalmist speaks of God's planting Israel as a vine out of Egypt. Israel was planted in the land of the heathen—the land of Canaan (v. 8). The vine grew and filled the land from the Mediterranean to the Jordan River (vv. 9-11).

But as the psalmist wrote this psalm, the nation had turned away from God. The Lord had removed His protection. Because of this, Israel's hedges were broken down, and heathen armies plucked her. Along her highways there was constant moving of armies (v. 12). Then in verse thirteen he speaks of the *"boar out of the wood"* wasting her. The wild boar was an emblem of Rome. God's protection being removed, Israel came under the terrible heel of Rome. A boar is a destroyer—it does not eat just the fruit but it eats the roots and destroys the plant. Rome endeavored to destroy Israel totally. The wild beast of the field devoured Israel. No wonder the psalmist prayed: *"Return, we beseech thee, O God of hosts: look down from heaven, and behold, and visit this vine" (v. 14).* Prayers like this brought God's protection to Israel.

Through the Bible in a Year: Proverbs 15; Isaiah 41–42

July 2

Read Psalms 80:14-19 and 81
Devotional Reading: Psalm 80:14-19

God's Restoration of His Own

Yesterday we saw how the enemies were out to destroy the vine, Israel. Even the wild boar came to try to destroy the vine at the root (v. 13). Verses fourteen and fifteen give a wonderful truth. The vine was not destroyed. The psalmist asked God to *"visit this vine."* The fact that God could visit it reveals that it still had life. In verse fifteen we find it had branches, and verse fourteen implies that it still had roots. Here is a wonderful truth: That which God plants never completely fails, and it never will.

> *"Being confident of this very thing, that he which hath begun a good work in you will keep it until the day of Jesus Christ" (Philippians 1:6).*

Two blessed doctrines stand out in our minds: (1) the perpetuity of the church, and (2) the eternal security of the believers. Both doctrines hinge on the sufficiency of Jesus Christ.

In these last verses of Psalm 80, we find that the vine (Israel) is restored. When the Babylonian captivity ended, the vine was replanted in the promised land, took root, and grew again. Israel, back in the land as a national entity, is proof that God cares for His own. Someone asked Mark Twain what proof he had that the Bible is the true Word of God. He answered: "The Jew." God has miraculously spared the Jews over the years.

God's hand is on the man of His *"right hand"* (v. 17). He calls this man the *"son of man,"* thus referring to Christ (v. 17). The word translated *"son"* in verse seventeen is the same word translated *"branch"* in verse fifteen. Christ is the Son; He is the Branch (Jeremiah 23:5; Zechariah 3:8); and He is the Vine (John 15:1).

Verse eighteen states that when God's people return to Him, they will be restored and will call on Him. The need is for God's people to turn, to repent, to confess sin, and to watch God do the work of restoration.

Through the Bible in a Year: Proverbs 16; Isaiah 43–44

July 3

Read Psalms 81–82
Family Reading: Psalm 81

Worshiping Him Who Saved Us

Psalm 81 is a song of worship. It was sung at one of the annual feasts—probably the feast of trumpets. Verse three commands that they blow the trumpets. The first three verses invite all of Israel to worship. This worship involved singing. Thus he exhorts in verse one, *"Sing aloud unto God our strength: make a joyful noise unto the God of Jacob."* This is also what we New Testament believers are to do: *"[B]e filled with the Spirit; Speaking to yourselves in psalms and hymns and spiritual songs, singing and making melody in your heart to the Lord"* (Ephesians 5:18-19).

Worship is personal. We are not worshiping some abstract intelligence or some kind of impersonal influence. We worship a Divine Person, God—*"the God of Jacob" (v. 1)*. Note that in verses one and four, He is called *"the God of Jacob."* This would mean that He is the God of grace, for the life of Jacob is a story of a sinner saved by grace. Verses four and five reveal that God's people were to sing praise, always to the Lord, for this was a *"statute,"* a *"law,"* an *"ordinance,"* and a *"testimony"* (vv.4-5). Thank God, today we worship not because of a law but out of a heart that is willing to worship because we are thankful for His grace and mercy.

The basis of their worship was praise for what the Lord had done for them. Verse six tells us that the Lord had delivered His people from the slavery of Egypt. God removed the Israelites from carrying the brick and mortar in Egypt. On the shoulders the slaves carried a rod on which hung the pot (a basket) that carried the brick. They were delivered from such bondage. The people of God could call on the Lord in trouble and He was ready to deliver them (v. 7). He answered them with thunder. God is able to deliver a nation without armies and military might.

Today, we who are saved know that we have been miraculously delivered from the bondage of sin. May we also glorify the Lord with heart-felt singing and worship.

Through the Bible in a Year: Proverbs 17; Isaiah 45–47

July 4

Read Psalms 81–82
Family Reading: Psalm 81

Missed Opportunities

Today, our devotion will center on Psalm 81:8-16. God pleads with His people to hearken unto Him.

Verse eight—*"Hear, O my people . . . O Israel, if thou wilt hearken unto me."*

Verse thirteen—*"Oh that my people had hearkened unto me . . . ."*

Note that verse eleven begins with the word *"but."* God wanted something different for Israel, and they would have received it if they had just heeded the Lord. But verse eleven reads, *"But my people would not hearken to my voice."* They would not listen. Nothing bothers a preacher more than to note that some people are not listening to his message. To fail to listen to the preacher is bad enough—but to fail to listen to God is much worse.

Because of Israel's failure to listen to God, she missed important opportunities for herself as well as others. Verse twelve is one of the saddest verses in all of the Bible. God gave them up to their own lusts. What a tragedy! God lets them go the way of their lusts to their own destruction. Missed opportunities! They could have been different but they were given up to their own lusts. Someone has well said, "The saddest word of tongue or pen are the words, 'It might have been.'"

Had they heeded God, idolatry would have been gone (v. 9). Had they heeded God, they would have been conquerors instead of the conquered (v. 14). Had they heeded God, they would have been much better off. Verse sixteen says God would *"have fed them also with the finest of the wheat: and with honey out of the rock should I have satisfied thee."*

Bible Truth for Today: *"Seek ye first the kingdom of God and His righteousness and all these things shall be added unto you."*

—Matthew 6:33

Through the Bible in a Year: Proverbs 18; Isaiah 48–50

July 5

Read Psalms 82–83
Devotional Reading: Psalm 82

Judgment of the Judges

Psalm 82 presents the judgment of the judges. These judges have an important position in this life. So important is that position that they were given the title of gods (v. 6). Jesus quoted from this psalm in John 10:34: *"Is it not written in your law, I said, Ye are gods?"* The Lord Jesus asked this question after Jews had tried to stone Him because He claimed to be God. He used this Old Testament truth about judges to show that He was not blaspheming. It was not blasphemy for Him to call Himself God when the Jews regularly referred to their judges as gods.

Judges are God's appointed representatives of Himself. Most of them fail to recognize their appointment literally came from God. Instead they are ignorant—*"They know not"* (v. 5). Moreover they are willful in their ignorance—*"neither will they understand"* (v. 5). Why are they willfully ignorant? Verse five again has the answer: *"They walk on in darkness."* And then let us note the result of their walking in darkness: *"[A]ll the foundations of the earth are out of course"* (v. 5). Social order is thrown into chaos by unrighteous judges. Today this is tragically true in our beloved United States of America.

This psalm calls the judges to realize they will face judgment by God. Verse one—*"God standeth in the congregation of the mighty; he judgeth among the gods."* The titles *"mighty"* and *"gods"* in verse one refer to the judges in Israel. Those titles are ascribed to judges in verse six. This does not mean they are literally God—for verse seven states that they will die like all men. But they can be certain they will be judged by God.

The question God asks these judges is *"how long will ye judge unjustly . . . ?"* (v. 2). They accepted bribes and played favoritism. God instructs the judges what they are to do: *"Defend the poor and fatherless: do justice to the afflicted and needy. Deliver the poor and needy"* (vv. 3-4). This has always been God's demand upon the judges. Be sure—God will set everything right. In the opening and closing of the psalm, He makes it clear: the judges shall be judged by God.

Through the Bible in a Year: Proverbs 19; Isaiah 51–53

July 6

Read Psalm 83
Devotional Reading: Psalm 83:1-5

The Enemies of God Attack His People

Psalm 83 is a very important psalm for believers to study. It reveals the faces of Israel and delineates their motives and goals. It is a psalm in which we should meditate in this church age. Satan lined up nations to stand against God's Old Testament people. And today he is working at motivating enemies against the church of God.

The psalmist begins with a prayer that God will act in dealing with the enemies. He asks that the Lord not keep silence (v. 1). We must remember that the fact that the heavens seem silent does not mean that God is non-existent or unconcerned. No—God may *seem* to be silent; but He is very capable of delivering His people, and He is also very interested in their welfare.

We should note that those who are the enemies of God in verses one and two are also the enemies of His people. In fact, they attack God by attacking His people. God recognizes that He and His people are one. In Acts 9:4 God spoke to Saul, who was persecuting the Christians; yet God asked, *"Saul, why persecutest thou me?"* An attack on God's people is considered an attack on God Himself. I think of the years that the Russian believers were severely persecuted, but now we see God has intervened and turned Russia completely around. Believers are not being persecuted, and the gospel is being received and honored.

The enemies of the Lord join together and take crafty counsel (v. 3). They did so against Israel. Their purpose was to *"cut them* [Israel] *off from being a nation" (v. 4)*. The verse further states that they wanted the name of Israel to be forgotten. They joined together in their severe hatred of the people of God. Satan was behind this; he was the one who energized these people in their determination to destroy Israel. Satan is doing the same thing against the church in this age. He would have enemies to pervert every Christian assembly into a *"synagogue of Satan"* (Revelation 2:9). May Psalm 83 alert us to our enemy and encourage us to be faithful to the Lord.

Through the Bible in a Year: Proverbs 20; Isaiah 54–56

July 7

Read Psalm 83
Devotional Reading: Psalm 83:5-12

God's People Surrounded with Enemies

Yesterday we noted the attitude of the enemies of God's people. We saw that in their enmity against His people they were really enemies of God. Today we are going to see who these enemies are and how the psalmist prayed for these enemies.

In verse five we read that all these enemies have come *"with one consent"* and *"are confederate"* against God. It is interesting to consider who these enemies are who had joined together *"with one consent."* Someone has said, "A common cause collects curious companions." These nations that often battled among themselves now came together against Israel—they all agreed that they hated Israel.

In the Persian Gulf War of 1991 we saw the "Coalition" that President Bush put together. Arabs were fighting against fellow Arab, Saddam Hussein. Muslims were fighting fellow Muslims. But everyone seemed to agree that if Israel attacked Saddam Hussein, the coalition could dissolve and all Muslims would stand together against Israel.

"Curious companions" are found in the New Testament. The Pharisees and Sadducees could not get along at all until Jesus came. Then they united against Him. Herod and Pilate were enemies, but of the trial of Jesus we read, *"And the same day Pilate and Herod were made friends together" (Luke 23:12).*

These enemies surrounded Israel. To the northeast were the Hagarenes and Ishmaelites, all descendants of Hagar; to the east, Moab and Ammon, descendants of Esau who hated Jacob; to the southwest, Amalek, also a descendant of Esau; on the west, the Philistines; in the northwest, Gebal and Tyre. Apparently the descendants of Lot were the leaders in the coalition, and they were joined with a super power in the north, Assyria (v. 8). As then, Israel today is a beleaguered state surrounded by enemies. Today these enemies would love to drive Israel out of the land. Keep your eyes on the Middle East. It is the place where prophecy is being fulfilled today. Also keep your eye on the church, for the enemies are joined together against God's people.

Through the Bible in a Year: Proverbs 21; Isaiah 57–59

July 8

Read Psalms 83–84
Family Reading: Psalm 83:9-18 and Psalm 84

A Godly Purpose for Praying That God Will Judge

In the last two days we have seen in Psalm 83 how the enemies of God's people are really the enemies of God. And we have noted that the enemies like to surround the people of God. In verses nine through eighteen we find the psalmist's prayer concerning these enemies.

He goes back in the history of Israel and asks that God's power be manifested again. He speaks of Sisera, the captain of the Canaanite army, who, the record states, was defeated by Barak; but actually he was defeated by two women, Deborah and Jael (vv. 9-10). His defeat came because God miraculously intervened (Judges 4–5). He also speaks of Gideon's defeating his enemies with only 300 dedicated men (vv. 9-11). The victory came because God miraculously intervened with a dream in the mind of one of the Midianite soldiers. God did it. He can do it again!

In verses thirteen through seventeen, the psalmist prays that God will intervene in this case. This was probably in the days of Jehoshaphat when the Moabites and Ammonites led a coalition against Israel. God again miraculously intervened (II Chronicles 20). The psalmist prayed that these enemies might be like *"a wheel"* (v. 13). The word *"wheel"* here is speaking of the spherical head of the wild artichoke. In the fall it becomes dry and light, and it breaks off. The wind drives it as it does our tumbleweeds in the western United States. The psalmist wanted to see these enemies driven like this. He wanted to see them burned on the hillside and hit by tempest and storm (vv. 14-15).

Someone may say, "That is terrible to pray like that." But, friend, please note the purpose of such praying. Verse sixteen states that the psalmist prayed this so *"that they may seek thy name, O Lord."* Verse eighteen reveals he prayed in this manner so *"that men may know that thou, whose name alone is JEHOVAH, art the Most High over all the earth."* He prayed for the defeat of the enemies so they could be convicted and come to know the Lord.

Through the Bible in a Year: Proverbs 22; Isaiah 60–63

July 9

Read Psalms 84–85
Family Reading: Psalm 84

Longing for Home Where Jesus Is

There are different ways to look at Psalm 84. In this devotion we are going to take it as a psalm to sing when we are finally home in Heaven with the Lord. The psalmist begins with these words: *"How amiable are thy tabernacles, O Lord of hosts!" (v. 1).* He was saying "How dear, how precious, is your dwelling place, O Lord." What makes a home so dear to us? Is it the well-decorated and appointed rooms? Is it the lovely furnishings? No—it is not. There are many people living in expensive fancy houses, and yet they are miserable. Things cannot satisfy. That which makes a house a home are those who live there.

In this case the Lord is in this home. In Psalm 84, there are twenty-three references to the Lord—different titles and different pronouns—but twenty-three in all. It is our Lord that really makes Heaven to be Heaven.

The psalmist states he longs for the courts of the Lord (v. 2). We can tell how spiritual we are by checking up on the wants we have. In Revelation 21 we find what makes God's sanctuary so special. It is true there will be no tears, no death, no sorrow, no crying, and no pain (Revelation 21:4). It is wonderful to think about. But that which makes Heaven Heaven is the presence of the Lord.

Revelation 21:23—*"and the Lamb is the light thereof . . . ."*

Revelation 22:4—*"And they shall see his face . . . ."*

The believer lives, trusting the Lord who is interested in the sparrow and the swallow. The psalmist could look up at the pillars of the temple and see birds' nests there. Surely God will care for His people also. So the psalmist could say, *"Blessed are they that dwell in thy house" (v. 4).* And then he could add, *"Blessed is the man whose strength is in thee; in whose heart are the ways of them" (v. 5).* The way is in his heart. Amen! Jesus said: *"I am the way . . . ."* He dwells in our hearts by the presence of the Holy Spirit. We have One to guide us all the way—none other than the Lord Himself.

Through the Bible in a Year: Proverbs 23; Isaiah 64–66

July 10

Read Psalms 84–85
Family Reading: Psalm 84

Lord, I'm Coming Home

In Psalm 84 the pilgrim believer is on his way from earth to his home in Heaven. He passes through the valley of Baca (v. 6). The word *"Baca"* signifies a balsam tree, one that grows in a very dry valley. The believer will go through some dry valleys. But God moves in with blessing—changing the valley of dryness to a well where rain fills the pools (v. 6).

"They go from strength to strength, every one of them in Zion appeareth before God" (v. 7). Those who trust the Lord move through the trials by God's strength, and continue on till they are home, appearing before God. Though they weep in the valley of verse six, they walk on the mountain in verse seven. Where is a real source of this strength? It is in prayer according to verse eight: *"O Lord God of hosts, hear my prayer: give ear, O God of Jacob."* So important is this truth concerning prayer that the psalmist wrote, *"Selah"—think of that!"*

How do we get home with the Lord? We arrive in Heaven because God looks upon the face of His anointed—the Lord Jesus Christ. We arrive in Heaven on His merit—not our own. What a privilege to be at home in Heaven. *"A day in thy courts is better than a thousand" (v. 10)*. The psalmist continues: *"I had rather be a doorkeeper in the house of my God than to dwell in the tents of wickedness" (v. 10)*.

Finally, when we are home, we will realize the blessing of God's presence and His purpose all the way through. We will know He was our strength, *"For the Lord God is a sun and shield" (v. 11)*. He has given grace, and following that will be glory. He withholds no good thing. In fact, the valleys of Baca will then be realized to have been good. In Heaven we will see the other side of the tapestry and we will exclaim: "It has all been good."

The psalm ends with praise: *"[B]lessed is the man that trusteth in thee" (v. 12)*.

Through the Bible in a Year: Proverbs 24; Jeremiah 1–2

July 11

Read Psalms 85–86
Family Reading: Psalm 85

A Plea for Revival

Psalm 85 is a song of pleading for revival. Verse six expresses the plea of the entire psalm: *"Wilt thou not revive us again: that thy people may rejoice in thee?"*

There seems to be a conflict in the psalm. Verses one through three praise God for what He has done. Verses four through seven reveal the sad condition of the nation. Some writers suggest these verses represent two different times; i.e., a time of gladness and later a time of gloom. I believe, however, the psalmist was writing about the nation shortly after the return from Babylon. They were back in their homeland—that surely was a blessing to bring forth praise. But they found their homeland in a sad state. The walls of Jerusalem were broken down. The temple was in ruins. The seventy-year period had given time for trees and undergrowth to grow up through the debris. They were glad for restoration but sad about the present condition.

Rotherham suggests that this psalm was sung with two choirs—one choir singing the verses of praise (vv. 1-3) and the second choir singing the verses of sadness (vv. 4-7). Many Jews, upon returning from Babylon, entered into the dispersion by not staying in the homeland but scattering to other nations where life would be easier. The first choir were the optimists of praise; the second revealed the pessimism of reality. The difference in these two sections is that verses one through three state of God, *"thou hast,"* six times; verses four through seven ask of God, *"Wilt thou,"* three times, and pray to God, *"Show us thy mercy"* (v. 7).

When we bask in the blessings of God, it is easy to forget His mercies and blessings. Our hearts can grow cold and indifferent so easily. A number of these Jews returned from captivity and they realized they must face hard work, hard times, and hostile neighbors. Lacking the godly pioneer spirit of Ezra and Nehemiah, they left their homeland and settled in Egypt, Persia, Rome, Greece, and Spain. There needed to be revival for which the psalmist prayed in verse six.

Through the Bible in a Year: Proverbs 25; Jeremiah 3–4

July 12

Read Psalms 85:6-13 and 86
Family Reading: Psalm 85:6-13 and 86:1-7; Devotional Reading: Psalm 85:6-13

Wilt Thou Not Revive Us Again?

Yesterday we noted the special prayer for revival in verse six: *"Wilt thou not revive us again: that thy people may rejoice in thee?"* A number of Israelites had returned from the Babylonian captivity and sincerely longed to see God's people revived so they would work at restoration of the homeland. But for many, their time in the homeland was temporary. They had tasted of the world and its ways in Babylon, and so they scattered to other lands—forgetting the land where God wanted them. The psalmist was concerned that these people, having been ransomed from bondage, would *"turn again to folly" (v. 8)*.

Those who did not have a heart for the homeland correspond to those today who have had reformation but not revival. What did the homeland need? It needed people who would *"fear him; that glory may dwell in our land" (v. 9)*. The people did not fear Him but rather had let their hearts grow cold and had turned again to folly. Renewal and revival follow this very same pattern. We can have a church revival or a national revival but the seeds of lukewarmness and the danger of indifference will creep back in. Satan and the flesh work against revival. Therefore, we need to live in a constant state of seeking a fresh touch from God in revival.

What is the absolute need for revival to be realized? Verse eight has the answer: *"I will hear what God the Lord will speak . . . ."* We need to hear the Word of God and obey it. God is ready to speak. We must be ready to obey. If we obey, we will turn from folly and begin to serve the Lord.

What is the result of revival? Souls will be saved. *"[H]is salvation is nigh" (v. 9)*, and *"Mercy and truth are met together" (v. 10)*. Truth will bring constant blessing (v. 11). The Lord will meet the needs of His people. *"Yea, the Lord will give that which is good; and our land shall yield her increase" (v. 12)*. We need revival—a turning from Babylon and Egypt to the Lord and His Word. Then *"Righteousness shall go before him; and shall set us in the way of his steps" (v. 13)*.

Through the Bible in a Year: Proverbs 26; Jeremiah 5–6

July 13

Read Psalms 86–87
Family Reading: Psalm 86

Praying in Severe Trial

Psalm 86 is a blessed psalm on prayer. David realized his great need, and he cried to the Lord to have that need met. He was facing trouble (v. 7). In fact, his trouble was so great that he needed to pray for his life to be preserved (v. 2). He was facing those who hated him and he needed God's grace and help (v. 17).

This is a psalm to which all of us can relate since trials and tribulations are our common lot. Very likely David penned these words when he was being chased and persecuted by Saul or maybe by Absalom. This psalm is the prayer of an afflicted soul in a time of real persecution. Thank God—David prayed! Prayer should be our first reaction, but too often it is our last resort. LeMoyne Sharpe wrote: "Prayer is much discussed, definitely needed, but seldom practiced." Therefore, we should examine a psalm like this with the prayer the Lord gave us in Luke 11:1: *"Lord, teach us to pray."*

David begins the prayer with this appeal: *"Bow down thine ear, O Lord, hear me . . ." (v. 1).* The picture here is that of a concerned doctor bending over a feeble patient to hear and learn the need. The patient needs the doctor's help; and we surely need divine help.

The psalmist was in trouble where even his life was in danger. In verse two he pleaded for God's protection. When he said, *"I am holy" (v. 2),* he was not pleading sinless perfection, but he was saying he had been set apart by God. Believers today can claim that—you see, that is what *"holy"* means—*"set apart by God."* The psalmist reminds God of his relationship and affirms that he trusts the Lord. Under deep trial, he can say, I trust in the Lord (v. 2). May we, too, regardless of the circumstances rest, with our trust in Him.

The psalmist reveals that answered prayer brings rejoicing to the child of God (v. 3). Jesus stated in John 16:24, *"Ask, and ye shall receive, that your joy may be full."* So David stated that God would make him rejoice by hearing his prayer.

Through the Bible in a Year: Proverbs 27; Jeremiah 7–8

July 14

Read Psalms 86–87
Family Reading: Psalm 86

Praising the Lord and Trusting Him for the Answer

In this great prayer of Psalm 86, we realize the very personal relationship between the believer and His Lord. Sixteen times in this psalm, David uses different titles of God, and he uses thirty pronouns referring to God—forty-six references to God and His power in this psalm. He speaks of himself thirty-five times. In all this we see the very personal relationship a believer has with the Lord.

Prayer involves not only requests of supplication but also praise. This prayer psalm is filled with praise. Note some praises David gives to the Lord.

> v. 5—*"[T]hou . . . art good and ready to forgive . . . ."*
> v. 5—*"[T]hou art . . . plenteous in mercy . . . ."*
> v. 7—*"[T]hou wilt answer me."*
> v. 8—*"[T]here is none like unto thee, O Lord; neither are there any works like unto thy works."*
> v. 10—*"[T]hou art great, and doest wondrous things . . . ."*
> v. 15—*"But thou, O Lord, art a God full of compassion, and gracious, longsuffering, and plenteous in mercy and truth."*

David cries, *"Be merciful unto me" (v. 3).* That is a correct prayer. We must plead on the basis of His grace and mercy—not on our merit. The psalmist wanted God to hear and answer (v. 6). He was confident God would do that very thing. In verse seven he stated, *"Thou wilt answer me."* What a blessed assurance! God will answer prayer. May we believe Him for it. David said the Lord would answer him right in the midst of his trouble. Therefore David could praise the Lord that He is God alone (v. 10).

A very essential part of our lives in seeking answers to prayer is that we believe His truth and be willing to have Him lead us according to His will (v. 11). He was anxious for the Lord to teach him the Lord's way so that he could walk in it.

Through the Bible in a Year: Proverbs 28; Jeremiah 9–10

July 15

Read Psalms 86:12-17 and 87–88
Family Reading: Psalm 86:12-17 and 87; Devotional Reading: Psalm 86:12-17

A Prayer of the Lord Jesus Christ

Today we will consider Psalm 86 as a Messianic Psalm, one that presents itself as a prayer the Lord Jesus could have prayed in those times when He withdrew from the crowd and was alone with the Father.

The Lord Jesus could have said and meant it in all of its fullest meaning: *"I am holy" (v. 2).* He alone could say of Himself and know that it was absolutely true: *"I will walk in thy truth" (v. 11).* In verse sixteen the prayer reads, *"and save the son of thine handmaid."* That could certainly refer to Christ for He came *"made of a woman"* (Galatians 4:4), and He was indeed the Son of Mary, who answered Gabriel in Luke 1:38: *"And Mary said, Behold the handmaid of the Lord . . . ."*

The Lord Jesus could say, *"O God, the proud are risen against me, and the assemblies of violent men have sought after my soul . . ." (v. 14).* The chief priests, scribes, and elders stood at the foot of the cross and said, *"Let him now come down from the cross, and we will believe him"* (Matthew 27:42).

When the storm clouds rise and disaster comes, we are so prone to turn from the Lord and even accuse Him of being unfair or even cruel. But note what Jesus would have prayed: *"But thou, O Lord, art a God full of compassion, and gracious, longsuffering, and plenteous in mercy and truth" (v. 15).* May we learn to pray as He would have prayed.

The prayer ends with the words, *"Show me a token for good; that they which hate me may see it, and be ashamed . . ." (v. 17).* God did give our Lord tokens for good; i.e., the salvation of the thief on the cross, the earthquake, the darkness, etc. Without question, many of those tokens for good bore fruit as witnesses of the cross received Christ at Pentecost and in the days of the early church in Jerusalem. Saul of Tarsas resisted the Lord, but he met Jesus Christ on the way to Damascus and then became the Apostle Paul—God's greatest witness during the church age. Jesus could certainly say: "The Lord has helped and comforted me" (v. 17).

Through the Bible in a Year: Proverbs 29; Jeremiah 11–13

July 16

Read Psalms 87–88
Family Reading: Psalm 87

God's Glorious City—Jerusalem

Psalm 87 presents the greatness of the city of Jerusalem. Verse three is a key verse: *"Glorious things are spoken of thee, O city of God."* Jerusalem is an amazing city. From a worldly standpoint we would never expect her to be a great city. It has no river, commands no strategic highway, and is located on a mountain top with a huge outcropping of rocks. All its roads lead into a desert area. The world would not locate a city in such a place.

The name *"Jerusalem"* means *"city of peace."* However, its history reveals that this city has suffered more sieges and sacking destructions than any other city. Many times Jerusalem has been almost totally destroyed. Babylonia, Egypt, Assyria, Greece, Rome, Arab countries, and European nations have all entered wars over Jerusalem.

Today Jerusalem is in the hands of Jews—the Arabs are insisting that Israel give the city up to Arab nations. As I write this Mr. Jim Baker, Secretary of State for the United States, is trying to lead the Arab nations and Israel to peaceful negotiations. Israel has made it known that she may negotiate some areas of concern, but Jerusalem is not negotiable. The day will come, however, when Israel will lose control of Jerusalem when the beast assumes his reign. But then the city will be restored again when the Lamb of Revelation 5 establishes His reign.

Psalm 87 speaks of Jerusalem. Its foundation is in the holy mountains, speaking of stability, security, and strength. The idea is that her foundations are in the Lord. Verse two states that the Lord loves the gates of Zion (Jerusalem). History will record the names of men born there (vv. 4-6). The singers and musicians will be there praising the Lord. What a city! Glorious things are spoken of her in the past and will be spoken of her in the future. In verse five God states that *"the highest himself shall establish her."* Jerusalem is the city God has honored and from which the Lord Jesus shall reign. Keep your eyes on the Middle East and Jerusalem.

Through the Bible in a Year: Proverbs 30; Jeremiah 14–15

July 17

Read Psalms 88

Praying When Trials Are Heavy

Psalm 88 is a most unusual psalm. It is the saddest of all the psalms. The entire passage is filled with the trials of a troubled soul. As the psalm progresses it seems that the gloom increases. The psalm ends with the word *"darkness."* As we have noted in reading through Psalms, many psalms begin with trouble and despair, but they always end in a note of joy. Not so with this psalm—it is different than all the rest.

Psalm 88 was penned by a saved man for he cried in the first verse, *"O Lord God of my salvation . . . ."* He was a believer with serious trials and deep troubles. He had cried day and night before the Lord (v. 2). His soul was full of troubles (v. 3). It was Spurgeon who wrote, "Trouble of the soul is the soul of trouble." There are those who believe the author of this psalm was afflicted with leprosy. He certainly was without friends for the people had counted him as one who had already died (vv. 4-5). He was close to death (v. 3). He saw himself almost as a corpse on the field of battle.

The writer of this psalm was an Old Testament Hebrew. He did not have the hope that we have because we live on this side of the resurrection of Christ. It seems he did not have the blessed hope Job had when he wrote: *"I know that my Redeemer liveth, and that he shall stand at the latter day upon the earth: And though after my skin worms destroy this body, yet in my flesh shall I see God" (Job 19:25-26).*

Even still, the psalmist did have *some* hope. No matter how feeble was the flicker, he still had some light. No matter how desperate he had become, he still had God and he still had a personal relationship with God. In the midst of these deep trials, he believed God and believed in prayer (vv. 1-2). Here is a man who seems to be peering into the grave as it yawns before him. He knew his only hope was to cry unto God. May we learn that is our only hope.

Through the Bible in a Year: Proverbs 31; Jeremiah 16–17

July 18

Read Psalm 88

Our Hope is in the Lord

Today we continue in Psalm 88, the saddest psalm of the Bible. Because of his trials the psalmist saw no hope of a future for himself. He stated in verses six and seven that he was in the lowest of the pits and that God's wrath lay heavy upon him.

Verse 8—*"Thou hast put away mine acquaintance far from me; thou hast made me an abomination unto them . . . ."*

There is reason to believe that the one who penned these words was afflicted with leprosy. That disease so plagues a person that he can have no friends to comfort and help. Instead the afflicted was to be put out of the camp.

"And the leper in whom the plague is . . . shall put a covering upon his upper lip, and shall cry, Unclean, unclean . . . . [H]e shall dwell alone; without the camp shall his habitation be" (Leviticus 13:45-46).

What a hopeless life is that of a leper! He was treated as though he were dead. In verses ten through twelve the psalmist asks a series of questions. He asks questions about the dead. Will they see wonders from God? Is there a possibility they will arise? He asks whether he will ever get to see God's lovingkindness and faithfulness. With all his friends, gone he feels the only One to Whom he may go is the Lord. In Leviticus 13 and 14, the chapters that present the miraculous healing God can give from leprosy, we find the priest is mentioned 121 times. The leper had to go to him and all the work had to be done by him. So today when the leprosy of sin grips us, we must turn to our High Priest, the Lord Jesus Christ—He is our only hope.

> My hope is in the Lord
> Who gave Himself for me,
> And paid the price of all my sin
> At Calvary.
> —Norman Clayton

Through the Bible in a Year: Ecclesiastes 1; Jeremiah 18–21

July 19

Read Psalm 89:1-24

God's Faithfulness Facing Man's Ruin

Today we begin reading Psalm 89, and for seven days we will have our devotions from this longer psalm. The psalm was written by Ethan the Ezrahite. He must have been a very wise man for when God speaks of the wisdom of Solomon, he states that Solomon was so wise that he was even wiser than Ethan (I Kings 4:31).

Ethan was a singer, who along with Heman and Asaph were principal musicians in the kingdom. It appears that Ethan lived to an extended age and was able to view the breakup of the kingdom under Rehoboam. He had sung during David's reign and then during Solomon's reign. He knew the kingdom in its gloriest days. But when he wrote this psalm it is apparent that he was disturbed concerning what he saw in the future of the kingdom.

Some have called this "The Covenant Psalm." The psalmist pleads that the covenant God made with David needed to be maintained. Ethan believed that what he saw was a great national disaster. He asked God to remember His covenant, and he expected deliverance because of God's faithfulness.

I recommend you read the entire psalm and underline the word *"faithful"* or *"faithfulness."* You should find it seven times in the King James Version. Also underline the word *"mercy"* or *"mercies"* and the word *"loving-kindness."* Again in the King James Version you should find these words seven times. The words *"mercy"* and *"loving-kindness"* are the same word—usually translated in the psalms as *"loving-kindness."* As the psalmist looks over the history of Israel, he finds it to be one continuous exposition of God's lovingkindness. Faithfulness and mercy are the undergirding truths of the Davidic covenant. II Samuel 7:9-16 reveal the promises of God and the surety of their fulfillment as part of the Davidic covenant.

Through the Bible in a Year: Ecclesiastes 2; Jeremiah 22–23

July 20

Read Psalm 89:1-24

The Faithfulness of God

Yesterday we considered the truths of God's faithfulness and mercy in His covenant with David. Both "faithfulness" and "mercy" shine forth in the first two verses of this great psalm.

The singer announced that he would *"make known* [God's] *faithfulness to all generations" (v. 1).* This truth that God in His mercy has proved His faithfulness to His people is the theme that permeates this psalm. Throughout the psalm God's faithfulness is related to past performance and to future promises. Psalm 89 is a commentary on two New Testament verses:

"If we believe not, yet he abideth faithful: he cannot deny himself."
—*II Timothy 2:13*

"Faithful is he that calleth you, who also will do it."
—*I Thessalonians 5:24*

The covenant mentioned in verse three is the covenant God made with David in II Samuel 7. That covenant assures that the family, the kingdom, and the throne of David would be established forever. Though David and his kingdom are now only history, the covenant abides and is fulfilled in the Son of David, the Lord Jesus Christ. The promise to David continues in verse four where we see confirmed that the seed of David would be established and his throne would be permanent.

The psalmist begins by revealing that God's faithfulness is manifest in many ways. He is faithful—more faithful and powerful than the gods of the pagans (v. 6). In nature God reveals His faithful power as the creator—there is none like Him (v. 8) and He rules the seas (v. 9). Both the heavens and the earth are the Lord's (v. 11). He created the north and the south (v. 12). Not only nature, but history also records His faithfulness. Verse ten states that He broke Rahab (Egypt) in pieces. What a miracle took place in Egypt when the Israelites were delivered from the hand of Pharoah.

Our God is faithful—He does not fail.

Through the Bible in a Year: Ecclesiastes 3; Jeremiah 24–25

July 21

Read Psalm 89:8-33

Praise in the Midst of Chaos

Beginning at verse eight we find the psalmist praising the Lord for His greatness and His relationship with the people of Israel. The key words in verses eight through nineteen are the person personal pronouns referring to the Lord: *"Thee," "Thy," "Thou,"* and *"Thine."* I recommend you underline them and count them. The psalmist is saying that the Lord maintains a special relationship with His people. He is their Saviour, their strength, their comfort—He is all in all to them.

Circumstances were dark. In verses thirty-eight through forty-four, the psalmist gives a picture of the darkness of that age. We will examine these verses in a later devotion—but let's just note them now. It was a dark day in Israel. The throne of David was gone (v. 44) and the country seemed in chaos with the strongholds in ruin (v. 40). With this in mind, the psalmist praised the Lord for His *power.* He has a mighty arm and a right hand held high (v. 13).

Further, he praises the Lord for His *principles.* Justice and judgment are the principles on which He works (v. 14). These two, *"justice and judgment,"* are effective only as *"mercy and truth"* (v. 14) accompany them. Every principle of operation must be based on truth and must be exercised with mercy!!

We should praise Him not only for His *power* and for His *principles* but also for His *people.* *"Blessed is the **people** that know the joyful sound"* (v.15). These people will walk in the light of the Lord's countenance (v. 15); they shall be exalted in His righteousness (v. 16).

In verse eighteen the psalmist praises the Lord for His *protection.* The Lord still is the defense of the righteous. Circumstances may be bad, but He is still working—still on the throne. We can rejoice in Him.

Today, we believers have known the joyful sound. We have heard the message of good news that Jesus saves. Now it is our privilege to walk in the light of His countenance. That light shines on our pathway as we study His Word, rest in His strength, and grow in His grace.

Through the Bible in a Year: Ecclesiastes 4; Jeremiah 26–28

July 22

Read Psalm 89:19-41

God's Covenant with David

Beginning at verse twenty we read of the specific covenant God made with David. In the first four verses God had spoken of the covenant and God's faithfulness to it. God made the covenant with David, and He will keep His covenant.

Note first of all that the covenant was initiated by God. *"I have found David my servant; with my holy oil have I anointed him" (v. 20).* Then in verse twenty-one God works with *"my hand"* and *"mine arm."* Verse twenty-three—*"I will beat down his foes . . . ."* Also note the *"I wills"* in verses twenty-five through twenty-nine.

David had not been born or reared in the court of a king. God chose him from out of the people (v. 19). The psalmist anticipated that David would face enemies from within, enemies such as Absalom. Therefore, he stated, *"The enemy shall not exact him; nor the son of wickedness afflict him" (v. 22).* Also the foes that would come against him from the outside would not conquer. *"And I will beat down his foes before his face, and plague them that hate him" (v. 23).*

Then the psalmist stated that God in His mercy would be faithful to David: *"But my faithfulness and my mercy shall be with him: and in my name shall his horn be exalted" (v. 24).* David was a great man—but he was still a man. The best of men are only men at the best. So the psalmist recognized that David failed; yet God had mercy upon him. And the psalmist could reason: "If God was merciful to David, then He would be merciful to David's kingdom now.

Then the psalmist looked forward to the future. The Davidic covenant would endure—and it would be fulfilled in Jesus Christ, the Son of David. Of Him, the psalmist wrote that God stated: *"Also I will make him my firstborn, higher than the kings of the earth" (v. 27).* The psalmist had genuine confidence that the covenant of David would stand and would be fulfilled in Jesus Christ.

Through the Bible in a Year: Ecclesiastes 5; Jeremiah 29–30

July 23

Read Psalm 89:25-45

Our Lord Is Faithful!

Yesterday we closed our devotional, stating that the psalmist was prophesying that Jesus Christ would come as the Son of David and He would reign above the kings of the earth (v. 27). Carrying on with that truth today, let's note first the truths concerning Jesus Christ, God's Messiah.

Verse twenty-five tells us that His reign will encompass the whole world from the rivers to the sea. He will rule even nature, for the winds and the seas are subject to His control (Mark 4:41). Verse twenty-six takes us further by telling us that He will cry unto God as His Father. This title, *"Father,"* was a characteristic title that the Lord Jesus used of God. It was not a familiar title in the Old Testament. These verses are stating that Jesus Christ will fulfill the covenant of David.

Verse twenty-eight reveals that this Davidic covenant will be fulfilled permanently in the Lord Jesus Christ. *"My mercy will I keep for him forevermore . . . His seed also will I make to endure for ever, and his throne as the days of heaven" (vv. 28-29).*

In verses thirty through thirty-four we find the problem with which the psalmist is dealing. The covenant is sure on the basis of God's faithfulness. But what happens when children of David fail? Suppose they forsake God's law and do not walk in His judgments—or break His statutes and do not keep his commandments (vv. 30-31). The psalmist answers that God will judge them—*"Then will I visit their transgressions with the rod, and their iniquity with stripes" (v. 32).* Then God states the great truth of this psalm: *"Nevertheless my lovingkindness will I not utterly take from him, nor suffer my faithfulness to fail" (v. 33).* God promised to keep His Word with David. He would not break His covenant or change what He had spoken. He had sworn and He would not lie to David (vv. 34-35). Amen! Our God keeps His promises. We can rest on His Word and claim His faithfulness. *"He abideth faithful; he cannot deny himself" (II Timothy 2:13).* This truth about God's abiding faithful is proved repeatedly in Old Testament history. Joshua announced: *"There failed not ought at any good thing which the Lord had spoken unto the house of Israel; all came to pass" (Joshua 21:45).*

Through the Bible in a Year: Ecclesiastes 6; Jeremiah 31–32

July 24

Read Psalms 89:38-52 and 90

Things Are Not Always What They Appear to Be

Psalm 89:38 begins with the word *"But."* There is a change in thought here. The psalmist had been speaking about the covenant God made with David, but there appeared to be a problem. It looked as though God had at least suspended the covenant if He had not indeed canceled it.

Verses thirty-eight through forty-five are characterized with the words, *"Thou hast."* The psalmist was saying that it appeared God had changed. It seemed that He had turned away and had not kept His promises.

Verse 38—*"[T]hou hast cast off . . . thou hast been wroth . . . ."*

Verse 39—*"Thou hast made void the covenant of thy servant . . . ."*

And thus the psalmist continues through verse forty-five. He said God had failed David. His mistake in these verses was that he was blaming God rather than man. It was not God who had changed but rather man. The kingdom was in jeopardy because of man's sins. Whenever this psalm was written, it was done so at a time when the royal line of David was in jeopardy because of the failure of kings in that royal line. The crown appeared to have been cast to the ground (v. 39). The country's defenses were broken. Strong holds had fallen into ruin (v. 40).

In addition to all of this, Israel had become a reproach to her neighbors. The enemies of the Lord rejoiced in the seeming destruction of Israel. The nation had become like an old man whose youthful zeal was gone; and now she seemed to be covered with shame.

Nothing seemed to be going according to the covenant of God. The simplest thing to do was blame God. But we need to remember that things are not always as they seem. No matter how things appear, we must always realize that God is still at work. He has a purpose for His actions. His covenant is being fulfilled even when it appears the opposite is true. May we learn to walk by faith and trust Him.

Through the Bible in a Year: Ecclesiastes 7; Jeremiah 33–34

July 25

Read Psalms 89:46-52 and 90

Trusting the Lord in All Circumstances

Today we center our meditation on the last verses of Psalm 89. The psalmist asks *"How long, Lord? Wilt thou hide thyself for ever? Shall thy wrath burn like fire?" (v. 46).* The situation looked hopeless. But there is one thing we must remember: God works on a bigger scale than just one man's lifetime. God sees the whole picture from beginning to end. He sees far beyond just my puny existence.

The psalmist reminded the Lord of the brevity of life. He requested that the Lord remember how short his life was (v. 47). Then the psalmist asked two very important questions: *"What man is he that liveth, and shall not see death? Shall he deliver his soul from the hand of the grave?" (v. 48).* The answers were obvious—no man shall live and not die. No man is able to deliver his soul from the hand of the grave.

The psalmist was pleading that God would intervene even during his lifetime. He adds the word "Selah" to verse forty-eight meaning—"Think on that again." How brief life is! May we constantly stop to meditate on the truth of the shortness of life. As we consider how uncertain life is, we should realize we must accept Christ as Saviour. If we have been saved, our realization of the brevity of life should bring us to surrender our lives entirely to the Lordship of Jesus Christ.

> Only one life, 'Twill soon be past;
> Only what's done for Christ will last.
> —Selected

In Psalm 89 we find the psalmist has confidence even in the most trying of circumstances. We must believe in Him and believe His Word. May we *Trust Him even where we cannot Track Him.* The psalm ends with the psalmist pleading for God to intervene even though the enemies are reproaching. In their reproach of God's servants they are literally reproaching His anointed (v. 51).

Let's trust Him and praise Him regardless of the circumstances.

Through the Bible in a Year: Ecclesiastes 8; Jeremiah 35–37

Read Psalm 90

The Greatness of God and the Infirmity of Man

Psalm 90 is the oldest psalm in the Bible. Next to the Book of Job it is the oldest portion of Scripture. It was written by Moses. As we have noted before, the Book of Psalms is divided into five sections—each one corresponding to a book in the Pentateuch. Psalm 90 begins the Fourth Book of Psalms—therefore it would correspond to the Book of Numbers, the book of the wilderness wanderings. Moses was their leader. In Numbers 13 and 14 we have the tragic story of the majority of the spies coming back with a report of fear, revealing an utter lack of faith. Chapter 14 gives God's response. He told them they would die in the wilderness and never enter the promised land (Numbers 14:29-37). It was at such a time as this that Moses wrote Psalm 90.

He begins the psalm by expressing the greatness of God and the infirmity of man. In verse one Moses announces that God is interested in man. He was the dwelling place for Israel in all generations. While they were wandering in the wilderness, they murmured against God. Even then, said Moses, He was their dwelling place. The Hebrew word translated "dwelling place" carried the idea of the "family room." It was not just a house to live in but a place of good fellowship. That is what our God wants to be to us.

Verse two speaks of the unchanging stability of God. We speak of the stability of the mountains—but God existed before the mountains, for he created them. Before they were created, they did not exist, but God has always existed. He is from *"everlasting to everlasting" (v. 2)*. Mountains will be only from creation until destruction—but God is eternal.

The next verses speak of the frailty of man. Verse three states that he will be turned to destruction. The word *"destruction"* is literally "dust." God will turn us back to dust, and He will do it at His will, when He commands, *"Return, ye children of men" (v. 3)*. Moses is saying that we must trust the Lord.

Through the Bible in a Year: Ecclesiastes 9; Jeremiah 38–40

July 27

Read Psalm 90

The Frailty of Man

Beginning with verse three, Moses presents the frailty of man. Verse three reminds us of two things: (1) The *certainty of death* and (2) the *uncertainty of the time of death.* To neglect to think on these two truths would be a tragedy, the biggest mistake any person can make.

Verse four reveals that time does not exist for God; it has no relation to Him. LaMoyne Sharpe has pointed out that time is a mere island in the sea of eternity. Verse four states that a 1000 years in God's sight are but as a *"watch in the night."* The twelve hours of night were divided into four watches—each being a three hour period. Think of it! A 1000 years to God is like three hours to man.

In verses five through six, the psalmist presents three pictures illustrating the brevity of life and the frailty of man. The first picture is that of a flood carrying man away. As I write this, just this past week a fifteen year old boy was swept away by the flood waters in southern California. Before the view of millions by television, he was swept down, and for eight battering, torturous miles they tried to save him. He would grab ropes or garden hoses thrown out to save him. But he could not hold on and he was added to the list of deaths because of the flood of February, 1992. Man is like that—caught in a flood, swept into the ocean of eternity. And think of this—the water that flows is gone never to return. So is life.

The second picture is that of sleep (v. 5). The night passes and it is over. So is the life of man.

The third picture is that of grass. It grows up, flourishes, and is cut down in the evening of the same day (vv. 5-6). Human life is frail and uncertain. What a mistake to trust in our life here rather than in the Lord for eternity. Job stated it this way: *"For we are but of yesterday, and know nothing, because our days upon earth are a shadow" (Job 8:9).*

Through the Bible in a Year: Ecclesiastes 10; Jeremiah 41–43

July 28

Read Psalm 90

May We Apply Our Hearts to Wisdom

In Psalm 90, Moses speaks first of the greatness of God (vv. 1-2). He then speaks of the frailty of man (vv. 3-6). Today we will note the fact that man is a sinner and that he dwells under the sentence of death. He was writing particularly of his generation of Israelites as they wandered in the wilderness. They had listened to the unbelief of the ten spies (Numbers 13) and had murmured against Moses' leadership and against the faith of Joshua and Caleb—even to the point of desiring to stone them to death (Numbers 14:1-10). God spoke out against the congregation, sentencing all those twenty years of age and older to death in the wilderness (Numbers 14:22-30).

That generation abode under the sentence of God's wrath. Moses stated in Psalm 90:7: *"For we are consumed by thine anger, and by thy wrath are we troubled."* Moses was writing of that generation, but the fact is, he was writing of all generations. We are all sinners, and unless we accept Christ's payment for our sin, we abide under God's wrath. Our iniquities are set before the Lord; and what's more—our sins we thought were secret are very open before Him. They are *"in the light of [His] countenance" (v. 8).* Just as the days of the Israelites in the wilderness passed away in His wrath, we too will find our days passing away under God's wrath, unless we come to Christ and walk by faith in Him—the very thing those Israelites refused to do (v. 9).

The last part of verse nine is very important: *"We spend our days as a tale that is told."* Moses includes Aaron and himself with those who were not going to see the promised land. Their tale was told—they had no future except to wander in the wilderness until they joined in the huge wilderness graveyard.

Verse twelve advises us what we should allow God to teach us about our lives. *"So teach us to number our days, that we may apply our hearts unto wisdom."* Verse twelve applies to both the saved and unsaved. If you are not saved, you need to come to Christ. But remember also that Moses and Israel had been redeemed from Egypt. They would correspond to us believers today who need to yield ourselves to the Lord in faith so we can be used by Him.

Through the Bible in a Year: Ecclesiastes 11–12; Jeremiah 44–46

July 29

Read Psalms 90:12-17 and 91

May We Neither Live Nor Labor in Vain

Psalm 90:12 is a great verse for our lives—*"So teach us to number our days, that we may apply our hearts unto wisdom."*

What does it mean to number our days? Is it simply to count them? The foolish farmer of Luke 12 tried to count. He said he had much goods laid up for many days. The fact was that for him, he did not even have a tomorrow. The Lord said: *"Thou fool, this night thy soul shall be required of thee . . ." (Luke 12:20).* To number our days does not mean to count them—it means to value them in the light of eternity.

In order to put the right value on the days of our lives, we must apply our hearts unto wisdom (v. 12). It is certainly a sad fact that most people do not realize why they were placed in the world. We are here that we might bring glory to God. We should use every minute to serve and honor Him. A poet wrote:

> Improve Time in time,
> While Time doth last,
> For all Time is no time,
> When the Time is past.

And how do we apply our hearts unto wisdom? First, we do so by coming to know the Lord in a personal relationship as Saviour. Second, we must accept the Bible as our guide for life. Third, we must obey the Bible and apply its truths to our lives.

In verses thirteen through seventeen, Moses prayed a lovely prayer concerning the needs of the Israelites in the wilderness. He asked God to return with His blessings upon the people if they would apply their hearts to wisdom. In the years they had left to them, Moses said they would need to rest on the mercy of God (v. 14). In verse seventeen he requested that the beauty of the Lord would rest upon the lives of the Israelites and that God would establish the work of their hands. He repeated the request that God would establish their works. May we desire, like Moses, to apply our hearts unto wisdom, and neither live nor labor in vain.

Through the Bible in a Year: Song of Solomon 1; Jeremiah 47–48

July 30

Read Psalm 91

God, the Lord, Our Dwelling Place

Psalm 91 is one of the greatest passages in all of the Bible. It is frequently quoted and often read at funerals. There is no superscription to tell us who is the author. I believe the author was Moses and this is a companion psalm to the previous one, Psalm 90. It is good to read Deuteronomy 32 and 33 and note the similarity in language. Deuteronomy 33:27 could give an outline for Psalms 90 and 91:

The eternal God is thy refuge—Psalm 90.
Underneath are the everlasting arms—Psalm 91.

There is so much in this psalm that I wish we could spend weeks on it, but space in this book does not permit that. So in brief form we will note truths from this psalm for three days. The psalm is Christ centered, and we can see Him as the great Protector of the Godly.

First we find the *Position Of The Godly* (vv. 1-2). When I write "the Godly," I do not mean those who are just saved. This individual who is blessed dwells *"in the secret place of the Most High"* and thus will *"abide under the shadow of the Almighty" (v. 1)*. He *"dwells"* there; he "abides" there. This is the believer who really desires to live, walking with the Lord. To have another's shadow *"abide"* on me means I must be close to that person. Oh friend, remember this: *Distance from God means Danger!* Someone has said that the promises of Psalm 91 are for "The Elect out of the Elect." All believers have access to this secret place, but only those who walk closely with Him abide there.

Please note the four titles for our Lord given in verses one and two. First, *"the Most High"*—Elyon—the God who possesses everything; second, *"the Almighty"*—Shaddai—the God who is all sufficient to supply our every need; third, *"the Lord"*—Jehovah—The God Who keeps His Promise; and fourth, *"my God"*—Elohim—the God Who is all powerful.

What a God we have! What a dwelling place for every believer!

Through the Bible in a Year: Song of Solomon 2; Jeremiah 49–50

July 31

Read Psalm 91

God, the Lord, Our Protection

Yesterday we considered the first truth presented in Psalm 91: *The Position of the Godly.* Now we note *The Protection of the Godly.*

The Lord delivers us from the snares of Satan and the enemies of the godly. He also delivers us from disease and its destruction. Note that the *"fowler"* of verse three is the *"terror by night"* and the *"arrow that flieth by day"* of verse five. The enemies of the Lord work day and night to hinder and to destroy the work of God. Also, note that the *"pestilence"* of verse three is the *"pestilence that walketh in darkness"* and the *"destruction that wasteth at noon day"* in verse six. God says those who "dwell" *in the secret place of the Most High" (v. 1)* need not be afraid of the evil work of enemies and pestilences (v. 5).

Why should we not be afraid? It is because the Lord covers us with his feathers, and under his wings we shall trust (v. 4). Wings and feathers speak of the loving concern of God's protection.

John Philips wrote: "Once, not far from a mission station in the heart of Africa, a forest fire swept through the brush, leaving death and desolation in its wake. After the fierce flames had subsided, a missionary took a walk down one of the trails, looking at the havoc wrought on every hand by the fire. He noticed a nest by the side of the way. Enthroned on the nest he saw the charred remains of a mother hen. Idly he kicked the poor heap with his foot, and, to his astonishment, out from under the burned and blackened carcass, there ran some baby chicks. Motherly love had taught that hen to give her life for her brood. Interestingly enough, on one occasion, the Lord Jesus likened Himself to a hen. Like that mother hen, the Lord Jesus spreads His pinions over His own. He deliberately gave Himself to the fierce heat, the blazing wrath of God at Calvary. We, sheltering beneath His wings, find eternal refuge from the flames."

> Under His wings, under His wings,
> Who from His love can sever?
> Under His wings my soul shall abide,
> Safely abide forever.
> —William O. Cushing

Through the Bible in a Year: Song of Solomon 3; Jeremiah 51

August 1

Read Psalms 91:9-16 and 92

The Security of the Godly

Today we continue our meditations in Psalm 91. We have seen *The Position of the Godly* and *The Protection of the Godly*. Next let us consider *The Place of the Godly*. Those who love the Lord have their refuge and habitation in the Lord (v. 9). They can rest in the Lord knowing that He protects them and permits in their lives only that which is for their profit. The godly do not have "accidents." They are only "incidents." Sharpe has written: "Losses enrich him, sickness teaches him, reproach is his honor, and death is his gain." Remember Romans 8:28: *"And we know that all things work together for good to them that love God . . . ."* No evil and no plague will touch the godly except as permitted by Him.

Next we note *The Path of the Godly*. God gives His angels charge over each one in all his ways (v. 11). The angels bear up the godly so that they will not dash a foot against a stone (v. 12).

Then consider God's *Pledge to the Godly*. He promises them absolute security. The godly individual is able to tread upon the *"lion and adder" (v. 13)*—he can trample the young lion and the dragon under his feet.

David Brainerd was a missionary to the Indians. He was weary after a long day's walk and he stopped by a stream to rest for the night. Indians hid in the forest waiting to attack and kill him. According to his custom and before the eyes of these hiding enemies, Brainerd knelt in prayer. The warriors saw a large rattlesnake glide along Brainerd's body and play with its forked tongue near his head. Brainerd was so engrossed in prayer that he was oblivious to the present danger. Then, miraculously, the snake turned and slithered into the brush. The Indians said, "The Great Spirit is with him," and they went back to their camp. The next day Brainerd walked into the Indian village and the whole tribe came out to meet him as a prophet. Through the godly life and prayer of David Brainerd, God revealed the security of one who rests in the dwelling place of the Most High.

Through the Bible in a Year: Song of Solomon 4; Jeremiah 52; Lamentations 1

August 2

Read Psalms 92–93

It is Good to Praise the Lord

We do not know who wrote Psalm 92 or when it was written. It undoubtedly became part of the Temple worship, for the superscription states it was "for the sabbath day." It is a psalm of praise to God for His righteous and moral government. The center verse, verse eight, is really the theme of the psalm: *"But thou, Lord, art most high for evermore."*

The psalmist begins with these words: *"It is a good thing to give thanks unto the Lord, and to sing praises . . ." (v. 1).* How we need to learn to praise the Lord. Verse two tells us when to praise Him—at least twice a day. We should praise Him in the morning, thanking Him for His lovingkindness. In the morning we should put the day into His hands. We do not know what the day may bring forth. There could be a tragedy, or a sudden temptation, or a wonderful opportunity. We need to commit the day unto Him.

Then in the evening we must review His faithfulness. I think it is permissible to look at verse two as some do, saying the morning speaks of prosperity and blessing while the evening refers to adversity and quiet. We should praise Him regardless of our circumstances.

Praise can be enjoyable. Verse three states we should sing praise with the accompaniment of musical instruments. These all were stringed instruments, and he warned that it must be *"with a solemn sound" (v. 3).* The word *"solemn"* is the word *"Higgaion"* (Psalm 9:16) which is translated *"meditation"* (Psalm 19:14). Our praise must be accompanied by meditation. Today some churches have gone too far with the song-leader saying: "Let's give Jesus a good cheer"—and there is clapping and foot stomping. We need to enjoy our worship, but we also need it to be *"with solemn sound."*

Verses four and five tell us that the believer is cheered and encouraged by the works of God. Verse six reveals that the unsaved or carnal man is bewildered by the same works of God. Men are going the wrong direction. They need to turn to God so they can understand His greatness, His goodness, and His grace.

Through the Bible in a Year: Song of Solomon 5; Lamentations 2–3

August 3

Read Psalms 92–93

Wicked Scattered—Righteous Strong Like Palms

Psalm 92 is a psalm of praise. Verse eight expresses the theme of the whole psalm—the Lord exalted and lifted up.

Verse nine continues the idea of praise by revealing what will happen to the wicked. The enemies of the Lord shall perish and be scattered (v. 9). In verse seven we read that they *"shall be destroyed for ever."* God has announced clearly that the Lord's enemies have no future. Those who insult and ignore the Lord will not last.

We saw communism rise up in Russia and considered it to be a threat to the whole world. As it shook its fist in the face of God, it was sowing the seeds of its own destruction. As I write this in 1992, we stand in amazement over the defeat of atheistic communism in Russia and the Eastern Block countries. By mocking God, they have denied the very purpose of their existence. Philips tells the story of the little girl that reminds us of the foolishness of those who mock God. She came home from school distressed because she had lost her birth certificate required at school. She sobbed to her mother, "I have lost my excuse for being born."

The wicked will be scattered and the horn of the righteous will be exalted as the horn of the unicorn. That wild ox lifts up its horn in triumph (v. 10). You see, the believer is on the winning side of God.

Then the psalmist praises the Lord for His mercy, grace, and power in the lives of the believer (vv. 12-15). While the wicked are destroyed like grass (v. 7), the righteous flourish as the palm tree (v. 12). The palm tree grows tall and erect. It grows slowly but the growth is sure. Both the palm and the cedar grow in adverse circumstances. Believers can also grow and will bring forth fruit in old age. The testimony of the righteous will be that the Lord is upright—there is no unrighteousness in Him (v. 13). Yes, it is a good thing to give thanks unto the Lord (v. 1).

Through the Bible in a Year: Song of Solomon 6; Lamentations 4–5; Ezekiel 1

August 4

Read Psalms 93–94

His Future Righteous Reign

Psalm 93 is the first of seven psalms that present the theocratic government of God, the others being Psalms 95-100. A theocratic government is one in which the Lord rules. Israel was a theocracy, but the people rebelled in Samuel's day and said they wanted a kingdom like the rest of the world (I Samuel 8:4-6; 19-20). From that day on Israel has faced problems. But the day is coming when the world will be under a theocracy again—Jesus Christ will be king and will rule in righteousness from Jerusalem. Psalm 93 is looking forward to that day.

Verses one and two state that the Lord will reign in majesty. He has the strength to rule the world and see His righteous rule established. What will be the result of His rule? The answer is that there will be stability. *"[T]he world also is stablished, that it cannot be moved" (v. 1).* How different that will be from what we see today!! There seems to be instability everywhere. As I write this early in 1992 we see instability in America with much talk of financial collapse; instability in the Middle East where they cannot agree on a peace treaty; instability in Russia with talk of unseating the new government of Boris Yeltsin; instability in Haiti; etc. When the Lord Jesus will reign in the future, He will do so from a throne established of old and as One Who is from everlasting (v. 2). What stability!

The floods being lifted up in verse three picture the nations of the earth endeavoring to rise up against the Lord Jesus Christ and His rule. They will come from the East and from the North against Him. But the Lord on high is mightier than these (v. 4). He will be the victor coming out of Megiddo with mighty triumph.

What will make His reign such a great one? It will be a righteous and moral reign because it will be built upon the sure testimonies of God's Word (v. 5). Holiness will be the feature of the house of our king, the Lord Jesus Christ (v. 5). Yes, He will have a reign of righteousness.

Through the Bible in a Year: Song of Solomon 7; Ezekiel 2–5

August 5

Read Psalm 94

The Vengeance of God

Psalm 94 is another psalm in which the psalmist asks questions about why the wicked prosper and the righteous suffer. This is a psalm where the psalmist requests the vengeance of God to actively deal with the wicked.

To understand the psalm we need to understand *"vengeance."* There is a big difference between *revenge* and *vengeance*. Revenge is that which a man will seek against another when he thinks he has been wronged. The Bible never justifies revenge but always condemns it. Vengeance, on the other hand, belongs only to God (v. 1). (Note also Deuteronomy 32:35 and Romans 12:19.) God's vengeance is the upholding of His justice and righteousness and is essential to the well-being of mankind. Vengeance in the hands of man degenerates into revenge, which is an act of passion rather than judgment, and stems from a desire to get even rather than exercise God's righteous judgment. The psalmist is not asking God to act with anger and hate, but he is asking God to punish the workers of iniquity after His own character. He asked God to *"render a reward to the proud" (v. 2).*

In verses three and four we find the psalmist asking three times, *"How long?"* Apparently the psalmist had suffered at the hands of the wicked. He notes that *might* seems to ally itself with the wrong and seems not to mete out justice. History bares him out. Joseph was a slave in a dungeon while his brothers lived peacefully. Pharaoh was on the throne standing against God while the Israelites were under the taskmasters. Saul was safe in his palace while David was hiding in caves. But then the scene changes. Joseph came into power, and his brothers fell trembling before him. Israel was set free and Pharoah's host was drowned in the Red Sea. Saul was defeated and committed suicide while David was enthroned.

How long?—Until God in His timing brings vengeance and until God in His wisdom vindicates the righteous. God knows what He is doing. We need to trust Him and leave all matters with Him.

Through the Bible in a Year: Song of Solomon 8; Ezekiel 6–8

August 6

Read Psalm 94

God Sees, Hears, Knows, and Will Judge

The wicked in their terrible acts against the righteous (vv. 5-6) make a very serious mistake when they say, *"The Lord shall not see, neither shall the God of Jacob regard it" (v. 7)*. They may not even say these words of blasphemy, but by their actions they manifest that they feel that way. They think there is no God to whom they must answer some day, or they think God will not look upon what they are doing.

In verse eight the psalmist has changed from speaking to God to speaking to these wicked persecutors. Because they think God will not see or regard their actions, the psalmist calls them what they are: *"brutish"* and "fools" (v. 8). They are fools and act like brutes because they leave God out of their thinking. Paul put it this way: *"Professing themselves to be wise, they became fools" (Romans 1:22)*.

Then the psalmist asks them some questions: "Would not the one who made our ears be able to hear Himself" (v. 9)? "Would not the one who formed our eyes be able to see Himself" (v. 9)? "Would not God who teaches men the knowledge they need be able to have knowledge Himself" (v. 10)? You see, the psalmist was saying that if someone does not believe the Lord is able to hear and see and know, he is really saying he does not believe in God at all.

Then in verse eleven the psalmist states that the Lord does know. He has been speaking to those who had persecuted the righteous, answering their foolish statements and objections. Now, in verse eleven he ends this section by stating that those who act as though God does not hear, or see, or correct, or know are really thinking empty, vain thoughts. They are sadly, dangerously, mistaken.

In verse twelve the psalmist returns again to speaking to the Lord: *"Blessed is the man whom thou chastenest, O Lord, and teachest him out of thy law."* This blessed man will have rest from adversity, for the Lord will not forsake His people (vv. 13-14). Further, the Lord will judge the wicked, the fools who lived as though there were no God. God will dig a pit for these wicked, and judgment will come. God is on His throne and sees the end from the beginning.

Through the Bible in a Year: Ezekiel 9–12

August 7

Read Psalms 94:15-23 and 95

The Righteous Delivered—The Wicked Doomed

Today our devotional will center on Psalm 94:15-23. In verse fourteen, the psalmist has the assurance that God will take care of His own. In verse fifteen, he manifests a further assurance: one day justice will rule and injustice will be put down.

We tend to get discouraged today when it seems the anti-God, anti-Bible, anti-Right forces prevail. Wrong seems to be on the throne and Right seems to be on the scaffold. But the day is coming when *"judgment shall return unto righteousness: and all the upright in heart shall follow it" (v. 15).*

The psalmist was undergoing severe testing at the time when he penned the words of Psalm 94. No one would help him (v. 16). He had to rely only on the Lord (v. 17). In a wonderful way he experienced the Lord's presence in holding him up when his foot slipped (v. 18). The psalmist had a trouble similar to those you and I have. His thoughts seemed to wander—there was a *"multitude of thoughts"* crowding his mind (v. 19). I find that to be a real problem in my life. I let my mind wander even when I should be intense in prayer. Even then the psalmist found the Lord met his need and became his delight (v. 19).

In verse twenty the psalmist asked the Lord whether the throne of iniquity would have fellowship with the Lord. It seemed to him that those in high places had swung to a position of iniquity. He asked: *"Shall the throne of iniquity have fellowship with thee . . . ?"* He stated that those in seats of government *"gather themselves together against the soul of the righteous, and condemn the innocent blood" (v. 21).* There is a constant battle between righteousness and iniquity. The oppressors keep on fighting, right up until the bitter end.

But the psalmist saw the deliverance of the righteous (v. 22) and the doom of the wicked (v. 23). The righteous shall be delivered and the wicked shall be destroyed. So this psalm which began with perplexity ends with peace. Faith lives for the present in the light of what will result in the future.

Through the Bible in a Year: Ezekiel 13–15 and 16:1-34

August 8

Read Psalms 95–96
Devotional Reading: Psalm 95

Come, Let Us Worship

Psalm 95 presents two different thoughts which are almost contradictory to each other. The first truth is given in verses one through seven. Here we are invited to praise God. Then in the middle of verse seven we find an abrupt change where the psalmist turns from *praising* the Lord to a warning against *provoking* the Lord.

The psalm itself does not give us the author of the quotation of Psalm 95:7b and 8. We know it is directly from God through the psalmist, for Hebrews 3:7-8 quotes the passage and ascribes it to *"the Holy Ghost."*

The invitation is, *"[L]et us sing unto the Lord: let us make a joyful noise . . . Let us come before his presence with thanksgiving . . ." (vv. 1-2).* We must worship Him with song and a joyful noise. We are to do this by proclaiming Him to be the Rock of our salvation (v. 1). They had been in Babylon, but now they had been delivered. God had proved Himself to be the Rock of their salvation.

> Oh, safe to the Rock that is higher than I,
> My soul in its conflicts and sorrows would fly;
> So sinful, so weary, Thine, Thine would I be:
> Thou blest Rock of Ages, I'm hiding in Thee.
> —William O. Cushing

Why should we come to Him? *"[T]he Lord is a great God and a great King above all gods" (v. 3).* What a great God we have and what a blessing to surrender all to Him!! He is mighty. *"In his hand are the deep places of the earth" (v. 4).* The very foundations of the earth have been laid by Him, and they are under His control. More than that, He is the strength of the hills. All the earth belongs to Him. *"The sea is his and he made it" (v. 5)*—all 200 million square miles of it! The dry land was formed by His hands. He is our great God. We must learn to praise Him.

May we accept the invitation to bow down and kneel before the Lord our maker (v. 6). *"O come, let us sing unto the Lord . . ." (v. 1).* *"O come, let us worship and bow down . . ." (v. 6).*

Through the Bible in a Year: Ezekiel 16:35-63 and 17–18

Read Psalms 95–96
Devotional Reading: Psalm 95

Don't Grieve God with Unbelief

Today we come to the second part of Psalm 95. We read of the *"provocation"* in verse eight. In the first part the theme is praising God; in the second, the theme is provoking God. We go from worship to warning, from exultation to examination, from the goodness of God to the severity of God. (*See* Romans 11:22.) The exhortation of verses seven and eight is given twice in the book of Hebrews (Hebrew 3:7-11 and 4:7). Therefore we realize this passage is written for us today.

The first part of Psalm 95 (verses 1-7a) looks forward to the future. We see what will take place during His millennial reign. From verse 7b on to the end of the psalm, the writer calls on Israel to remember its history. He states that history should teach us something. The psalmist realized full well that there was always a danger of history repeating itself. Someone has well said, "The only lesson we learn from history is that we seem to learn nothing from history." The psalmist wanted the Israelites to learn from history. He said, *"Today if ye will hear his voice"* *(v. 8)*. The writer of Hebrews quoted this for us today; therefore, this passage is for all believers in all ages.

The warning the psalmist gave was that we should not harden our hearts. Oh, the danger of allowing unbelief and disobedience to produce a hardening of heart. You cannot soften your heart, but you can harden it by repeated disobedience to His Word. When should we do something about this? *TODAY!* Remember, He who promises pardon **when** we repent has not promised preservation **until** we repent.

In verse eight the Hebrew word translated *"provocation"* is *"meribah,"* and the word translated *"temptation"* is *"massah."* Exodus 17:1-7 reveals that those two words spoke of the unbelief of the people. It was their unbelief that caused them to wander in the wilderness for forty years (v. 10) and to die in the wilderness, not entering into God's rest (v. 11). The speaker changes from the psalmist saying *"his voice" (v. 7)* to God saying *"Me," "My,"* and *"I"* in verses nine through eleven. God is pleading for believers not to grieve Him with unbelief. May we not allow history to repeat itself in our lives.

Through the Bible in a Year: Ezekiel 19–21

August 10

Read Psalms 96–97
Devotional Reading: Psalm 96

A Missionary Hymn

We have no trouble deciding who wrote this psalm and where it was first sung. I Chronicles 16 tells of the festival David led when the Ark of God was brought from the house of Obed-Edom to Jerusalem. David delivered a psalm to them that day. I Chronicles 16:7-22 are almost exactly the words recorded in Psalm 105:1-15. I Chronicles 16:23-33 is almost identical to Psalm 96.

This is a great missionary psalm. When I was a pastor, I often used this as a passage to read in opening a Missions Conference. It speaks of the whole world. The words *"gentiles," "nations,"* and *"people"* appear seven times. The words *"earth"* and *"world"* appear four times. Eleven times in thirteen verses the psalmist embraces the whole world. Therefore it is a missionary psalm and it is a millennial psalm. Today we should be carrying out The Great Commission to reach the world, winning them to Christ and teaching them to love the Lord. In the Millennium they will all *"go up from year to year to worship the King, the Lord of hosts . . ." (Zechariah 14:16).*

The psalmist invites all the earth to sing and bless the Lord (vv. 1-2). God has always been interested in the whole world. He wants *"all the earth" (v. 1)* to sing and to *"show forth His salvation from day to day" (v. 2).* The whole world should say, *"[T]he Lord is great, and greatly to be praised: He is to be feared above all gods" (v. 4).* The world should be warned that the gods of the nations are but idols. Jehovah, the LORD of Psalm 96, *"made the heavens" (v. 5)*—something the idols could never do!

If we had no other verses in the Bible, verses two and three should be enough to compel us to be missionary minded. It is our duty to go to pagan lands and declare His glory among the heathen (v. 3). May we not be content to sit in our pews and sing our songs when millions lie in darkness under the shadow of death. May we meditate in and sing the message of Psalm 96.

Through the Bible in a Year: Ezekiel 22–23

August 11

Read Psalms 96–97
Devotional Reading: Psalm 96

Sing! Give! Let!

Yesterday we noted the three invitations in the first two verses to *"Sing."* Now we come to verses seven and eight where we are commanded to *"Give."* We have said this could be called a missionary song. The key to missions is that we give. Missionaries give their lives to go. Those of us who stay behind in the homeland need to give of our substance so they can go. The greatest missionary, our Lord Jesus Christ, manifested His grace in that *"though he was rich . . . he became poor, that* [we] *through his poverty might be rich" (II Corinthians 8:9).* God revealed the spirit we should have in that He *"so loved the world, that he gave his only begotten Son . . ." (John 3:16).*

What should we give? First, we must give our **Praise in Worship**: *"Give unto the Lord the glory due into his name . . ." (v. 8).* Second, we give of our **Personal Wealth**: *"[B]ring an offering, and come into his courts" (v. 8).* Third, we give our **Practical Witness**: *"O worship the Lord in the beauty of holiness . . ." (v. 9).* God wants our praise. The world needs our practical witness of a holy life. And we need to give of our personal wealth. God does not need our gifts—but we need to give. The greatest gift we can give is to give our lives to His service.

We have another set of multiple commands in verses eleven and twelve:

> *"Let the heavens rejoice, and let the earth be glad; let the sea roar, and the fullness thereof. Let the field be joyful, an all that is therein . . . ."*

These four *"lets"* are looking forward to the future reign of our Lord Jesus Christ. They call for everything about planet earth to lift up voices in song praising God. He is coming to judge the world with righteousness and truth (v. 13). Let the whole earth rejoice. May we rejoice and be faithful in giving our lives in His work.

Through the Bible in a Year: Ezekiel 24–26

August 12

Read Psalms 97–98
Devotional Reading: Psalm 97

Rejoicing in His Reign

The first three words of Psalm 97, *"The Lord reigneth,"* are the theme words for the entire psalm. This psalm is looking forward to the day when the Lord will set up His millennial reign.

The first result of His reign follows those three theme words: *"[L]et the earth rejoice" (v. 1).* Amen! When the Lord reigns there will be rejoicing. Satan is now *"the god of this world" (II Corinthians 4:4).* The theme for Satan's reign is not rejoicing but slavery. He has the world confused, drugged by pleasure and fear, and enslaved to sin and self. Other reigns have produced oppression, injustice, terror, and death. But when our Prince of Peace comes to reign, perfect peace and rejoicing will be the result.

"Clouds and darkness are round about him" (v. 2). God dwells in the hidden place, for, in His glory, He must be veiled or we finite beings would be consumed. *"It is the glory of God to conceal a thing: but the honor of kings is to search out a matter" (Proverbs 25:2).* His reign will be not only in the hidden place but also in the holy place: *"righteousness and judgment are the habitation of his throne" (v. 2).*

There will be rejoicing when He reigns, and there will also be division. Verses three through five state His enemies will be destroyed and the obstacles to His program will melt like wax. He will reign and His reign will permeate every part of life. Today He longs to reign in each individual life. When He reigns supreme, the hills of problems melt like wax.

We have seen worldly reigns come and go. Hitler thought he would rule the world, but World War II solved that. However, though the western allies won the war they lost the peace. The Soviet Union was entrenched after World War II, and they violently oppressed the people. Now we have seen the U.S.S.R. and its satellites broken down—but still there is no peace. When the Lord comes there will be peace for *"The heavens declare his righteousness . . ." (v. 6).* He will handle easily the intercontinental ballistic weapons, for He is God. *"Even so, come, Lord Jesus" (Revelation 22:20).*

Through the Bible in a Year: Ezekiel 27–29

August 13

Read Psalms 97–98
Devotional Reading: Psalm 97

Hate Evil—So He Can Reign Supreme

Yesterday we noted from Psalm 97:1-6 that His reign will be one from the hidden place and from the holy place. He continues this theme of holiness in verses seven through twelve.

There will be those who endeavor to dethrone the Lord and who will set up their idols. In that day, when He reigns, He states this truth: *"Confounded be all they that serve graven images, that boast themselves of idols . . ." (v. 7).* The idolators will be judged and idolatry will be removed. Today we have idol worship in every corner of the globe. Isaiah wrote that those who worship idols are *"vanity"* and they have no *"profit"* from such worship (Isaiah 44:9). In fact Isaiah states that idolators *"feedeth on ashes" (Isaiah 44:20).* Sharpe has written: "A man who worships an image is but the image of a man—he must have lost his senses. He who boasts of an idol makes an idle boast." Idols and idol worship will have no place whatever in the righteous reign of the Lord Jesus Christ. The idol worshipers will be confounded. *"For thou, Lord, art high above all the earth: thou art exalted far above all gods" (v. 9).*

Verses ten through twelve give a clear revelation that the reign of our Lord Jesus will be a righteous one. *"Ye that love the Lord, hate evil: he preserveth the soul of his saints . . ." (v. 10).*

That will be true of His future millennial reign. It will also be true today when He reigns in any individual life. When the Lord is sovereign, there will be a hatred of sin. If we have been born again and have a genuine love for the Lord, we will hate evil. That hatred should not only deal with sin in society but also with sin in our own lives. Too often we are ready to censure others, and we fail to deal with personal sins in our lives. When we genuinely hate evil, we can claim the promises of His preservation in verse ten and rejoice and give thanks according to verses eleven and twelve. May we genuinely hate evil and thus exalt Him.

Through the Bible in a Year: Ezekiel 30–32

August 14

Read Psalms 99–101
Devotional Reading: Psalm 98

The New Song of Salvation

Psalm 98 is another invitation to sing a new song. We had the previous invitation in Psalm 96. Israel was to sing a new song. The "old song" they all sang was the song of Moses (Exodus 15). That was a song of redemption from Egyptian bondage. This *"new song"* of Psalms 96 and 98 is the song of salvation through the work of our Lord Himself (Psalm 98:1-2).

It is interesting to compare Luke 1:46-55 with Psalm 98. It would appear that Mary, this godly young Jewish maiden, had been meditating in Psalm 98 when she sang her song known as "The Magnificat." She was rejoicing in the knowledge that the Lord Jesus was to be born, who would show strength with His arm (Psalm 98:1 and Luke 1:51) and thus bring salvation (Luke 1:47 and Psalm 98:2).

Psalm 98 is definitely a song of rejoicing in the salvation provided in Jesus Christ. What do we read about the *"new song"*? *"And they sung a new song, saying, Thou art worthy to take the book, and to open the seals thereof: for thou wast slain and hast redeemed us to God by thy blood . . . Worthy is the Lamb that was slain . . ." (Revelation 5:9, 12).*

Psalm 98 is that new song. It praises the Lord for what He has accomplished: *"His right hand, and his holy arm, hath gotten him the victory" (v. 1).*

"The Lord hath made known his salvation" (v. 2) and then He has openly showed it to the heathen (v. 2). His salvation is based on His mercy. This truth is to be proclaimed to all the world (v. 3). Because of His salvation we should realize that the world of nature is rejoicing (vv. 5-8). But we must remember, He is not only the *Saviour* of the world but also the *Judge* of the world. He will come *"to judge the earth"* and His judgment will be one of righteousness (v. 9). The Lord has paid the price to save us. He will come back to rule and judge us with absolute equity.

Through the Bible in a Year: Ezekiel 33–35

August 15

Read Psalms 99–101
Devotional Reading: Psalm 99

The Lord Reigneth for He Is Holy

Psalm 99 is another one of these coronation psalms exalting the Lord Jesus Christ as the King who will reign. The fact is He does reign even now. Three of these psalms begin with the words, *"The Lord reigneth"* (Psalms 93, 97, and 99). Psalm 99 emphasizes that we must exalt Him who is our king.

Verse 5—*"Exalt ye the Lord our God . . . ."*

Verse 9—*"Exalt the Lord our God . . . ."*

Why should we exalt Him? The answer given in verses five and nine is that He is holy. Verse one mentions the cherubims and agrees with what we read of these creatures in Revelation 4:8 where these living creatures worship the Lord with these words: *"Holy, holy, holy, Lord God Almighty, which was, and is, and is to come."*

"Holy, holy, holy"—that is the way Psalm 99 presents Him. His name is holy (v. 3); *"he is holy" (v. 5);* and *"The Lord our God is holy" (v. 9).*

Therefore we see the theme of the psalm is to praise Him (v. 3) and to exalt Him (vv. 5, 9) because of His holiness. Where should we worship? Verse five states we should *"worship at his footstool,"* speaking of kneeling or bowing down in humility. Verse nine commands us to *"worship at his holy hill,"* thus to look up and exalt Him.

In verse eight, the psalmist speaks of three great men: Moses, Aaron, and Samuel. These three men interceded with God for the people. Since our Lord is the reigning King, men knew that *"he is high above all people" (v. 2).* But men are sinners and they did not worship Him as the Holy One with the *"great and terrible name" (v. 3).* These three men interceded with God for the people, and they received answers from God to their prayers (v. 6). But even these great men were still sinners needing forgiveness (v. 8). God forgave them because of His grace, but He did not excuse their sin. He is the same God today—*"Holy, Holy, Holy."* We must exalt Him.

Through the Bible in a Year: Ezekiel 36–38

August 16

Read Psalms 100–101 and 102:1-7
Devotional Reading: Psalm 100

A Day Coming With Universal Worship of Our Lord

Psalm 100 concludes the coronation psalms—Psalms 93, 95-100. This psalm definitely anticipates the coming reign of Jesus Christ.

We can view this psalm as being fulfilled in Jerusalem when Jesus is recognized as King-Priest of the world. Please note that the gates are flung open to all mankind (vv. 1-4). What a glorious day that will be! It will be easy to obey the command, *"Make a joyful noise unto the Lord"* *(v. 1)*. Our lives will be so changed that we will gladly enter into joyful song. It will be thrilling to see all lands *"Serve the Lord with gladness* [and] *come before his presence with singing" (v. 2)*.

The psalmist reminds us that when the world worships the Lord Jesus that worship must be intelligent. Verse three tells us: *"Know ye that the LORD He is God . . . ."* The world must recognize that Jesus Christ, the LORD Jehovah of the Old Testament is God. Further they will accept the truth of God's creation for *"it is he that hath made us and not we ourselves . . ." (v. 3)*. The theory of evolution will be a matter of history; and in that day it will no longer have followers.

Some men live as though they made themselves. Some even refer to themselves as "self-made men." But each one should see himself as Paul saw himself, *"But by the grace of God I am what I am . . ." (I Corinthians 15:10)*.

Verse three continues with the fact that we belong to the Lord: *"We are his people, and the sheep of his pasture."* He owns us, and He owns the pasture by which we are nourished.

What should we do today? We should come into His presence with thanksgiving and praise (v. 4). Then the psalm ends in verse five with three wonderful and blessed truths: (1) The Lord is good—that is an **essential premise**; (2) His mercy is everlasting—that is an **eternal promise**; and (3) His truth endureth to all generations—that is an **enduring praise**. We must be thankful that our LORD is not fickle or changeable. *"Jesus Christ the same yesterday, and today, and for ever"* *—Hebrews 13:8*.

Through the Bible in a Year: Ezekiel 39–40

August 17

Read Psalms 101 and 102:1-14
Devotional Reading: Psalm 101

A King's Resolutions—Part 1

Psalm 101 presents to us the resolutions of King David. He desired a righteous reign; therefore, we have the record of these resolutions he made in order that he might have that righteous reign. Nine times he states, *"I will";* six times he uses the word *"shall";* and once he says, *"I hate."* That makes a total of sixteen times he made a positive resolve of what he would do.

This psalm would be a good one to read at the beginning of a new year when people are thinking of resolutions. There is nothing wrong with making resolutions for our lives as long as we do not take the whole matter lightly with no apparent desire to keep the resolutions. Remember, Bible men made resolutions. Abraham said he had promised God that he would not take even a thread from the king of Sodom (Genesis 14:22-23). Jacob resolved to make an altar at Bethel (Genesis 35:3). Joseph's life proves he had determined he would not allow sin to come in. Joshua said, *"[A]s for me and my house, we will serve the Lord" (Joshua 24:15).* And Daniel purposed in his heart not to defile himself (Daniel 1:8). Psalm 101 presents David's resolves.

First, David made resolutions concerning his **personal conduct**. He begins by stating *"I will sing of mercy and judgment . . ." (v. 1).* That means he would sing with blessings or trials. No matter what came his way, David was going to rejoice. Paul put it this way: *"In everything, give thanks . . ." (I Thessalonians 5:18).* David vowed he would behave himself wisely and would be right in his actions at home (v. 2). Further, he stated he would set no wicked thing before him (v. 3).

Second, David made resolutions concerning his **private company**. He would not allow a froward heart —a wilfully obstinate person—to keep him company (v. 4). Neither would he know a wicked person (v. 4). The word *"wicked"* is the same word that would mean "pornography" today. He was not going to allow that wicked sin in his life. Moreover, he vowed not to keep company with those who engaged in slander (v. 5). These are good resolutions for all of us to make. Tomorrow we will look at more of David's resolutions.

Through the Bible in a Year: Ezekiel 41–43

August 18

Read Psalms 101 and 102:1-14
Devotional Reading: Psalm 101

A King's Resolutions — Part 2

Yesterday we considered the resolutions of King David. Generally I have written only one devotional on any psalm with only eight verses; however, the truths in Psalm 101 are so vital for today that I decided to write two devotionals on Psalm 101.

Psalm 101 is the very heart of the Christian life. We must be born again by faith in our Lord Jesus Christ. Following that, our lives should manifest a difference. We are to *"repent and turn to God, and do works meet for repentance"* (Acts 26:20). We are to turn *"to God from idols to serve the living and true God (1 Thessalonians 1:9).* Our lives after salvation must have rules of conduct. David outlined these for us in Psalm 101.

We had noted yesterday that there were resolutions concerning his *personal conduct*. Then we noted resolutions about his *private company*. One of these was that David would not tolerate slander (v. 5). The slanderer harms three people: himself, his listener, and the one his is slandering. Someone has said, "He that steals my purse steals trash; but he that steals from my good name robs me of that which will not enrich him and makes me poor indeed." Another person David said he would not allow in his personal company was the one with a proud heart (v. 5). The word translated *"proud"* here is the word *"rechab"* which means *"broad."* David desired to be careful of "broadminded people"—so broad they have no convictions.

Then third, David made resolutions about *public convictions* (vv. 6-8). His reign was not going to be one of trying to please men; rather he wanted his reign to please God. He would honor faithfulness in the land (v. 6). Further, he wanted men in positions of trust in the government who walked *"in a perfect way" (v. 6).* The word *"perfect"* in verse six and in verse two means "blameless." Those in high office should live so that no one could fasten blame on them. David also said he would not tolerate lying in his officers (v. 7). Amen! Suppose we had a governmental leader who followed in David's train today—What a difference our nation would experience!

Through the Bible in a Year: Ezekiel 44–46

August 19

Read Psalm 102

The Heavy Burden of the Psalmist

The inscription for Psalm 102 informs us of the subject of the psalm. It was written at a time when the psalmist was overwhelmed with deep affliction. The tone is that of a king burdened for his nation. Without question this is a Messianic Psalm, for Hebrews 1:10-12 quotes Psalm 102:25-27, applying the passage to our Lord Jesus Christ. Therefore, as we read the psalm we should seek to see Christ in it.

We do not know who wrote the psalm. It was probably written during the Babylonian exile when Jerusalem was in ruins. In verse sixteen the psalmist indicates Jerusalem needed to be rebuilt. Without a doubt it was penned in a time of great national disaster and distress. It is more a burden for the nation than for the psalmist personally. Note the word *"people"* in verses eighteen and twenty-two and the mention of *"Zion"* and *"Jerusalem"* in verses thirteen, sixteen, and twenty-one.

The psalmist was burdened for the nation—he carried a heavy burden. He asked God, *"Hear my prayer . . . let my cry come unto thee. Hide not . . . incline thine ear . . . answer me . . ." (vv. 1-2).* His distress is emphasized in verses three through five. *"[M]y days are consumed like smoke . . ." (v. 3)*—a figure of speech revealing how his life seemed to have been wasted away. *"[M]y bones are burned as a hearth" (v. 3)*—a high fever seems to have almost incapacitated him. His heart was withered like grass (v. 4), so severely that his appetite was gone. What a burden! It had affected him physically.

He felt the loneliness of it. He was *"like a pelican* [in] *the wilderness . . . like an owl of the desert . . . as a sparrow alone upon the housetop" (vv. 6-7).* He was totally out of his environment. A pelican belongs in the water, not the wilderness; an owl belongs in the forest, not the desert; and a sparrow is only alone when it has lost its mate. The psalmist carried the weight of this burden in sickness and loneliness. He was burdened for his nation.

Through the Bible in a Year: Ezekiel 47–48; Daniel 1

August 20

Read Psalm 102

Consolation Amidst the Gloom

Again today we look at Psalm 102 and feel the burden the psalmist has for his nation. First we saw the *psalmist's complaint.* Yesterday we noted that he was *distressed in his body* (vv. 3-5), and he was *desolate in his soul* (vv. 6-7). Today we note a third part of his prayer, in which he revealed he was *derided by men* (v. 8). Men reproached him all day long.

If this was written at the time of the Babylonian captivity we could use Daniel as an example of the scorn and derision men heaped upon any one who stood for God. The enemies had the kings come up with wicked decrees that threw three of Daniel's fellow Jews into the fiery furnace and that had Daniel himself thrown into the den of lions. In fact, there are some who believe that Daniel was the author of Psalm 102. These enemies made fun of the psalmist—their words apparently cut like a razor. He had inward sorrow as they inflicted on him outward reproach.

The psalmist's prayer also revealed that he was *disciplined by God.* His food was ashes and his drink was mingled with weeping (v. 9). He would appear to be lifted up by the Lord only to feel cast down (v. 10). His days were declining.

Next we see the *psalmist's consolation.* He took his consolation in the absolute security of the Lord—*"But thou, O Lord, shalt endure for-ever . . ." (v. 12).* The Lord will be remembered for ever by all genera-tions. No one can topple a throne that has its foundations in eternity. The psalmist was also encouraged by the strengthening of the Lord—God will arise and have mercy upon Zion (v. 13). God has settled the matter of time. He knows when He will favor His people.

Further, there was the secret desire of the servants of the Lord—they could look at the rubble of the stones in Jerusalem and take pleasure, for they knew what God could do (v. 14). Herein is the difference between a man of vision and a man of the world. The man of the world only sees the stones as rubble, whereas the man of vision sees the stones as a testi-mony of what God had done and rests on the fact that God can do it again. The psalmist was one who trusted God though the enemies encir-cled him.

Through the Bible in a Year: Daniel 2–3

August 21

Read Psalms 102:16-28 and 103:1-7
Devotional Reading: Psalm 102:16-28

A Glorious Future

In Psalm 102 we consider the future prospect God has for His people and the whole world. First we find that the psalmist assumes Zion (Jerusalem) will be rebuilt. He states it as a fact well known: *"When the Lord shall build up Zion, he shall appear in his glory" (v. 16).* Certainly God is stating here that Jerusalem will be rebuilt following the destruction wrought upon it by Nebuchadnezzar. But it goes far beyond that time to the future when Christ's millennial kingdom will come. Verse eighteen reads: *"This shall be written for the generation to come: and the people which shall be created shall praise the Lord."* That will be the future day when the name of the Lord will be declared in Zion (v. 21). The people of various nations will be gathered together—all the kingdoms to serve the Lord (v. 22). We can certainly look forward to that glorious day.

But before that day can come there will be the great tribulation when many will be destitute (v. 17). So serious will be their plight that they will groan as prisoners that they have been sentenced to death (v. 20). The Israelites underwent serious persecution when Nebuchadnezzar took them captive. Difficult as these experiences were, they will seem as nothing when compared with that which will be experienced in the great tribulation.

What do we learn of our blessed Lord and Saviour here? We learn that He is the compassionate One. He regards the prayer of the destitute; in fact, He will not despise their prayer at all—He will hear and listen to their cry (v. 17). He does take note of their groanings with a burden to loose them from their appointment unto death (v. 20).

In the Babylonian captivity we do not find a fulfillment of verse twenty-two—the peoples and the kingdoms of the worlds were not gathered together. The psalm is prophetic, looking into the future. We can rejoice in the knowledge that we have their hope for the future today. *"Even so, come, Lord Jesus" (Revelation 22:20).* May we look forward to that glorious day.

Through the Bible in a Year: Daniel 4–5

August 22

Read Psalms 102:22-28 and 103
Devotional Reading: Psalm 102:22-28

Our Eternal and Faithful God

Today we come to the last portion of Psalm 102. Certainly this is speaking of our Lord Jesus Christ. In our devotional for August 19, we mentioned that Psalm 102:25-27 is quoted in Hebrews 1:10-12 and is used to describe our Lord Jesus Christ. In Psalm 102, the writer has expressed his concern and burden for Israel. But now at the end, he expressed his confidence in the Lord. In verse twenty-three he revealed his consciousness of his own weakness and the brevity of his life: *"He weakened my strength in the way: he shortened my days."* Then he contrasts the shortness of his life with the eternity of God: *"[T]hy years are throughout all generations" (v. 24).* The psalmist was probably a leader in Israel—maybe a king or a prophet. He realized his life would be short, but he knew the nation was in the hands of the eternal God. Today, presidents and kings are often concerned about what place they will have in history. This psalmist was not worried about what value history would place on his work. Rather he rejoiced that history is really *HIS Story* and that government is ultimately in the hands of Him who watches human generations come and go.

Verses twenty-five through twenty-seven, verses that are quoted in the New Testament and applied to the Lord Jesus Christ, reveal that He is *"The Prince of Peace" (Isaiah 9:6)* and *"King of Kings, and LORD of Lords" (Revelation 19:16).* He laid the foundation of the earth; His hands made Heaven. But these places He created shall perish and become old as a garment (vv. 25-26). Though creation changes, He changes. *"But thou art the same, and thy years shall have no end" (v. 27).*

Verse twenty-eight sums the whole matter up by stating that God is trustworthy and that those who know Him will be used of God. He will keep His promises to His own. The future of Israel does not depend on a Joshua, nor an Ezra, nor a Nehemiah, nor a Daniel. The future of Israel is in the hands of our omnipotent God who is creator in the past, eternal in all time and space, and faithful to His promises. All will be fulfilled because God will keep His Word.

Through the Bible in a Year: Daniel 6–8

August 23

Read Psalm 103

Let's Praise the Lord

Almost trembling I come to write about Psalm 103. What a great portion of Scripture it is! Scroggie wrote of this psalm, "It expresses emotions of the heart in every hour when God becomes wonderfully real to us." Spurgeon said, "It is one of those all-comprehending Scriptures which is a Bible in itself, and it might alone almost suffice for the hymn-book of the church." Philips called Psalm 103, "David's Hallelujah Chorus."

I recommend you take the time to read through the psalm again and mark the title *"LORD"* when it appears, and the pronouns that refer to the the Lord—*"His," "Who," "He,"* and *"Him."* You will find *"Lord"* used eleven times and the pronouns used thirty-five times— a total of forty-six references to the Lord in this psalm.

This is a psalm of praise. Philips suggests: "Any time we have trouble praising the Lord we should turn to this psalm, get down before the Lord, and recite it back to Him. It is a paean of perfect praise." The psalm opens and closes with the words *"Bless the Lord."* How should I bless Him?—with *"my soul"* and with *"all that is within me" (v. 1).* I must bless the Lord with everything I have.

Please note that we should not forget *"**all** his benefits" (v. 2).* It would be impossible for us to remember **all** His benefits—but we should remember *some* of them. Unfortunately, there are those who appear to have forgotten **all** His benefits.

The psalmist lists some of the great benefits we receive in verses three through five. He forgives all our iniquities (v. 3). He heals *"thy diseases" (v. 3).* (It is important to note the word *"thy"* with *"diseases."* The *"thy"* refers back to the one addressed in verse two: *"O my soul."* He promised to heal all *soul* diseases—not all *body* diseases. Diseases of the soul are real: fear, guilt, lust, doubt, quiet, pride, anger, hate, jealousy, etc.). He redeems us from the destruction of Hell (v. 4). He crowns us with lovingkindness and tender mercies (v. 4). He satisfies (v. 5). And He renews our youth (v. 6). What wonderful blessings. Remember that those whom the Lord blesses should bless the Lord.

Through the Bible in a Year: Daniel 9–11

238

August 24

Read Psalm 103

The Song of the Soul Set Free

Yesterday we noted that this is a great psalm of praise. The basis for praise is God's mercy and grace. Verse eight tells us *"The Lord is merciful and gracious . . . ."* Oh, may we thank God for His mercy and grace!! Note that the verse states the Lord is *"plenteous in mercy"* but He is *"slow to anger."* He will chide but He will not *"keep His anger for ever"* (v. 9).

In verse ten, David tells us of a blessing in which we should always rejoice: *"He hath not dealt with us after our sins; nor rewarded us according to our iniquities."* Amen! What a blessing—we do not receive what we deserve. This is the song of a soul set free! If we trust His grace and mercy we do not get what we deserve—Hell—and we do get what we do not deserve—Heaven.

Then David tries to measure the mercy of God, but he concludes it is unmeasurable. Verse eleven states that His mercy is as high above the earth as the heavens. That is the vertical measure. It goes on into infinity. It is a distance no man can measure. Then David states: *"As far as the east is from the west, so far has he removed our transgressions from us"* (v. 12). When we go west, we keep going west and there is no time when we begin to go east unless we turn around. The psalmist did not say, "As far as the north is from the south," for if you go north far enough and keep on going you will start going south at the North Pole. Our sins have been removed as far as east is from west. There is no meeting place.

Then David measures mercy according to time. His mercy is not for a month or a year or a century or a millennium. It extends from everlasting to everlasting (v. 17). The Lord touched on that when He told Peter he should forgive seventy times seven, but that can be counted—490. How wonderful it is that the mercy of our God cannot be measured by numbers or by time. It is from everlasting to everlasting. We need to praise Him—we who are believers rest in His grace with our sins forgiven and forgotten, forever!!

Through the Bible in a Year: Daniel 12; Hosea 1–4

August 25

Read Psalm 103

Bless the Lord, All His Dominion

David reveals the expanse of God's mercy; and with it, he also reveals the frailty of man. The Lord knows the material of which we are made—dust (v. 14). How seldom do men stop to ponder that truth. We think we are great and important, but all God used to create men was the dust of the earth. And when we lay this body down, it goes back to dust. How weak and frail we really are.

The picture David gives us is that of a father looking at his infant children. They can do nothing without the parents' help. *"Like as a father pitieth his children, so the Lord pitieth them that fear him" (v. 13).* The Lord sees us in our weakness and manifests compassion on us. He is ready and anxious to meet every need in our lives. But so often man thinks he is strong and able to handle every situation. Jesus said, *"[W]ithout me ye can do nothing" (John 15:5).* May that truth be deeply imbedded in our minds.

The psalmist speaks not only of the frailty of man but also of the brevity of his life. *"As for man, his days are as grass . . ." (v. 15).* The wind passes over it and it is gone (v. 16)! So is man. In contrast to this brevity of life, David shows us that God's mercy is from everlasting to everlasting (v. 17). His righteousness extends to children's children (v. 17)—in other words from generation to generation.

Then David closes this psalm by speaking of the greatness of the Lord. He has His throne in Heaven and His kingdom rules over all (v. 19). There is none to compare with Him. He then lists those who should bless the Lord. They are the angels who do His commandments and hearken to His Word (vv. 19-20). Then in verse twenty-two David calls on all of God's creation in all of His dominion (Heaven and Earth) to exalt the Lord. And he ends the psalm the way he opened it in verse one by calling on his own soul to bless the Lord. It can be one continual song of praise because it ends just as it began. *"Bless the Lord, O my soul."* May we continually bless the Lord.

Through the Bible in a Year: Hosea 5–10

August 26

Read Psalm 104

Exalting the God of Creation

We will spend five days in meditating on Psalm 104. It is a great psalm presenting the facts of nature and creation in a poetic form. It is one of the most important chapters in the Bible presenting the origins and early history of the world. It begins and ends with the same words and same thought as Psalm 103: *"Bless the Lord, O my soul."* It is undoubtedly a companion psalm to the previous one; therefore, we would believe it has the same author, David. Believe me, I feel totally inadequate at trying to give you what God is saying in this psalm. Scroggie wrote of this psalm: "One might as well try to analyze a sunset, as a poem like this."

The psalmist began the psalm by breaking out into an excited exclamation of praise: *"O Lord my God, thou art very great; thou art clothed with honor and majesty" (v. 1).* With that he introduces the Lord, the Creator, and His creation. The first thing that happened in this universe was the entrance of God into it: *"Who coverest thyself with light as with a garment" (v. 2).* His first act of creation was the light (Genesis 1:3). With that light He clothed Himself. Paul stated that God *"only hath immortality, dwelling in the light which no man can approach unto . . ." (I Timothy 6:16).* Light is related to the electric impulses that operate the world. God is clothed in light—in fact *"God is light" (I John 1:5).*

Verse three speaks of God's chambers. We can understand from this verse that God does have an actual dwelling place. He laid beams upon which His chambers were built. All of this is surrounded by waters. God's presence does exist in a specific location in the universe He created. The Lord Jesus ascended and sat down at the right hand of the Father. There is a Heaven where God, the Father, and God, the Son, dwell today.

Then we read of specific acts of creation. As we go through Psalm 104, may we see Him in all of His power and glory manifested in creation.

Through the Bible in a Year: Hosea 11–14; Joel 1

August 27

Read Psalm 104
Family Reading: Psalm 104:6-27

The Universal Flood
And the Earth Following the Flood

Beginning at verse seven the psalmist continues to deal with creation and the primeval ages by speaking of the universal flood. In creation God called the earth out of the waters; in the universal flood God plunged the earth under the waters. The word *"coverest"* appears in verse two where it speaks of God's arraying Himself in light. The word *"coverest"* appears again in verse six when we read of God covering the earth with water. This word *"coverest"* comes from two different Hebrew words. The word translated *"coverest"* in verse six means *"hiding."* The first use means to array so that glory can be seen—the second means to hide or cover the shame that came from sin.

"[T]he waters stood above the mountains" (v. 6). That means the flood was universal with the whole earth covered. At the time of the flood there were violent natural phenomena that brought the mountains and valleys into existence. *"They go up by the mountains; they go down by the valleys unto the place which thou hast founded for them" (v. 8).* Dr. Henry Morris in his book, *Sampling the Psalms,* has written: "The eruption of the 'fountains of the great deep' and the pouring of huge torrents of rain on the earth from the 'windows of heaven' (Genesis 7:11) had left great empty caverns in the earth's crust and piled tremendous beds of sediments in all the antediluvian seas leaving the crust in a state of complex stress. Eventually, great faults and earth movements began to develop."

Verse nine refers to the fact that after the flood the Lord promised that he would never again judge the world with a universal flood (Genesis 9:11). In the next verses the psalmist presents God's provision for the earth and its occupants following the flood. He provides water so that all can have their thirst quenched (vv. 10-11). He will give the fowls a habitation in the trees that are watered by the springs (v. 12). And He waters the earth from the heavens so that every need may be met (v. 13). Our Lord is interested in and concerned for all of His creation.

Through the Bible in a Year: Joel 2–3; Amos 1–2

August 28

Read Psalm 104
Family Reading: Psalm 104:14-35

Our Great God Who Provides Every Need

The psalmist continues to glorify God in His creation as he looks at the earth following the flood. After the flood the earth was watered with the rains from Heaven. Verse thirteen states that God waters the hills from His chambers, and the earth is satisfied with these rains. God causes *"the grass to grow for the cattle, and herb for the service of man . . ."* *(v. 14).* God meets the needs of man so that man may *"bring forth food out of the earth" (v. 14).* Man receives the wine that makes heart glad, the oil that gives him health to make his face shine, and the food that gives him strength (v. 15).

Then the psalmist lifts his eyes from the hills of rolling grass to the forest lands: *"The trees of the Lord are full of sap; the cedars of Lebanon, which he hath planted" (v. 16).* It is a beautiful sight to visit Israel and see the forests that have sprung up over there. The Jewish government has led the people to plant millions of trees. The areas that were desolate areas of barren rocks have now become flourishing forests. For years I joined thousands of other tourists in planting some trees in Palestine to help these forests spring forth. Now Israel is again beginning to look as it did when the psalmist wrote this song.

The psalmist continues by noting the birds have nests in the hills covered by forests. Even the stork can find a home among the fir trees. Then he speaks of the cragged rocks in the high hills making a refuge for some creatures (v. 18). Those rocky outcroppings would be of no value for the dwellings of men. But they do have their purpose appointed by God.

And then he goes further and speaks of the moon and the sun. These two luminaries are faithful. The sun continues to know *"his going down" (v. 19).* The sun is on schedule—a schedule set by God. The same is true of the moon. What a great God we have to provide every need!

Through the Bible in a Year: Amos 3–7

August 29

Read Psalms 104:20-35 and 105:1-6
Family Reading: Psalm 104:20-35

Praising God for His Creation

As the psalmist discusses creation he mentions the fact that when darkness falls the beasts of the forest creep forth (v. 20). He says that God makes the darkness and He has a purpose in so doing. The beasts of the forest rest much of the day but they come forth as darkness comes. One of the beasts that does his prowling at night is the lion. He is out during the night seeking his prey. He goes about roaring seeking meat that God has permitted him to have. When the sun arises the lions return to their dens to lie down. They are beasts that work at night. And, of course, their stalking and their roaring is a picture of Satan, who goes about as a roaring lion seeking whom he may devour (I Peter 5:8).

Man is different. The lions work at night, but man is made to work in the daytime: *"Man goeth forth unto his work and to his labor until evening" (v. 23).* The difference between man and the animal world is found in the fact that man chooses to work. His working is proof of his superiority to the creatures which do not toil or spin.

The psalmist is praising the Lord. He cries out in verse twenty-four: *"O Lord, how manifold are thy works! In wisdom thou hast made them all: the earth is full of thy riches."* In these verses the psalmist blasts the theory of evolution. God has made all the works in the world. He is the Creator. Everything has come from His hand. He did it in His wisdom. His creation is perfect. Evolution claims that life on earth is the result of a random working of chance. "Not so!" says the psalmist. God has made it all and His wisdom is manifested in it all. The earth is full of God's riches (v. 24). The *"great and wide sea" (v. 25)* is filled with innumerable beings. The psalmist must have stood on the shore of the Mediterranean Sea and watched the ships set sail. He glorified God, who had made the earth and the sea. What a great God we have! May we join with the psalmist in praising Him.

Through the Bible in a Year: Amos 8–9; Obadiah; Jonah 1–4

August 30

Read Psalms 104:26-35 and 105:1-15
Devotional Reading: Psalm 104:26-35

Praise Him for His Sustaining of the Earth

Yesterday we noted that the psalmist praised the Lord for His creation. Today we will see how God in His wisdom has provided for the earth. Yesterday we stopped with the psalmist looking out across the Mediterranean Sea. He noted that there are huge creatures in the sea, one which he called *"leviathan"* which the psalmist said God had made to play in the sea. The seamen returning from their trips must have told the writer of these huge creatures, to be feared much more than even the crocodiles of the Nile. Yet these large, dangerous creatures must wait on the Lord to supply their meat (vv. 27-28).

These large creatures, along with the innumerable creeping things (v. 25), all die and return to dust (v. 29). As they lived, whatever sustained their life was that which was given them by God. They were created by God, and when they die they help to renew the face of the earth!! All ecologists need to read verse thirty: *"and thou renewest the face of the earth."* The Lord has made the earth a self-cleaning, self-renewing entity. God is continually at work. Of course man needs to recognize the danger of pollution—but many ecologically minded people have failed to realize that God is continually renewing the earth and its atmosphere. You see—*"The glory of the Lord shall endure forever: the Lord shall rejoice in his works" (v. 31).*

God knows what He is doing. He will keep the world. He does not need man's help. The eruption of a volcano helps to renew the atmosphere. The forest fire in Yellowstone Park has proved to be a blessing and not a catastrophe. God is in charge! God is at work!

Therefore, what should our attitude be? We need to praise God. The psalmist said he would sing unto the Lord as long as he lived (v. 33). And then he made the great announcement: *"My meditation of him shall be sweet; I will be glad in the Lord" (v. 34).* We must meditate on His greatness and on His love. The psalmist ends this great song encompassing God's creative and sustaining works. May we delight in His creation and praise Him as we look at all of nature.

Through the Bible in a Year: Micah 1–7

August 31

Read Psalm 105
Devotional Reading: Psalm 105:1-23

Rejoice—Return—Remember

Psalm 105 is another psalm of praise to the Lord. It opens with, *"O give thanks unto the Lord . . ."* and closes with *"Praise ye the Lord."* Psalms 103 and 104 fit together as a pair. Now we come to Psalm 105 and find that it fits very closely with Psalm 106. Professor Moulton calls Psalm 105 a National Hymn of the Promised Land and Psalm 106 a National Hymn of the Captivity. Both psalms are about God and His dealing with Israel. Here is the major difference: Psalm 105 tells how God treated Israel and Psalm 106 tells of the *people's disgrace.* These two psalms join with Psalm 78 as the three historical songs in the book of Psalms. God used singing to instruct the people.

This psalm opens with a three-fold call. It begins with a **Call to Rejoice**. *"O give thanks unto the Lord; call upon his name: make known his deeds among the people. Sing unto him, sing psalms unto him; talk ye of all his wondrous works" (vv. 1-2).* Israel had a purpose on earth, that being to announce to the world that God is faithful. It is very likely that this psalm was written following the Babylonian captivity. It would have been an ideal time for Israel to talk of His wondrous works before all the nations. But Israel did not. She was scattered among the nations and was no testimony to the grace, mercy, and faithfulness of God. The fact is that in many of our western lands it is Jewish people who lead out in anti-Bible rallies and programs. Communism came from the mind of a Jew, Lenin. He led out in the atheistic Bolshevik revolution.

Second, there is a **Call to Return**: *"Seek the Lord, and his strength: and seek his face evermore" (v. 4).* Today Jews are going back to their homeland. This is a testimony to the world. One day there will be 144,000 Jews to lead the world in turning back to God. Today Jews returning to their homeland need also to return to God.

And third, there is a **Call to Remember**: *"Remember his marvellous works that he hath done; his wonders, and the judgments of his mouth" (v. 5).* Oh, may we Rejoice, Return, and Remember today!

Through the Bible in a Year: Nahum 1–3; Habakkuk 1–2

September 1

Read Psalm 105
Family Reading: Psalm 105:7-28

God's Keeping and Protecting of Israel

Psalm 105:7 continues the thought that the seed of Abraham should remember God's works (vv. 5-6). The psalmist is speaking of the Abrahamic covenant into which God had entered with Abraham, the founding father of the Jewish people, and the nation of Israel.

Anyone who enters into a covenant would like to know something about the individual with whom he is dealing. God reveals that He is the sovereign with whom all of us have to deal (v.7). He is God, yet He is *our Lord.* His judgments rule the world and are vital for all of us to recognize. The psalmist speaks of three people who entered into this covenant: Abraham, Isaac, and Jacob (vv. 9-10). It was a great everlasting covenant. God will remember His covenant forever (v. 8). He is Sovereign and He keeps His covenants.

God made His covenant with Abraham, continued it as an oath to Isaac, confirmed it with Jacob, and it became the everlasting covenant with Israel. This covenant was narrowed down to be specifically with one nation, Israel. Abraham had other descendants—Ishmael, the father of Arab nations, and Esau, the father of the Edomites. But God did not confirm this covenant to Edom or to the Arabs. God confirmed it to Israel. The Edomites and Ishmaelites are joined together today as Arab nations standing against Israel. God extended His covenant with Abraham through Jacob which means it was specifically given to the nation of Israel. God said, *"Unto thee will I give the land of Canaan" (v. 11).* The land of Palestine belongs to Israel according to the covenant God made. No decision by the United Nations, no intervention by other worldly power, and no hatred of the Arab people is going to change that.

God reveals how He blessed, used, and protected Israel (vv. 12-14). First they were a very few people and had strangers with them (v. 12). But then they increased and saw God bless. They moved from nation to nation, permitting God to direct them (v. 13). More than that—God protected them. He dealt with kings that tried to reprove Israel. No man was able to do them wrong (v. 14). God kept and protected them by His grace and mercy. He will do the same for us today.

Through the Bible in a Year: Habakkuk 3; Zephaniah 1–3

September 2

Read Psalm 105
Family Reading: Psalm 105:13-36

God's Blessing on Joseph

In Psalm 105 the psalmist leads the people to sing the history of Israel. God reveals how He protected and kept Israel. They started as a small nation with Jacob and his family (v. 13), and God took care of them (v. 14). God delivered them from Laban (Genesis 31:38-55). He then delivered them from Esau (Genesis 33). Following that God had to save them from Hamor and Shechem (Genesis 34). He did not allow anyone to harm them, and He reproved kings for their sakes (v. 14).

Then God dealt with Israel through a famine (v. 16). Again God made provision for their deliverance. He sent Joseph before them to go into Egypt so that when the famine struck, Joseph would be in a position of authority—in the sovereign direction and authority of God (vv. 17-23 and Genesis 37–46). What a story it is! The psalmist directed Israel to sing the truth that God used Joseph. He was sold by his brothers into servanthood (v. 17). But God was actually *sending* him—*"He sent a man before them, even Joseph . . ." (v. 17).*

Joseph endured dreadful trials. His feet were hurt with the fetters he bore (v. 18). This is an additional fact we learn about the life of Joseph. Apparently he had to walk as a cripple because of the torture in the prison. He trusted the Lord to free him. There was a day when he had interpreted a dream for Pharaoh's chief butler. The butler was restored from prison to his former position and he agreed to remember Joseph as he ministered to the king. But he forgot all about Joseph (Genesis 40:23). Joseph had no one to whom he could turn except the Lord. He gave the Word of the Lord to the chief butler, but God let him continue in his trial, for the Lord was developing Joseph.

Finally, Joseph was released from prison and was promoted to be the chief ruler under Pharaoh for the whole land of Egypt. He had authority over all the princes and he had the responsibility of instructing the leaders of the land (vv. 21-22). History does not record another story as dramatic as this one—Joseph left dreadful persecution to become prime-minister of the land. It was under his sovereign rule that Joseph brought his family out of Canaan into Egyptian abundance (v. 23).

Through the Bible in a Year: Haggai 1–2; Zechariah 1–2

September 3

Read Psalm 105
Family Reading: Psalm 105:23-45

God Delivers the People of Israel

Beginning at verse twenty-three we read of Israel's going into Egypt and of the history of Israel in Egypt. Jacob became convinced it was God's will for him to go down into Egypt. The Pharaoh gave them a special area, the land of Goshen. And there God prospered the Israelites. *"And he increased his people greatly; and made them stronger than their enemies" (v. 24).* God had promised to bless the people of Israel and this blessing was very apparent in Egypt.

Not only did Israel see physical and material prosperity in Egypt, they also saw persecution. They became stronger than their enemies and this produced hatred on the part of the Egyptians. *"He turned their heart to hate his people, to deal subtilely with his servants" (v. 25).* Pharaoh had given Jacob and his family a very favored place in Egypt—the land of Goshen. This would have stirred some jealously. Further, we can be sure that some of the Jews were high government officials. The hatred of Joseph and his family grew until a new Pharaoh came to power, a Pharaoh that *"knew not Joseph" (Exodus 1:8).* Then the terrible persecution against the Jews was unleashed. This Pharaoh turned Goshen into a concentration camp and Pharaoh *"dealt subtilely with [God's] servants" (v. 25).*

This brings us to the time of Moses (vv. 26-45). Moses came on the scene to deliver the Israelites from the bondage of Egypt. Moses and Aaron showed signs to the Israelites to validate their leadership. The Israelites saw the signs Moses and Aaron revealed by the power of God and with the rod of God (v. 27). Then God showed His signs to the Egyptians (vv. 28-35). There was the awful darkness (v. 28); the waters changed to blood (v. 29); frogs covering the land, even going into the palace chambers of the kings (v. 30); flies and lice covering the land (v. 31); hail with powerful thunderstorms (v. 32); locusts that ate up what the hail had not destroyed (vv. 34-35); and the death of the first born (v. 36). No wonder they sang—they had seen a great victory.

Through the Bible in a Year: Zechariah 3–8

September 4

Read Psalms 105:36-45; 106:1-10
Devotional Reading: Psalm 105:36-45

God's Saves and Keeps His Own

The tenth and last plague that came to Egypt was the death of the firstborn (v. 36 and Exodus 11). It was this plague that God used to lead Israel to institute the Passover (Exodus 12). This last plague, like none other, convinced Pharaoh that he could not win against God. This was a terrible plague. Think of it—the first born in every family would die. I thought about the impact it would have on our immediate family if it were to happen today. It would mean that I would have to die, for I was the first born in my family; Kathy, our oldest child, would die; our two sons-in-law and two of our daughters-in-law would die; one grandson and four granddaughters would die—for all of these were the first born in their families. Add it up—there would be eleven funerals in our immediate family. It was a dreadful plague that touched every Egyptian family! The world has never seen anything like these ten plagues on Egypt since that time, nor will it see such plagues until the days when God pours out the vials of His wrath in the tribulation period. This tenth plague convinced Pharaoh to heed Moses' demand, "Let my people go."

As these Israelites left the land, the Egyptians were glad to see them go (v. 38). The Israelites asked the Egyptians to give them jewels of gold and silver (Exodus 11:2), and they came out *"with silver and gold"* *(v. 37)*. They left the land of Egypt with amazing strength—*"there was not one feeble person among their tribes" (v. 37)*. The fear of the Israelites fell across the land of Egypt (v. 38). In the last few years we have witnessed something similar—the deliverance of Christians and Jews from Russia. As far as I know, there are now no people incarcerated in Russian prisons for religious reasons. Just a few years ago there were thousands in prison, in exile, or in mental hospitals. God has again manifested His power to deliver right now in this twentieth century.

When the Israelites left, God again revealed His concern for them and His power in their lives. *"He spread a cloud for a covering; and fire to give light in the night" (v. 39)*. That cloud was there to lead them through the wilderness. It gave them shade from the burning sun by day and a fiery pillar to give them light at night. Our God leads, protects, and keeps His Own.

Through the Bible in a Year: Zechariah 9–13

September 5

Read Psalms 105:39-45; 106:1-15
Devotional Reading: Psalm 105:39-45

Praise God for His Salvation

Psalm 105:39-45 present a synopsis of God's dealings with Israel as they left Egypt and headed toward God's promised land. Much of Exodus, Leviticus, and Numbers is filled with the history of what God did for the Israelites as they were led from Egypt to settle in Canaan. From all of that vast store of history, God chose three items to record in this psalm. The first one we looked at yesterday. It was God's provision of leadership and protection given by the Shekinah cloud—the pillar of cloud by day to lead them and the pillar of fire by night to give them light (Exodus 13:21 and Psalm 105:39). That cloud also came between the camp of the Israelites and the camp of the pursuing Egyptians (Exodus 14:19-20).

The second illustration the psalmist used was the fact that God fed Israel in the wilderness. *"The people asked, and he brought quails, and satisfied them with the bread of heaven" (v. 40).* They had the manna miraculously provided by God on a daily basis. And when they requested meat, God brought them the quail (Exodus 16:12-22). God *"satisfied them" (v. 40)*—that is, He provided adequately that they should have been satisfied, but even then they complained.

The third illustration is that God provided them water in the wilderness (v. 41). Moses smote the rock and out gushed fresh, clean, pure spring water (Exodus 17:5, 6). The psalmist states, *"He opened the rock, and the waters gushed out . . ." (v.41),* and there was abundant water.

God provided protection, food, and drink for His people. This continued without fail for the forty years they wandered in the wilderness. They had asked, *"Can God furnish a table in the wilderness?" (Psalm 78:19).* Yes, He can and He certainly did just that.

Psalm 105 ends with the fact that God kept His promise to Abraham (v. 42). He brought forth His people and gave them the lands He had promised to them (vv. 43-44). Why did He do all this? *"That they might observe his statutes, and keep his laws" (v. 45).* That is the reason God saved Israel in the Old Testament and it is the reason God saves people in this present age of grace. He saves us so that we may glorify Him.

Through the Bible in a Year: Zechariah 14; Malachi 1–3

September 6

Read Psalm 106
Family Reading: Psalm 106:1-23

Praising the Lord for Him and His People

Psalm 106 is another of the "envelope" psalms—psalms that begin and end with the same words: *"Praise ye the Lord."* These last four words of the psalm indicate we could go back and repeat the psalm again. The truths of the psalm are vital to us, for it is a psalm where sin is recognized so that the sinner repents and confesses his sin.

The psalm opens with *"Praise ye the Lord" (v. 1).* Then the psalmist tells why we should praise the Lord and give thanks. It is because *"he is good: for his mercy endureth forever" (v. 1).* The word *"Lord"* in verse one is the Hebrew word "Jehovah." He is the One who by commitment has kept His covenant relationship with Israel. Our Lord is One who always remembers and never forgets His people. His mercy—His lovingkindness—endures forever. He never forgets us. His love is that of which the composer wrote: "O love that will not let me go."

So great is the Lord that the psalmist asks, *"Who can utter the mighty acts of the Lord? Who can show forth all his praise?" (v. 2).* As finite men, we are unable to praise Him as He deserves.

> Weak is the effort of our heart,
> And cold our warmest thought;
> But when we see Thee as Thou art,
> We'll praise Thee as we ought.
> —John Newton

The psalmist pronounces blessing on those *"that keep judgment"* and on those *"that do righteousness at all times" (v. 3).* He believes it is possible to keep judgment and do righteousness at all times. He prays asking the Lord to remember him and to bless him with *"favor"* (God's favor is God's grace). He realizes that only by God's grace can we have salvation (v. 4).

The psalmist wanted these blessings so that he could: (1) See the good of God's chosen people, (2) rejoice in the gladness of the nation, and (3) glory with God's inheritance (v. 5). All three of these are wrapped up in fellowship with the people of God. How important it is to have fellowship and to walk with God's people.

Through the Bible in a Year: Matthew 1–3

September 7

Read Psalm 106
Family Reading: Psalm 106:7-31

Israel and Her Sins

Yesterday we noted from Psalm 106 the truths of the greatness of the Lord. Today we will begin looking at the weakness of man as revealed in this psalm. Beginning at verse six we find confession of sin taking over in Psalm 106. The psalmist confesses the sin of the people three times: *"We have sinned with our fathers, we have committed iniquity, we have done wickedly" (v. 6).* In that confession he not only confesses the acts of sin but also the very nature of sin within each one of us. *"Iniquity"* speaks of the perverse nature we have, and *"wicked"* reveals the nature within us that craves to sin.

Following this introduction to the fact of sin in verse six, we find the psalmist's confession continues, and he catalogues the sins of the nation of Israel. Think of it—here is a national anthem that they sang frequently—a national anthem actually revealing national disgrace. This is unique—can you tell of a nation that has sung a national anthem of disgrace? It would be great if Washington, D.C., would do it and confess the sins of America. But Washington, D.C. has not—is there a possibility that Tokyo, London, or Paris would follow Washington's lead if she did confess the sins listed? From my vantage point, it does not look as though any capital in the world is ready or willing to confess sins.

The Lord divided the sins of Israel into three sections: sins in Egypt (vv. 7-12); sins in the wilderness (vv. 13-33); and sins in the land (vv. 34-46). Let us note the sins of Israel that are listed in this psalm: forgetting God's blessings (vv. 7, 13); unbelief (vv. 7-13, 24, 43); discontent (vv. 13, 14); envy (v. 16); idolatry (vv. 19-20, 36-38); murmuring against God (v. 25); lust (vv. 28-29); rebellion against God's lead (vv. 32-33); disobedience (vv. 34-35); wicked philosophy and desires (v. 29). In this list of ten sins, we find that at least eight of them were committed in the wilderness wanderings. Not much mention is made of their sins in Egypt. The reason for this is that Israel in Egypt pictures the unbeliever under Satan's domination before salvation. Then after salvation at the Passover and the Red Sea, Israel in the wilderness pictures the believer not yielding to the Lord and living a carnal life of sin and unbelief. Israel in the land pictures the believer coming to the place of victory.

Through the Bible in a Year: Matthew 4–5

September 8

Read Psalm 106
Family Reading: Psalm 106:7-31

The Danger of Leanness of Soul

In this national anthem of confession, the psalmist takes the Israelites back to their history in Egypt. He states that the people of Israel did not understand the wonders God manifested in Egypt; nor did they remember the multitude of His mercies (v. 7). Rather they provoked the Lord at the Red Sea. They complained to Moses saying that they had wanted to stay in Egypt. They made a ridiculous statement: *"Because there were no graves in Egypt . . ." (Exodus 14:11).* Actually there were many graves in Egypt. In fact today, when tourists visit Egypt, most of the attractions they see deal with death and graves: for example, the pyramids are elaborate graves for kings. There were many graves in Egypt. But these Israelites complained saying *"it had been better for us to serve the Egyptians, than that we should die in the wilderness" (Exodus 14:12).*

Psalm 106:8 and 10 tell us that the Lord *"saved them"* in spite of their complaining. He did this for His Name's sake (v. 8). In His grace and mercy, God forgave the sins of Israel (v. 8), He overcame their fears (v. 9), and gave them victory over their foes (vv. 10-11).

In the light of Egypt's defeat, the Israelites believed God's words and sang His praise (v. 12). But *"they soon forgot his works"* and did not depend on His counsel (v. 13). In this we see the *source* of sin: They forgot God's works and did not wait for His counsel (v. 13). Then we see the *force* of sin—they *"lusted exceedingly in the wilderness . . ." (v. 14).* They were not content with God's provision and they wanted more.

Now we come to verse fifteen—what a sad verse! What a powerful verse! *"And he gave them their request; but sent leanness into their soul."* It appears that prayer may be answered for evil as well as for good. God may give us what we request in our carnality, but then God lets us pay the penalty of a weak soul. How tragic! Yet, how often is that happening today.

What a contrast between these Israelites in the wilderness and Gaius in III John. The Israelites suffered lean unhealthy souls—but Gaius' soul prospered with good health because he walked in the truth (III John 2–3).

Through the Bible in a Year: Matthew 6–7

September 9

Read Psalm 106:12-35

Turn from Rebellion and Idols

In verses sixteen through eighteen, the psalmist writes of a serious sin on the part of Israel: the sin of envy. These verses are referring to the dreadful account in Numbers 16 where we read of the rebellion against the leadership of Moses. That rebellion was led by Korah, Dathan, and Abiram. This was a sizeable rebellion for it involved 250 princes of Israel, *"famous in the congregation, men of renown" (Numbers 16:2).* God dealt with this rebellion by having the earth open up to swallow Korah, Dathan, Abiram, and their company into the pit, and they perished (v. 17 and Numbers 16:29-33). Further, fire came out from the Lord and consumed the 250 princes who offered incense (v. 18 and Numbers 16:35). Remember, God brought this severe judgment because these men were stirring up and leading a rebellion against Moses and Aaron. God never looks lightly upon those who rebel against the leaders God has placed in His work. What was their sin? It was the sin of envy. Those who rebel against God appointed leadership are usually envying the person in leadership. They want that person unseated so that they can be in the place of leadership.

Beginning at verse nineteen, the Lord deals with the sin of idolatry. The psalmist states that *"they made a calf in Horeb, and worshiped the molten image" (v. 19).* He is referring to the time when Aaron led the people in melting the golden earrings and fashioning a calf to worship (Exodus 32:1-8). This took place while Moses was in the Mount receiving the tables of testimony from God. The psalmist recorded this saying the calf was made *"in Horeb"* Think of it! Horeb—the very place where God gave the law so man could have the knowledge of sin (Romans 3:20). Horeb—the place where Moses went to meet with God and the time when *"the sight of the glory of the Lord was like devouring fire on the top of the mount . . ." (Exodus 24:17).* In Psalm 106 God reveals His attitude about idolatry. The Israelites came out of Egypt where the Egyptians worshiped the Nile River, the bulls, crocodiles, etc. Now, when they can meet God, they turn to a golden calf. In changing the glory of God to be like an ox, they forgot God and His works (vv. 20-22). Oh, may I John 5:21 become a reality in all our lives: *"Little children, keep yourselves from idols."*

Through the Bible in a Year: Matthew 8–9

September 10

Read Psalm 106:21-48
Family Reading: Psalm 106:7-28

Do Not Play with Sin

In Psalm 106 we are reading the confession of the sins of Israel. Their great sin was that of unbelief in forgetting God and His commands. In their unbelief they went into idolatry (vv. 19-22). Their sin of idolatry caused God to desire to destroy them (v. 23). In the twenty-third verse we see the importance God places upon intercessory prayer. Moses interceded for the Israelites resulting in the fact that God did not destroy Israel, even thought He desired to do so.

Let's look at the sins that were confessed—sins that hold back God's blessings on His people today. First, they forgot God—they left him out of all their plans and priorities in life. Leaving God out of your life's philosophy and goals will bring serious results later. Second, as we noted yesterday, they went into idolatry (vv. 19-23). Third, *"they despised the pleasant land" (v. 24)*.

The *"pleasant land"* is a type of victory in the Christian life. They despised going on with God and growing in His love and grace. Next we come to the root of their sin: *"they believed not his word" (v. 24)*. God had promised them He would lead them, but they did not believe. Hebrews 3:19 states it clearly: *"They could not enter in because of unbelief."*

We see where unbelief leads: *"they believed not . . . but murmured in their tents" (v. 25)*. They complained about Moses, about Aaron, about their food, about God's provision, and about the place to which God was leading them. When ten of the spies came back with their evil report, the people were filled with fears and complaining.

They went further in their sin. They joined themselves unto Baalpeor and that involved the sin of whoredom (v. 28 and Numbers 25:1-3). The *"sacrifices of the dead"* are sacrifices offered to dead idols instead of to the living God. The Israelites hit bottom in Numbers 25. How far sin will lead! They bowed in the most vile way before the idols of Baal. Because of this, God's judgment had to fall. A plague broke out that killed 24,000.

May we learn the awful dangers inherent in sin! This psalm teaches us: Do not play with sin!!

Through the Bible in a Year: Matthew 10–11

September 11

Read Psalms 106:32-48 and 107:1-8
Family Reading: Psalm 106:32-48

Flee Pride, Worldliness, and Idolatry

For five days we have been reading and studying Psalm 106, this song of national confession. Israel had much to confess about events in her history. Sin had seemed to reign and consistently brought the people back to face their need. In verses thirty-two and thirty-three the psalmist calls our attention to the story in Numbers 20:7-13. God commanded Moses to strike the rock, but Moses, in his anger with the people, smote the rock twice and took credit to himself by saying, *"Hear now, ye rebels; must we fetch you water out of this rock?" (Numbers 20:10).* So the people sinned by murmuring and complaining—and Moses sinned in the way he reacted to the attitude and actions of the people. Moses spoke *"unadvisedly with his lips" (v. 33),* and that is the reason *"it went ill with Moses . . ." (v. 32).* In fact, because of Moses' reaction, he was not allowed to enter the promised land (Numbers 20:12; Deuteronomy 3:25-27). Leaders in God's work must be careful about sin in their lives or they may forsake their privilege of leadership. The people were guilty of provoking Moses by their sinful attitudes, and Moses was guilty of sinful reaction. Remember—our *reactions* are just as important as other people's *actions.*

A second sin listed in our passage today is the sin of disobeying God's command to be a separated Christian. The people *"did not destroy the nations"* as God commanded them but were *"mingled among the heathen, and learned their works" (vv. 34-35).* This Scripture is relevant for today. We must lead a separated life—separated from apostasy and its evil beginnings. Lack of separation leads us directly to idolatry (v. 36). By not separating from the sinful world and from idolatrous religion, we head right into the danger of dreadful idolatry. This idolatry listed here was so wicked that it brought the Israelites to do what other nations do—sacrifice their children to a pagan God.

How dreadful was their idolatry! But it is no surprise that God brought judgment (v. 40). Instead of following God's commandments to destroy the surrounding nations, Israel accepted their practices and came under the judgment of God. Oh, may we flee idolatry and its partner, worldliness.

Through the Bible in a Year: Matthew 12

September 12

Read Psalms 106:40-48 and 107:1-15

The Dangers of Sin

In Psalm 106:39 the word *"inventions"* means "pursuits." These Israelites became ensnared in sin, but it was not by accident. They pursued sin; they worked at being sinful; they planned with forethought and followed up with actions. They *"went a whoring with their own inventions" (v. 39)*—that is, they had well-planned, sinful ideas.

When the Israelites were in Canaan, they needed to be separated from the philosophy and actions of the Canaanites. Those Canaanites were dreadfully sinful with idolatry and its companion immorality ruling the people. The Canaanites used the vilest forms of sexual immorality in their worship. Pornographic symbols were seen everywhere. Male and female prostitutes were involved in the wickedness of religious rites—*"went a whoring"* literally took place. And the Israelites allowed this pagan wickedness to invade their religious ceremonies.

God hated this wickedness in the life of Israel (v. 40). His wrath was *"kindled against his people, insomuch that he abhorred his own inheritance" (v. 40)*. And what was the result? God *"gave them into hand of the heathen; and they that hated them ruled over them. Their enemies also oppressed them, and they were brought into subjection under their hand" (vv. 41-42)*. Those two verses sum up the entire book of Judges. The whole book is an account of recurring cycles: first, the people slipped into sin; then God judged by allowing a foreign king to take them captive; next the Israelites would repent and cry out to God; and then God sent them a deliverer. This cycle occurred repeatedly.

This section of Psalm 106 reveals the awful results of sin. Those who leave God turn from happiness to misery. God judges sin—no matter in whom it is found. The Israelites' leniency toward the Canaanites resulted in their being cruel to themselves. Judgment that comes into our lives is the result of sin. It is not something tacked on to sin, rather, it grows out of sin. Satan is a cruel taskmaster. He tempts and then he torments. Someone has said, "The Wicked man collects fuel for his own Hell-fire." Sinners forge rods which Satan will use to beat them. May we learn to hate sin.

Through the Bible in a Year: Matthew 13

September 13

Read Psalms 106:40-48 and 107:1-15

Praise God for His Deliverance

Yesterday we saw how the Israelites experienced God's judgment on sin in the time of the judges. They were repeatedly taken captive by foreign kings. But then the Lord gives the wonderful truth, *"Many times did he deliver them . . ." (v. 43).* Even then, they continued to provoke God, and the Lord had to continue with His judgments on sin. He *"regarded their affliction, when he heard their cry" (v. 44).* He was watching—He did know and understand.

Therefore, in verse forty-five, we read that *"he remembered for them his covenant, and repented according to the multitude of his mercies."* God does keep His covenants. He will not fail to be compassionate. He knows our frame and notes our weakness. Though he must deal with sin, He always acts in mercy. In fact, he has a multitude of mercies. Man may forget God, but God never forgets His covenant.

Verse forty-five states that God *"repented according to the multitude of his mercies."* It is important that we remember that God's repentance is not a change of His will, but of His work. God did not continue the destruction which He had commenced. Man repents by changing His will—God repents by willing a change.

The psalmist ends this psalm with a prayer and benediction. This psalm was likely written during the captivity and the prayer is a fervent one asking the Lord to deliver (v. 47). The request was, *"Save us."* Literally that means *"deliver us."* His appeal is directly to the Lord—*"O Lord our God" (v. 47).* The Lord alone is God, and we must rely only on His power to bring us deliverance. The purpose of the prayer was to glorify God—so they could *"give thanks unto thy holy name"* (v. 47). How important to bring all our burdens to Him and let Him deal with those who have persecuted and afflicted His people.

The result of that prayer is that there will be victory in any life that commits the matter to God—*"to triumph in thy praise" (v. 47).* And thus the psalm ends with praise, blessing the Lord. *"Blessed be the Lord God of Israel from everlasting to everlasting . . . Amen" (v. 48).* After recounting their sins in this National Anthem of confession, Israel praises the Lord for His mercy and His forgiving passion.

Through the Bible in a Year: Matthew 14–15

September 14

Read Psalm 107
Family Reading: Psalm 107:1-21

A Psalm We Need to Read

Psalm 107 is the first psalm of the Fifth Book. As we have mentioned before, Psalms is divided into five books which seem to follow the pattern of Moses' Pentateuch, the fifth book being Deuteronomy. Deuteronomy deals with the land and with the law of God. This Fifth Book deals with the same subjects. In Psalm 107 we find God's concern for the land and its people. Psalm 119, a vital part of Book Five, is the great psalm on the law of the Lord. It is very possible that Psalms 107 through 119 were sung in connection with the laying of the foundation of the new temple. (*See* Ezra 3:10-11.)

Psalm 107 was probably written to celebrate the Jews' return to Palestine following the Babylonian captivity. It is a psalm of gathering the people from lands in the east, west, north, and south (v. 3).

The psalm is a national song, but it is also a song with personal significance for all believers today. Verse forty-three presents the conclusion: *"Whoso is wise, and will observe these things, even they shall understand the loving-kindness of the Lord."* If we wish to be wise, God says it will be good to meditate on the truths in Psalm 107.

It is a psalm of praise. Four times we read these words: *"Oh that men would praise the Lord for his goodness, and for his wonderful works to the children of men!"* (*vv. 8, 15, 21, 31*). Also, four times we find that God hears and answers the cry of the oppressed (vv. 6, 13, 19, 28). God is able and willing to deliver His own. But He is also desirous of hearing our voices lifted in praise to Him for His lovingkindness and grace.

The psalm begins with an encouragement to praise the Lord. *"O give thanks unto the Lord, for he is good: for his mercy endureth forever"* (*v. 1*). The Lord **wants** our praise, so He commands, *"O give thanks unto the Lord."* We can give Him our money and He will use it. He rewards faithful stewardship, but He does not need it. However, He does long for our praise. We can give Him thanks. Oh that we might constantly give thanks to the Lord.

Through the Bible in a Year: Matthew 16–17

September 15

Read Psalm 107
Family Reading: Psalm 107:4-32

Delivered by the Lord

Today we begin looking at the large portion of this psalm, verses four through thirty-two. This section states four times that men need to *"praise the Lord for his goodness, and for his wonderful works to the children of men!" (vv. 8, 15, 21, 31).* We believers have much for which to be thankful, and it is good for us to praise Him for His goodness and His wonderful works to the children of men. There are many ungrateful people in the world who do not stop to praise the Lord for His goodness and His wonderful works. May we be sure to be thankful. One of the marks of a spirit-filled life is a thankful spirit (Ephesians 5:20 and Colossians 3:17). We will note four distressing situations for Israel in verses four through thirty-two. In every case God provided deliverance.

The first distressing plight is found in verses four and five where the Israelites were fainting travelers lost in the desert *needing a guide*. *"They wandered in the wilderness in a solitary way . . ." (v. 4).* The *"solitary way"* meant literally *"a pathless waste."* They had no path to follow—and they were lost. There was no city in which to dwell. They became hungry and thirsty. They cried out asking God for help (v. 6). And God graciously met their need. *"[H]e delivered them out of their distresses" (v. 6).* Then He became their leader so that they might go to *"a city of habitation" (v. 7).* He met their need. He satisfied the longing soul and He gave them food so that they were filled (v. 9). Surely they should have done what God longed for them to do: *"Praise the Lord for his goodness, and for his wonderful works."*

The second distressing plight is found in verses ten through sixteen where the Israelites were in a dungeon *needing a deliverer*. They had come through the captivity which was like sitting in the darkness of a dungeon, bound with irons (v. 10). But God delivered them when they cried unto Him (v. 13). He brought them out of the dark dungeon and broke the gates of brass and cut the bars of iron (v. 16). Certainly, again, it was only appropriate that the psalmist should write: *"Oh that men would praise the Lord for his goodness, and for his wonderful works to the children of men!" (v. 15).*

Through the Bible in a Year: Matthew 18–19

September 16

Read Psalm 107
Family Reading: Psalm 107:16-36

Trusting the Lord for Healing

Yesterday from this psalm we noted distressing plights in which the Israelites found themselves. Those situations apply to us today. We answer to the same God to which Israel answered, and God has established principles of operation in the world that deal with sin in our lives, just as they dealt with sin on the part of Israel.

The Lord speaks of fools in verse seventeen. He states that *"because of their transgression, and because of their iniquities,* [they] *are afflicted."* Physical sickness can come as a result of sin. The truth is that often suffering is self-produced—people who suffer often bring it upon themselves. However, not all affliction is self-produced. God may permit affliction to come to build us up in faith. But many physical afflictions are the direct result of sin. Because of their sickness, these fools lost their appetite for food. Then with their lack of nourishment and with the destructive power of the disease, they come to the very gates of death (v. 18).

If at that time these fools will disown their foolishness and *"cry unto the Lord in their trouble" (v. 19),* He can act and save *"them out of their distresses" (v. 19).* Someone has said, "Prayer is a salve for every sore." Prayer is just as effective in a sick bed as it was in the wilderness (vv. 4-9) and in prison (vv. 10-16). Verse twenty speaks of those who are spiritually sick. They have lost their appetite for the Word of God. They, too, may turn to Him in prayer and find healing mercy. He will deliver them from their destruction. The Lord is the Great Physician. Medicine and therapy are good—but it is the Lord who directs healing. Therefore, when healing comes, we should adopt the exhortation of verse twenty-one: *"Oh that men would praise the Lord for his goodness, and for his wonderful works to the children of men!"* And then should follow the actions given in verse twenty-two: *"And let them sacrifice the sacrifices of thanksgiving . . ."* How often men are restored to health and never thank the Lord. Only one out of ten lepers that were healed returned to give God praise (Luke 17:11-19). May we learn to trust Him for healing and then praise Him.

Through the Bible in a Year: Matthew 20–21

September 17

Read Psalm 107
Family Reading: Psalm 107:23-43

Our Lord Quiets the Storms

In these devotions on Psalm 107 we have seen three dreadful situations from which the Lord delivered Israel. They were lost in the desert, bound in prison, and afflicted because of sin. Today we consider a fourth plight that men face—that of being like a ship lashed on a stormy sea (vv. 23-32).

God permits men to be caught in a storm at sea. The winds blow and the waves are lifted high (v. 25). The men on board the ship feel the ship rise high *"up to the heaven"* and then sink down into the depths (v. 26). The sailors strive hard, but the fearful condition of the floundering ship causes their hearts to melt (v. 26). They cannot walk on board—they stagger around as though they were drunk (v. 27). All hope is gone. They are at their wits end! (v. 27). Their ability as seamen has not helped. It looks hopeless. Human ingenuity and skill have done their best and failed. What then?!

The answer is simple—it is the same answer given in the preceding three seemingly hopeless conditions: *"Then they cry unto the Lord in their trouble, and he bringeth them out of their distresses" (v. 28)*. God answers prayer. The storm becomes a calm and the waves are still (v. 29). How wonderful! God sees the storm—He hears their cry—He brings calm.

What is the result? The seamen are glad because the sea is quiet (v. 30). God has quieted the situation miraculously, and He brought them to the very haven they desired—they came safely to the seaport they desired (v. 30). The Lord will see us through all the tempests and tests of this life. He can calm the inner tempest so that the winds and waves of anxiety and terror are put to rest. Then He will take us to our desired port—we will be brought to the harbor of Heaven. Again the psalmist calls on men to *"praise the Lord for his goodness, and for his wonderful works to the children of men!" (v. 31)*. What should our response be? Verse thirty-two has the answer: *"Let* [us] *exalt him . . . and praise him."*

Through the Bible in a Year: Matthew 22–23

September 18

Read Psalms 107:33-43 and 108

God Has Power to Bless or Blight

Psalm 107 is a Psalm for us.

1. If we seem lost in a spiritual desert, He is the One to lead us out (vv. 4-9). Remember, these verses are written to God's people—not unsaved people. Sometimes God's people feel lost not knowing which way to turn.

2. If we feel as though we are locked in a spiritual dungeon, He can deliver (vv. 10-16).

3. If we realize we have spiritual sickness because of sin, only He can bring healing and miraculous delivery (vv. 17-22).

4. If we are almost defeated by the storms of life, we can cry to Him and He will bring the calm we need (vv. 23-32).

This psalm applies to us today!

In verse thirty-three, we find a change in the psalm. The psalmist now gives truths of God's providential government that help us know why God does deliver.

God has power to change conditions and situations. He can change rivers so that they dry up and become a wilderness; watersprings can be changed to be dry ground; a fruitful land can be changed to be absolutely barren because of the wickedness of those who dwell in the land. May we never take our situation for granted. If we are realizing blessings from God, we must praise Him and walk humbly with Him. How often have I seen churches enjoying the blessings of God and then they become proud of what they have done. They begin to think they have accomplished this by fleshly energy. It does not take long until the spring is stopped and the place is changed to dry ground. A fruitful field can become barren because of sin.

God also has the power to do the opposite. He can turn the wilderness into a lake and the dry ground into a spring. Remember God alone has the power to bless and use our lives. May we look to Him and trust Him.

Through the Bible in a Year: Matthew 24

September 19

Read Psalms 107:33-43 and 108

God's Righteous Government

Today we have our last devotion in Psalm 107. The psalm ends with these words: *"Whoso is wise, and will observe these things, even they shall understand the loving-kindness of the Lord" (v. 43)*. Therefore, we need to look at the truths and principles God gives in this psalm—then we will be able to understand the lovingkindness of the Lord.

As we review the psalm, we note that in every distress the Israelites cried unto the Lord; and in every case the Lord saved them out of their distresses. Who is it that understands the loving-kindnesses of the Lord? It is that person who, because he carried a heavy burden, cried unto the Lord and saw the Lord deliver him out of the distress. To become wise, we need to observe this truth. We are all going to find ourselves in difficult situations. We must learn to roll the burden on the Lord and watch Him miraculously deliver us from the burden.

Those who are proud of their position are not going to realize the blessings of His mercy and grace. Verse forty states that the Lord poureth contempt upon princes. Why? Because they are proud and not willing to humble themselves before the Lord.

In contrast, the poor will have a special place of blessing with the Lord. Verse forty-one reads: *"Yet setteth he the poor on high from affliction, and maketh him families like a flock."* The Bible puts an emphasis on the fact that God blesses the poor. *"The common people heard Him gladly" (Mark 12:37)*. The reason the poor and common people hear him is that they recognize their poverty and their need of the Lord. Remember, the princes in this psalm are not condemned because they are princes but because they are godless. Likewise, the poor are not exalted because they are poor but because they are godly. Therefore, we should not exalt those of high estate, nor should we despise those who are poor. God has a way of changing the condition of both. *"The righteous shall see it, and rejoice" (v. 42)*. The manifestation of God's righteous government is a source of rejoicing to the righteous and of sadness to the wicked.

Through the Bible in a Year: Matthew 25

September 20

Read Psalm 108

A Fixed Heart

We must note that we have seen Psalm 108 before. The fact is this psalm is composed from two previous psalms. Verses one through five are found in Psalm 57:7-11; and verses six through thirteen are taken from Psalm 60:5-12. Charles Spurgeon wrote, "The Holy Spirit is not so short of expressions that He needs to repeat Himself; thus there must be some important reason for the combining of two former utterances into this new setting."

The historical setting of the two previous psalms is different then the setting for Psalm 108. It is very likely that Psalm 108 was composed at the time of the Jews return from Babylon. Many centuries had lapsed since Psalms 57 and 60 were written in David's day. Truth does not change—truth has always been truth. Inspired in David's time, the truth in the two psalms was still truth to be applied to the time of the release from captivity.

The first and last verse of Psalm 108 speaks of God. The way we can have victory is to recognize the need for God's blessing in our lives. Every believer must battle with the lusts of the flesh and the attacks of Satan. Our faith and our victory must be only in the Lord.

David begins the psalm with the truth of a heart steadfast in its purpose. *"O God, my heart is fixed . . ." (v. 1).* The word *"fixed"* means to be erect and stand upright. When our heart is set upon God, there is no fluctuation. The course of life is fixed. This is the steadfastness about which we read in I Corinthians 15:58: *"Therefore, my beloved brethren, be ye steadfast, unmoveable, always abounding in the work of the Lord"* But now the heart is fixed, and the psalmist says the result of such a fixation is joy and praise (v. 1).

His praise would be not be only private but also public—*"among the people" (v. 3).* His praise would be focused on God's mercy and truth: *"For thy mercy is great . . . and thy truth reacheth unto the clouds" (v. 4).* What a blessing it is to stand unflinchingly on the mercy and truth of God. It was because of this that David could say: *"Be thou exalted, O God . . ." (v. 5).* We should sing praises because of his mercy and truth—lifting him up before the people.

Through the Bible in a Year: Matthew 26

September 21

Read Psalms 108 and 109:1-7

Victory Through Christ's Victory

In Psalm 108:6, there is a change from praise to prayer. The psalmist prays *"save with thy right hand, and answer me."* Then the writer speaks of past victories that God had given the nation of Israel. He wrote of the fact that God had given the land to Israel and on both sides of Jordan—Succoth, Gilead, and Manasseh being on the east side and Shechem, Ephraim, and Judah being on the west side (vv. 7-8). God had given the victory.

Then the psalmist wrote of three powerful enemies: Moab, Edom, and Philistia (v. 9). Moab was an accursed race (Deuteronomy 23:3-4). Edom was a powerful force with a seemingly impregnable city, Petra. The Philistines remained in the land and were a perennial enemy to Israel. Just as Israel had three powerful enemies, so do believers today—the world, the flesh, and the devil. Israel defeated her three powerful enemies, and believers can realize the same victory today. The fact is that our enemies have already been defeated at Calvary. If we will only appropriate the blessing of Calvary in our lives, we too will see the enemies defeated.

Moab became Israel's washpot (v. 9)—a picture of utter servitude. Over Edom the shoe could be cast (v. 9)—a picture of servants waiting on a master. The servants washed the master's feet with a washpot and then took the shoe and washed it. God will give blessed victory if we will surrender to Him.

Edom looked impossible. It's strong city, Petra, was known to all nations as being impregnable. But God can do that which seems to be impossible with man. You may be looking at an almost impossible problem today. The Lord is able to meet that need and give the victory.

The psalmist gives an important caution in verse twelve: *"Give us help from trouble: for vain is the help of man."* Oh, recognize this. When we cease trusting the strength of man we have opened the door for God to work. Verse thirteen promises, *"Through God we shall do valiantly: for he it is that shall tread down our enemies."* God is able to give victory—claim this psalm and His victory today.

Through the Bible in a Year: Matthew 27

September 22

Read Psalm 109
Family Reading: Psalm 109:1-20

Follow David's Godly Example

Psalm 109 was written by David when he was suffering severe trial and criticism. This psalm is the last of the imprecatory psalms. David was greatly disturbed over the disloyalty of one individual—probably Ahithophel. This man became on Old Testament picture of Judas. Ahithophel betrayed David, and Judas betrayed David's greater Son, the Lord Jesus Christ.

Please note how the psalm begins. David pled, *"Hold not thy peace, O God of my praise" (v. 1).* David begged God not to hold His peace when David was being viciously attacked. But then David added, *"O God of my praise."* God was the one whom David praised. David gives us a blessed example. He praised the Lord in the midst of dreadful adversities. He had learned to praise the Lord no matter what happened.

In verse two he identifies the type of attack he faced. Those who were attacking were deceitful, and they had spoken with lying tongues. One who particularly cursed David was Shimei (II Samuel 16:5-14). Shimei was probably influenced by lies from Ahithophel. Oh, the damage that one deceitful tongue can do. May we all be sure to beware of deceitful and hateful tongues. Verse three states that these enemies encompassed David with words of hatred.

David had difficulty understanding their lies and hate. He showed them love—but for his love they became his adversaries (v. 4). David's godly attitude was manifested in verse four. When they opposed him, David said he would give himself unto prayer. There—that is the answer! Opposition arises against us—let us give ourselves to prayer. Even then, these adversaries were so wicked that they rewarded David's good with evil and his love with hatred (v. 5). How can men become so wicked that they return evil for good and hatred for love?

To return evil for good is devilish. The Lord manifested His spirit to be the opposite—that is to return good for evil. In Luke 6:27 He commanded us: *"Love your enemies, do good to them which hate you."* Let's have Jesus as our example (I Peter 2:21). Then we will not follow the actions of the enemies who stood against David.

Through the Bible in a Year: Matthew 28; Mark 1

September 23

Read Psalm 109:6-31

God Will Deal with Sin

Verse six begins a dreadfully serious imprecatory portion. This part of the psalm has given difficulty to many commentators. It does not seem to fit the character of King David, a gracious man who twice spared the life of his enemy, King Saul (I Samuel 24–26). He is referred to as a man after God's own heart. Would he speak forth these judgments as given in this psalm?

An easy way out of this dilemma is one taken by some commentators. They teach that this is not David calling forth judgment on his enemy, but rather it is David's enemy reviling David and calling forth courses on him. That might be a good explanation if it were not for the fact that there are other similar imprecations in the psalms. I believe the best way to understand this is that this is an Old Testament occurrence under law. Today we are in the age of grace and the New Testament knows nothing of this type of calling forth judgment.

Even though it is not a New Testament type message, there are truths in this section of the psalm that are eternal truths that apply today. David here is praying for judgment on one individual. In verses six through nineteen the words *"he," "him,"* and *"his"* are used three times. And five times the words *"them"* or *"their"* refer to his children. This portion is spoken about one man. The man referred to was probably Ahithophel who, when he had defected to Absalom, did so with bitter hatred in his heart against David.

David begins by asking that someone be placed over his adversary just like the enemy himself. This passage reveals that those who serve Satan should not be surprised to have his company here on earth (v. 6) and his condemnation hereafter (v. 7). Just as this adversary judged and condemned others, the psalmist requested that he also be judged and condemned. The idea expressed here is the same that we have in the statement we make often: "What goes around comes around." Our way of dealing will come back to deal with us. Verse eight is quoted in Acts 1:20 as applying to the arch-traitor of all time, Judas Iscariot. God is the one who works vengeance. We must learn to leave every situation with Him.

Through the Bible in a Year: Mark 2–3

September 24

Read Psalm 109:11-31

Calling on God to Deal with Sin

In Psalm 109:6-20, we read a very serious imprecation against an adversary given by King David. In that portion we read the word *"let"* twenty-one times. David is asking that this man be dealt with in the same manner he has dealt with others in this life.

David's adversary was one who did not show mercy (v. 16). Instead, he persecuted the poor and needy. Therefore, David prayed that as his adversary had shown no mercy, even so he should not receive mercy now. His enemy slew the broken hearted—even so he could expect the very same thing to take place in his life.

This man loved cursing and did not give out blessings (v. 17). David prayed that the cursing would come back upon his own head and that blessings would be far from him (v. 17). A tyrant has a poor memory, but David urged God not to forget his sins. Let the adversary have what he loved. It is the truth of Galatians 6:7-8:

"Be not deceived; God is not mocked: for whatsoever a man soweth, that shall he also reap. For he that soweth to his flesh shall of the flesh reap corruption; but he that soweth to the Spirit shall of the Spirit reap life everlasting."

We will reap what we sow. This adversary had sown fleshly activity and David asked that he receive of the flesh in return. *"As he clothed himself with cursing like as with a garment, so let it come into his bowels like water, and like oil into his bones. Let it be unto him as the garment which covereth him, and for a girdle wherewith he is girded continually" (vv. 18-19).*

Today we would say, "He made his bed—let him sleep in it," or perhaps, "May all his chickens come home to roost."

Another Scriptural example of this principal can be found in the book of Esther. Haman built the gallows on which to hang Mordecai, but those gallows became the very ones on which Haman was hanged.

David rested his case with the Lord (v. 20). He concluded the denunciation of his adversaries by asking God to deal with them in His way. Today we are to leave vengeance with the Lord. (*See* Romans 12:19—*"Vengeance is mine; I will repay, saith the Lord."*)

Through the Bible in a Year: Mark 4 and 5:1-20

September 25

Read Psalms 109:21-31 and 110

David's Need of the Lord's Mercy

After David had committed his adversaries to the Lord, he then called upon God for help in his own life. He first asked that God would act according to His character. David requested: *"do thou for me, O God the Lord, for thy name's sake . . ." (v. 21).* David called on *"God"* —Adona—the sovereign God who is the God of power and can do all things according to His will. He also called on "the Lord"—Jehovah— the God of promise. When he asked that the Lord do this for His name's sake, he was saying that he trusted the Lord to work according to His character revealed in His power and His promises. He knew the Lord was both willing and anxious to save him. Then David recognized that God's mercy was good and that He could rely on God to act in mercy in his life. Thus he could pray with confidence, *"deliver thou me" (v. 21).* Twice he pled for God to work according to His mercy (vv. 22, 26).

After calling on God to act according to His character, David further requested that God would act according to David's need (vv. 22-26). David was experiencing a dreadful low time in his life. He was depressed and sick. His heart was wounded within him (v. 22). He had lost his courage and determination. The spirit of his will was crushed. He was totally discouraged: *"I am gone like the shadow when it declineth . . ." (v. 23).* He seemed to have no stability, for he felt tossed up and down (v. 23). He was in deep mental distress and depression gripped his being. He was facing physical exhaustion: *"My knees are weak through fasting" (v. 24).* And he was losing weight: *"[M]y flesh faileth of fatness" (v. 24).* I wonder if he did not feel that death was approaching. As we have noted from other psalms, it appears David was afflicted with a serious illness after his sin with Bathsheba.

To make his situation even worse, David realized he was a reproach to those about him. *"When they looked upon me they shook their heads" (v. 25).* They looked at this weakened old man in astonishment and asked, "Is this the man who defeated Goliath."

In this condition, David prayed *"Help me, O Lord my God" (v. 26).* David turned to the right person—the Lord alone who could help in this trying situation.

Through the Bible in a Year: Mark 5:21-43 and 6

September 26

Read Psalms 109:26-31 and 110–111

David Gives God the Glory for Victory

Today we will consider the last part of Psalm 109. David pled for God's mercy in his life. He made his plea so that the Lord might be glorified.

"Help me, O Lord my God: O save me according to thy mercy: That they may know that this is thy hand; that thou, Lord, hast done it" (vv. 26-27).

David wanted all to know that God had performed the miracle. He wanted them to recognize God's hand in the healing and strengthening of David. This was his longing—that God might be glorified. The rebellion of Absalom was strong. He had most of the army and also had the cleverest man in the nation as his private counselor. The situation was desperate and looked hopeless for David. The only One who could deliver David was the Lord.

That is true in every one of our lives. Sin has its grip on us. Our only hope and help is in the Lord. We need to trust Him. Then following the victory that He gives, we must give Him the glory and recognize our own weakness and unworthiness.

David committed his enemies to the Lord. He asked that those adversaries be clothed with shame. Ahithophel, his chief and most dreaded adversary, committed suicide. He covered himself with his own confusion as with a mantle (v. 29). God dealt with David's adversaries even according to David's prayer.

And what did David say his response would be?

He announced he would greatly praise the Lord, and he would see that His praise would be known among the multitude of people (v. 30). David was a man *"after God's own heart" (I Samuel 16:7).* One proof of this was the fact that he trusted the Lord and then always gave God the glory for any victory that came. He closed the psalm by stating the truth that God is ready and anxious to stand at the side of the poor to deliver them from adversaries that condemn. May we trust the Lord for deliverance and give Him the glory for victory.

Through the Bible in a Year: Mark 7–8

September 27

Read Psalms 110–111
Devotional Reading: Psalm 110

Our Glorious Priest-King

Psalm 110 is a unique psalm because:

1. Its entire content presents the Lord Jesus Christ. It has no primary application to any king or priest in Israel.
2. It is quoted more often in the New Testament than in any other psalm.

The psalm presents two comings of our Lord Jesus Christ. His first coming was as a prophet and priest. God, the Father, gave him the title of *"priest for ever after the order of Melchizedek" (v. 4).* Then in verses five and six, He is presented as king and judge.

Psalm 110 opens with an unusual statement: *"The Lord said unto my Lord . . ." (v. 1).* Here David is permitted into the councils of the Trinity where David hears God's secret conversation with His co-equal Son. David calls the Son, *"my Lord."* So David sees beyond the fact that he would have an earthly son who would reign over Israel. He saw that this *Son* would reign forever with his kingdom established by God (II Samuel 7:12-13). Christ was a descendant of David through Mary; but in this psalm, David recognizes Him as more than a son—He is David's Lord. Verse one further states that He will be the Conqueror who is now sitting at the Father's right hand. David therefore saw beyond the birth of Jesus, yes, even beyond the cross, to the resurrection and ascension where He was seated in Heaven.

The words of verse four address the very heart of this psalm and the very center of our faith: *"The Lord hath sworn, and will not repent, thou art a priest for ever after the order of Melchizedek."* God has made Jesus our High Priest—God will never change that. He sits today, as David saw Him prophetically, at the Father's right hand, ever living to make intercession for us (Hebrews 7:25). His priesthood can never be revoked, and His authority can never be removed. His priesthood is forever *"after the order of Melchizedek."*

Who is He? He is the Priest-King. He will rule and judge the world (vv. 5-6). This will be *"in the day of his wrath" (v. 5).* Wickedness will not go unpunished. All kings and peoples will either yield to His authority or be crushed by it.

Through the Bible in a Year: Mark 9

September 28

Read Psalms 111–112

Worship the Lord

Psalms 111 and 112 begin with the same word. It is one word in the Hebrew language, *"Hallelujah."* In our King James Bible it is translated with four words, *"Praise ye the Lord."* These psalms could be called twin psalms because their structure is the same. In the Hebrew each psalm contains twenty-two lines, each line beginning with a different letter of the Hebrew alphabet, thus making up the complete alphabet.

From Psalm 111 we learn much about worship. What is *worship?* It is the ascribing of *worthship* to the Lord. It involves realizing all that God is and praising Him for His person and His work. Worship is actually an automatic instinct of mankind. As archeologists have uncovered the ruins of former civilizations, they found one thing that was universal in all past societies—a place of worship. The ruins may reveal that the civilization had a market and other buildings necessary to their civilization. Some did not have a marketplace; others lacked something else; but they all had a place for worship. Maybe it was a temple, maybe an altar, but they all had some type of worship.

The psalmist commands us all to praise the Lord. To aid in this he next gives us his own personal example: *"I will praise the Lord with my whole heart" (v. 1).* His worship was to be done with his *"whole heart."* When we sing, we need to think of the words we sing. When we pray, our hearts should enter into the prayer. The psalmist stated that His praise of the Lord would be done personally and publicly—*"in the assembly . . . and in the congregation"* of the righteous (v. 1).

What would make up the basis for the psalmist's worship?

First, he would praise the Lord for His works. These would involve His creation with great works. Please note the contrast between verses two and three. In verse two, he praises the Lord for His **works** (plural), whereas in verse three he praises the Lord for His **work** (singular). The **works** are those of creation. His **work** is the work of redemption. This work is *"honorable and glorious"* and it involves His righteousness (v. 3). We, too, must praise the Lord for His great works in creation and His one greatest work, redemption, which brings us into fellowship with Him.

Through the Bible in a Year: Mark 10

September 29

Read Psalms 111–112

The Wonder that Leads us to the Wisdom of Praise

Yesterday from Psalm 111, we noted the definition of necessity for worship. From this same psalm, today we are going to consider the wonder and wisdom of worshipping the Lord.

The psalmist speaks of works of the Lord that need to be remembered (v. 4). One of the saddest things in the Bible is that Israel forgot the blessings the Lord had poured out. They did not remember! God had warned them not to forget: *"Only take heed to thyself, and keep thy soul diligently, lest thou forget the things which thine eyes have seen, and lest they depart from thy heart, all the days of thy life . . ."* *(Deuteronomy 4:9).* We forget, we have revival, and then we often forget again! Jonah tells of a great revival that came to Nineveh. Then, 150 years later, Nahum wrote of the sure judgment that would come on Nineveh because of her gross sins. You see, great things happened in Nineveh under Jonah—but the people forgot, became lukewarm, and lost the joy of the blessings they once had.

We need to remember—for God remembers. *"[H]is righteousness endureth **for ever**"* *(v. 3).* *"[H]e will **ever** be mindful of his covenant"* *(v. 5).* *"The works of his hands are verity and judgment . . . They stand fast **for ever and ever** . . ."* *(vv. 7-8).* *"[H]e hath commanded his covenant **for ever** . . ."* *(v. 9).* *"[H]is praise endureth **for ever**"* *(v. 10).* God is faithful; therefore, we need to become faithful.

The works to which the Lord calls our attention are those that have to do with Israel's redemption. In the wilderness God miraculously gave them manna from Heaven to eat (v. 5). Time after time God revealed Himself strong and faithful. All that He did was done in truth and uprightness (v. 8). God sums it all up in verse nine by speaking of it as the *"redemption"* He sent unto His people. Therefore they should remember that *"holy and reverend is his name" (v. 9).* Thus in verses two through nine, God commands us to praise the Lord because of the *wonder* of His work.

In verse ten He speaks of the *wisdom* of praising the Lord. He gives a good understanding to those who praise Him. May we praise the Lord.

Through the Bible in a Year: Mark 11 and 12:1-27

September 30

Read Psalms 112–113

Another Look at the Blessed Man

Psalm 112 is a companion psalm to Psalm 111. In the Hebrew they both had twenty-two lines, each beginning with a different letter in the Hebrew alphabet. It appears that they were written by the same author. The last verse of Psalm 111 and the first verse of Psalm 112 fit together very well. Both verses speak of fearing the Lord and of obeying His commandments. Psalm 111 places the emphasis on the *Saviour* while Psalm 112 features the *saint*. Psalm 111 gives us the Lord's *person* and in Psalm 112 we see the Lord's *people*.

Psalm 112 bears resemblance to Psalm 1. Both begin with *"Blessed is the man"* and end with a call for the *"wicked"* or *"ungodly"* to perish. Psalm 112 presents that which makes one a blessed man. Remember, the word *"blessed"* means *"happy"* or *"rejoicing."* We will note several truths about this blessed man today and tomorrow.

First we see *Explanation* for his being blessed—a twofold explanation from verse one. He is blessed because he fears the Lord. Men look everywhere for happiness, but the secret is very simple—*"Blessed is the man that feareth the Lord" (v. 1).* When this fear of the Lord is applied to God's people, it is never a slavish fear. It is really a love for the Lord and a desire to please Him who is love. Men look for the pot of gold at the end of the rainbow, and they never find it. What they need to do is follow the arch of the rainbow and look up. In fearing the Lord they will find happiness. God says a second part of this explanation for blessedness is obedience to the Word—the blessed man *"delighteth greatly in his commandments" (v. 1).*

Second, we see the *Extension* of this blessed man. His children carry on his testimony and life style. *"His seed shall be mighty upon earth: the generation of the upright shall be blessed" (v. 2).* Not only does he influence his children, but he also influences later generations—grandchildren and great-grandchildren.

Third, we note his *Expectation.* He will have needs met and *"his righteousness endureth for ever" (v. 3).* That is the same statement made about the Lord in Psalm 111:3. Material things do not destroy the holiness of the righteous man—he carries forth God's character.

Through the Bible in a Year: Mark 12:28-44 and 13

276

October 1

Read Psalms 112–113

Blessings in the Life of the Blessed Man

Yesterday we noted three truths concerning the blessed man. First, we saw the *Explanation* of the secret that makes him blessed: his fear of the Lord and his obedience to God's Word *(v. 1)*. Second, we realized the *Extension* of his being blessed came to his posterity *(v. 2)*. And we also saw his *Expectation (v. 3)*.

Next we will look at his *Experience* of God's guidance: *"Unto the upright there ariseth light in the darkness . . ." (v. 4)*. Light in the darkness—that is our need today for we are living in a very dark world. As saved people, because we have this light, we know where we are and where we are going.

Also we will note his *Excellency.* There are wonderful truths given here about the blessed man. First, *"he is gracious and full of compassion" (v. 4).* The one who enjoys the blessing of God is one who is not spiteful or revengeful. Rather he is forgiving and kind. (Please read Ephesians 4:30-32 concerning the one who is not to grieve the Holy Spirit.) Then, too, this blessed man is a good man, showing favor and lending (v. 5). This man is ready to help someone in need. If someone asks for a loan, he is sympathetic to that person. But the psalmist is careful to note that this man is also wise: *"[H]e will guide his affairs with discretion."* Being willing to help others does not mean that this man is foolish, exposing himself to fraudulent men.

Now let us consider the *Example* of this blessed man. He is an example of a man whose heart has been established (v. 8). Therefore, this man *"shall not be afraid" (v. 8).* He is not moved. He knows that he is secure in the Lord; therefore, he does not need to fret or worry. He may not have much of a name here, but in eternity *"the righteous shall be in everlasting remembrance" (v. 6)!* *"[H]is heart is fixed" (v. 7);* therefore, bad news does not overthrow him—*"He shall not be afraid of evil tidings" (v. 7).* He is *"trusting the Lord" (v. 7).* His righteousness carries on in this life, enduring for ever (v. 9).

Lastly, we see his *Exaltation.* *"[H]is horn* [the power of his life] *shall be exalted with honor" (v. 9).* This blessed man is in distinct contrast to the wicked man whose very *"desire . . . shall perish" (v. 10).*

Through the Bible in a Year: Mark 14

October 2

Read Psalms 113–114

Praise the Lord

Psalms 113–118 are known as the "Hallel Psalms." We could say that these psalms compose Israel's "Hallelujah Chorus." They were sung often during the year and in their entirety at the feasts of Passover, Pentecost, and Tabernacles. Being sung at Passover, they call our attention to Gethsemane and Calvary. It is believed that Psalms 113–115 were sung before the Passover meal began. Psalms 116–118 were sung after the meal.

The psalm begins and ends with praise. Particularly, servants of the Lord are to praise Him (v. 1). What a privilege it is to serve the Lord! Regardless of how important our place of service is, we need to praise Him, for He has commanded His servants to praise Him. Our Lord desires smiling service—not surly service. Servants of the Lord often become jealous of others or are so busy that they do not take time to praise the Lord.

Please note these truths about praise:

1. Whom should we praise? *"The Lord" (vv. 1, 3, 9)*.
2. Who should praise? *"The servants of the Lord" (v. 1)*.
3. What in particular should be praised? *"The name of the Lord" (vv. 1, 2, 3)*.
   Please notice that three times in the first three verses, the psalmist commands us to praise His name. This can imply that we are to praise the Father, the Son, and the Holy Spirit.
4. When should we praise the Lord? *"For evermore" (v. 2);* throughout the whole day (v. 3).
5. Where should the Lord be praised? Everywhere—*"From the rising of the sun to the going down thereof" (v. 3);* in other words, "from East to West."
6. What is the cause for praise? *"He raiseth up the poor out of the dust, and lifteth the needy out of the dunghill" (v. 7)*. The Lord humbles Himself (v. 6) to reach down to us in our need. He not only lifts us from the mire, but also seats us among princes (v. 8).
7. Why should we praise Him? Because He is the great God! *"Who is like unto the Lord our God, who dwelleth on high" (v. 5)*. He has no peers. There is none like Him. We should praise Him.

Through the Bible in a Year: Mark 15–16

October 3

Read Psalms 114–115
Devotional Reading: Psalm 114

Spiritual Power from God

When I read Psalm 114, I sit amazed and thrilled with the power of God. This psalm is speaking of real power needed in our lives, in our churches, in soul winning, in missions, and in revival meetings. Verse seven commands: *"Tremble, thou earth, at the presence of the Lord, at the presence of the God of Jacob."* Here is power!

Philips, in *Exploring the Psalms,* entitles this psalm: "How God Gives Power." He calls this a song of spiritual power and divides it with two main points: "The roots of spiritual power" and "The results of spiritual power." We will follow that outline today.

The Roots—what brings spiritual power? First, they were separated. Verse one tells us that *"Israel went out of Egypt."* She was not *forced* out—she *went* out. Egypt is a picture of the world, and Israel separated from the world. In citing history, this psalm speaks of the exodus from Egypt—the entire nation of Israel moved out. The psalm does not cite the exodus from Babylon where only a portion of the Israelites came out. From Egypt they came out of slavery. That exodus was the event that Israelites regarded as the central and great truth of Israel's history. They came out *"from a people of strange language" (v. 1).* The world has a different language than believers. The world cannot speak the language of Heaven. Spiritual power comes as we turn from the world to the Lord.

Second, they were sanctified: *"Judah was his sanctuary" (v. 2).* Sanctification is the positive side of separation. Paul wrote that he was separated unto the gospel of God (Romans 1:1). We need both separation from the world and separation to the Lord.

The results reveal God's power over nature—*"The sea . . . fled; Jordan was driven back" (v. 3).* This speaks of the Red Sea at the beginning of their exodus and the Jordan River at the close of their forty years of wandering. God delivered them in both cases. Who made this possible?—God and His power (v. 7). He brought water and met their need (v. 8). Spiritual power comes when we separate from the world, are sanctified in Him, and submit to His dominion (v. 2).

Through the Bible in a Year: Luke 1

October 4

Read Psalm 115

Rely on the Lord—Not Idols

Psalm 115 is an exposure of the insanity of idolatry and the wisdom of relying on the Lord. Verse two is a key verse for the entire psalm in answer to the question of that verse: *"Wherefore should the heathen say, where is now their God?"* This was a question that the heathen were asking. Therefore, this psalm must have been written in a time of great national trial. Some believe it was written in the days of Ezra when only a portion of the Jews returned from the ease and luxury of Babylon to the rigors of discipleship to serve God. Others believe it could have been written and sung in the days of Hezekiah. We do not know when it was written, but it is certain that the Jews respected this psalm, for it was part of the hymn that was sung at each Passover feast. Psalms 115–118 are likely the hymn that was sung at the last supper the Lord Jesus Christ had with his disciples (Matthew 26:30). We also know it was written in a time of great stress on Israel with the heathen mocking as they did in verse two.

The psalm begins with a *Recognition of the Importance* to trust the Lord. Twice in verse one the psalmist says to God: *"Not unto us"* should glory be given. They recognized that without the Lord they could do nothing. The singers confessed glory should be given only to the Lord's name because of His mercy and His truth (v. 1). Logically they asked, *"[Why] should the heathen mock"* (v. 2). They answered that question very clearly in verse three: *"But our God is in the heavens: he hath done whatsoever he hath pleased."* God is in charge—His sovereign will is always being done. Seeming delays on His part do not mean desertion. Instead such delays are given to teach us valuable lessons. He has not promised us a smooth voyage, but he has promised us a safe landing. He does what He pleases. Therefore, He deserves all the praise.

Then the psalm continues with the *Revelation of the Impotence* of idols. Men turn to idols—how foolish!! Idols are made by men (v. 4). They appear to have organs of sense but they cannot speak, see, hear, smell, handle, or walk. Most tragic of all, the men who make them become like them (vv. 5-8). We must keep ourselves from idolatry.

Through the Bible in a Year: Luke 2

October 5

Read Psalm 115

The Lord—Our Help and Shield

Psalm 115 is a great passage on the folly of idolatry. Verse eight states clearly that those who trust the idols become like the idols. Maclaren wrote, "Men make gods after their own image, and when made, the gods make them after theirs."

In his book *Preaching the Psalms,* LeMoyne Sharpe has written the following comparisons between God and idols: "*First,* idols vary in every age and among various nations. But God remains the same. *Second,* idols are numerous and conflicting. God is one, and in harmony with Himself. *Third,* idols are the work of men's hands. God is eternal and uncreated. The same power which can make an idol can destroy it. But the living God is untouchable by His creatures. *Fourth,* idols at best can occupy only temples made with hands. But God is in the heavens. *Fifth,* idols are senseless. God is keenly sensitive of the needs of His creatures. Thus the issue should be settled once and for all."

In verses nine through eleven the psalmist appeals to three groups to trust in the Lord. He has proven that idolatry is folly; therefore, he summons these groups to turn from folly to faith. The first group to whom he appeals are the people of Israel, God's own covenant people. The psalmist pleads with Israel to trust the Lord because He is Israel's help and shield (v. 9).

The second group to whom these appeals are given is the family of Aaron, those who make up the family of the High Priest (v. 10). His summons to these, the religious leaders of Israel, is that they trust in the Lord. The word *"trust"* in verse nine and ten means *"to commit oneself to another, and to leave oneself there."*

Verse eleven pleads with all who fear the Lord to trust in the Lord. In all three cases God's invitation to these groups is given on the basis that the Lord is their help and shield. May we learn this lesson as well. The Lord is our help in every need and our shield against every attack. He is our help and shield!

Through the Bible in a Year: Luke 3–4

October 6

Read Psalms 115:12-18 and 116
Devotional Reading: Psalm 115:12-18

He Will Bless Those Who Fear Him

Yesterday we noted the appeals given in Psalm 115:9-11. Verse twelve gives us the assurance that the Lord has blessed in the past and will bless in the future. *"The Lord hath been mindful of us"*—that is spoken by those who fear the Lord in verse twelve. We look back and we can see how God has blessed. And then we look to the future for the assurance that He will bless all three groups given in verses nine through eleven: "us"—those who fear the Lord (v. 11); the house of Israel (v. 9) and the house of Aaron (v. 10).

Whom will He bless? Verse thirteen answers with *"He will bless them that fear the Lord, both small and great."* The blessing of the Lord does not depend on how much we know nor on our family heritage. Nor does it depend on whether we are in full time ministry. It depends only on whether we trust Him. He is faithful, and we can rest on His faithfulness.

Who is the one blessing? Verse fifteen answers that question: *"Ye are blessed of the Lord which made heaven and earth."* The one who created all things is the one who is giving the blessings. Certainly He is able. He who flung myriads of stars thousands and millions of light years into space is able to control all things that affect my life and yours.

Why do we need His blessing? We are on earth: *"The . . . heavens are the Lord's: but the earth hath he given to the children of men"* *(v. 16).* And what a mess men have made of the earth. We need help—help from Him who is Creator and Redeemer. We need His help now. Therefore, we should bless Him now while we have life. Soon life will be over for us—and we will be silenced as far as giving praise to Him is concerned (v. 17). Our praise of the Lord should begin now and continue throughout eternity—*"from this time forth and for evermore"* (v. 18). May we be faithful to praise Him.

Through the Bible in a Year: Luke 5 and 6:1-38

October 7

Read Psalm 116

God Answers Prayer

We do not know when Psalm 116 was written, nor do we have any record of who wrote it. We realize from reading the psalm that it was written after the psalmist had been delivered from some serious and tragic illness. The psalm is intensely personal—the writer refers to himself with the pronouns *"I," "me," "my,"* or *"mine"* thirty-five times. But the writer is not sinfully thinking only of himself; the titles *"Lord"* and *"God"* along with pronouns referring to Him appear thirty-six times. In Psalm 116, the psalmist is thanking the Lord for His deliverance from the penalty and results of sin.

The psalmist had been so ill that he felt he was at the point of death (v. 3). He had faced a very difficult time that brought him to the very place of death. Trouble and sorrow were on every hand (v. 3).

He begins the psalm by announcing in verse one: *"I love the Lord."* Why did he love the Lord? The reason given in verse one is that God heard the voice of his supplications. He emphasizes that truth by adding, *"Because he hath inclined his ear unto me, therefore will I call upon him as long as I live" (v. 2).* It is good to love the Lord for the reasons that the psalmist gave. The love the psalmist manifested was a love given in return for God's favor.

Because God answered, verse two reveals that the psalmist pledged to continue to call upon the Lord. In verse three the psalmist tells us the circumstances out of which he had been delivered by God: *"The sorrows of death compassed me . . ."* He experienced either dreadful sickness or extreme danger. Out of this deep anguish, the psalmist's faith came forward leading him to pray in verse four: *"Then called I upon the name of the Lord; O Lord, I beseech thee, deliver my soul."* And God answered. His answer surpassed the psalmist's appeal, as it often does, so that he could confidently say, *"Gracious is the Lord, and righteous; yea, our God is merciful" (v. 5).* May we consistently turn to the Lord in prayer and see Him work miraculously in our lives.

Through the Bible in a Year: Luke 6:39-49 and 7

October 8

Read Psalms 116–117

Faith Through Dreadful Trials

In Psalm 116 we find the author undergoing a difficult trial. He had been brought low (v. 6). In verse ten he states that he was greatly afflicted. We can realize how low this individual was when we read, *"For thou hast delivered my soul from death . . ." (v. 8)*. The psalmist had faced death and had seen God miraculously deliver him.

The psalmist knew that his only answer was to rest in the Lord and to rely on His gracious strength. The Lord had delivered him through the dreadful experience. Now he could praise the Lord for His bountiful deliverance (v. 7). He would not only rest in the Lord, but also walk before the Lord in the land of the living (v. 9). Someone might ask, "How can you rest while walking?" Remember this—spiritual rest makes no one idle; therefore, it is no enemy to walking. Spiritual walking makes no one weary; therefore, it is no enemy to rest. In the service of God there is a rest about which the world knows nothing. Our walk is before *"the land of the living" (v. 9)*. The world is going to watch to see how a believer comes through the trials of life.

Verse ten opens with two words, *"I believed."* No part of his trial had robbed the psalmist of faith. What did his faith cause him to do: *"I believed, therefore have I spoken . . ." (v. 10)*. He confessed before others the blessing of God's sustaining grace. The heart and tongue go together. Jesus said, *"[O]ut of the abundance of the heart the mouth speaketh" (Matthew 12:34)*. The psalmist had a heart filled with praise, and he spoke what he knew by faith.

In verse eleven the psalmist confessed a problem that we all face. He judged others hastily for the trials he was enduring. *"I said in my haste, All men are liars" (v. 11)*. Now he recognized that he spoke in haste. Far too many of us get our exercise by jumping to conclusions. We all need to think a matter through and then speak thoughtfully.

The psalmist realized what God had done for him. He wondered what he could do for the Lord in return (v. 12). Like the psalmist we all should stop and meditate on the many benefits God has bestowed on us.

Through the Bible in a Year: Luke 8

October 9

Read Psalms 116–117

Surrender to God Because of Blessings Received

We closed yesterday's meditation with the question given in Psalm 116:12: *"What shall I render unto the Lord for all His benefits toward me?"* He thought he needed to do something in return. However, he answered the question in verse thirteen: *"I will take the cup of salvation, and call upon the name of the Lord."* Before he goes any further asking what he should do in return for God's blessing, he resolves that he will continue to receive more of what God is freely giving. Actually, nothing pleases the Lord more than for us to open up our hearts and lives so that we can receive more of His blessings. In addition, the psalmist resolves that he will call upon the Lord in prayer. In verse fourteen he adds another of his resolves—*"I will pay my vows unto the Lord now in the presence of all his people."* The psalmist resolves to be totally surrendered to the will of God. He states he will pay his vows. How often have I heard someone in a time of serious illness tell the Lord that he will serve the Lord if the Lord will heal him. I have seen God bring healing, and the individual forgets all about his vow. Not so with the psalmist. He planned to keep his vows.

"Precious in the sight of the Lord is the death of his saints" (v. 15). When one of His own is called out of this life to be with Him, it is precious to God. Had he been taken from his sick bed into the presence of the Lord, the psalmist realizes his homecoming would have been precious to the Lord.

The last four verses of Psalm 116 review what he has been discussing in the previous verses. He was freed from the trials he had undergone—*"Thou hast loosed my bond"* (v. 16). Therefore, he gave his life to be the Lord's servant (v. 16). Because of the freedom he received and his desire to be God's servant, the psalmist could again say that he would yield all to the Lord and would keep his vows. May we, like the psalmist, rejoice in the salvation our Lord has given us and dedicate our all to Him.

Through the Bible in a Year: Luke 9

October 10

Read Psalms 117–118

A Call to All to Praise the Lord

Psalm 117 has the distinction of being the shortest psalm in the Psaltery and the shortest chapter in the Bible. Some would say it is so short it really is not significant. Not so! This psalm is placed here for a purpose. It is not just an adjunct to the psalm before it or the psalm after it. Psalm 117 probably was sung often in the way the doxology is sung in our services today.

It is a psalm of praise. It is seventeen words long in the Hebrew and three of those words are *"praise."* The matter of praise is commanded. It is not just an option for us to consider. In the Old Testament there is no duty more pressed upon us than the duty of praise. Yet it seems to be one of the duties least practiced by us. We can't praise Him too much, but we can praise Him too little. A forgiven people should be a happy people; and a happy people should be a praising people.

Whom should we praise? In all three commands in this short psalm, we are told to praise the Lord. He is the one worthy of our praise.

Who should praise the Lord? The psalmist tells us that all people should praise Him—*"all ye nations"* and *"all ye people" (v. 1).* How different this is from the isolated bigotry of the Jews who lived during Jesus' earthly ministry. The Lord invites all nations and tongues and people to know and praise Him.

Why should we praise the Lord? The psalmist gives two reasons. First, we should praise Him because of His merciful kindness (v. 2). In verse two he states that that mercy is great toward us. That mercy is given us in His grace today. The second reason for praise is that the truth of the Lord endureth forever (v. 2).

We need to praise the Lord for His grace that works in our lives and for His Word that instructs and directs our lives. May we praise Him today. Remember that praise, or the lack of praise, is a good indicator of our spiritual condition. So let's obey God's command and praise the Lord.

Through the Bible in a Year: Luke 10 and 11:1-13

October 11

Read Psalm 118
Family Reading: Psalm 118:1-20

Praise Him for His Enduring Mercy

Psalm 118 is another psalm of which we have no statement concerning its author. It could well have been written during the days of Ezra and Nehemiah following the Babylonian captivity. The first and last verses of this psalm are identical, and are to similar to Ezra 3:11: *"[G]iving thanks unto the Lord: because he is good, for his mercy endureth forever."* It could well be that this psalm was written to celebrate that occasion.

The psalm was sung as part of the temple worship—probably at the Feast of Tabernacles. The psalmist was celebrating a great deliverance, thankful for the mercy of the Lord.

The psalmist invited us all to give thanks to the Lord because of His goodness and His grace. Verse one states that *"he is good: because his mercy endureth forever."* Goodness is one of our Lord's attributes, and out of His goodness flows His mercy. The wonderful truth is that His mercy endureth forever. In this age, where we have all types of disposable items—disposable containers, disposable flashlights, even disposable cameras—it is great to find something enduring forever. The psalmist invites Israel to say that *"his mercy endureth forever"* (v. 2). That same invitation is given to the priestly family, the house of Aaron in verse three. And then it is extended to all of us who fear the Lord—we, too, are to say, *"[H]is mercy endureth forever"* (v. 4). So we see the Lord invites public praise, priestly praise, and personal praise.

The psalmist then states in verse five the reason we should praise the Lord. The psalmist said he did so because when he was in distress he called on the Lord and the Lord answered, setting him a large place. That testimony can be repeated by those of us who have come to know Him. We were distressed in the bondage of sin. We cried unto Him and He delivered us, saving us—and we can know that the mercy that reached out and saved us endures forever. Let's praise Him for His goodness to us and His mercy that endures forever.

Through the Bible in a Year: Luke 11:14-54 and 12:1-21

October 12

Read Psalm 118
Family Reading: Psalm 118:1-20

Deliverance by God's Help

Yesterday we noted the *goodness* of God as revealed in the fact that His mercy endureth forever (vv. 1-4). Today we will consider the *greatness* of God in His ability to meet every need in the life of the believer (vv. 5-13).

When he wrote this song the psalmist was in deep distress. Note verse five: *"I called upon the Lord in distress . . . ."* Also note verses ten through thirteen where we see that this psalmist was compassed about with many enemies. Without question the psalmist was a king against whom nations gathered to destroy him.

The psalmist's answer in such distress was to call upon the Lord. The Lord answered him (v. 5). Surrounded by the enemy, it was as though he was hemmed up in a narrow canyon. He prayed and the Lord answered. Then he wrote that the Lord *"set me in a large place" (v. 5)*. The Lord moved him out of the narrow gorge into a large open plain.

Prayers that come out of distress are usually prayers that come out of the heart, and prayers out of the heart go directly to the heart of God. With this answer the psalmist boldly announced: *"The Lord is on my side; I will not fear: what man can do unto me?" (v. 6)*. Further he stated, *"The Lord taketh my part . . . therefore shall I see my desire upon them that hate me" (v. 7)*. The psalmist stated confidently: *"It is better to trust in the Lord than to put confidence in man . . . [or] princes" (vv. 8-9)*. In verse seven the psalmist said he had friends to help him—but the Lord did not just leave him to his friends; rather the Lord entered into the fray Himself.

In verses ten through twelve the psalmist notes that he was compassed about with enemies as numerous as bees. He was one person against a great crowd. However, there is one word in verses ten and eleven—the word *"but."* *"But in the name of the Lord I will destroy them" (vv. 10, 11)*. He was one—***BUT*** he had the Lord. One with God is a majority in any situation. Here the Lord comes to the aid of his prayerful, trusting hero. The apparent loss became a sure gain.

Through the Bible in a Year: Luke 12:22-59 and 13

October 13

Read Psalm 118
Family Reading: Psalm 118:8-29

Delivered by God's Right Hand

The middle verse of the entire Bible is Psalm 118:8, and this verse certainly ought to become a central truth is all our lives: *"It is better to trust in the Lord than to put confidence in man."* Any person who is honest with himself knows he cannot even trust himself—much less his fellow man. I remember when I was asked to wear a big button that said "100% for . . . " a certain preacher. I said, "I am not even 100% for Ed Nelson because I am just a sinner saved by grace. The only one for whom I could ever be 100% for is the Lord Jesus Christ."

The psalmist does not dream of boasting of his works, but rather speaks of the strength and salvation of the Lord—the One who is the source of all blessings. *"The Lord is my strength and song, and is become my salvation" (v. 14).*

He exalted the Lord, recognizing that all victory comes from Him. In verse sixteen he wrote: *"[T]he right hand of the Lord doeth valiantly."* In fact he makes the statement, *"the right hand of the Lord doeth valiantly"* twice in verses fifteen and sixteen.

The psalmist reveals how severe his trial was by writing in verse seventeen, *"I shall not die, but live, and declare the works of the Lord."* Apparently his trials had brought him to the very gates of death. But God speaks of His "right hand." In fact He mentions the right hand of the Lord three times. It is His right hand that defends saints and defeats Satan. God protected and kept His servant. Enemies had encompassed the psalmist—but God had delivered him. Even when enemies plot the death of a servant of God, they cannot succeed when it is God's will for the man to live. The servant doing the will of God is immortal until the work of God is completed in his life.

> Plagues and death around me fly.
> Till He please I cannot die;
> Not a single shaft can hit,
> Till the God of love see fit.
> —Selected

Through the Bible in a Year: Luke 14–15

October 14

Read Psalm 118
Family Reading: Psalm 118:8-29

Christ, Our Cornerstone

In Psalm 118:18, the psalmist realized that the encircling enemies were really a chastening by God.

"The Lord hath chastened me sore: but he hath not given me over unto death."

God permits chastening for our own good. But the Lord puts the limit on how extensive the chastening will be. Our pains are for our instruction—not for our destruction. Trials should make us better—not bitter.

The psalmist came to the gates of the Temple. In verse nineteen he requested: *"Open to me the gates of righteousness: I will go into them, and I will praise the Lord."* In verse twenty he defined those gates as those into which the righteous enter. The gates to the place of worship are called *"the gates of righteousness."* We all need to come to those gates and enter into worship. It is sad today to see how many there are that fail to come to the church building, the house of God for the purpose of public worship. Remember, those who neglect public worship will almost always fail to engage in any worship whatever.

In verse twenty-one, the psalmist gives the reason for his praise: *"I will praise thee: for thou hast heard me, and art become my salvation."* He had seen the Lord do the miraculous in delivering him from his enemies. It was surely an event worthy of praise.

When we come to verse twenty-two we recognize immediately that it is a verse quoted often in the New Testament: *"The stone which the builders refused is become the head stone of the corner." (Matthew 21:42; Acts 4:11; Ephesians 2:20; I Peter 2:6-8)* This Stone is revealed as being the Lord Jesus Christ. The cornerstone was the most important stone in the building. It capped the building and bonded the walls together. Jesus Christ, being that Cornerstone today, is the head of the church and the One who supports the individual believer and the body of Christ in weakness, trials, and even unto death. May each of us believers as a small living stone rest in Him, our chief Cornerstone (I Peter 2:4-5).

Through the Bible in a Year: Luke 16–17

October 15

Read Psalms 118:22-29 and 119:1-16
Devotional Reading: Psalm 118:22-29

The Lord at Calvary Became Our Cornerstone

Yesterday we considered the truth of the head stone of the *"corner"* in Psalm 118:22. Today we will consider more about that cornerstone. It is presented many times in the New Testament as referring to Jesus Christ. There are six places where it is quoted almost verbatim. But there are many more verses in the New Testament in which it is referred to as presenting Christ as the true and only foundation of the Church. He was the stone that was rejected by the builders—the religious and political leaders of Israel and of the world. He was rejected then, and He is being rejected by the same people today. But this One, *"despised and rejected of men" (Isaiah 53:3)* became the one to whom all men must come in order to be saved.

Verse twenty-three states that this exalted position of Christ was the work of God and not of man. *"This is the Lord's doing; it is marvellous in our eyes."* God in His wisdom designed it; God in His justice instituted it; God in His love provided it; and God by His power laid this Cornerstone.

Verse twenty-four is often quoted as referring to Sunday. Surely it includes Sunday as the Lord's day—but it refers to more than just Sunday. It refers to every day of a believer's life. But I believe it also refers to something more than that. In its context it is referring to this age of grace, the time when we come to the Lord Jesus Christ as our Saviour from sin and the Cornerstone of our lives. You see, verse twenty-six refers to the day when Christ made His Triumphal entry into the city of Jerusalem just before His crucifixion (Matthew 21:9). This passage is definitely referring to the time when God gave His Son at Calvary to die in our place.

The psalm ends with the psalmist acknowledging God as His Lord. Verse twenty-seven: *"God is the Lord."* Verse twenty-eight: *"Thou art my God . . . I will exalt thee."* Acknowledging the Lordship of God in his life, the psalmist confesses that he willingly bound his life with the cords of love as a sacrifice. When the light has come, a believer should willingly and joyfully give his life to the Lordship of Christ.

Through the Bible in a Year: Luke 18 and 19:1-27

October 16

Read Psalms 119:1-24

Brief Introduction to Psalm 119

Today we begin meditations in Psalm 119. Frankly, I feel totally inadequate to write these devotionals on Psalm 119. We will spend several days on the psalm—it will take us until November 13 to complete the psalm. This is a psalm with which we should come to be very familiar. Matthew Henry relates that his father, Philip Henry, required his children to quote one verse of this psalm each day. They quoted the entire psalm in less than half a year, and they repeated this many times. It is no wonder that Matthew Henry wrote the great Bible commentary known by his name.

Psalm 119 is the longest psalm in the entire Psaltery and the entire Bible. It is a unique psalm in that it is divided into twenty-two stanzas, each one having eight verses. Each stanza begins with a different Hebrew letter, and each of the eight verses in a stanza begins with the same letter.

We do not know who wrote the psalm, nor do we know when it was written. It has been ascribed to David, Ezra, Hezekiah, Jeremiah, Nehemiah, Daniel, and Malachi. It could have been David. David suffered much, and the psalmist mentions his sufferings at least sixty-six times. It could have been Ezra, for he is the one who *"prepared his heart to seek the law of the Lord, and to do it, and to teach in Israel statutes and judgments" (Ezra 7:10)*. That for which Ezra prepared his heart is the subject of this psalm.

Whoever wrote the psalm undoubtedly had resolved to love the Word of God and to make His Word and law the governing principle of his life. God's Word is referred to in 173 of the 176 verses. God is referred to in every verse except verse 121, and in that verse it is implied that the psalmist is making request of God.

As we read through Psalm 119, we can note it is an intensely personal psalm. The psalmist makes reference to himself 325 times using such words as *"I," "my," "me," "mine," "myself,"* and *"Thy servant."* May we receive personal instruction as we look at this psalm together.

Through the Bible in a Year: Luke 19:28-48 and 20

October 17

Read Psalm 119:1-8; 25-40
Note Particularly: Psalm 119:1-2

The Psalm of Superabounding Blessing

Psalm 119 presents a great challenge of anyone deciding to preach it or to write an exposition of it. Augustine said that Psalm 119 seems "not to need an expositor, but only a reader and listener."

This psalm is divided into twenty-two groups of eight verses each. Why eight? Remember that numbers in the Bible hold significance for us. *Seven* in the Bible is the number of completeness. The Hebrew word for seven is *"sheba"* which means *"to be full, to be satisfied, so to have enough."* Revelation, the book that completes the Bible is a book of *sevens*—*seven* churches, *seven* Seals, *seven* Trumpets, and *seven* Golden Bowls. The Hebrew word for eight, however, is *"sh'monch,"* which means *"to make fat, to superabound."* Seven is enough, but eight is more than enough. It goes beyond seven, thus it represents a new beginning. Christ rose on the first day of the week which was the Jewish eighth day, Saturday being the seventh day. Psalm 119 reveals that the Word of God, the Law of the Lord, superabounds beyond completion. It is that which we must have in our lives in order to live to glorify God. This psalm, with twenty-two stanzas of eight verses each, reveals the fullness and fatness of the Word and will of God.

Remember that the Word of God is given us in His written Word, the Bible, and in His living Word, the Lord Jesus Christ. The psalm begins with *"Blessed are the undefiled . . . Blessed are they that keep his testimonies . . ." (vv. 1-2).* The word *"Blessed"* is the same word that opens the Psalms in chapter one: *"Blessed is the man . . ."* We saw that Psalm 1 spoke of the Lord Jesus Christ as the One most surely blessed. Psalm 119 does the same. We can see Jesus all the way through the psalm as the one who is our example (I Peter 2:21) for living and obeying the Word of God (Matthew 4:4 and Hebrews 10:7).

The word *"blessed"* in the Old Testament means *"happy."* It is written in the plural which means the person has many blessings—is very happy— has joy that abounds. This psalm, like Psalm 1, will reveal to us that which makes the individual truly happy.

Through the Bible in a Year: Luke 21 and 22:1-18

October 18

Read Psalm 119:1-8; 41-56
Devotional Reading: Psalm 119:1-8

The Way of Genuine Happiness

The first stanza of Psalm 119 (vv. 1-8) deals with the way and the walk of a believer. *"Blessed are the undefiled in the way, who walk in the law of the Lord" (v. 1).*

The words *"way"* and *"ways"* appear fifteen times in this psalm. Two of those times the psalmist speaks of an evil or a false way (vv. 101, 104). The word *"way"* presents the idea of a life lived according to the path marked out by God's law revealed in God's Word.

Who are those who are blessed? They are the ones who are *"undefiled in the way"* of life. Remember that the word *"blessed"* means "happy." The ones who have kept themselves undefiled in the way are the ones who are really happy. How different this is from the idea of the world. They think that no one can be happy if he remains undefiled. They would suppose that Daniel was not a happy person because he decided not to defile himself with the king's meat (Daniel 1:8). Real happiness does not come from sources such as pleasure, wealth, popularity, or position. It comes from knowing the Lord and living according to His will. Robert Burns expressed the futility of looking to human sources of happiness when he wrote:

> Pleasures are like poppies spread,
> You seize the flower, the bloom is fled,
> Or like a snowflake on the river,
> A moment white then gone forever.

Those who are undefiled are those who *"keep his testimonies"* and *"walk in his ways" (v. 2-3).* The psalmist knew that real happiness, that is genuine joy, comes only from turning from sin to walk in the way of the Lord. He prayed, *"O that my ways were directed to keep thy statutes!" (v. 5).* He longed to be this one who would enjoy the blessing of the Lord—real happiness in living for Him.

Through the Bible in a Year: Luke 22:19-71

October 19

Read Psalm 119:9-16; 57-72
Devotional Reading: Psalm 119:9-16

The Effect of God's Word in a Committed Believer

Psalm 119:9-16 is a portion of Scripture to which Bible believers often refer. Verse eleven is one of the most quoted Scripture verses in the Bible: *"Thy Word have I hid in mine heart, that I might not sin against thee."* By having God's Word stored in his heart, many a believer has been delivered from temptation. Someone has said, "This Book will keep you from sin, or sin will keep you from this Book." How true! The Bible is an important part of our continual victory in Christ. Psalm 119:9-11 present three effects that the Word of God will have in the life of a young person. First, it will have a *Cleansing Effect.* Verse nine reads, *"Wherewithal shall a young man cleanse his way? By taking heed thereto according to thy word."* Young people need to live clean lives. What will produce a clean life? The answer is clear—it is the Word of God. *"Now ye are clean through the word which I have spoken unto you" (John 15:3).* Everyone of us, young and old, need to daily experience the cleansing effect of the Word of God as we spend time in His Word.

Second, it will have a *Controlling Effect.* The psalmist states in verse ten: *"With my whole heart have I sought thee: O let me not wander from thy commandments."* Verse ten holds the secret to a life lived right: *"With my whole heart."* God desires total commitment. Anyone who tries to keep God's Word in a half hearted way will fail to be the holy person God wants him to be.

Third, God's Word will have a *Correcting Effect.* Verse eleven states that God's Word hidden in our heart will deliver us from sin. Then verse twelve crowns the passage with, *"Blessed art thou, O Lord: teach me thy statutes."* It is as I receive and apply the Word of God that I have victory over sin.

Please note the words *"I have"* and *"I will"* in verses ten through sixteen. The psalmist's strong commitments to what God has done and will do in his life came out of his commitment to the Word of God. Each of us will do well to meditate on these verses and make them part of our lives.

Through the Bible in a Year: Luke 23

October 20

Read Psalm 119:9-16; 73-88
Devotional Reading: Psalm 119:9-16

Letting God's Word Work in our Lives

We are going to be reading and considering Psalm 119 through November 13. As you have noticed, each day we will read an eight verse stanza from which we will have our devotional. In addition we will read two other eight verse stanzas consecutively through Psalm 119. Upon completing the psalm we will begin at verse one and read through the psalm again. We will read through the entire psalm three times. Four times we are going to give two days of devotions to an eight verse stanza. This second stanza, verses nine through sixteen, is the first one to which we will give a second day for our meditation on the passage.

The psalmist gives the priceless worth of the Bible in verse fourteen. *"I have rejoiced in the way of thy testimonies, as much as in all riches."* There is nothing in this life to compare with the riches inherent in the Word of God.

Then in verse fifteen, the psalmist tells us in what he will meditate and why. *"I will meditate in thy precepts, and have respect unto thy ways."* The word *"ways"* speaks of the paths we follow. Meditation in God's Word will lead our feet into right paths. The psalmist states this truth again in verse fifty-nine: *"I thought on my ways, and turned my feet unto thy testimonies."* It is important to get our feet on the right path. There are many slippery places in life. We need to have a sure footing and not be trying to travel in slippery areas. I remember driving our pick-up and fifth-wheel trailer over Wolf Creek Pass in southern Colorado during the winter. About two miles from the top of the pass the snow packed highway became so slippery that our wheels spun out and the rig stopped. I set all the brakes, but the whole rig began to slide down the steep grade backwards! Dangerous—but God delivered us. Life is like that—many slippery places. Therefore, we need the Bible.

The stanza ends with the psalmist saying, *"I will not forget thy Word"* (v. 16). We must do the same—always remember God's Word.

Through the Bible in a Year: Luke 24

October 21

Read Psalm 119:17-24; 89-104
Devotional Reading: Psalm 119:17-24

Opportunities in the Word—
Opposition to the Word

In verse seventeen we are given a vital truth of the Christian life: *"Deal bountifully with thy servant, that I may live and keep thy word."* The truth *"that I may live and keep thy word"* is actually a New Testament truth. The Old Testament principle was: "Do this, and you will live." But in the New Testament we find something importantly different. We live to keep God's Word. First we receive life and then we have action: "If you live you will do this." We must first live through the new birth, and then we have grace and strength to live the life.

Following that we need to daily study the Word of God. Thus, we need God to open our eyes to behold wondrous things out of His law (v. 18). We receive life—then we grow through feeding on His Word. Verse eighteen is a good prayer for pastors and Sunday School teachers to pray. We need to get profit from the Word of God that will appear unto all those we teach (I Timothy 4:15)

Another wonderful benefit from the Word of God is that it will dispel our loneliness and keep us from feeling like a stranger in the earth. Suicide is very prevalent in our society. Individuals feel rejected and alone. If they would only turn to the Word of God, that loneliness would flee. We should pray, *"[H]ide not thy commandments from me" (v. 19).*

These first verses of the third stanza (vv. 17-19) reveal the great opportunities we can find in God's Word. Beginning with verse twenty-one we have the second half of this stanza. It reveals great opposition to the Word of God. We find the proud erring from God's commandments (v. 21); reproach and contempt for the Word of God (v. 22); and princes speaking against the truth of the Lord (v. 23).

What is the answer to this opposition? Verse twenty-four gives that answer: *"Thy testimonies also are my delight, and my counselors."*

Through the Bible in a Year: John 1

October 22

Read Psalm 119:25-32; 105-120
Devotional Reading: Psalm 119:25-32

Dealing with Sin in our Lives

Today we come to the fourth stanza of Psalm 119. Verses twenty-five through thirty-two form a prayer for God to quicken the life of the psalmist. He was enduring some great trial or grief. He had gone so low that he opened this prayer with the words, *"My soul cleaveth unto the dust . . . " (v. 25).* The psalmist was in the grip of depression, very likely overcome, with his own guilt. In todays's society when one is troubled with guilt, the principle recommendation is to see a psychiatrist. These experts often encourage their clients to let everything "hang out"—that is, they are to confess openly their problems to others in the same therapy group. In such a group everyone comments on the problems. They criticize each others attitudes, personality traits, and shortcomings.

But this is not what the psalmist suggested. He was going to bring his problems out in the open—but only before God. He prayed to the Lord: *"[Q]uicken thou me" (v. 25).* He would come to a counselor all right—that counselor being the Lord through His Word. The Bible will meet every need in our lives: *"[Q]uicken thou me according to thy word" (v. 25).* This request to *"quicken"* meant to put new life into him. As we read the Bible and exercise faith, God gives wonderful results.

The psalmist confessed his sin to God: *"I have declared my ways, and thou heardest me . . . " (v. 26).* He confessed his sin to the Lord. He is the One to whom we can go when we are dealing with sin. Our God is the Great Psychiatrist who, through His Word, can meet the need in every life.

The psalmist prayed that he would understand the precepts of God. With that understanding he could give testimony of the wondrous works of God (v. 27). With his understanding of God's precepts, the psalmist realized the wickedness of his sin and his soul melted—that is, he wept (v. 28). Then the psalmist asked God to remove the way of lying from him. This is a need in all our lives. We need to be honest with one another in our relationships. What a need in every life—recognition and confession of sin out of an honest heart.

Through the Bible in a Year: John 2–3

October 23

Read Psalm 119:33-40; 121-136
Devotional Reading: Psalm 119:33-40

Four Pictures of a Man of God

Today we will look at four pictures of a Man of God as found in Psalm 119:33-40.

1. A Sojourner (vv. 33-34)

   The psalmist pictures himself as being on a journey and needing to know the proper way. He asks the Lord, *"Teach me . . . the way of thy statutes"* (v. 33), and then he promises, *"I shall keep it unto the end" (v. 33).* Often I ask directions to a place in unfamiliar territory, trust my memory, and fail to write the directions down. Soon I find myself wondering where I am to turn and which direction. Not so with the psalmist—he said he would take God's directions and follow them closely. He prayed for God to not only show him the way, but also to give him understanding in walking the way (v. 34).

2. A Soldier (vv. 35-36)

   The psalmist indicated that he fought a battle in his life. He asked God to make him to go in the path of God's commandments (v. 35). And then he said he delighted in those commandments (v. 35). Why would he have to ask God to make him do something in which he delighted? The answer is that every believer has a battle within himself. He has *"the old man"* and *"the new man"* (Ephesians 4:22-24 and Colossians 3:9-10). The psalmist wanted to live according to the new man; therefore he prayed: *"Incline my heart unto thy testimonies, and not unto covetousness" (v. 36).*

3. A Spiritual Man (vv. 37-38)

   To be a spiritual man we need to turn away our eyes *"from beholding vanity" (v. 37).* Temptation often comes through the eye gate. We must also have God's Word established in our hearts (v. 38).

4. A Sanctified Man (vv. 39-40)

   The psalmist prayed that he would not bring reproach on the name of the Lord (v. 39). The secret of a holy life is that we long after the precepts of the Lord (v. 40).

Through the Bible in a Year: John 4

October 24

Read Psalm 119:41-48; 137-152
Devotional Reading: Psalm 119:41-48

Trusting the Lord to do His Will

The psalmist had just prayed in verse thirty-nine that God would turn away his reproach from him. The world is watching every child of God to see if he brings reproach on the name of the Lord. The psalmist recognizes this, and in verse forty-two he states that he will have an answer to give to the one who reproaches him because of his faith in the Lord. That answer comes from our salvation through God's mercies. *"Let thy mercies come also unto me, O Lord, even thy salvation, according to thy word" (v. 41).* Men will endeavor to mock and bring reproach on the name of the Lord. The wisdom of this world is opposed to the truth of God's Word, and we are thus given an answer of the hope that is in us (I Peter 3:15).

Therefore, the psalmist prayed: *"And take not the word of truth utterly out of my mouth; for I have hoped in thy judgments" (v. 43).* By resting on the Word of God we can hope in the blessing and justice of God's judgments. He will keep His Word. Therefore, the psalmist could say, *"So shall I keep thy law continually for ever and ever" (v. 44).* He said that he had hoped in God's judgments; therefore, regardless of what would take place in his life, he would rest on the Word of God.

Often, we feel that God is not bringing his judgments to pass. It seems to be taking too long—we ask ourselves, "Is God really working?" The psalmist said he would not be troubled by seeming delays. He would trust the Lord no matter what did or did not happen. Abraham waited a long time for Isaac. He even resorted to fleshly means to help God out. But in God's timing, Isaac was born miraculously. Abraham *"staggered not at the promises of God through unbelief; but was strong in faith, giving glory to God" (Romans 4:20).* In God's time, Isaac was born. We need to hold on to the Word of truth and realize that God will accomplish His will.

Through the Bible in a Year: John 5

October 25

Read Psalm 119:49-56; 153-176
Devotional Reading: Psalm 119:49-56

Hoping in God's Word

As we read through Psalm 119 we note many verses that reveal the psalmist was facing adverse circumstances. These difficult times existed because there were wicked men who hated his godly stand. Psalm 119:49-56 again presents this problem.

He begins this section by stating in verse forty-nine that his hope was in the Word of God. Our relationship to Christ presents us a wonderful hope. Often we think of hope as something rather weak. For example, we consider it a poor answer when we ask someone if he is saved and he says, "I hope so." But hope does have a positive meaning. It relates us to the future and is definitely certain when our hope is placed on the Word of God. The Bible is sure and hope based on Biblical promises is sure and stable.

In verse fifty the psalmist states that the Word of God became his comfort in his affliction. When we face affliction we need to do what the psalmist did—he turned to the Word of God. He wrote: *"[T]hy Word hath quickened me" (v. 50)*—that is, God's Word had given him new life. Often, instead of turning to God's Word in times of affliction, people turn everywhere else. They go to the doctor if they face sickness; to the lawyer if they face problems; to employment agencies if they are without a job; or to the government if they need money. Please understand—doctors and lawyers and employment agencies can help—but we ought to go to God and His Word *first*. The psalmist found new life through the Word of God.

Verse fifty-one states that the psalmist faced great derision by the proud who hated him and his God. They undoubtedly scorned him as did Goliath when he saw David coming to meet him: *"Am I a dog, that thou comest to me with staves?" (I Samuel 17:43).* The psalmist stated his answer to their scorn and derision was that he had not declined from God's law (v. 51). He hoped in God's Word, trusted that Word for new life even when afflicted, and refused to turn from God's law. He hoped in God's Word and saw God's deliverance in his life.

Through the Bible in a Year: John 6

October 26

Read Psalm 119:1-16; 49-56
Devotional Reading: Psalm 119:49-56

Comforted by God's Judgments

Yesterday we noted that the psalmist received his hope from the Word of God. In Psalm 119:52, he states that God's judgments brought comfort to him. We do not get much comfort from the judgments of men. I am writing this in May, 1992, and am watching the people rioting in Los Angeles. Said to be the worst civil unrest in the United States in the twentieth century, these riots were sparked because people could not accept the decision of a jury. What a blessing it is to be a believer, and to comfort ourselves with the knowledge that the judgments of God are always right because they reflect His character. We have volumes of laws on the books of our states and nation. They are supposed to accomplish what God effected in ten commandments.

Men break God's laws. The psalmist stated in verse fifty-three that horror had taken hold upon him *"because of the wicked that forsake thy* [God's] *law."* The psalmist lived in Israel, a nation that received the laws it spurned from the very character of God. Men break God's laws constantly without any thought as to the consequences their actions will bring. The psalmist observed men breaking God's laws, and it brought horror to his heart. Well it should! The AIDS epidemic today is a direct result of man's forsaking God's law. Like the psalmist, you and I should be filled with horror at the realization that men are forsaking God's law.

The believer lives a different life than the one who forsakes God's law. He makes the statutes of the Lord his songs in his home (v. 54). He remembers God's name in the night and then pledges to keep God's law (v. 55). The Word of God becomes very precious and important to him. In fact, the precepts of God become his very life. He had the comfort of the Word of God and the blessing of remembering the name of the Lord even in the night because he had kept the precepts of God (v. 56).

Through the Bible in a Year: John 7

October 27

Read Psalm 119:17-32; 57-64
Devotional Reading: Psalm 119:57-64

A Robbery that Awakened the Soul

The psalmist had been robbed by the bands of the wicked (v. 61). What was his response? It was the same as that of the believers who had seen *"the spoiling of their goods"* in Hebrews 10:34. They took the loss of material possessions joyfully for they realized that in Heaven they had *"a better and an enduring substance" (Hebrews 10:34).*

The psalmist realized also that he had something the robbers could not take—his relationship to the Lord. He stated it clearly in verse fifty-seven: *"Thou art my portion, O Lord."* Amen! The robbers cannot take that away. Matthew Henry was robbed; he told everyone that he was thankful! Thankful? For what could a person be thankful when he has been robbed? Henry gave several reasons, and one of them was, "I am thankful that I was robbed and was not the robber." You see, robbers lose far more than the ones they rob. Their victims lose their possessions and purse; thieves lose their integrity.

The psalmist announced that since the Lord was his portion he would keep God's word (v. 57). He intreated the Lord's favor and requested that God's mercy would be shown (v. 58). Apparently the robbery brought him up short and made him do some thinking. In verses fifty-nine and sixty he stated: *"I thought on my ways, and turned my feet unto thy testimonies. I made haste, and delayed not to keep thy commandments."* It seems that he may have grown cold and backslidden. The robbery made him think and caused him to come back to God.

He thought (v. 59). The devil does not want us to think. He wants to detract us. To *"muse"* is *"to think."* But what do we have on every hand?—amusement. The word *"amuse"* means *"don't think."* And so we amuse ourselves to death. Thank God the psalmist thought and turned his feet unto the testimonies of the Lord. The bands of the wicked had helped him come to himself and hasten without delay to keep God's commandments. God's mercy worked in his life causing him to turn back to the Lord. He ended this stanza in verse sixty-four by announcing, *"The earth, O Lord, is full of thy mercy."*

Through the Bible in a Year: John 8

October 28

Read Psalm 119:33-48; 65-72
Devotional Reading: Psalm 119:65-72

Blessing Through Affliction

Often when we face affliction, we foolishly feel sorry for ourselves. We would rather not experience affliction. But in this stanza we find the psalmist stating twice the benefit affliction brought to him.

Verse 67—*"Before I was afflicted I went astray: but now have I kept thy word."*

Verse 71—*"It is good for me that I have been afflicted; that I might learn thy statutes."*

The psalmist realized that God does use affliction to bring forth fruit in our lives. Remember: Trials should make us better—not bitter! It is the same truth we find in James 1:2: *"My brethren, count it all joy when ye fall into divers temptations* [various testings].*"* So when the tests of affliction come we should rejoice. Peter gives us the same truth in I Peter 4:12-13: *"Beloved, think it not strange concerning the fiery trial which is to try you, as though some strange thing happened unto you: But rejoice, inasmuch as ye are partakers of Christ's sufferings; that, when his glory shall be revealed, ye may be glad also with exceeding joy."*

The psalmist regarded his affliction as good: *"It is good for me that I have been afflicted"* (v. 71). We should be able to say the same thing. The key is that we not rebel against affliction. Affliction which drives us to our Bible and to our knees is good for us.

The afflictions the psalmist faced not only involved physical sickness but also persecution: *"The proud have forged a lie against me . . ."* (v. 69). There is nothing worse than to have people begin lying about you! What did the psalmist do? In that same sixty-ninth verse he gave the answer: *"I will keep thy precepts with my whole heart."* As he rested in the truths of the Word of God, he became an overcomer. In fact, he could say with confidence: *"The law of thy mouth is better unto me than thousands of gold and silver"* (v. 72). He trusted the Lord and His Word. Therefore, he saw his afflictions as blessings bearing profit for his soul.

Through the Bible in a Year: John 9 and 10:1-30

October 29

Read Psalm 119:49-64; 73-80
Devotional Reading: Psalm 119:73-80

Man Created Directly by God

"Thy hands have made me and fashioned me . . ." (v. 73). The psalmist declared that he believed in creation—that he was made by the direct act of God. Man is not the product of evolutionary change with all of its inherent chances. The psalmist said that God's hand had made him. We are thrilled when we can purchase something that is hand made. That which is made by hand displays the most tender loving care. Machines may turn out work faster—but a handmade object has an intrinsic value that never comes with the volume production of a machine.

In creation God spoke and creation took place. God said, *"Let there be light: and there was light" (Genesis 1:3);* God said, *"Let there be a firmament* [atmosphere]*"* and the atmosphere existed (Genesis 1:6-7); God said, *"Let the waters under the heaven be gathered together into one place,"* and seas and oceans appeared and so did the dry land (Genesis 1:9-10). Read farther in Genesis 1 and you will note that God spoke plant life into existence; He spoke to create the sun, moon, and stars; and He spoke, commanding the earth to bring forth living creatures. However, when He came to create man, the Bible states that He did more than speak. He said, *"Let us make man in our image . . ." (Genesis 1:26).* He reached down into the dirt and fashioned man's body by hand (Genesis 2:7). All foul and fish were created together (Genesis 1:20-21), and all beasts and creeping things were created together (Genesis 1:24-25)). BUT MAN was different—he was special and was set apart from the rest of creation. We might say that God mass produced the universe—but He made man by hand.

The psalmist goes further. He states that God's hands fashioned him personally. Every person is different—fashioned specially and particularly by God. It is so much more wonderful to believe that each of us is a special creation by God and not the product of an evolutionary process of chance. We did not come form a one-celled amoeba through apes and monkeys. No!! We are created by God. His hands fashioned us. You and I are "hand made." What a blessing to know that we are His special creation.

Through the Bible in a Year: John 10:31-42 and 11

October 30

Read Psalm 119:65-80
Devotional Reading: Psalm 119:73-80

Proper Requests When We Face Trials

The psalmist was sure about many things. In verse seventy-five he stated one *certain knowledge* he had: *"I know, O Lord, that thy judgments are right, and that thou in faithfulness hast afflicted me."* As we have noted several times in Psalm 119, he was undergoing severe trials and persecution. He may have been very ill, and certainly he had enemies attacking him. He accepted these as judgments of a sovereign God. He recognized God's faithfulness in all his afflictions. This is the blessing all of us need. When trials come, we need to ask what God is endeavoring to teach us. Paul, too, had a certain knowledge about this: *"And we **know** that all things work together for good to them that love God, to them who are the called according to his purpose" (Romans 8:28).*

Then the psalmist lists five requests he made to God, each beginning with the word "Let."

"Let, I pray thee, thy merciful kindness be for my comfort . . ." *(v. 76)*. The psalmist knew that real comfort could come only from God, and only on the basis of His mercy.

"Let thy tender mercies come unto me, that I may live . . ." (v. 77). God is One of tender mercies—and we can know these mercies even as did the psalmist.

"Let the proud be ashamed; for they dealt perversely with me without a cause . . ." (v. 78). The psalmist recognized that it was proud men who fought against him. But he knew he would win the battle by meditating in the precepts of God.

"Let those that fear thee turn unto me . . ." (v. 79). The psalmist was a marked man, being persecuted by the proud in power as we noted in the previous verses. He felt keenly the need of the fellowship of those who loved the Lord. How precious is fellowship with loving believers when we are experiencing severe trials.

"Let my heart be sound in thy statues . . ." (v. 80). The psalmist knew full well that he needed to have his heart right and grounded in God's Word.

Through the Bible in a Year: John 12 and 13:1-20

October 31

Read Psalm 119:81-104
Devotional Reading: Psalm 119:81-88

Clinging to God's Word in Difficult Circumstances

In Psalm 119:83 the singer stated, *"For I am become like a bottle in the smoke; yet do I not forget thy statutes."* We must remember that they did not have glass or plastic bottles in those days. Instead they had wineskins. The skins of animals were used to make containers for liquids. Smoke would really affect those wineskin containers. Let smoke fill your house—you will find that every fabric in the house takes on the odor of the smoke. If I buy a used car, I want one that has not had tobacco smokers using it. That odor of smoke permeates everything and is almost impossible to remove from the car. A wineskin would pick up the odor of smoke and transfer that to the contents inside the wineskin. The writer said he was that wineskin. He felt he was absorbing the contamination of the world. There was one way to get rid of that *"smoke"*—to always remember God's statutes (v. 88). The pollution of the world can only be overcome with the cleansing of the Word of God. We cannot escape the contamination of the world—it is on every hand. But we can see cleansing by turning to the Word (the statutes) of God.

To the psalmist it seemed as though God were delaying His dealing with the writer's enemies for a long time. He wondered *"How many are the days of thy servant? When wilt thou execute judgment on them that persecute me?" (v. 84)*. But then, again, the psalmist declares his trust in the Lord and His word: *"All thy commandments are faithful . . ." (v. 86)*. He states it again in verse eighty-seven: *"I forsook not thy precepts,"* and again in verse eighty-eight: *"[S]o shall I keep the testimony of thy mouth."* He was *"almost consumed . . . **but** . . ."* (v. 87). Note those two words, *almost* and *but.* Apparently the writer was looking back at some experience through which God had delivered him. The enemy wanted him to deny God, but what did they find? The psalmist said, *"[B]ut I forsook not thy precepts."* Praise God for that *"but."* The more the enemies attacked, the more the psalmist clung to the Word of God.

Through the Bible in a Year: John 13:21-38 and 14–15

November 1

Read Psalm 119:89-96; 105-120
Devotional Reading: Psalm 119:89-96

The Word: Forever Settled in Heaven

This stanza, Psalm 119:89-96, presents the greatness and importance of the Word of God. It begins with the tremendously important words, *For ever.* The Word of God is for ever. *"For ever, O Lord, thy word is settled in Heaven" (v. 89).* Think of that! God's Word is settled—it is stable, well grounded as a foundation—and it is *forever,* settled eternally!! God's Word is lifted above the changes of time and the temporary framework of everything on earth. God's Word is settled in Heaven. That means it is settled! No one dare tamper with it. Voltaire held up the Bible and announced, "In fifty years I'll have this book in the morgue." However, in fifty years he was in the morgue and the Geneva Bible Society owned his house using it as a place to store and distribute Bibles.

Not only is the Word of God settled in Heaven, it also abides on earth. *"Thy faithfulness is unto all generations: thou hast established the earth, and it abideth" (v. 90).* When God created everything, He did it by speaking His Word—*"And God said, Let there be light . . ." (Genesis 1:3).* Today the earth continues to operate by the Word of God. *"They continue this day according to thine ordinances . . ." (v. 91).* Everything on planet earth works only according to God's Word. Men speak of "Mother Nature" or "the laws of nature" or "providence." They are really speaking about God. He created the earth and it operates according to His ordinances. The last of verse ninety-one states that the generations of the earth are really God's servants.

Verse ninety-six makes the following important statement: *"[T]hy commandment is exceeding broad."* Many speak of Christians as being narrow minded. They think the Bible is a narrow-minded book. But this verse states that God's commandment is *"exceeding broad."* Actually, it is the philosophies of men that are narrow. Men try to explain the universe with the theory of evolution. When evolution is logically applied to mankind, it fosters "isms" such as Naziism, Communism, and Humanism. The theory is narrow because it refuses to accept the broad dimension of creationist truth. The Bible gives us an acceptable answer to all problems men face. May we thank God for His Word and accept its breadth in our lives.

Through the Bible in a Year: John 16–17

November 2

Read Psalm 119:97-104; 121-136
Devotional Reading: Psalm 119:97-104

Wisdom from God's Word

Psalm 119:97-104 is a great portion of Scripture!! I feel like Moses—I must take off my shoes for I am standing on holy ground. (*See* Exodus 3:5.) This passage contains the secret for a life that enjoys the blessing of God. The secret is that the blessed individual delights in the Word of God. *"O how love I thy law! It is my meditation all the day" (v. 97).*

What does the Word of God do for us? First, it gives us God's wisdom. The psalmist states that through God's commandment he had been made wiser than his enemies. A Bible believer does not need to fear his enemies. He has wisdom beyond them and can see them defeated. David is a classic example. Three times in I Samuel 18 we find that David behaved himself wisely (I Samuel 18:5, 14, 30). Because he loved the Word of God, he actually behaved himself more wisely than all the servants of Saul (I Samuel 18:30).

Not only was the psalmist wiser than his enemies, he was also wiser than his teachers: *"I have more understanding than all my teachers: for thy testimonies are my meditation" (v. 99).* Please note that the Bible does not say that the psalmist had more *knowledge* than his teachers—it says he had more wisdom. *Wisdom* should be our goal—not just knowledge. Proverbs 4:7 states: *"Wisdom is the principal thing; therefore get wisdom: and with all thy getting get understanding."* The Bible student is going to have wisdom from God. The psalmist also said that God's Word had given him more understanding than the elders (v. 100).

The Word of God had kept the psalmist from evil (v. 101) and had led him to accept the judgments of God (v. 102). What was it that gave this singer such wisdom? Verse 103 has the answer: *"How sweet are thy words unto my taste! yea, sweeter, than honey to my mouth."* He loved the law of God (v. 97) and he found God's Word to be sweet to his taste (v. 103). It is the sweetness of the food that seems to satisfy. God's Word gives wonderful satisfaction and rest to everyone who believes and practices it.

Through the Bible in a Year: John 18–19

November 3

Read Psalm 119:105-112; 137-152
Devotional Reading: Psalm 119:105-112

The Bible—Our Guide in Life

Psalm 119:105 is a very familiar verse to most believers. *"Thy word is a lamp unto my feet, and a light unto my path."* In many Christian schools in America, students recite in the opening of the chapel service a pledge to the Bible. A part of the pledge says, *"I will make it a lamp unto my feet, and a light unto my path."* The danger is that they say this as a form so often that they give no thought as to what it really means.

It should mean they are going to let the Word of God guide their lives. His Word is a lamp to our feet and a light to our path. A light on the path shows us the direction we should go, but it does not show us all the twists and turns ahead of us. It points us in a general direction, but we cannot discern all the bumps and hazards ahead. When our boys were growing up we had four-wheel drive vehicles that we used for trips into the "back country" of the Rocky Mountains. I can remember driving up some of those rough and difficult "four-wheel drive only" trails at night. Our lights would shine ahead but not around the bends nor on the other side of a hill. There were times when we would "crawl" over rocks, climbing a hill. When we got to the crest our lights would not shine on the trail that went down the other side—they would shine far off into open spaces. We would get out of our four-wheel drive vehicle to look at the rugged path on the hill going down with a flashlight. That flashlight was our "lamp." We had a light on the path, but we needed a lamp to guide our steps.

The Bible does not unfold the whole map of life's journey before us. If it did we would be too fearful to face the future. But God does give us the Bible to be a lamp unto our feet—and He guides us one step at a time. Someone has said that Easterners in the Psalmist's day strapped a little lamp to their feet to show them the next step. May we accept the Bible as a light on our path and then look to it as a lamp for each step we take.

Through the Bible in a Year: John 20–21

November 4

Read Psalm 119:105-112; 153-168
Devotional Reading: Psalm 119:105-112

The Bible—Our Heritage

Psalm 119:105-112 is a great stanza on the purpose of the Bible in our lives. Yesterday we saw that verse 105 speaks of God's guidance in our lives: His general guidance—*"a light unto* [our] *path,"* and His specific guidance—*"a lamp unto* [our] *feet."*

Then the psalmist explains what he did with God's guidance—he followed it. *"I have sworn, and I will perform it, that I will keep thy righteous judgments" (v. 106).* He made promises to God, and he kept them. I have heard people promise God something when they were undergoing a trial; but then when the trial is over, they seem to forget the promise. Not so with the psalmist, and it should not be so with us.

The psalmist did not allow circumstances to "get him down." He stated in verse 107, *"I am afflicted very much."* Enemies beset him on every hand. The way he handled the problem was by asking God to *"quicken"* him *"according unto* [His] *word" (v. 107).* He turned to the Word of God for reviving (quickening) power that gave him inner strength to overcome the trials. Even when the wicked laid a snare to trap him, he erred not from the precepts of God (v. 110). He relied constantly on the Word of God for strength to meet every foe and realize victory in every circumstance.

Our relationship with God depends on our having the right offering to present to God. The psalmist went beyond just the offering of a sacrifice by asking God: *"Accept, I beseech thee, the free will offerings of my mouth . . ." (v. 108).* He realized that our worship must be more than form or ritual—it needs to be what Jesus said: *"in spirit and in truth" (John 4:24).* The psalmist wanted his heart to overflow with praise to the Lord as an acceptable sacrifice.

A good motto for any believer is given in verse 111: *"Thy testimonies have I taken as a heritage for ever: for they are the rejoicing of my heart."* The most priceless heritage any of us can have is the Bible. Oh that its truths might bring great joy to our hearts continually. Let's make the Bible our heritage.

Through the Bible in a Year: Acts 1–2

November 5

Read Psalm 119:1-8; 113-120; 169-176
Devotional Reading: Psalm 119:113-120

The Lord and His Word—Our Only Hope

In verses 114-116, the psalmist spoke of the claim he had on God for protection. As we have seen previously in this psalm, the writer faced many enemies, and he had to rely on the Lord for powerful victory. By faith he accepted the Lord as follows:

"My hiding place" (v. 114)—A place one would prepare in case it was needed.

"My shield" (v. 114)—The hiding place was prepared for future help, but the shield was that which was used right at the time he faced the enemy.

"My God" (v. 115)—He relied totally on the Lord.

"My Hope" (v. 116)—The Lord and His Word were the only hope the psalmist had.

The writer was ready for whatever attack might come. His first hope was in the Lord and His Word, and his last hope was in the Lord and His Word. If the Lord and the Bible failed, he had nowhere else to turn.

John Philips tells the story of a pioneer missionary in the Yukon. Finding it necessary to walk through desolate country, he often had to face fierce, wild animals. He decided to carry a gun for protection. He would stop to visit in lonely homes in desolate areas, give a witness for Christ, and leave gospel literature. When he called on one home, the woman challenged him: "You tell me that you trust in God and that He is all powerful—then why do you carry a gun?" The missionary thought the challenge through carefully and decided to throw his gun into a ditch and claim Matthew 28:20—*"[L]o, I am with you alway."* Not too long afterwards he came face to face with a grizzly bear. Both stopped dead in their tracks. The missionary claimed God's promise and then remembered something he had learned in his days in the army—surprise often is the winning element of victory. He yelled, waved his arms, and flourished his Bible—then he charged straight at the bear. It turned tail and fled! May we learn that the Lord is the One who can protect us even in dangerous circumstances.

Through the Bible in a Year: Acts 3–4

November 6

Read Psalm 119:9-24; 121-128
Devotional Reading: Psalm 119:121-128

Believing God Will Work

In this stanza of his song, Psalm 119:121-128, the psalmist manifests his concern about the evil doers of his day. In verse 126 he states that these wicked men have made void the law of God. What should a believer do when he sees the evil doers working contrary to God's law? The psalmist stated what he would do in verse 127: *"Therefore I love thy commandments above gold; yea, above fine gold."* The more men depart from the Word of God, the more we should cling to it.

The psalmist knew that the Lord was the only One who had the answer to the need of that day. In verse 126 he prayed, *"It is time for thee, Lord, to work."* Amen! *"When the enemy shall come in like a flood, the Spirit of the Lord shall lift up a standard against him" (Isaiah 59:19).* In these dark days in our nation and in our world, we believers need to trust the Lord and request of Him, "Lord, it is time for thee to work."

The psalmist was able to tell the Lord that he had endeavored to do what was right. Yet it appeared that conditions were not changing. He said, *"I have done judgment and justice: leave me not to mine oppressors" (v. 121).* He believed God could overcome, yet he wondered why this did not take place. Verse 122 is the only verse in the entire psalm that the writer does not use any of the synonyms for the Word of God. Instead he speaks to the Lord, the living Word, telling Him that he is accepting the Lord as the guarantee of the promises: *"Be surety for thy servant for good . . ." (v. 122).* He said that he needed the Lord to stand behind His promises and give assurance they would come true. It was like Abraham who *"staggered not at the promise of God* [the promise of a son] *through unbelief; but was strong in faith, giving glory to God; And being fully persuaded that, what he had promised, he was able also to perform" (Romans 4:20-21).* So the psalmist went directly to God as the *"surety"* (guarantor) of all His promises. May we also not stagger at God's promises but believe them.

Through the Bible in a Year: Acts 5–6

November 7

Read Psalm 119:25-48; 129-136
Devotional Reading: Psalm 119:129-136

God's Word—The Light We Need

Psalm 119:130 states a very important truth for all our lives: *"The entrance of thy words giveth light . . . ."* How necessary it is for us to have light when darkness is all about us. My dear wife and I spend much of each year traveling around the United States ministering to churches. We usually park our fifth-wheel trailer in a church parking lot. Beside the door of the trailer is a small light to help us see the steps and the keyhole to unlock the door. It is usually still daylight when we leave the trailer to walk into the church for the nightly service. Since we still have the daylight, we often forget to turn on our little "porch" light. It is dark when the service is over, and often we are parked in an area where there are no lights in the parking lot. On a very dark night we have real trouble getting to the trailer without bumping our shins on the steps or hitting some object in the parking lot. What a difference even that tiny bulb makes when it is on!!

Like the psalmist, we are in a very dark world. We need the light of God's Word. When we open our hearts to His Word, light floods into our lives. Light reveals *dirt.* We cannot see the dust on the counter top until the light hits it. Light reveals *disorder.* The room may be a mess, but in the dark we do not see the muddle.

Please note who it is that receives the light: *"[I]t giveth under-standing to the **simple**" (v. 130).* It is light—not to the sophisticated but to the simple. The one who comes by faith to receive the Word and obey it will receive the light that only God's Word can give. God's Word is given not for debate but for obedience. The psalmist longed for the Word of God. *"I opened my mouth, and panted . . ." (v. 131).* He desired God's Word, and his whole being longed for it. Would it not be wonderful if God's people today had that same longing? Far too many people have a Bible in the home that they never open. If they do not open it, they cannot have its light. May we love and long for the Word of God.

Through the Bible in a Year: Acts 7

November 8

Read Psalm 119:49-72; 137-144
Devotional Reading: Psalm 119:137-144

The Bible—Our Delight

These verses in Psalm 119:137-144 reveal that the testimonies of the Lord are righteous because they are given by a righteous God. In these eight verses the word *righteous* and *righteousness* appear five times and the word *upright* appears once. Verse 137 begins the stanza by stating that God in His very nature is righteous: *"Righteous art thou, O Lord."* Therefore, any word that comes from God is going to spring out of His righteous character. God is **always** right; therefore, He is right in His commands and testimonies.

Verse 140 reads: *"Thy word is very pure: therefore thy servant loveth it."* From a fountain of pure water nothing impure can come. So the Bible is a pure book because it comes from our righteous Lord. The psalmist stated that he loved the Word of God because of its righteous and pure character. What a blessed book it is!

"Thy testimonies that thou hast commanded are righteous and very faithful" (v. 138). Think of it—the Word of God, without editing and revision, is faithful and never changes.

"Thy law is the truth" (v. 142).

"The righteousness of thy testimonies is everlasting" (v. 144).

When men write books, they need to be edited, proofread, corrected, retyped, and probably retyped again. Not so with God's Word. It came out of His righteous character. There will be no future revelations to invalidate what has already been written. His Word is *"very faithful"* (v. 138), *"truth"* (v. 144), and endued with everlasting righteousness (v. 144).

Therefore, the psalmist revealed what God's Word meant to him. He loved it (v. 140); he delighted in it (v. 143); and he claimed it so that he could live by it (v. 144). Though trouble and anguish would come, the psalmist knew he could turn to the Word and have help. He knew He needed the Word, and its commandments to really know the delights that could come into his life. With an understanding of the Bible, he knew that he could live to honor the Lord. May the Bible be our delights also as we live each day.

Through the Bible in a Year: Acts 8–9

November 9

Read Psalm 119:73-96; 145-152
Devotional Reading: Psalm 119:145-152

Fervent Prayer When Troubled

In this portion of Psalm 119 we find the psalmist crying unto God with fervent prayer. In verses 145-147 we find the word *"cried"* three times. The psalmist realized the seriousness of his plight. He cried with his whole heart (v. 145)—his prayer was fervent. He cried, *"Save me"* (v. 146)—he recognized the only One who would help him was the Lord.

Note that with these pleas he immediately stated: *"I will keep thy statutes" (v. 145)* and *"I shall keep thy testimonies" (v. 146).* These are necessary ingredients to prayer. If I cry unto the Lord, then with that cry I must be walking with the Lord. Not only must I say, "I am desperate," but I must also manifest, "I am determined." I cry, "Rescue me," and with it I must cry, "Rule me." I John 5:14-15 puts it this way: *"And this is the confidence that we have in him, that, if we ask any thing according to his will, he heareth us: And if we know that he hear us, whatsoever we ask, we know that we have the petitions we desired of him."*

The psalmist's prayer burden filled his whole life. He *"prevented"* (v. 147) or "anticipated" the dawning of the morning with his cries for help. He could not sleep, so he arose and prayed. His heart was burdened. Prayer was the order of the day for him. Not only did he anticipate the morning with prayer—he did the same at night: *"Mine eyes prevent the night watches . . ." (v. 148).* He lifted his prayer unto God constantly and he meditated in the Word of God (v. 148).

His enemies were constantly attacking. They drew *"nigh"* to the psalmist, but they were far from God's law (v. 150). But the psalmist knew something better— the Lord was near (v. 151). The last stanza of "How Firm a Foundation" sums it up well:

> The soul that on Jesus hath leaned for repose
> I will not, I will not desert to his foes;
> That soul though all Hell should endeavor to shake,
> I'll never, no never, no never forsake.

The psalmist's trust was in the eternal Word of God (v. 152). Remember that the passing storm which sways the branches does not disturb the roots.

Through the Bible in a Year: Acts 10–11

November 10

Read Psalm 119:97-120; 153-160
Devotional Reading: Psalm 119:153-160

Revival Through the Lord, the Living Word

The psalmist begins this section by asking God to consider his afflic-tion (v. 153). Not all suffering and affliction are given by God as a judg-ment on our sins. Today there is a lot of teaching and preaching that says that if we face trouble it is because God is judging us for our sins. On television we hear the idea that health and wealth can be equated with spirituality. If one were right with God he would not be ill. If he just had faith, there would be instant and miraculous healing. One tele-vision evangelist has opened his program with, "Something good is about to happen to you." That *"something good"* that God can give might be sick-ness or financial reverses. Paul said, *"[A]ll things work together for good"* *(Romans 8:28)*. So if we are believers, we can know that everything that comes our way, whether a blessing or apparent affliction, is for our good.

The psalmist wanted God to consider his affliction, and then he request-ed that God might quicken him. Four times in the passages for yesterday and today (vv. 145-160) we find the word *"quicken"* (vv. 149, 154, 156, and 159). We find this word five more times in Psalm 119. It means "give me life" or "keep me alive." The idea is that of revival. Revival comes in our lives as we pray with the psalmist, *"quicken me according to thy word" (v. 154)* or *"quicken me according to thy judgments" (v. 156)*. However, there is more to revival than just coming to the Word of God. We must come into a vital relationship with the Lord Himself. Thus the psalmist also prayed, *"quicken me, O Lord, according to thy lovingkindness" (v. 159)*. The Bible, in and of itself, does not save us nor does it sanctify us. The Bible points us to Christ. We can love the Word of God and still need revival by a closer personal relationship with the Lord. Jesus Christ is the Way. The Bible is the signpost pointing to the way. The psalmist loved and honored the Word of God, but yet he needed to come to the Lord Himself for the quickening he needed. May we love Him to whom the Word of God points us.

Through the Bible in a Year: Acts 12–13

November 11

Read Psalm 119:121-144; 161-168
Devotional Reading: Psalm 119:161-168

Standing in Awe of God's Word

Throughout the first 160 verses of Psalm 119, we have found repeated references to the trials and persecution the psalmist was undergoing. In this section, from verse 161 to the end of the psalm, we find a change. The writer mentions the persecution one more time in verse 161, and that is the last time. He closes out the psalm singing about the peace he has by trusting the Word of God. In verse 165 he speaks of that peace: *"Great peace have they which love thy law: and nothing shall offend them."*

Peace?—when princes are persecuting him without a cause (v. 161)? Yes, he had peace because his heart stood in awe of the Word of God. The princes of this world might demand us to stand in awe before them. But we will be wise to say with the apostles, *"We ought to obey God rather than men" (Acts 5:29)*. Though they were beaten, the apostles rejoiced that they were counted worthy to suffer shame for His name, and they continued to witness for Christ (Acts 5:41-42). Daniel and his three companions were commanded by the king to stand in awe of him, but they chose rather to stand in awe of God's Word.

Did the psalmist fret over his decision to stand in awe of the Word of God? No—definitely not! Instead he wrote in verse 162, *"I rejoice at thy word, as one that findeth great spoil."* He counted the Word of God as valuable as any treasure that man could discover.

The psalmist went further. In verse 163 he stated, *"I hate and abhor lying: but thy law do I love."* Here are two contrasts: *"I love"* and *"I hate,"*—also *"thy law"* and *"lying."* He is speaking of lying as being that which is contrary to God's law. He calls false religion *"lying."* That is exactly what it is. Those who propagate it know nothing about the way to Heaven, but they act as though they do. Jesus Christ is *"the way, the truth, and the life" (John 14:6)*. False teachers present another way which is not truth—therefore it is a lie. The psalmist said he hated lying. He hated false religion—not the persons of the false religion but the lies they propagate. May we love God's law and hate the lies leading away from His Word.

Through the Bible in a Year: Acts 14–15

November 12

Read Psalm 119:145-168
Devotional Reading: Psalm 119:161-168

The Blessing of Great Peace

Please note again today verse 165: *"Great peace have they which love thy law: and nothing shall offend them."* The psalmist has reached a place of peace in his life. He was resting on God's Word. Those who love God's law will have a peace that the world does not understand. Note that verse 165 states that *"nothing shall offend them."* The word *"offend"* means "to make them stumble." Nothing will cause them to stumble because they are relying wholly on the Word of God. Satan is busy throwing his fiery darts, but they do not stumble—they love God's law. There is no peace like this *"great peace"* (v. 165) which comes to a believer who loves God's law.

The psalmist gives us some characteristics that come to the life of that one who has this *"great peace."* First, this one praises God. *"Seven times a day do I praise thee, because of thy righteous judgments"* (v. 164). This is a good example for us to follow— pausing repeatedly during the day to praise the Lord. The psalmist said he praised the Lord because of His *"righteous judgments"*—His overruling and controlling the way in our lives day after day.

With this *"great peace"* we could say with the singer: *"Lord, I have hoped for thy salvation, and done thy commandments"* (v. 166). *"Salvation"* in this verse is referring to our future deliverance from this life when we meet the Lord. That is the *"blessed hope"* of the Church when we are raptured into the presence of the Lord.

Then the psalmist said he loved the testimonies of the Lord exceedingly (v. 167). That is both a definite cause and a sure result of *"great peace."* What a blessing to love His testimonies exceedingly— with every part of our being.

That brings us to the last characteristic: *"I have kept thy precepts and thy testimonies"* (v. 168).

May we know this great peace and manifest the characteristics of it daily in our lives! May we praise Him, long for His second coming, love His testimonies, and keep His precepts.

Through the Bible in a Year: Acts 16–17

November 13

Read Psalm 119:169-176 and 120–121
Devotional Reading: Psalm 119:169-176

A Great Writer Needed the Lord

Today we meditate on the closing stanza of Psalm 119. We have been considering truth from this great psalm for almost a month. Now in these last verses we find this psalmist continuing to pray and praise the Lord. In verses 169 and 170, he asks the Lord to hear his prayer: *"Let my cry come near before thee, O Lord"* and *"Let my supplication come before thee" (v. 170).* Think of it—at the close of this wonderful psalm, the singer cries out again, "O Lord hear me." He knew very well that he needed the Lord to bless if there was to be blessing.

The psalmist made two promises to God. First, he promised that he would praise the Lord: *"My lips shall utter praise, when thou hast taught me thy statutes" (v. 171).* The word *"utter"* means *"to bubble over."* When God teaches his child, his heart is so full that it will bubble over with praise.

The second promise is found in verse 172: *"My tongue shall speak of thy word: for all thy commandments are righteousness."* When our tongue speaks God's Word, it means that the Word of God must be put in the heart. *"[O]ut of the abundance of the heart the mouth speaketh"* *(Matthew 12:34).* In computer programming the phrase "Garbage in, garbage out," refers to the fact that if you program a computer with garbage, then expect to retrieve garbage. In our lives an equally true phrase would be, "Godly thoughts in, Godly thoughts out."

First the psalmist cries, *"Hear me" (vv. 169-172).* Then he prays, *"Help me" (vv. 173-176).* In verse 173 he requested: *"Let thine hand help me."* He realized that the only One who could give effective help was the Lord.

It is interesting that Psalm 119 ends with a confession of need in verse 176. The psalmist confessed that he had gone astray like a lost sheep. Think of it! He who wrote this great passage of Scripture did not consider himself a super-saint. He admitted he was a sinner in need of grace. He wrote great passages concerning the Word of God, under God's inspiration; however, he still recognized his need for God's grace and power. Oh, how much each of us needs the grace of God.

Through the Bible in a Year: Acts 18–19

November 14

Read Psalms 120–122
Devotional Reading: Psalm 120

The Dreadful Opposition of a False Tongue

Today we begin a series of fifteen psalms: Psalms 120–134. Each of these psalms has the title, "A song of degrees." There are various ideas about the origination and use of these psalms. Four of them are ascribed to David and one to Solomon. We are not sure who wrote the other ten. A number of good Bible teachers believe Hezekiah compiled all fifteen and actually wrote the ten that are not ascribed to David or Solomon. As we look at these psalms we will show how some of them certainly could have been written by Hezekiah.

Psalm 120 is a particular case in point. King Hezekiah could have written this as a prayer when he was under the attack of Sennacherib and Rabshakeh from Assyria. Rabshakeh threatened the nation of Judah with his speeches in which he defied the Lord God of Israel. (Please note II Kings 18:13-37, where Rabshakeh lies about the Lord, even claiming in verse twenty-five that the Lord sent him to destroy the land of Judah.

It could well be that Hezekiah did write Psalm 120. He prayed to be delivered from lying lips and a deceitful tongue (v. 2). Those lips and that tongue could have definitely been those of Rabshakeh. In verse three, the psalmist asked an important question: *"What shall be given unto thee? Or what shall be done unto thee, thou false tongue?"* A lying tongue is always difficult to deal with. Often the only thing that can be done is to remain silent and not to try to answer.

One thing I learned long ago was that you cannot argue with lies. This lying tongue was a big problem, for the psalmist called it *"Sharp arrows of the mighty with coals of juniper" (v. 4)*. The juniper was used to make the charcoal which made the hottest fire. What a tongue!—just what James said about it: *"And the tongue is a fire . . . that . . . setteth on fire the course of nature; and it is set on fire of hell" (James 3:6)*. We need to do what this psalmist did—keep working for peace, even when we are being cut to shreds by a false, fiery tongue (vv. 6-7).

Through the Bible in a Year: Acts 20–21

November 15

Read Psalms 121–123
Devotional Reading: Psalm 121

Our Lord—Able to Keep Us

From Psalm 120 to Psalm 121 we have a dramatic change. In Psalm 120 we find the apparent lack of peace because of a slandering tongue. In Psalm 121 we look up with hope because we can rest in the Lord and His keeping power.

The psalmist lifted up his eyes unto the Lord. He looked at the mountains (v. 1), but he was literally looking to the Lord to see Him as the only One who could give help. The psalmist stated the truth which we all need to affirm daily in our lives—our help comes from the Lord who made heaven and earth (v. 2). He is the God *"Who hath measured the waters in the hollow of his hand, and meted out heaven with the span, and comprehended the dust of the earth in a measure, and weighed the mountains in scales, and the hills in a balance"* (Isaiah 40:12). Surely He is able to help us regardless of the straits in which we may find ourselves.

The Lord is our keeper (v. 5). He is busy at keeping us from falling. First, the psalmist prays that his foot will not slip (v. 3). The third verse literally was a request from the psalmist, "May He not suffer thy foot to be moved." We need to look daily to the Lord for His keeping power to deliver us from slipping. We may believingly trust the Lord to keep us, but we need that keeping power constantly. Therefore, the psalmist states that the Lord is always there—always alert to our every need. *"[H]e that keepeth thee will not slumber. Behold, he that keepeth Israel shall neither slumber nor sleep" (vv. 3-4).* Tempters and dangers are awake and all about us—but so is our Protector!

The believer is kept by the power of God. He delivers from sun stroke, something that was always a danger in the Middle East (v. 6). More than that, He is able to deliver *"from all evil" (v. 7).* What does He deliver? Not just our body but also our soul (v. 7)! When we go out—the Lord preserves us; when we come in—He is also keeping us (v. 7). Someone has called Psalm 121 "The Traveler's Psalm." We can trust Him to keep us in all our ways.

Through the Bible in a Year: Acts 22–24

November 16

Read Psalms 122–124
Devotional Reading: Psalm 122

The Blessing of Corporate Worship

These songs of degrees were very likely sung as the Israelites gathered for worship at the Temple. Psalm 122 was written by David, probably soon after the Ark was removed from Obed-edom's house and brought to Mount Zion (II Samuel 6:12-18). He rejoiced over the privilege of coming to Jerusalem for worship and wrote the psalm to encourage the people to be faithful in their worship.

Not every part of the Bible was written directly to us who are living today in this church age, the age of grace. However, every part of the Bible was written for our benefit. Therefore, today we will consider truths from this psalm that we can apply to our lives today. We, too, should be glad when we can join with others with the thought, *"Let us go into the house of the Lord" (v. 1)*. Often today we find many believers who are not glad when they are invited to worship with other believers. It is easy for a believer's heart to become cold toward spiritual things and cause him to be absent from the place of worship. Remember that today we do not worship in a building but in our hearts. Jesus said, *"God is a Spirit: and they that worship him must worship him in spirit and in truth" (John 4:24)*. Jesus was telling the Samaritan woman that worship is not dependent on a certain mountain or a certain building—worship is from the heart. Corporate worship involves the assembling and fellowshiping of believers together. When we are called to assemble ourselves together, we should rejoice as David did.

The fellowship in Jerusalem was a blessing. The city was built *"compact together" (v. 3)*. For there to be worship there must be unity of mind and purpose. Verse four reveals that this corporate worship was a witness to the other nations.

The psalmist prayed for the peace of Jerusalem and then gave the promise that all those who love Jerusalem will prosper (v. 6). The peace for which the psalmist prayed will come as one is faithful to worship the Lord by being in the fellowship of God's people. The New Testament admonishes us not to forsake *"the assembling of ourselves together . . ."* *(Hebrews 10:25)*.

Through the Bible in a Year: Acts 25–26

November 17

Read Psalms 123–125
Devotional Reading: Psalm 123

Seeing the Lord Above Our Circumstances

We find an ascent to these songs of degrees. Many believe that the Israelites sang these songs as they mounted step after step of the Temple. The first four psalms of this group are certainly on ascending scale. The psalmist began in Psalm 120 disturbed over his troubling surroundings. He climbed from that to the place where he lifted up his eyes unto the hills in Psalm 121. Then in Psalm 122 he rose to the place where he was thrilled to be in fellowship with God's people in the house of the Lord. Now we come to Psalm 123, and we find the psalmist lifts up his eyes directly to the Lord. Certainly he has revealed definite progress in the right direction. He rises from being troubled by his circumstances to the place where he is trusting the Lord, the One above all circumstances. The psalmist told the Lord: *"Unto thee lift I up mine eyes, O thou that dwellest in the heavens" (v. 1).* He was facing trouble (vv. 4-5). In the midst of the trouble he looked to the Lord. It is important that we see the Lord above circumstances—then we can have victory.

Please note the word *"Behold"* in verse two. We saw that same word in Psalm 121:4 where it called attention to God's keeping power in our lives—is was God's *"Behold."* In Psalm 123:2 we have the *"Behold"* of God's servants—they will keep their eyes watching the Lord. Oriental servants would obey just by a movement of the master's hand (v. 2). Servants had to keep their eyes on the master. So should we! May we learn to wait on the Lord, looking for His mercy to be revealed in our lives.

Verses three and four reveal the contempt of those who are enemies of the people of God. They are *"at ease" (v. 4).* That phrase refers to believers who grow cold and indifferent; they often become the most difficult enemies of those who love the Lord and really want to live for Him. How often have I see those who professed salvation slip into an *"at ease"* mode and do great harm to an assembly of believers. May we all keep our eyes on the Lord!

Through the Bible in a Year: Acts 27–28

November 18

Read Psalms 124–126
Devotional Reading: Psalm 124

A Song of Gratitude

David wrote Psalm 124 as a song of gratitude to the Lord for delivering of His people. The people of God are still faced with trouble from enemies. We believers live in hostile territory. Enemies lurk on every hand. There are haters of God and his people at work right now. We need to be delivered from danger.

Thank God we have the Lord who watches over us, protects us, and wins the battles for us. David had experienced many victories—some personal and some national. In this psalm he gives credit for the victory to the Lord. As he wrote Psalm 124 he was so excited he was almost incoherent. He was ecstatic over victory. He knew full well that there was no human way he could have triumphed in the danger he faced.

Men rose up against David. They could easily have overpowered him, but the Lord was on his side. Please note the word *"if."* He uses it twice in the first two verses: *"If it had not been the Lord who was on our side."* David then gives the results *if* the Lord had not been on his side (vv. 3-5). In those three verses please note the word *"Then."* He gives the results in dramatic picturesque language. He pictures the enemies acting as wild beasts attacking and swallowing up God's people (v. 3). He speaks of the enemies coming as a raging flood carrying everything before it to destruction (vv. 4-5). But God delivered. Isaiah 59:19 gives this great promise for us to claim: *"When the enemy shall come in like a flood, the Spirit of the Lord shall lift up a standard against him."*

David realized the victory given by God. Therefore he praised the Lord for what He had done: *"Blessed be the Lord, who hath not given us as a prey to their teeth" (v. 6).* The enemies thought they had David trapped, but he realized blessed deliverance as a bird that escaped the snare. Only another power could deliver a trapped bird. So it is with us—God must deliver us from the snares set to entrap the soul.

David sums it up in verse eight: *"Our help is in the name of the Lord, who made heaven and earth."* A God who can create heaven and earth can do anything. We simply must trust Him and watch Him working by His delivering power.

Through the Bible in a Year: Romans 1–2

November 19

Read Psalms 125–128
Devotional Reading: Psalm 125

Secure in Christ

Psalm 125 reveals the security that believers can know. We rest secure in His grace. How secure are we? *"They that trust in the Lord shall be as mount Zion, which cannot be removed, but abideth for ever"* *(v. 1).* Zion is the place that God has appointed as the ultimate seat of sovereign power on earth—the place where our Lord Jesus Christ will set up His millennial reign.

Think of it—those who trust in the Lord will be as Mount Zion, abiding forever. Every believer is secure in Jesus Christ. Jesus stated it this way: *"My sheep hear my voice, and I know them, and they follow me: And I give unto them eternal life; and they shall never perish"* *(John 10:27-28).* Paul wrote this truth in Romans 8:38-39: *"For I am persuaded, that neither death, nor life, nor angels, nor principalities, nor powers, nor things present, nor things to come, nor height, nor depth, nor any other creature shall be able to separate us from the love of God, which is in Christ Jesus our Lord."*

The *"Lord is round about his people" (v. 2);* therefore, *"the rod of the wicked shall not rest upon the lot of the righteous . . ." (v. 3).* God has promised that those who trust in Jesus Christ will never experience the rod of the wicked. David could pray confidently asking the Lord to do good unto those who are upright in heart (v. 4).

Not so with those following crooked ways. We probably all remember the nursery rhyme:

> There was a crooked man and he went a crooked mile,
> He found a crooked sixpence beside a crooked stile;
> He bought a crooked cat, which caught a crooked mouse,
> And they all lived together in a little crooked house.

Does that sound like a nonsensical rhyme? Well, it is more—it shows that those who are crooked and devious will end up with crooked and devious people. They will be led *"forth with the workers of iniquity" (v. 5).* Thank God we who trust Him can know He will lead in righteous paths and keep us by His grace.

Through the Bible in a Year: Romans 3–5

November 20

Read Psalms 126–129
Devotional Reading: Psalm 126

The Rejoicing of the Ransomed

Psalm 126 was written following a time when there was a national deliverance. Very likely it was written by Hezekiah following God's miraculous deliverances of Jerusalem as recorded In II Kings 19:32-37, II Chronicles 32:21-22, and Isaiah 37:33-38. *"[T]he Lord turned again the captivity of Zion" (v. 1).* It was such a miracle that the people could hardly believe it. They were *"like them that dream" (v. 1).* Their mouths filled with laughter (v. 2). They found it difficult to express their deep emotions upon realizing that God had delivered them. When they were able to give expression to the blessing God had poured out, they did it with singing (v. 2).

This miracle pictures the miracle of salvation in the lives of believers today. God brought us *"up out of a horrible pit, out of the miry clay and set* [our] *feet upon a rock and established* [our] *goings. And . . . put a new song in* [our] *mouth, even praise unto our God" (Psalm 40:2-3).* The miracle of our salvation is as great a miracle as the fact that 185,000 Assyrian troops were slain in Hezekiah's day. Even the heathen were amazed and they said, *"The Lord hath done great things for them" (v. 2).* The people answered in verse three, the key verse of this chapter, *"The Lord has done great things for us, whereof we are glad."*

In verse four the psalmist prayed, *"Turn again our captivity, O Lord, as the streams in the south."* Even after the Israelites had seen the miraculous deliverance God had given, they had backslidden and their lives had become cold. Sin had brought them into slavery again and they needed the Lord's deliverance. The *"streams in the south"* could be absolutely dry, and then God could send rains that would make the streams run over their banks. The psalmist knew that God had the power to turn the captivity just as the streams in the south (v. 4).

The psalmist was praying for revival. One of the essential ingredients in revival is to have tears over the lost (vv. 5-6). In verse six we find a tremendous promise—that a believer who goes with tears bearing the Word of God will come again with rejoicing, bringing souls with him (v. 6). May we claim this promise in our lives.

Through the Bible in a Year: Romans 6–8

November 21

Read Psalms 127–130
Devotional Reading: Psalm 127

Building with God as Partner

The heading for Psalm 127 states that it was written by Solomon. Had this ascription not been given, we could still have easily known that Solomon was the author. In the first two verses he uses the word vain three times, a word that he used often. The words *"vain," "vanity,"* and *"vanities"* are used nine times in Proverbs and thirty-eight times in Ecclesiastes. Solomon had learned that many things the world thinks are marks of success are really vanities when considered in the light of eternity.

Solomon said that if the Lord does not build the house *"they labor in vain that build it" (v. 1).* But then he goes further and states that if the Lord does not *"keep the city, the watchman"* will not be able to keep it either (v. 1)—his work will be *vain.* And in verse three he adds that diligent labor which leaves God out is also vain (v. 3). Whether we are building a life, a house, a city, a nation, a business, or a church, we will do well to have God as our partner. Further, we cannot keep that which is built without God's blessing. We appoint men to be watchmen in the city, but still riots break out. If the Lord were to withdraw His presence, society would be impossible.

I wrote this in 1992. Los Angeles thought its watchmen could handle the city, but the worst riots of this twentieth century broke out. In Communist countries the governments had many watchmen, but they left God out. As I write this we are witnessing what some call the breakdown of communism. Why? They left God out. In fact they boasted they would build without God. One reason the tribulation period will be so terrible is that the Holy Spirit will be withdrawn—they will be building without God.

Society needs God. So do our families. *"[C]hildren are a heritage of the Lord" (v. 3).* Their lives are dependent on their parents' trusting the Lord to lead and direct. A man who endeavors to build a home without consistently seeking the Lord is going to find he is building in vain. Let's honor God in our homes and have Him as our partner in building.

Through the Bible in a Year: Romans 9–10

November 22

Read Psalms 128–130
Devotional Reading: Psalm 128

A Fruitful Home

We have here two psalms that fit together: Psalms 127 and 128. They both emphasize the home. Psalm 128 presents these facts: The welfare of the state depends on the welfare of the home, and the welfare of the home depends on the spiritual condition of the head of that home.

The psalm begins, as do many others, with the word *"Blessed."* That word is in the plural and means many joys shall come to the person called *"blessed."* His blessing is first of all in his fearing the Lord (v. 1). That is the center of his life—a reverence for and an awe of God. This refers to his inner being. Another requirement for blessing is that a person walk in His ways (v. 1). This refers to his outward behavior. The fact is that no one really fears the Lord if he does not walk in His ways.

If one will fear the Lord and walk in His ways, he receives a wonderful guarantee from God: *"For thou shalt eat the labor of thine hands: happy shalt thou be, and it shall be well with thee" (v. 2).* Talk about a guarantee—you have never needed a better one. One car manufacturer guarantees its product for 60,000 miles, another for 70,000 miles. Those are good guarantees—but they are only peanuts compared to this one given by God. Fear the Lord and walk in His ways, and He guarantees *"it shall be well with thee" (v. 2).*

Verse three continues the guarantee: *"Thy wife shall be as a fruitful vine by the sides of thine house"* Here is an excellent picture of a blessed home. The wife is likened unto a vine. A vine does not support itself but clings to its support. The feminist movement would like to do away with this picture of a wife as a clinging vine—but it is in the Bible, given to us by God. Once a vine has found its support, it climbs up the support. A wife who takes her scriptural place clinging to her husband for support will have plenty of opportunity to grow and realize her potential. Together, she as a Scriptural wife, along with a husband who fears the Lord, will see the children grow to be like fruitful olive plants (v. 3).

Through the Bible in a Year: Romans 11–13

November 23

Read Psalms 129–131
Devotional Reading: Psalm 129

Nations of the Earth— Beware!

Today we consider Psalm 129. These eight verses are very important verses in our Bible. They state graphically the fact that God has a covenant tie with Israel that He does not have with any other nation on earth. The nations of the world have not recognized this fact, and they have been dealt with by Almighty God.

The psalm begins by declaring emphatically that the nation of Israel can say, *"Many a time have they afflicted me from my youth" (vv. 1, 2).* In the Hebrew language there is no comparative or superlative degree such as we have in the English language. We speak of great or greater or greatest. But not so with Hebrew. If one desires to have a superlative degree, he simply repeats what he just said. *"Many a time"* in verses one and two means that the persecution was to the superlative degree, and the psalmist could not count the number of times that Israel was persecuted. The affliction had begun when Israel was just a young nation—the psalmist repeats it was from Israel's youth. The nation spent its youth in Egypt and there grew to manhood. The Pharaoh tried to destroy Israel, but his army was drowned in the Red Sea by God's miraculous intervention. From that day till now, nations that have attacked Israel have been destroyed. Though verse three states that persecutors plowed the back of Israel, verse four states the Lord cut asunder the cords of the wicked nations who performed such dreadful persecution.

History is replete with examples of nations attacking Israel. This psalm says those nations will become as grass on the housetops. They put dirt on their roofs; seeds blow onto the roof, sprout, spring up, and then die for lack of depth of earth. In effect, God says that nations that defy Israel will die just like the grass on the rooftop. God covenanted with Abraham that He would *"bless them that bless thee, and curse him that curseth thee" (Genesis 12:3).* History has proven that God has kept that covenant. Psalm 129 states definitely: "Nations of the earth beware—don't allow anti-Semetic hatred and don't fight against Israel."

Through the Bible in a Year: Romans 14–16

November 24

Read Psalms 130–132
Devotional Reading: Psalm 130

Who Could Stand?—None!

This is another of those psalms we designate as the Penitential Psalms. Psalm 130 takes us from the depths of anguish to the heights of assurance. We do not know for sure who the author was, but we know he was deeply convicted over sin. He may have been convicted of his own sin, or he may have been carrying the burden of the sin of the nation on his shoulders. It is a wonderful portion of Scripture that gives us the grace of God.

The psalmist begins by stating that he was in the depths of despair. Where should he turn? He gives the answer in verse one, *"I cried unto thee, O Lord."* Then he amplifies that with the very first word of verse two, *"Lord."* He pleaded, *"Lord, hear my voice: let thine ear be attentive to the voice of my supplications."* He realized his sin, agonized over it, and recognized the only one who could help was the Lord.

In verse three he asked an important question: *"If thou, Lord, shouldest mark iniquities, O Lord, who shall stand?"* The answer is obvious—none of us could stand. The Bible teaches we have all sinned and come short of the glory of God (Romans 3:23). Suppose the Lord would reveal on a screen before a crowd the entire story of every one of our lives. He would show our secret thoughts, our hidden actions, our motives, etc. If he did, I believe it would be as it was with elders in John 8:9—they *"went out one by one, beginning at the eldest, even unto the last . . . ."* None of us could stand.

The Lord is not going to do that. Verse four reads, *"But there is forgiveness with thee, that thou mayest be feared."* God sees our sins—but when we cry out to Him from the depths, he hears, forgives, and gives us rest. Salvation does not come just because we pray a desperate prayer. We receive it when we trust the Lord. That is what the psalmist did. He knew that the Lord would *"redeem Israel from all his iniquities" (v 8)*. He waited for the Lord, and his hope was in God's Word (v. 5). There we find assurance in His Word.

Through the Bible in a Year: I Corinthians 1–3

November 25

Read Psalms 131–132
Devotional Reading: Psalm 131

A Humble Believer

Psalm 131 is a short psalm, but that does not mean it is unimportant. It stands out in Israel's hymnbook as one from which we all must learn. David speaks of his own life and what God had accomplished in him. He had grown and, in this psalm, speaks of maturity in the Lord.

I wonder if David ever planned for this psalm to be sung by others. Some say it is likely that King Hezekiah is the one who compiled these fifteen songs of degrees. Maybe David had written it down, never planning for others to see the words. He was a truly humble man and could honestly write, *"Lord, my heart is not haughty" (v. 1)*. Humility is one of the highest attainments in a spiritual life. However, just when we are sure we have it, we most often lose it. Someone has said that there are four kinds of pride: pride of face, of lace, of race, and of grace. The last one, pride of grace, can be the most subtle and most dangerous. You see, that which first overcame man is the last thing man overcomes.

David did not allow himself a haughty heart or lofty eyes (v. 1). While the world tells people to "get ahead" and "think of number one," David said he did not seek things for himself. He defeated Goliath, not by his own strength, but because God delivered Goliath into his hand (I Samuel 17:45-46). Then the women began to sing that Saul had slain his thousands, but David his ten thousands (I Samuel 18:7). This produced jealous wrath in Saul (I Samuel 18:8-9), but David *"behaved himself wisely" (I Samuel 18:5, 14, 15)*. He was in Saul's court and was lifted up in the eyes of the people, but he did not exercise himself *"in great matters, or in things too high for me" (Psalm 131:1)*. He acted as a weaned child (v. 2)—that is, like one who has gained some independence but still must look to his mother for help. His wise behavior meant that he quieted himself (v. 2). He did not attempt to rush ahead; rather, he simply waited on God. Though he had already been anointed king, he humbly and patiently waited for God's timing. This psalm is one of the shortest to read, but one of the longest to learn.

Through the Bible in a Year: I Corinthians 4–6

November 26

Read Psalms 132–133
Family Reading: Psalm 132; Devotional Reading: Psalm 132:1-7

Yielding Our Lives to be Used of God

This psalm speaks of David in the third person—so we know it was not written by David. It was probably written by one of the kings who endeavored to have a righteous reign. This writer longed for the house of David to be established with its godly rule of the land.

The writer prayed that David's purpose in life would be realized, a purpose in which the psalmist states *"afflictions"* were involved (v. 1). The word *"afflictions"* in this case means *"concerns."* David had one all consuming concern in his life—that was his desire to build a temple for God in Jerusalem. The psalmist states that David vowed to the Lord that he would see this longing to build the temple brought to fruition (v. 5).

David made a *solemn vow* to the Lord, the mighty God of Jacob (v. 2). Jacob had made his vow to God in Genesis 28—God had fulfilled that vow in founding the tribes of Israel. David made his vow to the same Lord and made it clear he planned to keep that vow as one spoken in truth before God.

His vow was also a *serious vow.* He would labor at seeing it accomplished regardless of the cost. If it meant sleepless nights and being away from home, he was going to see it accomplished. He would not give up until he saw the vow performed (vv. 3-4).

And then we note that it was a *successful vow.* David said he would not give sleep to his eyes until he found *"a place for the Lord, a habitation for the mighty God of Jacob" (v. 5).* It took a long time, with David facing wars, disloyalty, family troubles, and discouragements. But David did not quit.

David found the ark. People had heard of the longing of his heart, and the psalmist wrote, *"Lo, we heard it at Ephratah: we found it in the fields of the wood" (v. 6).* Others heard of it. They told him where he would find the ark. Israel had been without the ark for twenty years (I Samuel 7:1-2). David's vow was known by others. Our dedication, like David's, will make an impact on others for good. May we yield ourselves to the Lord so we, too, can be a blessing.

Through the Bible in a Year: I Corinthians 7–9

November 27

Read Psalms 132–133
Devotional Reading: Psalm 132:8-18

God's Sure Promise to David

Psalm 132 divides itself into two sections: the first deals with David's promise to God to build the Lord a house in Jerusalem (vv. 1-10); the second reveals God's promises to build a house for David— that is the dynasty that would come through his life and descendants (vv. 11-18).

In verse eight the prayer is made: *"Arise, O Lord, into thy rest; thou, and the ark of thy strength."* That very prayer was made by Solomon in II Chronicles 6:41 when he was dedicating the temple. The ark had been moved to Jerusalem to what David hoped would be its resting place. David longed to have such a place of worship. He wanted it to be a place of holiness. Therefore, the prayer is given in verse nine: *"Let thy priests be clothed with righteousness; and let thy saints shout for joy."* David knew that for a nation to have joy, it needed to have holy living. The priests that led the nation needed to be men of righteousness. With the ark at the center of the nation and the priests honoring the Lord with lives surrendered to the Lord, David was sure that the nation would have the blessing of God.

In verse eleven we begin the second section that reveals the surety of God's promise to David—*"The Lord hath sworn in truth unto David"* *(v. 11)*. His descendants could rest assured that God would not turn from His promise. David could be certain that his line would continue on the throne in Israel: *"Of the fruit of thy body will I set upon thy throne"* *(v. 11)*.

The Lord has chosen Zion for His habitation (v. 13). He will reign from Zion. God chose the place for His dwelling place. When we deal with Jerusalem, we are dealing with the very place God has called His place of abode. God promised that David's children would abide on the throne. God required David's children to keep God's covenant and His testimony (v. 12). Then He assured them that the children would continue to sit upon the throne. Part of that promise included the last two words of verse twelve—*"for evermore."* God promised David the throne forever (II Samuel 7:13, 16). That promise continues in Psalm 132 and is fulfilled in Jesus Christ (Luke 1:32-33).

Through the Bible in a Year: I Corinthians 10–11

November 28

Read Psalms 132:8-18 and 133–134
Devotional Reading: Psalm 132:13-18

Are You Clothed with His Salvation?

In Psalm 132:14 God is speaking of the blessing that will come to Zion. It is this place that He has chosen for His dwelling. He states, *"This is my rest for ever: here will I dwell . . ."(v. 14).* God has put His name there—the name of Jehovah. The temple site belongs to God and to His chosen people the Jews. Today, His name is associated with a Muslim mosque—the Mosque of Omar. Therefore, the day will come when the Mosque of Omar, now standing on the temple site, will come down.

In verse fifteen we read a millennial promise: *"I will abundantly bless her provision: I will satisfy her poor with bread."* This promise anticipates that day when the Lord Jesus Christ will set up His reign. Zion and Jerusalem will become the center of world rule. It will be obvious to all that God's blessing abides there.

God promises to *"clothe her priests with salvation" (v. 16).* This speaks of today. Every believer in the Lord Jesus Christ is a priest. What a privilege to be a priest of the Lord—saved by grace (I Peter 2:5, 9).

In Zion there will be life. The horn of David will bud (v. 17). If we wonder whether a plant has life, that question is answered when we see the buds come forth. Life will come as leaves or flowers or fruit. In Zion, David's horn (the symbol of strength) will bud, revealing that life is in the house of David forever (v. 17). Christ is the seed of David that brings life to those who trust Him. Further light comes forth out of Jerusalem, and light certainly comes from Jesus Christ, the Light of the world. God states He ordained a lamp through the house of David (v. 17).

Psalm 132 speaks of two ways to be clothed. Verse sixteen reveals the clothing of salvation, and verse eighteen speaks of the clothing of shame. Which clothing will you wear for all eternity? What a tragic end to be clothed with shame forever! Today you can turn to the Lord and be clothed in His righteousness (v. 9) and with His salvation (v. 16). That will bring joy forever.

Through the Bible in a Year: I Corinthians 12–14

November 29

Read Psalms 133–135
Devotional Reading: Psalm 133

The Blessing of Unity

Psalm 133 is a blessed psalm with a message for all ages—and surely a message for us today. David called for unity in the nation of Israel. Our need in our churches today is a *"unity of the Spirit" (Ephesians 4:3)*. Very likely this psalm was composed at the time when David was anointed king over Israel (II Samuel 5:3-4 and I Chronicles 12:38-40). Please note that in I Chronicles 12 the people were *"of one heart to make David king"* (v. 38) and *"there was joy in Israel" (v. 40)*. David saw the kingdom begin with a blessed unity. That unity was *"good"* and *"pleasant" (v. 1)*. Later David saw that unity destroyed by Absalom's rebellion. Solomon's kingdom was also wrecked by disunity led by Jeroboam. Today there is a great need for unity among the people of God. As I visit the local churches across America, and around the world, I find many of them with their testimony damaged because of a lack of unity.

Please note that this psalm speaks of *unity—**not** uniformity.* There are those today who endeavor to force a uniformity on the people of God. They would have professed believers unite around a cause regardless of what they believe. God does not honor an imitation ecumenism, that is, a unity brought about by doctrinal compromise or organizational efficiency. The church is an organism, not an organization, and its New Testament picture is a body, not a business.

The Lord uses two pictures to describe unity. It is as the precious ointment used to anoint Aaron (v. 2). That ointment was made from God's divine recipe (Exodus 30:23-25). It left a lovely fragrance as it covered Aaron. Though it flowed down, its fragrance rose upward. And it was like the dew that settled upon Mount Hermon and Mount Zion (v. 3). Life in the Middle East depends on that dew. Remember that both of these came from above. They gave life and fragrance. Unity must come from God, with the result being life and fragrance from our Lord through believers in an ungodly world.

Through the Bible in a Year: I Corinthians 15–16

November 30

Read Psalms 134–135
Devotional Reading: Psalm 134

Dedicated Servant Yielded to Him

Today we come to the last psalm of these Songs of Degrees. They end with Psalm 134, a psalm of special praise to the Lord. Again this psalm begins with, that same word, *"Behold."* It calls on all of us to take special notice. This is very important—*"Behold."*

What is it that is important? Blessing the Lord. And who is to bless the Lord? The answer is, *"all ye servants of the Lord" (v. 1).* Please note that He says *all* servants should bless the Lord. Regardless of our position, we need to bless the Lord, from the least servant to the greatest.

Why is it that the servants need to bless the Lord? Do they not bless the Lord with their very work for Him? These servants stood through the night watches (v. 1). They sacrificed in serving the Lord. Yet, God calls on them to *"bless the Lord" (v. 2).* You see, there is always a danger of becoming unduly familiar with holy things and taking for granted our privileges in Christ. Far too often we start complaining or grumbling about our service. Oh that we could enjoy serving the Lord in whatever capacity He gives us.

In blessing the Lord, they were to lift up their hands (v. 2). Lifting up their hands revealed three things. First, it revealed that their hands were *clean. "Who shall ascend into the hill of the Lord? . . . He that hath clean hands . . ." (Psalm 24:3-4).* God does require clean hands of his servants. We do not need clever hands, but we must have clean hands. Second, it showed that the hands were *whole*, without blemish. There were areas in which an Old Testament priest could serve if there were blemishes in his life—but not in the sanctuary. This is also true today. Leadership requires a life that is blameless (I Timothy 3:2). Third, lifting up the hands revealed that they were *dedicated* to the Lord. He desires all three—cleanness, wholeness, and dedication.

These Songs of Degrees began with the psalmist groaning in distress (Psalm 120). They close with him glorifying the Lord with unity in the fellowship (Psalm 133) and dedication of the servants (Psalm 134). The last verse (Psalm 134:3) states clearly that all blessing comes from the Lord. May we love Him and yield to Him.

Through the Bible in a Year: II Corinthians 1–4

December 1

Read Psalm 135

Praise Him, Ye Servants

Psalm 135 is a psalm devoted to the worship of the Lord and is for those who are servants of His. He calls *"O ye servants" (v. 1)* to praise the Lord. The title *"Lord"* appears nineteen times. There are twenty other references to Him using the title *"God,"* the words *"his name,"* or using pronouns referring to Him—thirty-nine references to our Lord—thus making this a "Godly" psalm.

The first three and the last three verses of this psalm are verses of praise to the Lord. The first four and last four words are *"Praise ye the Lord."* Who is it that the psalmist is calling to praise the Lord? Verse one calls on the *"servants of the Lord"* to praise him. He identifies these servants in verse two: *"Ye that stand in the house of the Lord, in the courts of the house of our God."* These were the Levites and the priests who served in the tabernacle and the temple. Therefore, this psalm can be applicable to believers today, for in this church age the believers are the priests.

Please note two characteristics of those addressed. First, they have access to the Lord. Verse two says they *"stand in the house of the Lord."* Every believer today has access to God through Jesus Christ. We *"enter into the holiest by the blood of Jesus" (Hebrews 10:19).* Second, they serve God; they are called *"servants of the Lord."* They minister as they stand in His presence. The Christian looks to Christ not only as a Saviour to be trusted but also as a Sovereign to be obeyed.

Why should His servants praise Him? In verses 3-5, God uses the word *"for"* in each verse and gives us three reasons to praise Him.

1. *"[F]or the Lord is good"* and His name *"is pleasant" (v. 3).*
2. *"For the Lord hath chosen Jacob . . . and Israel for his peculiar treasure" (v. 4).*
3. *"For . . . the Lord is great, and . . . our Lord is above all gods" (v. 5).*

The psalmist desires that saved people praise the Lord. Therefore let us praise Him not just with *words,* but with *witness;* not only in *church,* but in the *community;* not only on *Sunday,* but *every day* of the week.

Through the Bible in a Year: II Corinthians 5–8

December 2

Read Psalm 135

The Greatness of Our God

In Psalm 135:5, the psalmist wrote: *"For I know that the Lord is great . . . ."* He then calls on two witnesses to prove that greatness. First, he reveals God's sovereignty through the witness of creation. *"Whatsoever the Lord pleased, that did he in heaven, and in earth, in the seas, and all deep places" (v. 6).* Please note that from the farthest reaches of space (heaven) to the deep places of the seas, God's creation pleased him. All of creation was made to please the Lord; and because it pleased Him, we as His creatures find creation pleasing to us. In verse seven the psalmist continued giving the witness of creation, revealing that God causes the evaporation of the seas to take place so that He can give water to the earth in the rain He sends. He makes the powerful lightning bolts to flash and the winds to come out of His treasures (v. 7). What a great God we have as we see Him revealed in creation.

Second, the psalmist brings forth the testimony of history. He begins with the fact that His people were delivered from Egyptian bondage (v. 8). He lists the last of the judgment-miracles first because it was the most dreadful of all—the death of the firstborn. In verse nine he speaks of the other nine miracles of judgment that came upon Egypt because of Pharaoh's hard heart. He calls those judgments *"tokens."* Think of it—changing water to blood; bringing frogs, lice, and flies; disease in livestock and boils on men; destructive hail and locusts; and horrible darkness—all of these are just *"tokens"* of His power. Further, in verses ten through twelve, he speaks of the nations God smote, turning their land over to Israel.

Verse thirteen tells us that God is eternal. He does not age and therefore does not weaken. *"Jesus Christ the same yesterday, and today, and for ever" (Hebrews 13:8).* He can judge the world by His might, but He will also discipline His people to bring forth the fruit they need in their lives (v. 14). The words *"repent himself"* in verse fourteen mean *"show compassion"*— and so He will. He will discipline His own with compassion. What a great God we have!

Through the Bible in a Year: II Corinthians 9–11

December 3

Read Psalms 135:15-21 and 136
Devotional Reading: Psalm 135:15-21

Our God is Alive and Deserves Praise

As we have noted in previous devotionals, Psalm 135 begins with three verses of praise to the Lord and also ends with the psalmist praising the Lord in the last three verses. Prior to verse fifteen the psalmist gave us reasons for praising the Lord. In verses fifteen through eighteen, he gives us a comparison between God and idols. God is full of mercy, concerned for His people, and works miracles on their behalf. The idols of the heathen, however, are dumb, blind, deaf, and actually dead. He presents the stark contrast between idols and our Jehovah God. Let's note some contrasts:

1. The idols are manufactured by men: *"The idols of the heathen are silver and gold, the work of men's hands" (v. 15).* It may be a big fat Buddha or a serene, composed virgin—they bear the label, "made by man."

2. The idols are lifeless. They have mouths that do not speak and eyes that cannot see (v. 16). Their ears hear nothing and they have no breath (v. 17). How foolish to worship such a god. They can be made of precious metals such as silver and gold, but they have no life.

    Our God, on the other hand, is alive. We have a resurrected Saviour.

    > To own a god who does not speak to men,
    > Is first to own, and then disown again.
    > Of all idolatry the total sum
    > Is having gods that are both deaf and dumb.

When we see how God in His greatness has worked on our behalf, we should let our hearts burst out in praise. When we compare our great God to the idols of the heathen, again our lips should utter praises to the Lord. So the psalmist ends this psalm with three verses calling all Israel to exalt the Lord with blessing and praise. The psalm ends the way it began: *"Praise ye the Lord."*

Through the Bible in a Year: II Corinthians 12–13; Galatians 1–2

December 4

Read Psalm 136

All Creation Reveals His Mercy

Psalms 135 and 136 are companion psalms and have many things in common. The first and last verses of each begin and end with the same words: Psalm 135—*"Praise ye the Lord,"* and Psalm 136—*"O give thanks unto the Lord."* They each give us part of Israel's history. Psalm 135 rehearses history to show us the folly of worshiping false gods. Psalm 136 emphasizes the wisdom of worshiping the Lord, the true God.

Very likely Psalm 136 was sung by two groups. The priests and Levites sang the first part of each verse; then the congregation antiphonally sang the second line or the refrain, *"for his mercy endureth for ever."* That last statement is a part of every verse—it was sung twenty-six times! The Holy Spirit seldom repeats Himself, but when He does, it is for a good reason. God wanted to remind us that everything we have comes because of God's mercy.

The psalmist begins by calling on God's people to give thanks. We are to give thanks to the *"LORD"*—Jehovah (v. 1), to *"God"*—Elohim (v. 2), and to the *"Lord"*—Adonai (v. 3). We are to give thanks unto Him because He is good (v. 1). Also we are to give thanks unto Him because of His greatness (vv. 2-3). He is *"the God of gods" (v. 2)*—that is, He is greater than the idols of the heathen mentioned in Psalm 135:15-18. Also, He is *"the Lord of lords" (v. 3)*—that is, He is greater than any of *"the rulers of the darkness of this world"* or the *"spiritual wickedness in high places" (Ephesians 6:12).*

He is our great God who created all things because His mercy endures forever. He alone is the creator, and His creation is referred to as *"great wonders" (v. 4).* Verses four through nine deal with creation. Our God acted in mercy by never leaving man to the doom of chance. His creation is perfect, manifesting His wisdom, and revealing His sovereignty. The sun, moon, and stars move according to His plan. All this took place because He is the God of mercy who is interested in us.

Through the Bible in a Year: Galatians 3–4

December 5

Read Psalm 136

Israel's History Reveals His Mercy

Praise the Lord, for His mercy endureth forever! That is the theme of Psalm 136. Yesterday we noted His mercy manifested in creation. Today we will consider His mercy as we have seen it presented in God's deliverance of His people from Egyptian bondage. Just as in the first nine verses we saw God's glory in the creation of the world, beginning at verse ten we see His glory in the creation of the nation of Israel.

The children of Abraham had gone down into the land of Goshen. What a blessing that appeared to be. But that seeming *"land of plenty"* was turned into a *"house of bondage."* The persecuted nation was glad to be freed from slavery. God delivered Israel by His mercy revealed in miraculous acts.

First, He smote the firstborn of Egypt (v. 10). God's mercy is revealed in His delivering Israel—but His mercy is also revealed in the fact that He used ten plagues to offer Pharaoh an opportunity to repent. God's patience with Egypt in this case is one historical fact that reveals that in wrath God remembers mercy (Habakkuk 3:2). Verse eleven speaks of God's bringing His people out of Egypt because His mercy endures forever. Verse twelve gives the manner by which He did it: *"With a strong hand, and with a stretched out arm."* God's stretched out arm reveals an extraordinary display of His power. Today we see it as the power by which the Lord Jesus could say, *"I give unto them eternal life; and they shall never perish, neither shall any man pluck them out of my hand" (John 10:28).* His arm was outstretched on the cross to give us this great deliverance.

Second, the psalmist speaks of God's parting the Red Sea, delivering Israel through the Red Sea and destroying Egypt in the Red Sea. What a miracle! It is the miracle most frequently referred to in all the Bible. The psalmist sang of it in verses thirteen through fifteen.

Third, we read of God's miraculous leadership of this new nation of Israel through the wilderness (v. 16). Over and over again in Exodus, Leviticus, Numbers, and Deuteronomy, we find God in His enduring mercy leading, protecting, and delivering Israel.

Through the Bible in a Year: Galatians 5–6; Ephesians 1

December 6

Read Psalms 136:17-29 and 137
Devotional Reading: Psalm 136:1; 17-29

Israel's Victories Because of His Mercy

Today we conclude our meditations in Psalm 136. Verses sixteen through twenty state that God led His people through the wilderness; and as He did so, He slew the famous kings, Sihon and Og. These two kings were famous because of their large armies and the victories they had won. But the Bible records that the Lord who smote Pharaoh at the beginning of Israel's wilderness experience was well able to smite Sihon and Og near the end of Israel's march. (*See* Numbers 21:21-35.)

The destruction of Sihon was fatal and final. These nations never arose again to oppose God's people. The Lord dealt with them in His sovereign grace and power. God led His people through the *trials* and *testings* so that they could enter the land *triumphantly.* God won the victories for Israel, and then He gave them the land of the defeated kings as a heritage for them to possess (v. 21).

In the last verses of Psalm 136, the Lord presents the fact that He deals with us today on the basis of His mercy, just as He dealt with Israel in those days. It is all on the basis of His unchanging mercy. Let's note what He has done for us.

First, He remembered us in our low estate (v. 23). Thank God, He remembers and deals with us justly and fairly on the basis of His mercy that endures forever. Second, He rescued us from our enemies (v. 24). The word *"redeemed"* in verse twenty-four is translated from a Hebrew word, which means *"to break."* That is our need. We must be broken.

By His mercy He will protect us and use us for His glory. For these mercies, we should certainly give thanks unto the God of Heaven (v. 26).

Through the Bible in a Year: Ephesians 2–4

December 7

Read Psalms 137–138 and 139:1-6
Devotional Reading: Psalm 137

Cherish the Blessings of God

Psalm 137 has been called the tale of three cities—or we could say two cities and a neighboring nation. The two cities are Jerusalem and Babylon. The country of Edom is mentioned (v. 7) because of the hatred that nation consistently manifested against Israel. Jerusalem was the capital of the country of God's people, Israel. Babylon was the head waters of apostasy. It was, and will be, one of Satan's world capitals. Babylon is the place where Nimrod and his companions formed the first league of nations endeavoring to build common political, religious, and cultural ties. In contrast, Jerusalem has been, and will be, God's religious capital. Therefore, these two capitals have always been at enmity with each other.

This psalm is one of the captivity. The Jews had departed from God, and He had allowed them to be taken captive by Nebuchadnezzar and his Chaldean empire. There in captivity, the Jews wept over their homeland around Jerusalem. Verse one states their weeping came when they *"remembered Zion."* The fact that they *"remembered"* automatically implies they had forgotten. While they were at Jerusalem with its peace and plenty, they did not treasure what they had. The well is seldom prized until it is dry. These Jews in captivity came closer to Zion than they did when they were in Jerusalem.

They could not sing in this foreign land. They hung their harps on the willows in mourning (v. 2). The heathen of Babylon taunted them by requiring them to sing. They could not sing the songs of Zion without a song in their hearts (vv. 3-4). While in Babylon, they came to love Jerusalem. They no longer wanted to be lukewarm about the blessings of God. They wanted Jerusalem, the place of the temple where they met God, to became their chief joy (v. 6).

The last three verses present the feeling of these Jews toward those who had shown great enmity against them. I suggest you read and reread this psalm. Be sure now that God and His presence is the chief longing of your life. Do not let spiritual blessing become commonplace or allow your life to be engulfed in lukewarmness.

Through the Bible in a Year: Ephesians 5–6; Philippians 1

December 8

Read Psalms 138–139
Devotional Reading: Psalm 138

Praise to God for His Control and Power

With Psalm 138 we begin a group of eight psalms, all written by David and all presenting the truths of victory in any life yielded to God. This group of psalms has been referred to as "the devout Israelite's manual of private prayer and praise." Psalm 138 presents a definite contrast to the preceding psalm. In Psalm 137 the Israelites could not sing, but in Psalm 138 singing is spontaneous, with praise given to God. In Psalm 137 trouble brings tears, but in Psalm 138 trouble leads to triumph.

In the first two verses of Psalm 138 David announced three times that he would (*"I will"*) praise the Lord. David promised to praise the Lord with his whole heart (v. 1). He would come to the temple and worship because of God's lovingkindness and His truth (v. 2). In verse two he made a tremendous statement about the value of the Bible: *"[T]hou hast magnified thy word above all thy name."*

David recalls a time of special need when he turned to the Lord (v. 3). God answered and met the need, giving strength to David's soul. That is our need today—soul strength. Every servant of the Lord has the need to be made fit for the work of the Lord. Be assured, we can have strengthening of the soul, for with God's command comes the power to perform it.

David speaks of God's power over the kingdoms of men. He recognized that truth in seeing Absalom and others miraculously defeated by God. In verse six the Lord gives a truth that David had come to realize—a truth that is vital for spiritual power today: *"Though the Lord be high, yet hath he respect unto the lowly: but the proud he knoweth afar off."* God honors humility, but He resists the proud. The Lord holds the proud at arm's length. He will resist the proud, but he will bless the humble with a reviving from their trouble (v. 8). He will accomplish His purpose in the lives of those who trust Him (Psalm 138:8 and Philippians 1:6).

Through the Bible in a Year: Philippians 2–4

December 9

Read Psalm 139

God Knows All about Me

Today we come to a great portion of Scripture, Psalm 139. We will spend four days reading in this psalm. During our reading, I suggest you underline every reference where you find the name of God, every reference where He is referred to by personal pronoun, and every reference the psalmist makes to himself. You will then find this to be a highly personal psalm where the singer recognizes his close relationship to the Lord. The writer is David. He wrote this at a time when he had experienced great victory from the Lord. His heart was full of the blessings of God. David expressed some important truths about God, truths on which all of us will do well to meditate. This psalm reveals some of the great attributes of God—omniscience, omnipresence, and omnipotence. The average man may have difficulty pronouncing and explaining these attributes, but he has no problem experiencing them.

The first attribute David presents is God's omniscience—the fact that God is all-knowing. He has the ability to know everything about each of us. In verse one, David says that the Lord had searched him—that is, God "pierced through" or saw right through him. God knows all about each one of us. He knows my walk, my every step. He knows when I sit down and when I rise up (v. 2). Think of it—He knows every movement I make. He compasses my path and knows where I walk and where I stop (v. 3).

He knows my will—every motive I have. He understands every thought I think (v. 2). Do you remember that the Lord Jesus knew the very thoughts the Pharisees were thinking (Matthew 12:25)? He could know these thoughts because He was God. He is acquainted with all our ways (v. 3). Also He knows my every word (v. 4). He states there is not one word I use but what the Lord knows all about it.

In verse six David exclaims that this knowledge is too wonderful for him. It is so high he can not reach it. He recognized that God had all knowledge and that he could not escape the fact of that knowledge. We need this same understanding of God's power to know us completely so that we can live to please him.

Through the Bible in a Year: Colossians 1–3

December 10

Read Psalm 139

God is Everywhere Present

This is the third day we have been assigned to read Psalm 139. We will read it again tomorrow—four days reading the same psalm in its entirety. And on the fifth day we will read the last eight verses. Some may say, "That is a lot of time given to reading just Psalm 139." Actually, it is so great a portion of Scripture with vast oceans of truth that we would benefit by camping on its ground much longer. Herder wrote of this psalm, "Language utterly fails me in the exposition of this psalm." Philips noted, "The psalm is so full, intricate, detailed, grand in concept, and thrilling in its statements and stanzas, it seems a crime to leave any word unexplored." May we realize we are on holy ground and ask the Lord to make this psalm a part of us. I recommend you memorize the psalm.

Today we come to another of God's attributes presented in this psalm, His omnipresence. "Omnipresence" means that God is everywhere. David asks the questions: *"Whither shall I go from thy spirit? Or whither shall I flee from thy presence?" (v. 7).* In verse eight he answers those questions with these words appearing twice: *"Thou art there."* The believer will meet Him in Heaven, but the unbeliever will also face him in Hell (v. 8). There is no place on earth but that God is present (v. 9). The believer finds comfort in that fact. Wherever he goes, he finds the Lord leading and His right hand holding him (v. 10).

An infidel father wanted to instill his unbelief into his young son. He wrote in huge letters on a wall in the house: "God Is Nowhere." The boy studied the words for a little while, and then said, "That is what my teacher tells us, that 'God is Now here.'" Yes, David said, "God is Here." He is the center and He is the circumference.

Death will not remove us from His presence (v. 7). *Distance* will not remove us from His presence (vv. 9-10). Finally, *darkness* will not hide us from His presence (vv. 11-12). This should shock the unbeliever into turning to God. Suicide is folly—for it does not solve problems nor does it cause the individual to escape the presence of God. This truth also gives confidence to the believer.

May we believe it and turn everything over to Him.

Through the Bible in a Year: Colossians 4; I Thessalonians 1–3

December 11

Read Psalm 139

God's Power is Manifested in Each Human Body

Psalm 139 presents three of God's great attributes: His omniscience (vv. 1-6); His omnipresence, which we considered yesterday (vv. 7-12); and His omnipotence, which will be the basis of today's meditation (vv. 13-18). "Omnipotence" means "all powerful."

David spoke of the fact that no one could hide from God's presence (v. 12), and then he continued with these words, *"For thou hast possessed my reins . . ." (v. 13)*. The word *"reins"* speaks of our very innermost being, the seat of all desires and longings. David is describing the intimacy which God had with him. God knows all about every one of us and has the power to control our inner being.

Today we learn from microbiology that our bodies are made up of microscopic cells, so small that the letter "O" in this type size would contain about 30,000 cells. Each such cell contains about 200 trillion microscopic atoms. Each cell has its own function and operates on a definite time table. Each day about three billion cells in the body die and are replaced by three billion new cells. Every seven to nine years we have a new body made of all new cells. *"WE ARE FEARFULLY AND WONDERFULLY MADE"!! (v. 14)*. We can say with David: *"Marvellous are thy works" (v. 14)*.

Verses fifteen and sixteen give a clear Bible explanation that abortion is murder—murder because abortion takes the life of an innocent person. David said God knew all about each of us right from conception (v. 15). All our members were written in God's book, even before there were any (v. 16). They were created by God and continued to be fashioned (v. 16). The Bible teaches that the newly formed baby in the womb of the mother is a person. To take the life of that innocent, unborn child is to commit murder. The pro-abortion people want to remove personhood from that unborn child. But God's Word makes it clear; that which is in the mother's womb is a person. God fashioned all the members of that body and knew every member, even before they existed (v. 16). We are fashioned by God, even in the womb—a wonderful example of his omnipotence. To take that life is to take the life of a human being.

Through the Bible in a Year: I Thessalonians 4–5; II Thessalonians 1–2

December 12

Read Psalms 139:17-24 and 140
Devotional Reading: Psalm 139:17-24

Judgment Must Begin at God's House

In the first sixteen verses of Psalm 139, David acknowledged the life changing truths of God's omniscience, omnipresence, and omnipotence. In verse seventeen he continues his consideration of God as the all-powerful One. God had the power to create him in the womb and to deliver him in birth. But now David speaks of God's power to keep him in all of life's ways. God constantly thought of David, and He constantly thinks of each of us: *"How precious also are thy thoughts unto me, O God! How great is the sum of them! . . . they are more in number than the sand" (vv. 17-18).*

At verse nineteen the psalm seems to take an abrupt change. Some think these verses are almost unchristian, but they fit well into the psalm. David states that in His love for the Lord he has had to take his stand against wickedness (vv. 19-22). He first presents the consummation of the wicked—*"Surely thou wilt slay the wicked, O God" (v. 19).* God has promised judgment of the wicked. David considered them to be *"bloody men."* Then he speaks of the character of the wicked. They speak against God and take His Name in vain (v. 20). There is no more wicked sin than taking God's name in vain. It reveals a deep ingrained hatred of God.

David states that there is such a thing as holy hatred—a hatred of sin and an abhorrence of those who attack God, the Creator and Maintainer of the universe (vv. 21-22). David made it clear that he wanted no companionship with the wicked. He stood against those that hated God (v. 22).

In the last two verses David prayed for God to deal with him. He first asked God to search him and to know him (v. 23). He said he had a perfect hatred for the wicked (v. 22), but he knew that hatred can soon grow into bitterness if a person is not careful. He wanted God to reveal sin in his life so that he could be delivered from a revengeful spirit. He asked God to see if there was any wicked way in his life (v. 24). Then he asked God to lead him in the way of life everlasting. All of us should use Psalm 139:23-24 often in our prayers. We need to let God search us so that His righteous judgment can be done.

Through the Bible in a Year: II Thessalonians 3; I Timothy 1–3

December 13

Read Psalms 140–141
Devotional Reading: Psalm 140

Prayer for Deliverance from Evil

We come to four psalms that stand together dealing with a common theme—a theme which meets needs in the life of every believer. That theme is "Our answer to the trouble caused by the enemy of our souls." All four psalms, 140-143, deal with the need we have to be delivered from the evil one and to be preserved by the Lord.

Psalm 140 begins, *"Deliver me, O Lord, from the evil man . . ." (v. 1).* That fits well with the disciple's prayer as given in Matthew 6 and Luke 11. Jesus taught us to pray, *"Deliver us from evil"* (literally, the evil one) (Matthew 6:13; Luke 11:4). David had to pray for deliverance just like we believers need to do today.

The enemy against whom David was praying was strong, cunning, crafty, and steadfast in attacking. It could have been one individual who hated David and led in attacking him—one such as Absalom, his son; or maybe Doeg, the Edomite; or maybe Saul. Whoever it was connived mischief in his heart and gathered others to help in the attack (v. 2). Together they acted like serpents who were ready and waiting for opportunity to attack (v. 3). David understood much about serpents. They use their forked tongue to detect the scent of potential nearby victims. When the snake's mouth bites, the muscles in its jaws press the poison glands and force venom to flow from glands beneath the lips through the hollow fangs. The victim is poisoned, and paralysis and death will follow quickly. The wicked are like that; they use their mouths to send forth the poison. Their words are often more deadly than their actions.

David had the answer. He prayed for God to deliver. These wicked persevere in their attacks, but we can rest on our faithful Saviour and God to keep us. He is ready to keep us from the hands of the wicked and preserve us from the violent man. They may hide a snare and set nets by the wayside, but our God is faithful to deliver and give victory.

> And though the world with devils filled,
> Should threaten to undo us;
> We will not fear, for God hath willed
> His truth to triumph through us.
> —Martin Luther

Through the Bible in a Year: I Timothy 4–6

December 14

Read Psalms 140–141
Devotional Reading: Psalm 140

David's Confidence That God Will Deal Fairly

Yesterday we noted how wicked men attacked David, trying to trap him and destroy him. In verse six we see his trust and hear his prayer, *"I said unto the Lord, Thou art my God: hear the voice of my supplications, O Lord."* Verse seven reveals David's recalling battles of the past in which he recognized God was the One who gave the victory. He prayed, *"O God the Lord, the strength of my salvation, thou hast covered my head in the day of battle."* Undoubtedly he was thinking of the day when God gave him the victory over Goliath. God covered his head. The helmet of salvation and the shield of faith are better protection than those of brass (Ephesians 6:13-17). Also, we can be sure that David thought of the many times that he had been miraculously delivered from Saul's tyrannical schemes. He could say confidently, *"Thou art my God" (v. 6).*

In verses eight through eleven David prays another of his imprecatory prayers. In these prayers David is simply asking God to deal with sin and sinners according to His character. They are prayers that fit with the Mosaic Law: *"[L]ife for life, eye for eye, tooth for tooth, hand for hand, foot for foot" (Exodus 21:23-24).* It also stands with the truth revealed in Galatians 6:7: *"[W]hatsoever a man soweth, that shall he also reap."* David asked that God deal according to His character with justice and fair play. God did exactly that when the men who put Shadrach, Meshach, and Abednego in the fiery furnace were burned to death by the flames of that very furnace (Daniel 3:22). We see it again when Haman was hanged on the very gallows he had designed for Mordecai (Esther 7:10). God deals fairly, and David claimed that truth. Wicked men may rise to prominence, but they will not come to permanence.

David closes this psalm with his statement of confidence that the Lord will bless. In verse twelve David states the truth that the Lord will maintain *"the right of the poor,"* a truth presented in Matthew 5:3: *"Blessed are the poor in spirit: for theirs is the kingdom of heaven."*

David ends this psalm, written while he was enduring severe attacks by the enemy, with acknowledgement of the truth, *"the righteous . . . shall dwell in thy presence" (v. 13).* The future makes it worth it all.

Through the Bible in a Year: II Timothy 1–3

December 15

Read Psalms 141–142
Devotional Reading: Psalm 141

How to Face Trouble

Psalm 141 is a companion psalm to Psalm 140. Yesterday, in Psalm 140, we noted the serious trouble David faced. Psalm 141 reveals how David faced that trouble. Psalm 140 presents that which came to David from outside. Psalm 141 reveals what David did within himself when that trouble came. David was a man after God's own heart (I Samuel 13:14 and Acts 13:22). Psalm 141 gives us definite clues as to what made David such a man.

First, when David faced trouble he prayed. In verse one, he states twice, *"I cry unto thee."* In verse two we read the fact that he lifted his prayer as incense in the morning and as the sacrifice in the evening. David was not an Old Testament priest. He dared not do what Uzziah did in II Chronicles 26:16-21. Uzziah, as king, was never given permission to do the work of the priests. He rebelled against God's order and was smitten with leprosy. In verse two David reveals his heart in tune with God by personally entering into New Testament truth where each believer is his own priest under our High Priest, the Lord Jesus Christ (I Peter 2:5, 9).

Second, David recognized he must guard his mouth. He prayed that God would set a watch before his mouth (v. 3). He knew his heart—to sin with the mouth is a subtle sin; it can raise its ugly head in our lives even when we are praying. We are well acquainted with the command, "Watch your step!" We would do well to heed also, "Watch your mouth!" Further, David asked God to deliver him from practicing iniquity (v. 4). Satan would love to defeat our prayer life. We must guard our own inner attitudes when we are facing enemies from without.

Third, David realized that he must accept the rebuke of righteous men. He said that such rebuke would be *"an excellent oil"* (v. 5). He viewed the rebuke of godly friends as did Solomon in Proverbs 27:6: *"Faithful are the wounds of a friend."* Even when they reproved him, David stated that he was going to pray for them in their calamities. No wonder God said he was a man after His own heart.

Finally, David kept his eyes fastened on the Lord (v. 8). His trust was in the Lord. By faith and prayer he had victory.

Through the Bible in a Year: II Timothy 4; Titus 1–3

December 16

Read Psalms 142–143
Devotional Reading: Psalm 142

God is With Us in No Man's Land

Psalm 142 is the last of the "Maschil" (instruction) psalms. Surely this psalm gives excellent instruction to us. David was in deep trouble. He had gone to hide in a cave (the ascription tells us it was written in the cave). David had found it necessary to flee from Saul, who in his anger was driven to rid the nation of David. Also David had found it necessary to flee the Philistines (I Samuel 21:14-15 and 22:1). As he wrote this psalm he was in the cave—sought by foes and deserted by friends. In verse four he said, *"[N]o man . . . would know me."* He did not say *"no man knew me."* They knew who he was; but by a deliberate act of his will, they "would not" know him. He felt alone—destitute. He said, *"[N]o man cared for my soul" (v. 4).* No wonder he cried out, *"[M]y spirit was overwhelmed within me" (v. 3).* David had hit "bottom."

Thank God verse three has not only a *"when"* but also a *"then."* *"When my spirit was overwhelmed within me, then thou knewest my path" (v. 3).* In the midst of his despair, David knew that there was One who cared. God knew his path and would lead him and sustain him all the way.

David knew that he had to look to the Lord. He saw his enemies as being stronger than he (v. 6). Therefore, he resorted to prayer, saying of the Lord, *"Thou art my refuge and my portion in the land of the living" (v. 5).* The enemies may have been stronger than David, but they were not stronger than God. King Saul had the power of the government with his court and armed forces behind him. But David had God. In the end, there lay Saul's headless body, stripped of his armor, dead in the mount of Gilboa (I Samuel 31). David had trusted the Lord, and the Lord had delivered him. David had no doubt that God would see him through all his trials. Though he was in "no man's land," he was also in God's land and was led by God's hand. He had confidence that God would bless: *"[T]he righteous shall compass me about; for thou shalt deal bountifully with me" (v. 7).* David's faith in the Lord had brought the victory.

Through the Bible in a Year: Philemon; Hebrews 1–3

December 17

Read Psalms 143–144
Devotional Reading: Psalm 143

David Turns All Over to the Lord

As in the previous psalms, David was falling into deep trouble and distress in Psalm 143. Again, his only resort was to turn to the Lord in prayer. He called on the Lord to hear and answer prayer: *"Hear my prayer, O Lord, give ear to my supplications" (v. 1).* In this psalm he may have been facing the rebellion of Absalom. His days of fleeing from Saul did not present as many deep seated anxieties for David as did the problems that came with Absalom's rebellion. Under Saul's persecution, at least David knew he was being persecuted unfairly. With the rebellion of Absalom, David surely remembered the words of Nathan, *"Now therefore the sword shall never depart from thine house . . ." (II Samuel 12:10).* David was not only facing unfair persecution but also problems because of the sin he had committed. Therefore in Psalm 143, David has sunk even deeper into depression. He makes the same statement as in Psalm 142 that his spirit is overwhelmed within him; but now in Psalm 143 he adds this statement, *"[M]y heart within me is desolate" (v. 4).* Certainly David had hit bottom. He had nowhere to go but to the Lord.

In this psalm David not only pleads God's mercy but also God's faithfulness and righteousness (v. 1). David knew what later Paul would state clearly: *"If we believe not, yet he abideth faithful: he cannot deny himself" (II Timothy 2:13).* David knew he had a sin nature, for he said, *"in thy sight shall no man living be justified" (v. 2).* Notice in verse two that he refers to himself as God's servant. Undoubtedly his mind was going back to the time when Nathan had delivered God's message to David in which God called him His servant (II Samuel 7:5, 25). Now he claims that relationship with God.

In verse five he wrote, *"I muse on the work of thy hands."* The word *"muse"* means *"to think"* or *"to talk with oneself."* Some say that is a sign of insanity. Actually, here it is a sign of sanity. So it was with the prodigal son in Luke 15. David and the prodigal talked to themselves about God. They realized God's dealing and turned to Him. That is sane thinking—something we all need.

Through the Bible in a Year: Hebrews 4–7

354

December 18

Read Psalms 143:7-12 and 144
Devotional Reading: Psalm 143:7-12

David's Prayer When Facing Trials

In Psalm 143:7-12 we have one of David's prayers. In it he makes five requests of God. Today we will note these requests.

1. *"Hear me" (v. 7)*. David was facing troubling circumstances and deep depression. He knew the only place to turn was to the Lord.

2. *"Cause me" (v. 8)*. He gives two requests with the words, *"Cause me."* First, he asks that God will cause him to hear the Lord's lov-ingkindness. He not only wants God to hear him, but he also realizes he needs to hear God. Second, he asks God to cause him to know the way he should walk. This is a request we all need to present to God—"Show us the way to walk." This request would involve an understanding of God's Word. It would be the request of Psalm 119:18: *"Open thou mine eyes, that I may behold wondrous things out of thy law."*

3. *"Deliver me" (v. 9)*. David requested deliverance from his enemies. This is the request the Lord taught us to make in His model prayer for us, *"[D]eliver us from evil" (Matthew 6:13)*. The evil enemy from which we all need to be delivered is Satan with all his devices.

4. *"Teach me" (v. 10)*. David asks God to teach him to do God's will. David did not simply ask God to teach him *to know* God's will, but rather *to do* God's will. To do God's will we must be taught of God. David knew that God's will was best, for he said, *"[T]hy Spirit is good."* Sometimes we get the idea that God's will would be difficult and hard. No!—if we do God's will we will find it is the very best thing for our lives. Therefore, verse ten is a prayer that I should make an important part of my life.

5. *"Quicken me" (v. 11)*. David knew he was facing the possibility of death. Both Saul and Absalom had plans to kill him. He prayed, *"Quicken me"*—that is, "Make me alive." He trusted God for his life. For us it should be a request for spiritual reviving.

Here are five requests we would do well to present to the Lord.

Through the Bible in a Year: Hebrews 8–10

December 19

Read Psalms 144–145
Family Reading: Psalm 144

The Lord, Our Help and Defender

Psalm 144 gives us a view of David's meditation about God and about himself. The psalm was written shortly after David had won a battle and had seen God subdue the people under his leadership (v. 2). Therefore, this is a psalm of praise. It appears that it is a psalm of praise because of God's answering the prayer of the preceding psalm: *"And of thy mercy cut off mine enemies, and destroy all them that afflict my soul: for I am thy servant" (Psalm 143:12).* Psalm 144 begins with *"Blessed be the Lord my strength . . ." (v. 1).* David had seen a great victory and he was ascribing it to God. The Lord had done it all. He was David's strength and had taught David how to fight the battle (v. 1). David had been used to a staff and a harp. He had to learn to use the sword and the spear.

Not only was God David's strength, but also in verse two David ascribed five other virtues to God. The Lord was David's *"goodness"*—that is the lovingkindness David needed each day; He was David's *"fortress"*—his wall of protection; He was David's *"high tower"*—the place of safety beyond bow shot range; and He was David's *"shield"*—his protection in the actual battle. Today, that *"shield"* is our faith, and with it we quench the fiery darts of the wicked (Ephesians 6:16). With the Lord being all of this to David, it is no wonder he could say in verse two that the Lord is *"he in whom I trust."*

In verses three and four, David reveals the emptiness of the energy of the flesh. We are nothing without God—in fact our *"days are as a shadow that passeth away" (v. 4).* King David, with all his ability and strength, had to come to the place where he realized the energy and strength of the flesh is vanity. He realized that power belongs unto God (Psalm 62:11). Therefore he prayed for the Lord to bow the heavens and cast forth the lightning (vv. 5-6). He asked that God would send forth His hand from above (v. 7). David realized that in war, the Lord was his only strength, and in peace, the Lord was his only preservation.

Through the Bible in a Year: Hebrews 11–12

December 20

Read Psalms 144–145
Family Reading: Psalm 144; Devotional Reading: Psalm 144:9-15

A Happy People

Psalm 144:9 begins a new note in the book of psalms—a note that continues right on through to the end of Psalm 150. That note is one of praise unto God. Psalm 145 is entitled "David's Psalm of Praise," and then we note that the following five psalms all begin and end with the words, *"Praise ye the Lord."* This rising crescendo of praise to the Lord begins in Psalm 144:9 where David announced, *"I will sing a new song unto thee, O God: upon a psaltery and an instrument of ten strings will I sing praises unto thee."*

Throughout the previous psalms we have seen David facing great trouble. His burden has been heavy and his spirit depressed. But now it changes with a new song. From here on, David will live above his troubles. He will take his stand on the highlands of faith. David now sees clearly that it is the Lord who must be enthroned. *"It is he* [the Lord] *that giveth salvation unto kings: who delivereth David his servant from the hurtful sword" (v. 10).* David had seen victory over the terrible sword of Goliath and the tyrranical sword of Saul. When he wrote Psalm 144, he had been undoubtedly facing the treacherous sword of Absalom. But now he had victory—a new song of praise. He believed that God would bless the nation, giving deliverance from enemies without and within (v. 11), and that He would bless families with children that would grow up as godly young people (v. 12). Also the Lord would give such a nation prosperity with every need being met (vv. 13-14).

This brought David to verse fifteen, the high point of the psalm: *"HAPPY IS THAT PEOPLE, WHOSE GOD IS THE LORD."* Oh, that those words could be inscribed in the thinking of our nation's leaders. Those words should be the basic philosophy of our president and vice-president, our state governors, our legislators, our judges—certainly the justices of our Supreme Court. It should be the underlying philosophy of our school teachers and the curriculums for our school children. It should be the first and essential plank of every political platform. We need it drilled into the consciousness of every citizen, *"HAPPY IS THAT PEOPLE, WHOSE GOD IS THE LORD."*

Through the Bible in a Year: Hebrews 13; James 1–2

December 21

Read Psalm 145

David's Great Psalm of Praise

Psalm 145 is a unique psalm of praise. We can see it is unique because it has a unique superscription: "David's psalm of praise." Of no other psalm is that written. David wrote many psalms, but this must have been his favorite. Psalms 146–150 are filled with praise, but none of them is ascribed to David. This may be the last of his psalms, and he did not just call it, "A psalm of David," but rather, "David's psalm of praise."

In the first and last verses of this psalm we find another mark of its uniqueness—both verses have the words *"for ever and ever."* This psalm is stamped with the mark of eternity.

What did David say he would do? Note verse one: *"I will extol thee, my God, O king."* To *"extol"* means "to set preeminently on high; to exalt above all others." It expresses the greatest possible admiration. David continued, *"I will bless thy name . . . I will praise thy name for ever and ever" (vv. 1-2).* Praise is the only present duty of man that will continue for ever and ever. We now pray, but there is coming a time when prayer will be no longer necessary. Please note that praise is a duty for *"every day" (v. 2).*

David said he would praise the Lord because of a relationship: *"my God" (v. 1).* Also he would praise the Lord because of His rule in David's life. He calls God, *"O King,"* in verse one. David had submitted himself to the sovereign authority of God.

David said he must praise the Lord because of His greatness, and he adds that God's greatness is *"unsearchable" (v. 3).* In Psalm 139, David had said God should search David, but here he says that no one can search God. Praise should be a continuing virtue and action with one generation training the next to praise God (v. 4). David said that he would speak of God's glorious majesty and His wondrous works (v. 5). Men may speak of God's terrible acts, but David said he would declare God's greatness (v. 6). David's declaring God's greatness and leading out in praise would cause others to utter the memory of God's goodness and to sing of His righteousness (v. 7). May we all learn to extol and praise our God.

Through the Bible in a Year: James 3–5; I Peter 1

December 22

Read Psalm 145

God's Greatness, Goodness, and Glory

Yesterday we noted that Psalm 145 was a very special psalm to David—his own "psalm of praise." He praised God first for His *unsearchable greatness* (vv. 1-7) and also for His *unrestricted goodness* (vv. 7-13). David refers to God's great goodness and states clearly that *"the Lord is good" (v. 9).* David links God's goodness with His righteousness (v. 7). God's goodness springs from His righteousness. He always does what is right. He is never the author of sin. He must always punish sin because He is good. However, He never punishes sin vindictively.

His goodness is not only a righteous goodness, but it is also a merciful goodness. *"The Lord is gracious, and full of compassion; slow to anger, and of great mercy" (v. 8).* The righteousness of God brings judgment against sin; but the mercy of God offers His forgiving grace to all. Please note in verse nine these words: *"to all"* and *"over all."* God's mercy is unbounded—like a sea without a bottom and without a shore. There is blessed truth in this children's chorus:

> Wide, wide as the ocean,
> High as the heavens above,
> Deep, deep as the deepest sea;
> Is my Saviour's love.

Then we note God's *unspeakable glory* (vv. 11-13). Men shall forever speak of the glory of His kingdom (v. 11). The fact of His mighty power is revealed to the children of men by His mighty acts (v. 12). As I write this I am sitting in a park in southern Indiana. The clouds are black; the thunder is rolling. God, by His mighty acts, is revealing His power just as He did to David centuries ago.

"Thy kingdom is an everlasting kingdom, and thy dominion endureth throughout all generations" (v. 13). How different from earthly kingdoms, they rise and fall. History is replete with examples—Babylon, Medo-Persia, Greece, Rome, etc. Today we have seen the collapse of the Soviet Union and we are witnessing the decline of America. Thank God, His kingdom is forever. Men come and go like shadows on the wall, but God reigneth eternally. Let's praise Him!

Through the Bible in a Year: I Peter 2–4

December 23

Read Psalms 145:14-21 and 146

Praise God for His Government and Grace

Today we consider the last part of Psalm 145. We have considered His greatness, His goodness, and His glory. Today we will look at His government and His grace.

His government is based first on *His power.* He has the power to uphold all that fall and raise up those that are bowed down. David, the psalmist, certainly knew all about that. No one was ever bowed down by a greater load of conviction and guilt than was David after he fell in his shameful sin. He knew well that God had lifted him up and had kept him. *Second,* His government is based on *His provision.* *"The eyes of all wait upon thee; and thou **givest them their meat** in due season. Thou openest thine hand, and **satisfiest the desire** of every living thing" (vv. 15-16).* God provides! And please note the words in verse fifteen, *"in due season."* God will meet our need in plenty of time—and He knows the right time. *Third,* God's government is based on *His purity.* *"The Lord is righteous in all his ways, and holy in all his works" (v. 17).* His government will be absolutely righteous and just. Just as God deals the same with all, satisfying the desire of every living thing (v. 16), so He deals the same with all in the administration of justice (v. 17). In His kingdom there will be no favorites, with one law for some and another law for others. There will be no executive privilege—no diplomatic immunity.

Appropriately the psalm ends with *His grace.* God *"is nigh unto all them that call upon him" (v. 18).* He hears the cry of them that fear Him and saves them (v. 19). His grace stands ready to save all that call upon Him. Verse twenty presents the sharp contrast between those that love the Lord and the wicked. The Lord preserves those who love Him, but He destroys the wicked. It is important to remember that God holds His government and His grace in perfect balance. His grace will not interfere with His government, neither will His government interfere with His grace.

Thus David closes his "psalm of praise" with his mouth speaking *"the praises of the Lord" (v. 21).* And his final words are an invitation for all to praise Him, *"for ever and ever."*

Through the Bible in a Year: I Peter 5; II Peter 1–3

December 24

Read Psalms 146–147
Devotional Reading: Psalm 146

Praise Him Now While We Live

Psalm 146 begins the last five psalms, often referred to as the double Hallelujah psalms. They each begin and end with the words, *"Praise ye the Lord."* Actually, in the Hebrew they begin and end with the one word, *"Hallelujah." "Hellelu"* means "praise" and *"Jah"* is an abbreviation of the title, "Yahweh"—"Jehovah". Therefore, *"Hallelujah"* means "praise Jehovah."

The title *"Jehovah"* means that God is the One who has become our salvation. The first time we find it in scripture is in the first song in Exodus 15:2. Moses led the children of Israel to sing after the defeat of Pharaoh's hordes: *"The Lord* [Yahweh] *is my strength and my song, and he is become my salvation."* The name appears 49 times in the Old Testament—7 times 7, which indicates the perfection of perfection. Now the Psalmist announces he will personally praise Jehovah. He states he will make praise of the Lord a top priority in his life—*"While I live"* and *"while I have any being" (v. 2).*

Then he contrasts trust in the Lord with false trust. First he shows the danger of misplaced trust. *"Put not your trust in princes, nor in the son of man, in whom there is no help" (v. 3).* These psalms were very likely sung at the opening of the restored temple. The Jews realized how they had trusted Cyrus and other princes of Persia. But those princes failed and the temple building was stopped. They dared not trust in man—neither should we trust anyone but the Lord. Man will fail (v. 4).

Where should we put our trust? Verse five gives the answer. *"Happy is he that hath the God of Jacob for his help, whose hope is in the Lord his God."* Note he says, *"the God of Jacob,"* and not the God of Israel. Jacob signified the weak, natural man who had to come by grace to trust the Lord. Jacob pictures us sinners in need of grace and mercy. He can be our God as He was Jacob's God. We cannot go wrong trusting Him, for He is the One who had the power to create all things (v. 6).

Through the Bible in a Year: I John 1–4

December 25

Read Psalm 147
Devotional Reading: Luke 2:1-20

Praising the Lord for the Coming of Jesus Christ

Today is Christmas day. Often have we read the passage called "The Christmas Story"—God's inspired account of the night in which Jesus Christ came to earth via the virgin Mary. The shepherds were awakened as they slept with their flocks on the hills near Bethlehem (Luke 2:8-9). They saw the glory of the Lord shine round about them (v. 9). They heard the angel's announcement of the birth of the King of kings (vv. 10-12). And then they heard *"a multitude of the heavenly host **praising** God, and saying, Glory to God in the highest, and on earth, peace, good will toward men" (vv. 13-14).*

There was great praise that night when Jesus was born. Today, will we praise the Lord or will we simply party and exchange gifts and leave the Lord out of our thinking and activity?

Our regular schedule for reading today is Psalm 147. The Lord commands us to praise Him (v. 1). He says that praise is good, pleasant, and comely (v. 1). *"Good"* means "profitable or beneficial"; *"pleasant"* means "delightful"; and *"comely"* means "to be at home." We should be right at home praising the Lord for His benefits and the delights they bring.

Psalm 147 reveals some major reasons why we should praise the Lord. A first reason is that He heals the broken hearted (v. 3). That is exactly what our Lord Jesus stated was one of His major purposes for coming to earth. When the Lord Jesus stood in the temple in Luke 4:16-19, He read from Isaiah that He had come to heal the broken-hearted. No wonder the heavenly host praised Him. In Psalm 147:3 we read that we should praise the Lord because He binds up the wounds of those who are broken in heart. Jesus came to do exactly that: He sets at *"liberty them that are bruised" (Luke 4:18). "A bruised reed shall he not break, and smoking flax shall he not quench . . ." (Matthew 12:20).* Jesus is to be praised because He heals the broken hearted.

We should lift our voices in praise to our God today for sending His Son that we might be redeemed.

Through the Bible in a Year: I John 5; II John; III John; Jude

December 26

Read Psalms 147

How Great Thou Art!

Yesterday we considered reasons that the Psalmist gives for us to praise the Lord. In the first verses of Psalm 147 we see that we should praise the Lord because of His *GRACE*. He heals the broken hearted and binds up their wounds. Today we will find that we should praise the Lord because of His *GREATNESS*.

Psalm 147 tells us a bit about how great is God. Verse four states that he *"telleth the number of the stars."* The word *"telleth"* is an Old English word that meant "to count." We still call those in the bank who receive our deposits and disburse funds to us, "tellers." They are busy counting the money. God has counted the stars and knows the exact number. Scientists tell us there are one hundred billion stars in our galaxy and that there are one hundred million galaxies in space. Figures that stagger our imagination! But God has counted them, knows how many there are, knows where each one is and where it is headed, and knows *"their names"!!* So the psalmist exclaims: *"Great is our Lord, and of great power"* (v. 5).

God covers the heavens with clouds, causes rain to fall on every hill and valley, and with the rain He makes the grass to grow (v. 8). With that grass he feeds every beast and every baby bird (v. 9). He is GREAT.

In His greatness, He has not forgotten the meek, but He lifts them up (v. 6). He blesses the meek and deals with the wicked. He is great— but He considers each of His own and cares for them. He is not looking for strength in men but rather for men to put their trust in Him. He takes pleasure in those that fear Him and hope in His mercy (vv. 10-11).

Therefore we should praise the Lord. We should *"Sing unto the Lord with thanksgiving; sing praise upon the harp unto our God"* (v. 7).

> O Lord my God! When I in awesome wonder
> Consider all the works Thy hands have made,
> I see the stars, I hear the mighty thunder,
> Thy pow'r thro' out the universe displayed,
> Then sings my soul, my saviour God to Thee;
> How great thou art, how great Thou art!
> —Carl Boberg

Through the Bible in a Year: Revelation 1–3

December 27

Read Psalms 147:12-18 and 148

Israel Should Praise the Lord

In Psalm 147:12 we find the Lord's third summons for the people to praise Him. This time the invitation is to His people, the nation of Israel. His summons is to Jerusalem and Zion. The Jewish people are under special obligation to praise the Lord, for God had made them His special people. Verse nineteen refers to this: *"He showeth his word unto Jacob, his statutes and his judgments unto Israel."* Moses asked the Israelites this question in Deuteronomy 4:8: *"And what nation is there so great, that hath statutes and judgments so righteous as all this law, which I set before you this day?"* The answer is an obvious, "None." Israel is God's special nation.

Israel could claim God's *Protection.* *"[H]e hath strengthened the bars of thy gates . . . He maketh peace in thy borders" (vv. 13-14).* The iron gates and the stone walls will be only ornamental in the millennium, for the Lord will be Israel's protection. Also, Israel could claim God's *Provision.* He *"filleth thee with the finest of the wheat" (v. 14).*

Finally, Israel can realize God's *Purpose.* They were the recipients of His Word. Through His Word the Lord accomplishes His purposes. He may send snow, frost, ice, or cold (vv. 16-17). God asks an important question: *"Who can stand before his cold?" (v. 17).* Two men who could answer that are Napoleon and Hitler. They both lost armies on the frozen plains of Russia because they were not prepared for the cold. God has power to stop armies—all He needs is to send some snow and ice.

Israel has had and will have God's special protection. Verse twenty states that God has *"not dealt so with any nation."* Israel has the special privilege among nations of being bound to heaven by a treaty with the living God. God has no such treaty with the United States, nor with Germany, nor Great Britain, nor any nation other than Israel. God does not have an embassy in Washington, nor does He have one in Rome. It is true that God has blessed America because of its identification with God and the Bible in its history. But the only nation in which God has promised to make His capital is Israel, and Jerusalem will be that capital. Therefore the psalmist could shout, *"Hallelujah."*

Through the Bible in a Year: Revelation 4–8

December 28

Read Psalms 148–149

All of Heaven—Praise Him

Psalm 148 is a psalm entirely of praise. There is not one petition of prayer in it. The psalmist is calling on all of creation to praise the Lord. In these fourteen verses we find the word *"praise"* thirteen times. The psalm can be divided into two sections. The first section (vv. 1-6) begins in heaven (v. 1) with angelic beings (v. 2) and moves down to earth in verse seven. The second section (vv. 7-14) begins on earth (v. 7) and moves to heaven (v. 13).

God commands all the beings of Heaven to praise the Lord. He is to be praised from Heaven—and also in the heavenly heights (v. 1). In verse two the Lord calls on the highest of created beings to praise the Lord—the angels. All are to praise Him—*"all his angels"* and *"all his hosts."* Not only are the created heavenly beings to praise the Lord, but also the heavenly bodies are to praise Him. Verse three calls upon the sun, the moon, and the stars to praise Him. How can they praise Him? They do so by moving in perfect order and timing. The sun praises the Lord as it warms the earth and brings growth and life. The moon praises Him as it tugs on the tides and as it reflects the light of the sun. The stars praise Him by following ordained paths across the sky.

Then the psalmist says the Lord should be praised because of God's power and perfection in creation. He created the heavens and the vast oceans of water that move about through the sky. How were they created? The answer is given in verse five: *"Let them praise the name of the Lord: for he commanded, and they were created."* What a miracle! How can people not believe that God created all things. To me it seems much easier to accept the Biblical account of creation rather than to accept men's foolish theories of origins.

We should praise the Lord because of His creation. Then, too, we should praise Him because of His control. *"He hath also stablished them* [the sun, moon, and stars] *for ever and ever: he hath made a decree which shall not pass"* (v. 6). God is creator and He is controller. For these reasons we should continually praise the Lord. May we become faithful in our praise to Him.

Through the Bible in a Year: Revelation 9–12

December 29

Read Psalms 148–149

All of Earth—Praise the Lord!

Again today we look at Psalm 148. Yesterday we noted in the first six verses that all heaven should praise Him. Today we will see the psalmist's invitation for all of earth to praise Him. This begins with verse seven: *"Praise the Lord from the earth."* Then the psalmist lists all of creation that should enter into this crescendo of praise rising from planet earth.

First, he calls on the denizens of the deep, sea monsters living in the deep seas, totally alien to man (v. 7). One of those *"dragons"* praised the Lord by transporting Jonah to Nineveh. Another small fish from the sea took Peter's hook and provided the money he needed to pay Caesar. These creatures were praising the Lord.

Then we find that fire, hail, snow, vapor, and stormy wind must praise Him (v. 8). And they did so many times in Scripture. The disciples stood in amazement and said: *"[E]ven the winds and the sea obey him:" (Matthew 8:27)*.

Next, the psalmist calls the mountains and hills with their fruit trees and cedars to praise Him (v. 9). The writer of Psalm 121 stated that he would lift up his eyes unto the hills. Those hills pointed him to the Lord from whom came his help. When I am at home in Colorado, I love to look to those towering peaks as they point me heavenward.

Then the psalmist calls on earth's created beings to praise Him— beasts, all cattle, creeping things, and birds of the air (v. 10).

Last, the psalmist invites the crown of God's creation, man, to praise the Lord (vv. 11-13). The call is for all men—kings and all people, princes and judges, men and women, young and old—to praise Him. Men should praise the name of the Lord because His name alone is exalted (v. 13). His glory is above the earth and the heaven, which the psalmist has just said should praise Him also.

The psalmist closes this call to praise by saying that the people of Israel should praise Him. Verse fourteen emphasizes the Scriptural truth that the children of Israel are *"his people," "his saints,"* and *"a people near unto him."*

All of Heaven and earth—Praise the Lord!

Through the Bible in a Year: Revelation 13–16

December 30

Read Psalm 149; Revelation 4:8-11 and 5:8-14

Praise by His Favored Ones

For these last two days in the year we will read one of the last two psalms and also a portion from the book of Revelation. Psalm 149:1 calls for a *"new song"* of praise. Revelation 5:9 speaks of a new song in Heaven sung by the twenty-four elders celebrating the Lamb (the Lord Jesus) taking the scroll (the title deeds of earth) saying, *"Thou art worthy to take the book, and to open the seals thereof: for thou wast slain, and hast redeemed us to God by thy blood . . . ."* This *"new song"* in Psalm 149, like others mentioned in the Bible, anticipates the millennium, when Christ Jesus will reign.

In verses one and two we are told who will sing this song—*"the congregation of saints"* and *"the children of Zion."* He is referring both to God's people, Israel, and to His spiritual assembly, all the redeemed of all ages. The title *"congregation"* suggests "a military assembly of favored or beloved ones." Those who know the Lord may appear to be a very small group in comparison to earth's billions, but they are God's favored ones. Jesus said, *"Fear not, little flock; for it is the Father's good pleasure to give you the kingdom" (Luke 12:32).* Remember He also promised, *"[W]here two or three are gathered together in my name, there am I in the midst of them" (Matthew 18:20).* There are assemblies of true believers in the Lord Jesus Christ scattered throughout the world. May we never forget that we are not just a group of nobodies in the world; but we make up the congregation of His favored ones.

We join in praise because the Lord takes pleasure in His people (v. 4). He will beautify the meek with salvation. He will deliver us, and we will sing aloud in glory. The world may trample on the believers today, but the world does not have the last say.

Instead, in the end, the Lord will bring judgment on those who persecuted His favored ones on earth. The *"two-edged sword" (v. 6)* is the Word of God (Hebrews 4:12). This is the weapon God has given us by which to see Satan defeated. We have His Word. Let's use it and thus fulfill the command that ends the psalm: *"Praise ye the Lord."*

Through the Bible in a Year: Revelation 17–19

December 31

Read Psalm 150; Revelation 7:9-12 and 19:1-10

The Grand Finale of Praise

Today we come to the closing of the Hebrews' Hymnbook with a glorious song of repeated and resounding praise. This could be called "The Hallelujah Chorus" of the psalms. The last five psalms, 146-150, are psalms of praise. Through each one rises a crescendo of praise until we come to this last psalm. It rises as the doxology to all psalms with a glorious voice of praise to God. Thirteen times in six verses we note the word *"praise."* This is the grand finale of a great book of music.

Praise is the theme of the psalm:

> Who should be praised?—the Lord God (v. 1).
> Where should He be praised?—*"in his sanctuary"* (heaven) and *"in the firmament of his power"* (earth) (v. 1).
> Why should He be praised?—for *"his mighty acts"* and *"his excellent greatness"* (v. 2)
> Who should do the praising?—*"everything that has breath"* (v. 6)

The Psalms begin with God's blessing an individual man (Psalm 1) and end with every creature praising God (Psalm 150). All through Psalms we have heard the notes of sorrow, distress, and trial. But with this song we have the note of eternity—praise for His mighty acts, His power, and His excellent greatness. Praise should rise from His earthly temple and it does rise from Heaven, the abode of God and His ministering angels.

The psalmist calls for all musical instruments to be incorporated into this great chorus of praise. What a time of praise it will be throughout the expanse of eternity! We hear that praise in Revelation 7:9-12 and 19:1-10. May we, who are still on earth, learn to praise Him now.

> Crown Him with many crowns, the Lamb upon His throne;
> Hark! how the heavenly anthem drowns all music but its own.
> Awake, my soul, and sing of Him who died for thee,
> And hail Him as thy matchless king through all eternity.
> —Matthew Bridge

Now we close this book of 366 devotionals from Psalms. I have received a great blessing in writing them. I trust you have been blessed as you allowed me to share them with you. Let me say it again: May we learn to praise Him!

Through the Bible in a Year: Revelation 20–22